# CHÂTEAU LÉOUBE

CAROLE BAMFORD

# CHÂTEAU LÉOUBE

PROVENCE LIVING

PHOTOGRAPHY BY MARTIN MORRELL

VENDOME

NEW YORK · LONDON

'Provence has always held
a special allure for me.
Anthony and I had been
looking for a house for a while
when we eventually found
*Léoube*, our sleeping beauty.'

- CAROLE BAMFORD

17 INTRODUCTION
41 THE HOUSE: ENTERTAINING SPACES
87 THE HOUSE: LIVING SPACES
123 THE POOL AND POOLHOUSE
155 THE GARDEN
183 VILLA MARIA
205 THE VINEYARD AND OLIVE GROVE
249 THE BEACH AND CAFÉ
275 THE CHAPELLE SAINT-GEORGES

286 ACKNOWLEDGEMENTS

Dedicated to my grandchildren,
in memory of all the meals
around our Provençal table.

OPPOSITE Umbrella pines, with their unmistakable silhouettes – towering trunks topped with graceful wide canopies – are an emblematic sight on Provence's coastline and a commanding feature of the skyline at Léoube.

OVERLEAF The turquoise waters at the Plage du Pellegrin.

# INTRODUCTION

Provence has always held a special allure for me. The drama and variety of its changing landscapes, the beauty of the soft golden light, the heady scent of lavender drifting on the breeze and its proximity to the sea have all been huge draws. And yet my husband and I had been looking for a house in Provence for about 15 years until we eventually found Château Léoube, our sleeping beauty.

Nestled on a rocky peninsula along the Côte d'Azur, it felt like we'd happened upon a hidden treasure. The house is set back from a quiet bay along what I still consider to be one of the region's most breathtaking and beautiful stretches of coastline. When we first went to view it, you couldn't see the house from the sea, so it really did feel like a secret with all the privacy and seclusion we had been looking for. The château had been owned by the same family for years and hadn't been touched in a while, so it needed work but we could see it had so much potential. There was of course a lot of interest in it, but the lady owner, who was very elderly, had loved the house and its land and she wanted to sell to somebody who would care for the estate the way she had. I still meet people in the local villages today who have fond memories of visiting her café or staying at the beach house she rented out. Léoube has been a treasured place since long before we became its guardians. The day we met the owner, she walked around the property with us to try and assess whether we were the right people to sell to. While we'd like to think we found Léoube: in reality it chose us.

When we first walked into the house, we didn't plan to do very much to it: we thought we'd replace a few chimneypieces, change some tiles and freshen it up a little, but, as we started to peel back the layers and uncover what lay beneath, we realised the scale of what we'd undertaken. It was then that we brought in Alain Raynaud, our wonderful architect.

I'd met Hubert de Givenchy at a dinner party some years before. My husband and I had been staying with a friend who lived next door to him and we were invited for supper at Le Clos Fiorentina, his summer house in St-Jean-Cap-Ferrat.

I remember feeling very nervous about meeting him. He was so elegant – very tall with an imposing stature – and his taste was impeccable, which meant that there was something intimidating about that first encounter. But he was charming – funny and warm – and we became friends. Hubert's reputation as somebody who defined glamour is often spoken about and of course it's true; I've never met anybody who could do anything as beautifully refined in such a considered yet seemingly effortless way. I used to go and visit him and his partner, Philippe Venet, at their hôtel particulier in Paris, and it remains one of the most exquisite houses I've ever seen – a beacon of style and a lesson in how to furnish and inhabit a home.

Hubert was such a huge inspiration for me. When we bought Léoube, he came to visit me the first summer we were there. I remember the wry smile and the earnest note in his voice as he said, 'It's wonderful. But you're very brave…'. He offered to help me with the renovation and one of his greatest blessings was his connection to Alain, who had worked with Hubert on his own houses.

I have loved working with Alain. To this day, I am in awe of how his practised eye has the ability not only to be able to conceive proportions in a house but also to truly understand how people use and live in spaces. The most complex thing for him to address at the outset was the layout of the château. On the ground floor in particular, the house had been a tangled muddle of tiny rooms that ran into each other. Alain wanted to open up the space and make it more suitable for the needs of a large family – for living but also for entertaining. As we walked around together for the first time, I remember watching as his eyes traced the light, gauging how he could work with it to flood the rooms with its golden lustre and transform the spaces. For Alain, working with a building is a dialogue – it speaks to him. He works organically and holistically, but also in a very practical way, an approach that very much echoes my own and I feel very grateful to have met such a kindred spirit.

The renovation took us 14 years. We started with Villa Maria, the guesthouse right next to the beach, so that we would have somewhere to stay while we worked on the château. Villa Maria was just beautiful – perfectly formed, tucked on the edge of the bay just metres from the waves – and suddenly I felt like we didn't need the château: tackling such a huge project seemed quite insurmountable.

But with Alain, I had formed a little team to help me with Villa Maria and we all just got stuck into the bigger task. I worked with Wendy Nicholls on the interior decoration, Tommaso del Buono performed miracles on the garden and its landscaping and our friend Bosie (John Bowes Lyon) generously accompanied me on visits to France to provide moral support and a second opinion. We would all fly out about once every six weeks or so to meet with Alain and check on progress, and the renovation just became part of our lives. We'd spend our days going to markets or galleries to source furniture, ceramics or local artworks, or combing France in search of exceptional or specialist artisans to create bespoke linens or chandeliers or chimneypieces. And then, as the dusk drew in, we'd have an evening cocktail, watching the sun set over the cypress trees and slipping into the gentle, soothing rhythm of Provençal life. There didn't seem any need for rush and we took our time. And it was a very happy time.

Throughout those fourteen years, Provence and its storied history provided the backdrop to our lives but also gently guided the architectural vernacular of the house and the way we chose to decorate its interiors. My own style when starting a renovation or refurbishment project is always to consider the character and sensibilities of the building itself as well as its surroundings, so Léoube is infused with Provençal influence. We've sought to honour the architectural traditions and styles of houses like this in the area. The region's celebrated heritage of attracting artists is reflected in the many local pieces and paintings we've collected and its colours and combination of rustic and refined style have all informed the decisions we've made. But our situation has, of course, also governed practical decisions to enable us to navigate the challenges of living in a Mediterranean climate. The progression of rooms follows a rhythm as you move from dim, shaded hallways into sun-drenched living spaces, configured to allow the air to flow and keep the rooms cool during the heat of the day.

ABOVE Vine leaves are an emblem of the estate's identity and its enduring connection to the land.

Provence offers everything you could possibly want in a place to live: lively markets and colourful local produce; vibrant towns and cities alongside sleepy picturesque villages; a rich tradition of art and culture. But one of the most beloved elements of Léoube is its setting by the sea. We knew from the outset that one of the biggest changes we wanted to make to the property was to take advantage of the chateau's position by the water. The previous owners had allowed the gardens to grow untamed in the stretch of land between the house and the water, creating a dense screen that completely obscured the view of the sea. Months of careful clearing and Tomasso's thoughtful landscaping allowed us to create an unobstructed panorama of the Mediterranean from the house. That sight offers an ever-changing canvas of blues that shift from deep cobalt to brilliant turquoise depending on the light and the season and I never tire of watching its mutations. The sea is woven into the fabric of our life at Léoube: I begin every morning with a swim in the crystal-clear waters; the rhythmic sound of the waves provides a constant lull and a gentle soundtrack to our days; the abundant seafood from coastal villages and nearby markets takes centre stage on our plates, reminding us of the sea's generous bounty.

Peter Mayle wrote that: 'Provence unlocks the poetry within our souls and inspires us to see the world with new eyes.' For me, that is the magic of Château Léoube. As someone with a busy, inquisitive mind, he captured what is perhaps most treasured of all for me in this piece of paradise: it is a home full of stories, discoveries and memories, each corner imbued with the rhythm of nature but above all with the simple pleasure of slowing life down. That expansive horizon and the arresting Provençal landscape calm my mind, offering me peace and perspective.

In writing this book, I hope to share not only the path we took to restore the house and the interiors that now give voice to those stories but also a glimpse into the essence of Provence. Like the countless writers and artists who were drawn to its mysticism and captivated by its beauty before me, it is a place that nourishes and inspires those who embrace it. I hope you too will find a measure of Provençal inspiration in these pages.

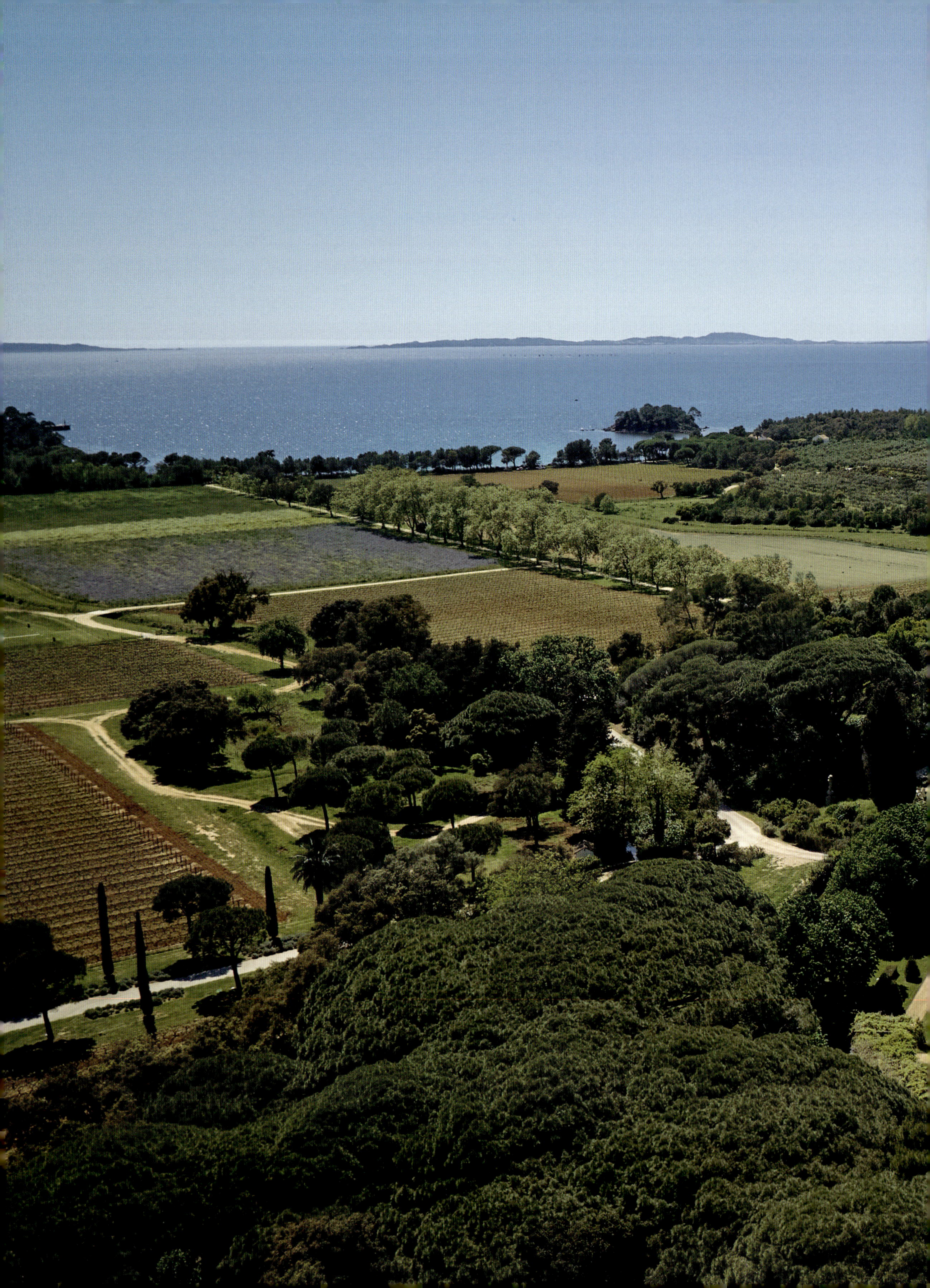

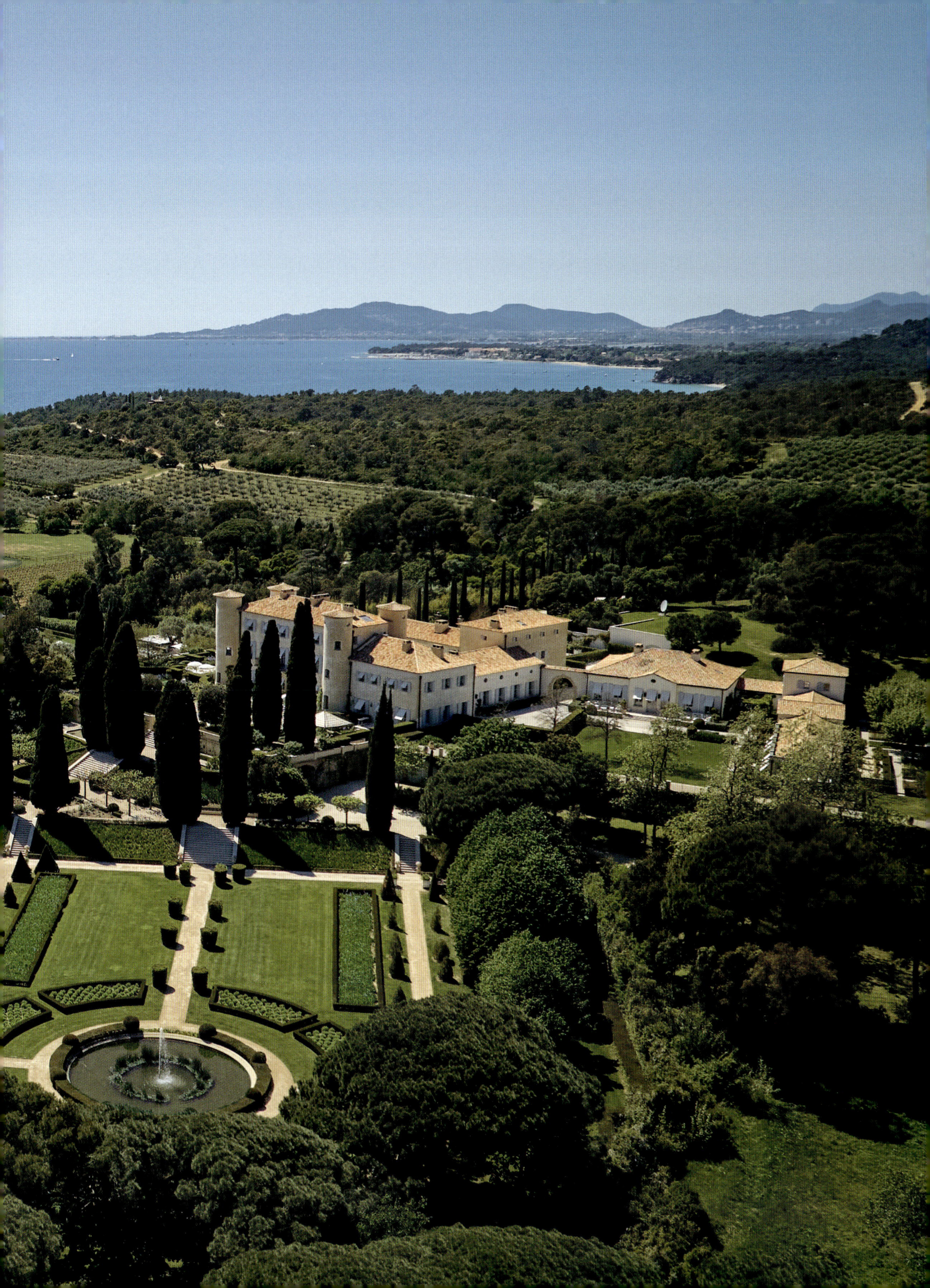

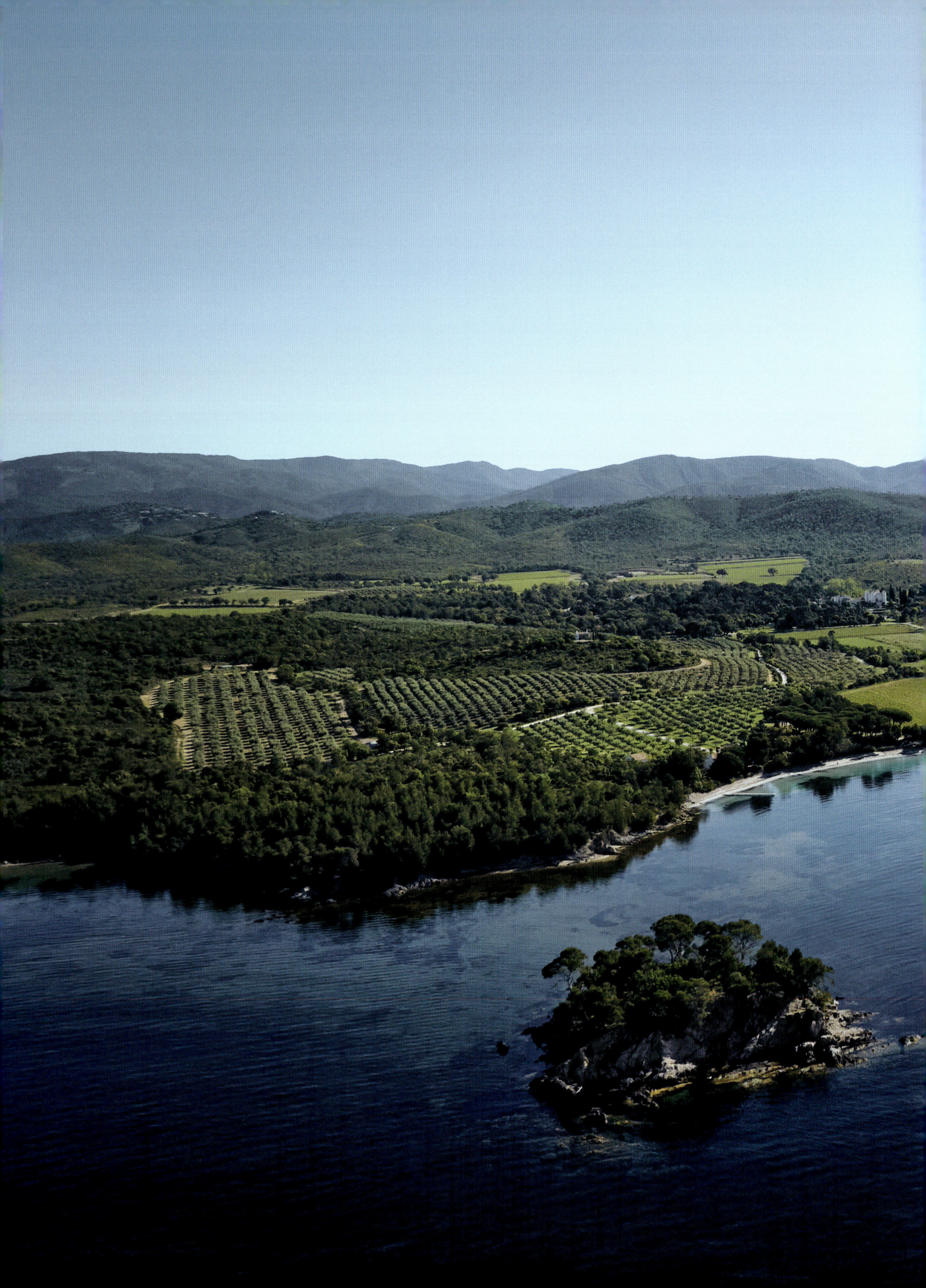

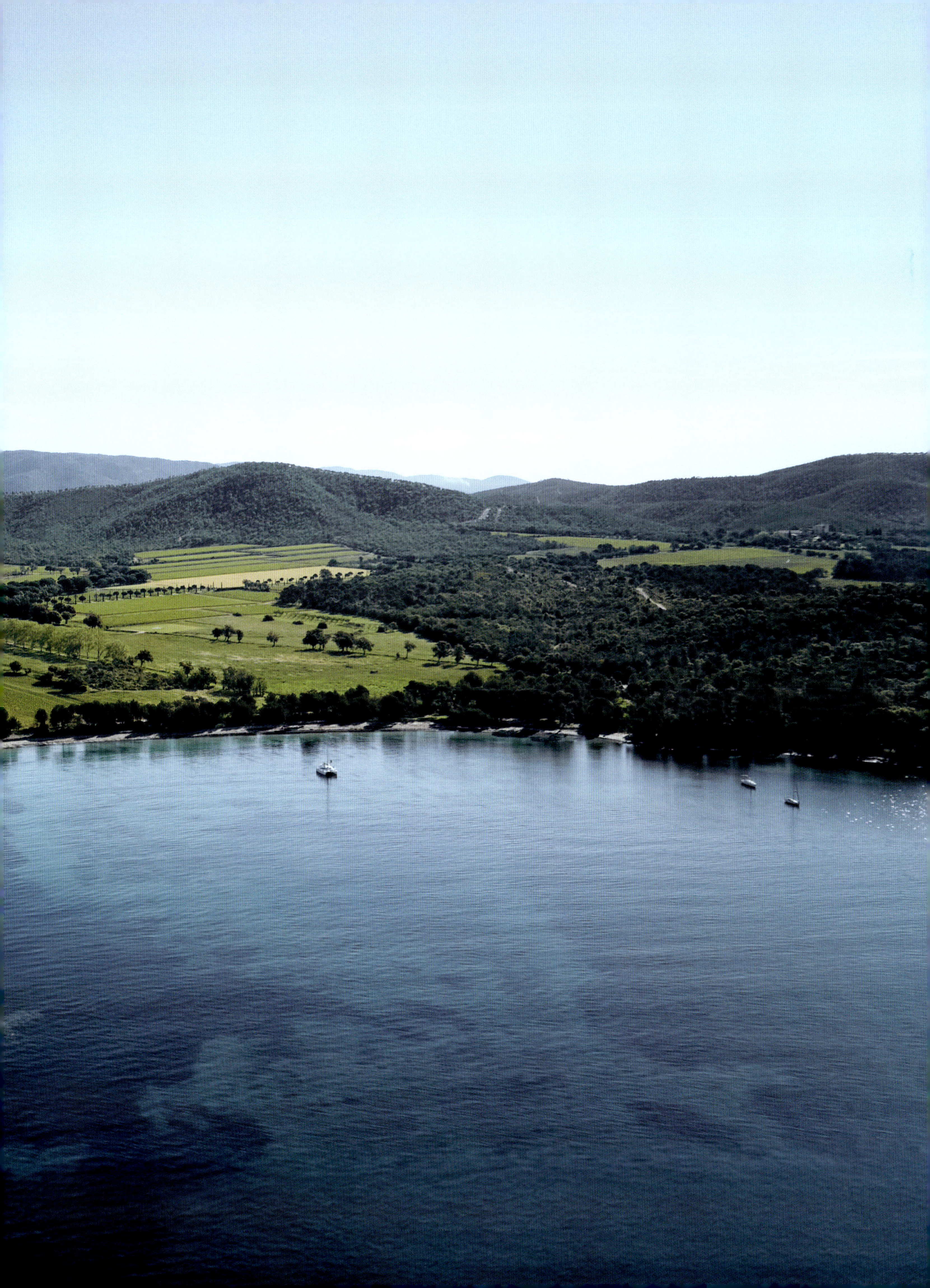

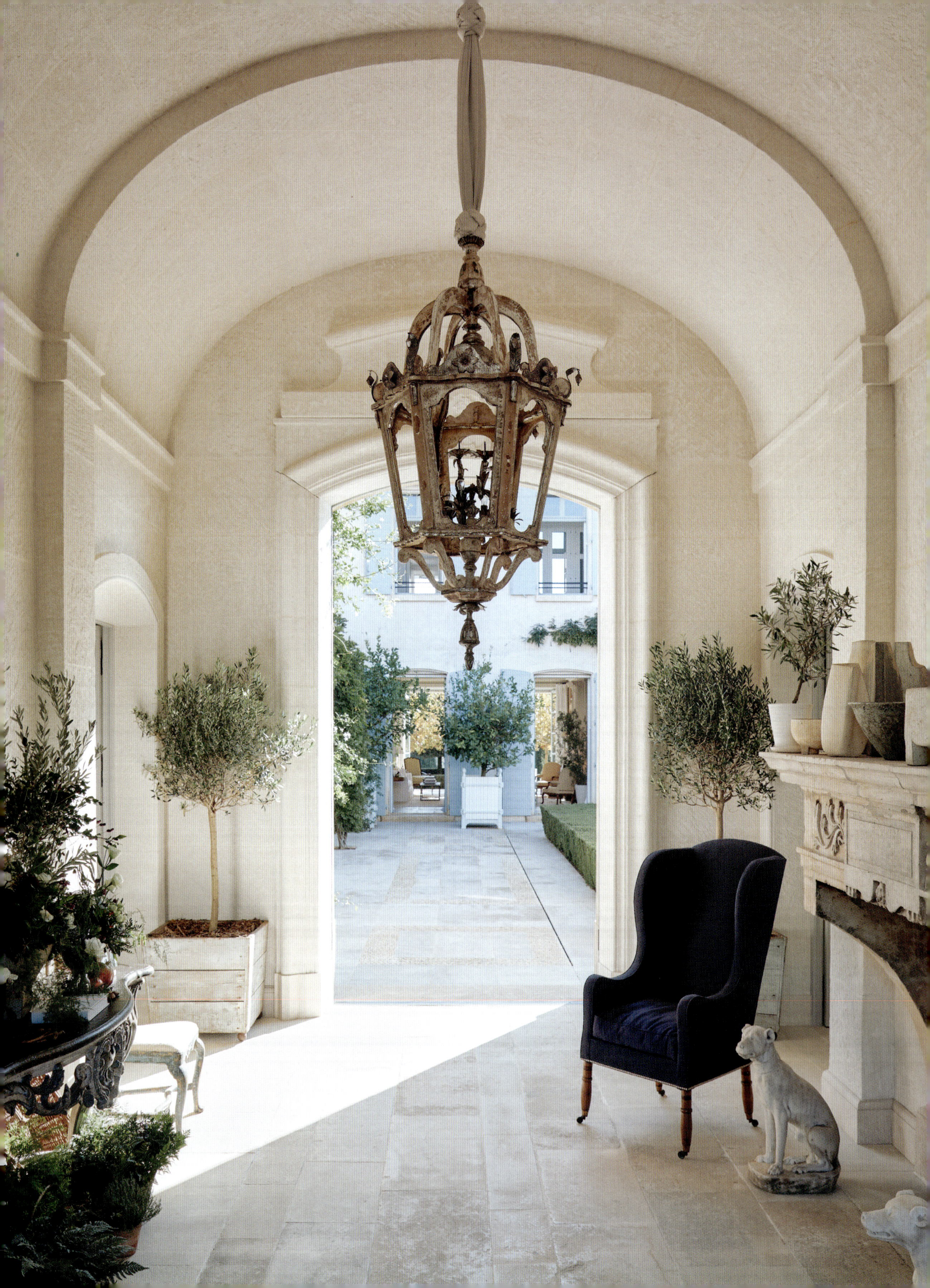

# THE HOUSE

ENTERTAINING SPACES

Restoring and decorating a house of this scale might seem like quite a daunting task. Lots of people have said to me they would have felt overwhelmed by the number of decisions needing to be taken but, while there were times when the task did feel formidable, working with spaces, reimagining them and breathing life into them is a passion that ignites my imagination and I draw so much energy from that form of creative expression.

Working with a building and outlining a style for a home isn't solely about aesthetics. While our tastes and personalities help define them, how we shape our homes is mostly about feelings – how we want to feel and how we want others to feel on entering our spaces. For me decorating a home is about the stories you tell through your choices. When I look around these rooms, there are objects and pieces that I find beautiful or am drawn to because of their meaning and significance to my life. There are so many stories within these walls and, for me, that's the difference between a home and a house. Many people can design beautiful houses but this home is a tapestry – fragments of lives pieced together through the objects, photographs, fabrics and furniture that fill it.

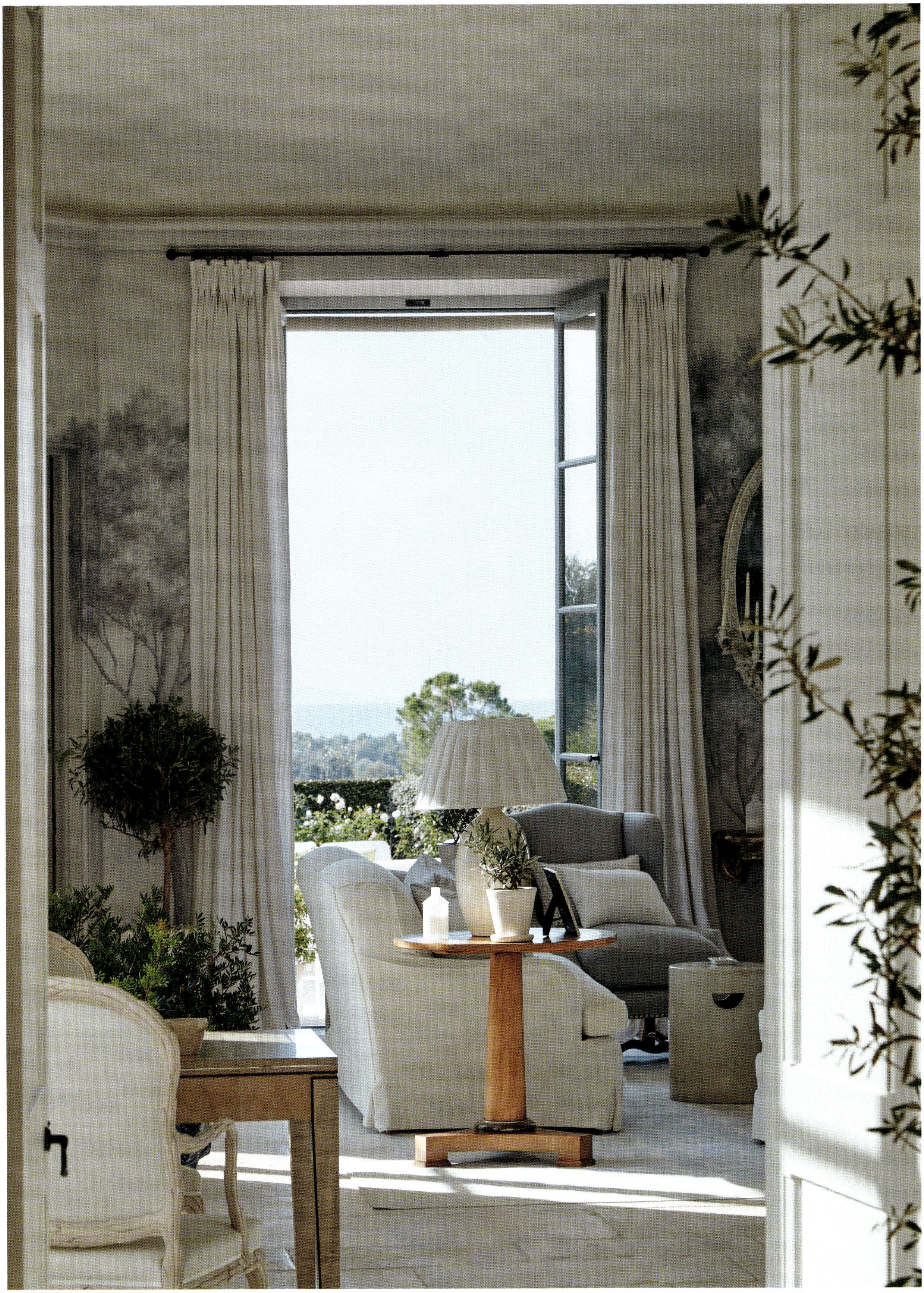

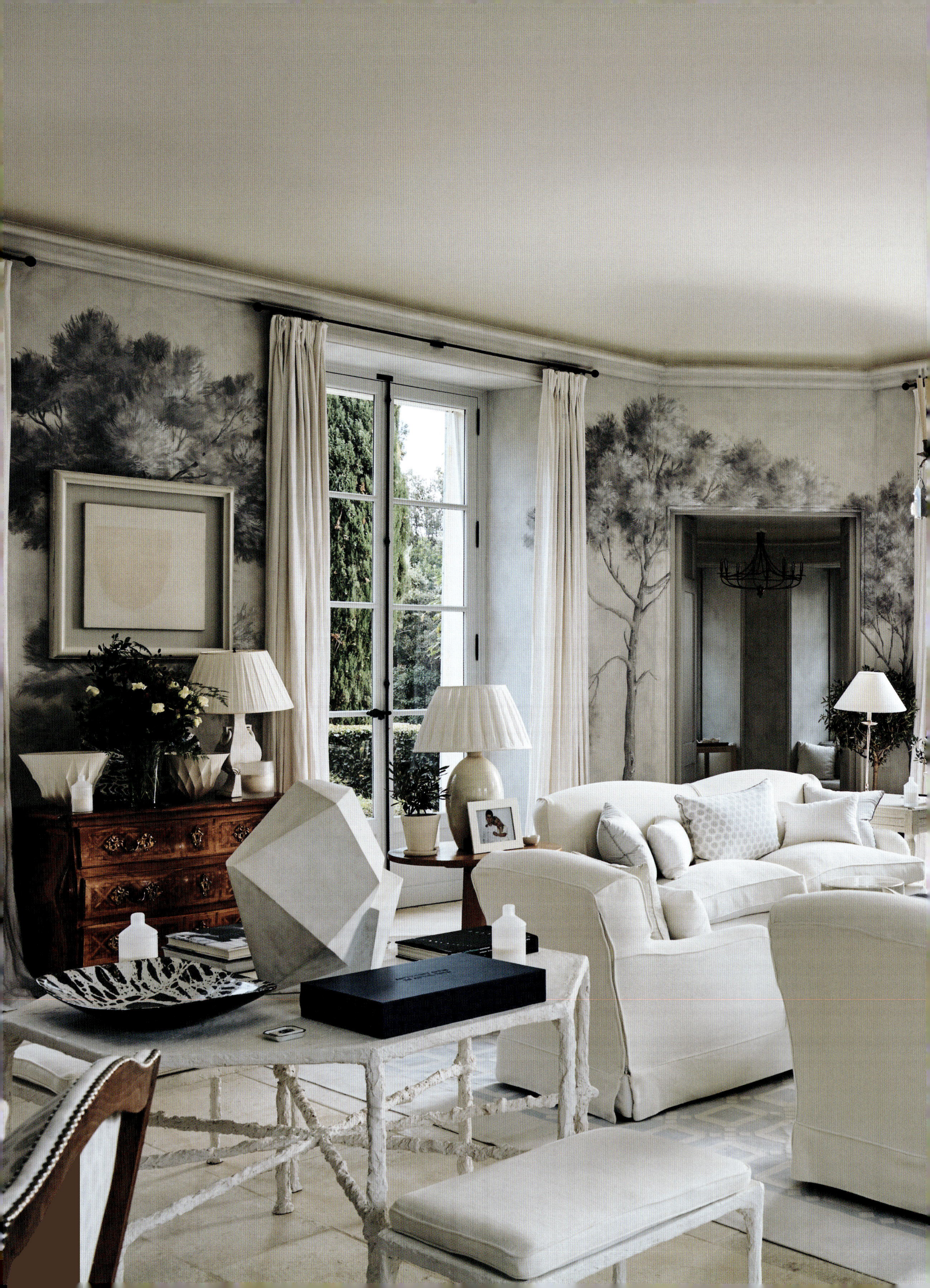

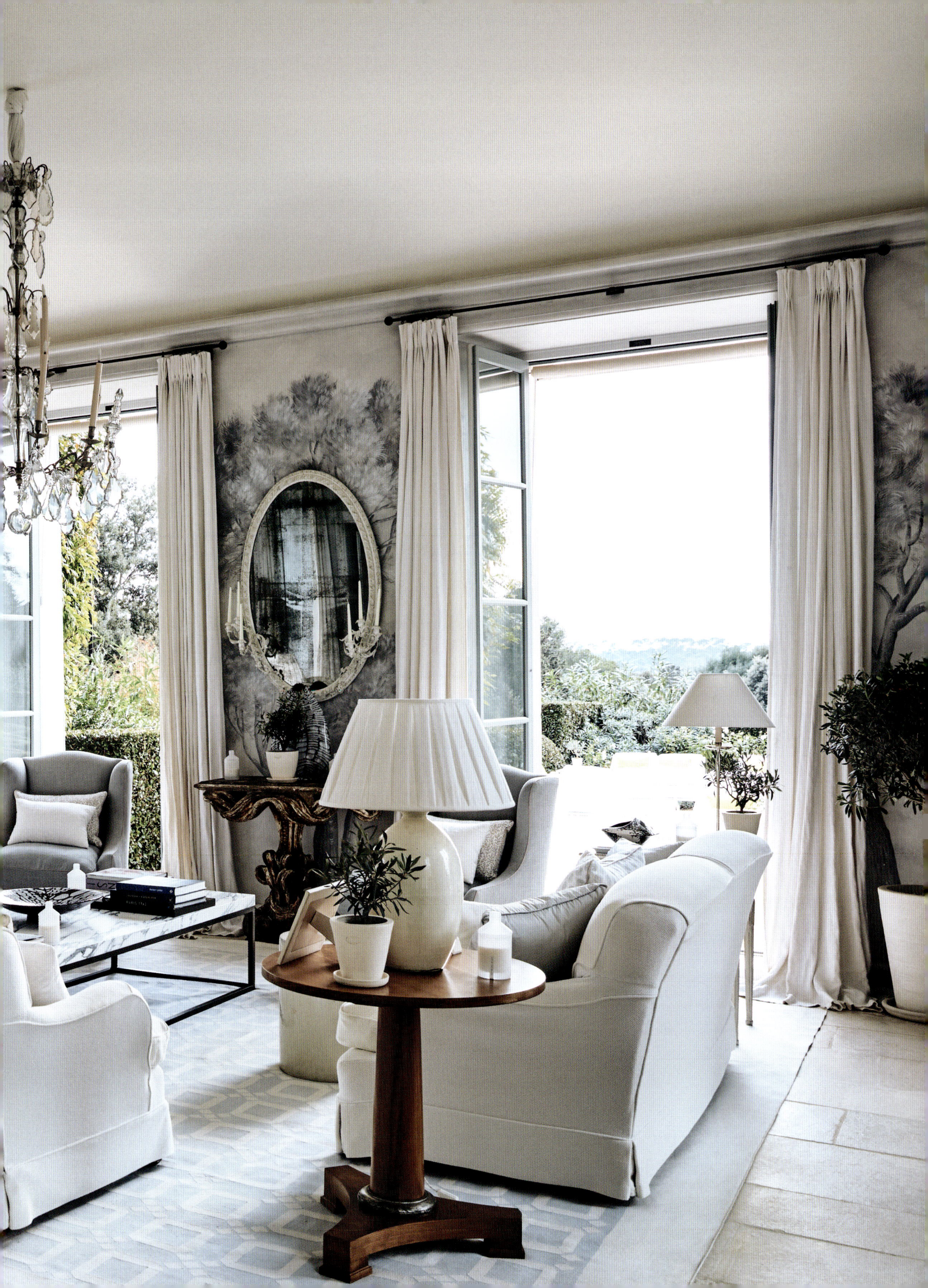

ABOVE A group of hand-thrown porcelain vessels by Andrew Wicks. He usually creates groups of vessels to establish a visual relationship between the forms. OPPOSITE AND OVERLEAF The umbrella pines on the drawing room walls were hand-painted by decorative artist Lucinda Oakes.

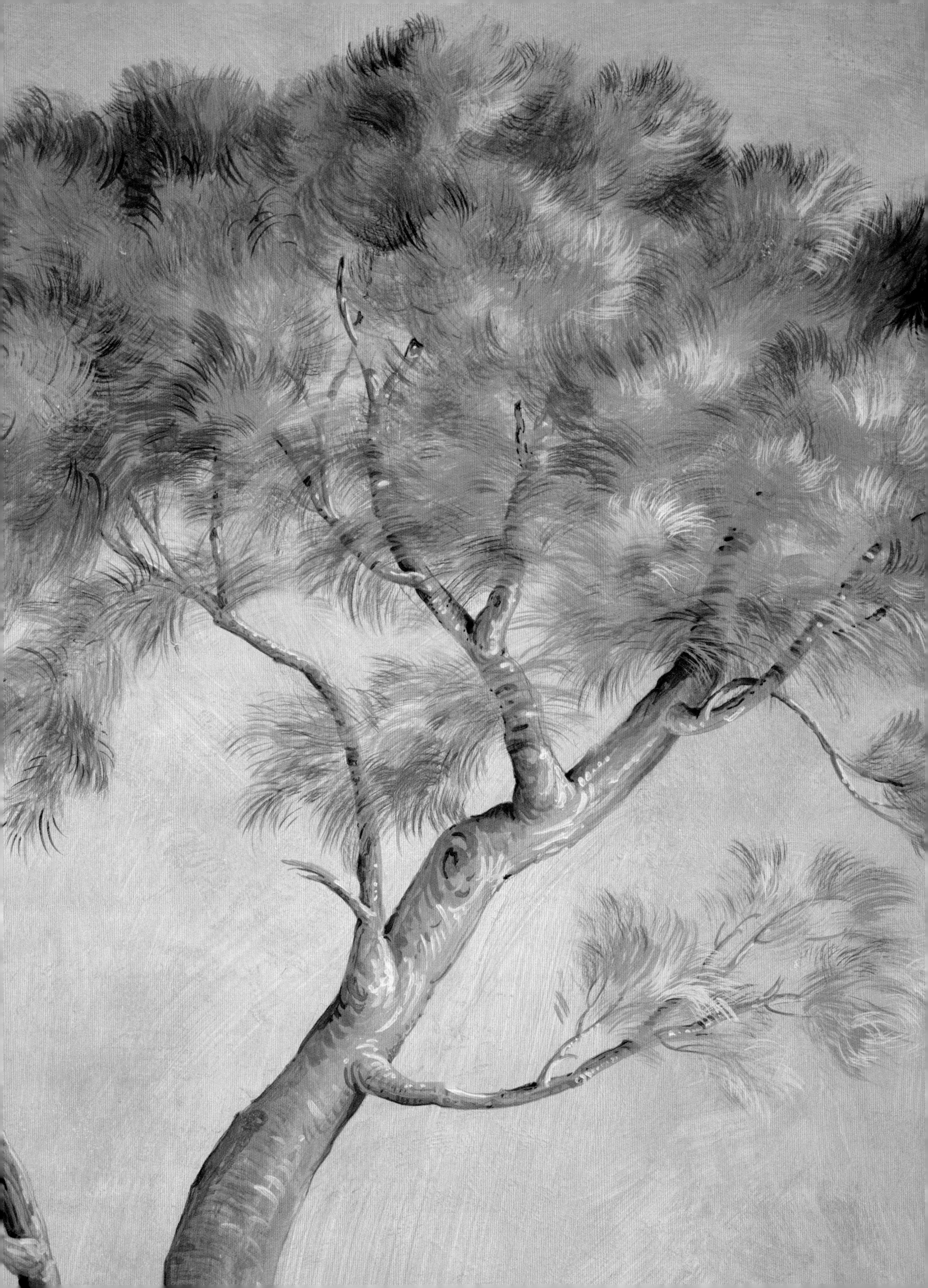

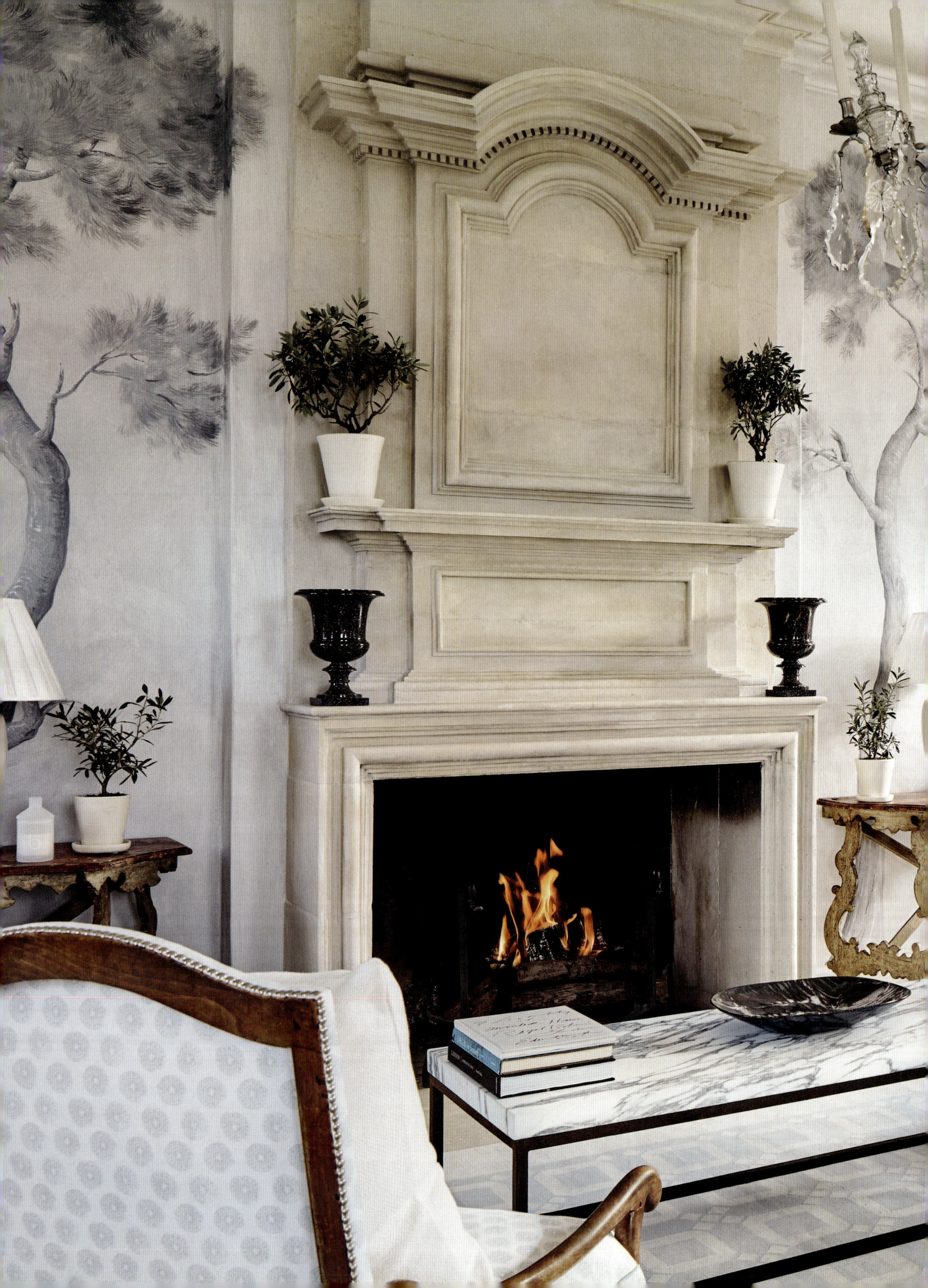

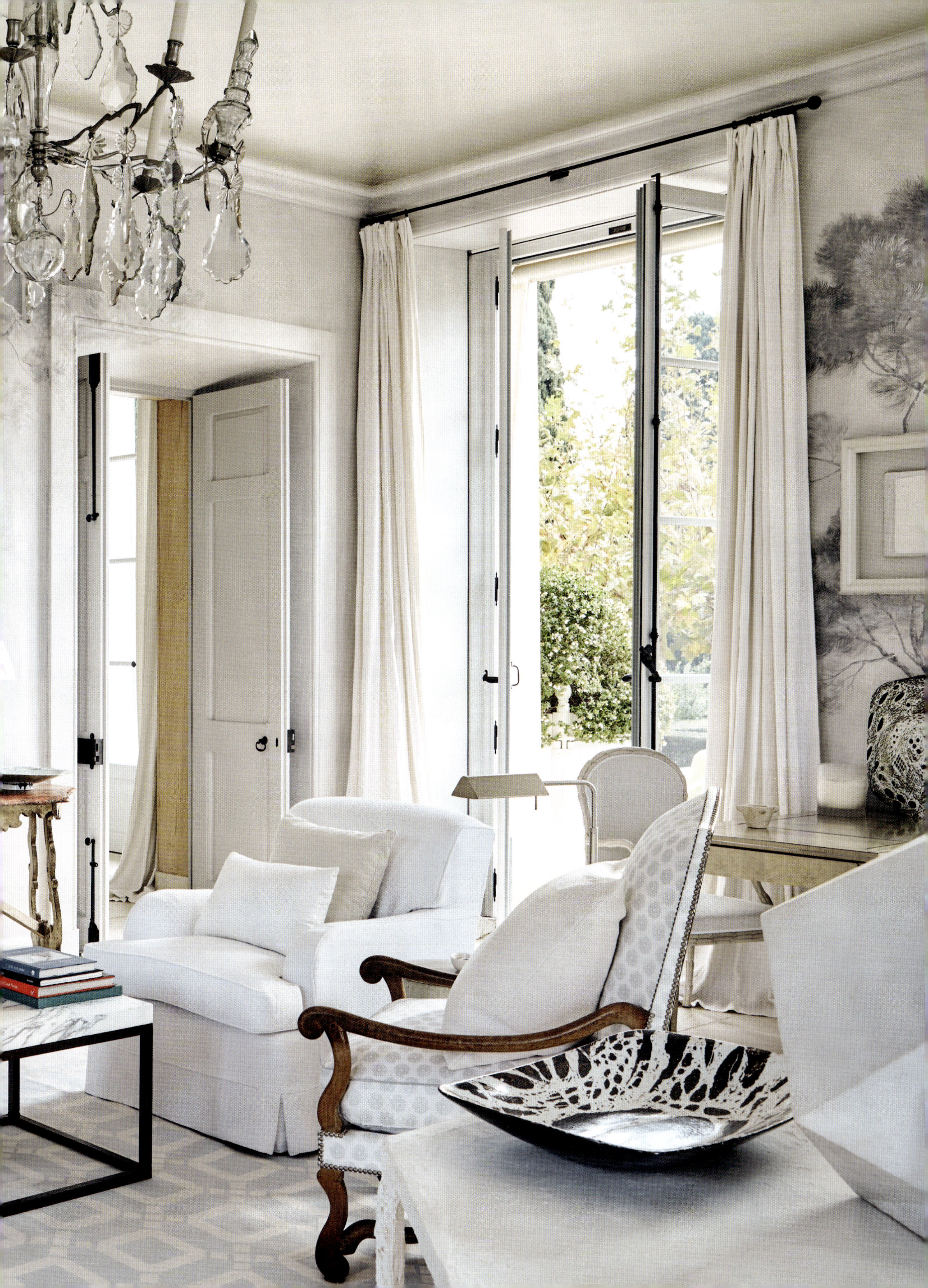

ABOVE The chandelier makers we worked with for many of the glass chandeliers were from Mathieu Lustrerie based in Gargas in Provence. OPPOSITE An Egyptian carved marble water jar from Hawker Antiques.

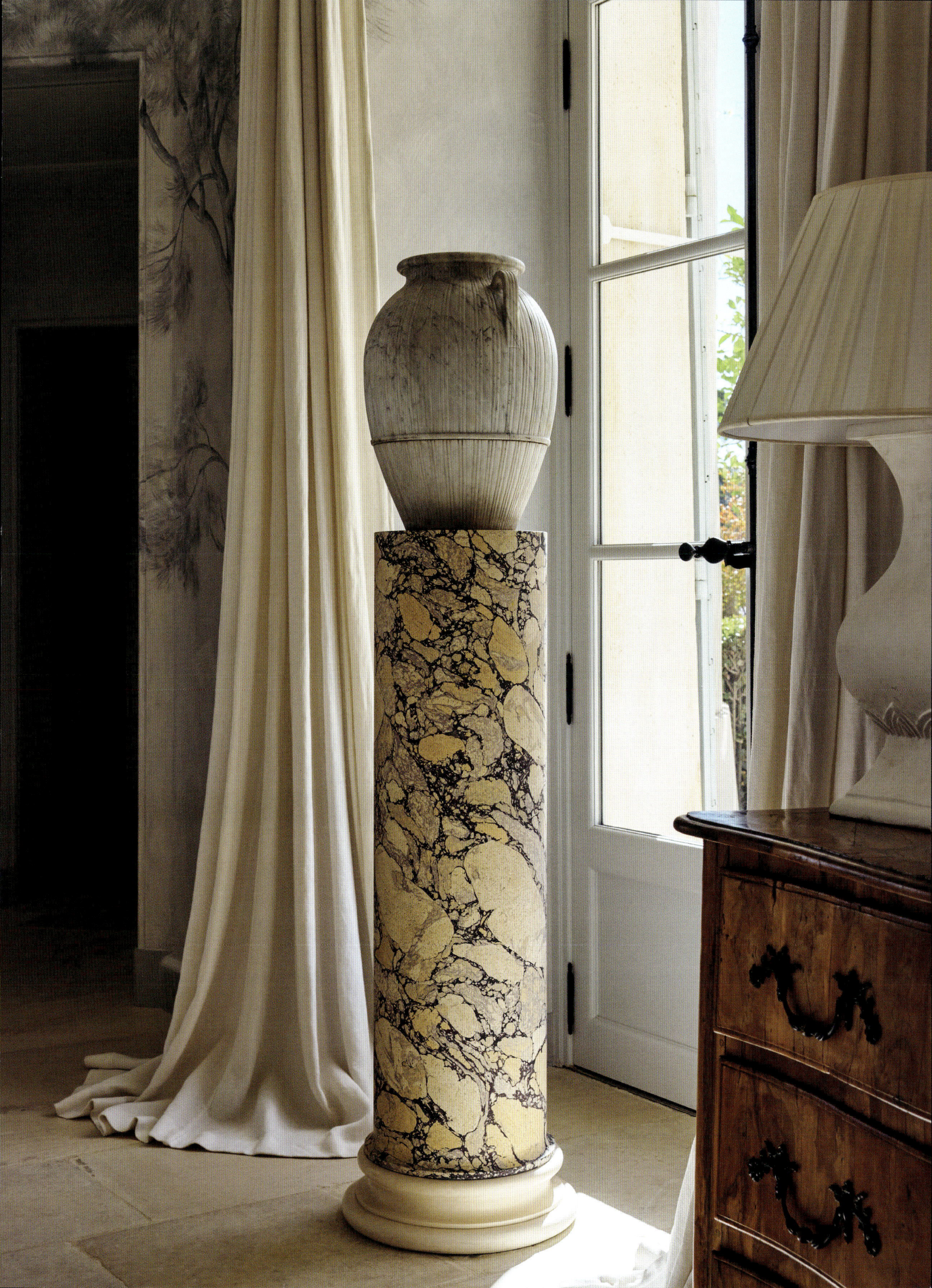

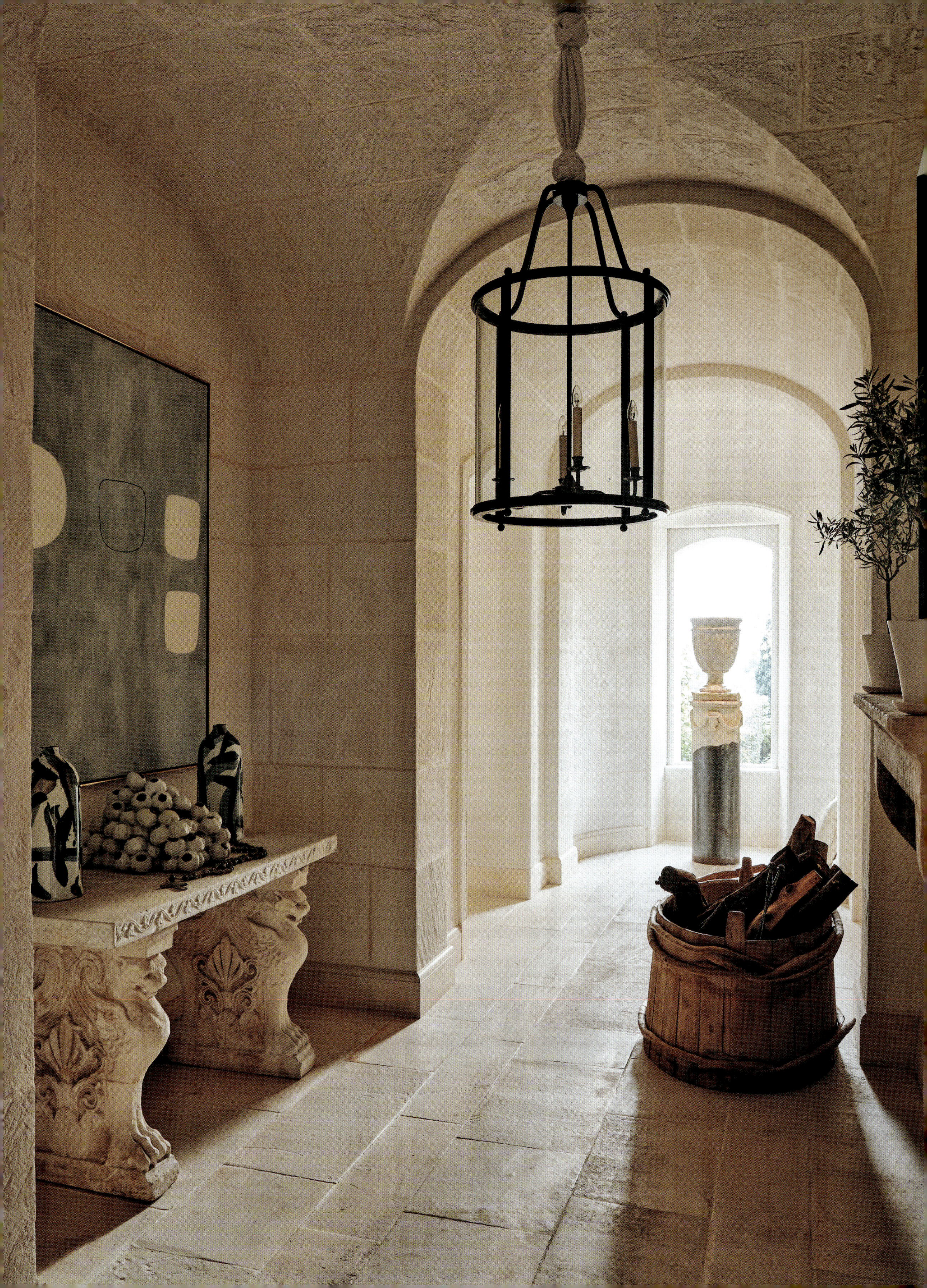

THE HOUSE: ENTERTAINING SPACES

'Art is a manifestation of emotion,
and emotion speaks a language that
all may understand.'

– W. SOMERSET MAUGHAM

Taking on a project like this requires a willingness to embrace both the challenges and rewards of working with old buildings but it is just as much about permitting yourself the freedom and permission not to be constrained by its history, allowing spaces to evolve with a renewed sense of purpose. I'm drawn to the past and to the heritage and tradition they represent but I also want to bring something fresh and modern to design. That blend is particularly marked at Léoube in the entertaining spaces.

Each room – the drawing room, morning room, dining room, library and ballroom – were not simply rooms to be decorated, but had defined roles to play within the rhythm of our life. As such, they have elements that acknowledge and honour the heritage of this style of château and France's architectural tradition, but include more contemporary elements and pieces that meet the needs, comforts and function of modern living in a warm climate.

Some decisions were governed by the mood I wanted to instil in each room – comfort, calm or a sense of occasion. The walls in the drawing room were painted by decorative artist Lucinda Oakes. Wendy and I had spoken about having one room painted in grisaille and we felt that it would bring a sense of serenity to this room which is a more formal space for entertaining guests. The towering umbrella pines – such an integral part of the Provençal landscape – are rendered in a way that is very soothing, as if nature is inviting you to pause and to breathe. The palette of greys, white and green developed from the paint colours set the tone for the rest of the room.

The table in the centre I adore; it is a copy of a little maquette of a Giacometti table that Hubert de Givenchy had on his desk at Le Jonchet, his house in the country, and we thought that it would look wonderful in the middle of the drawing room in a larger size. This house has so many memories of happy times with friends and this table will also make me think of Hubert, whose legacy and friendship has been a huge part of my life and whose style and counsel have informed much of the house.

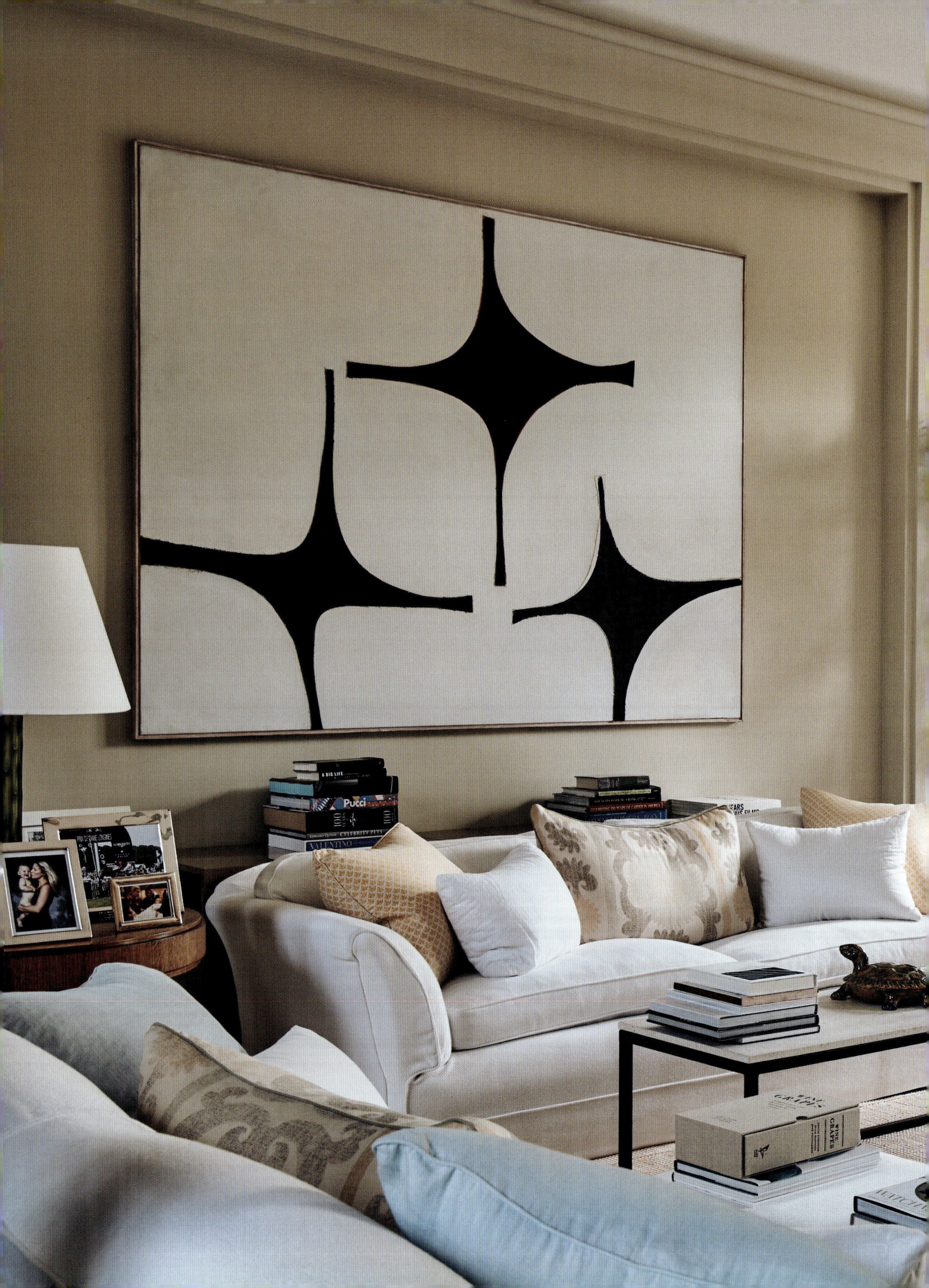
Pucci
VALENTINO

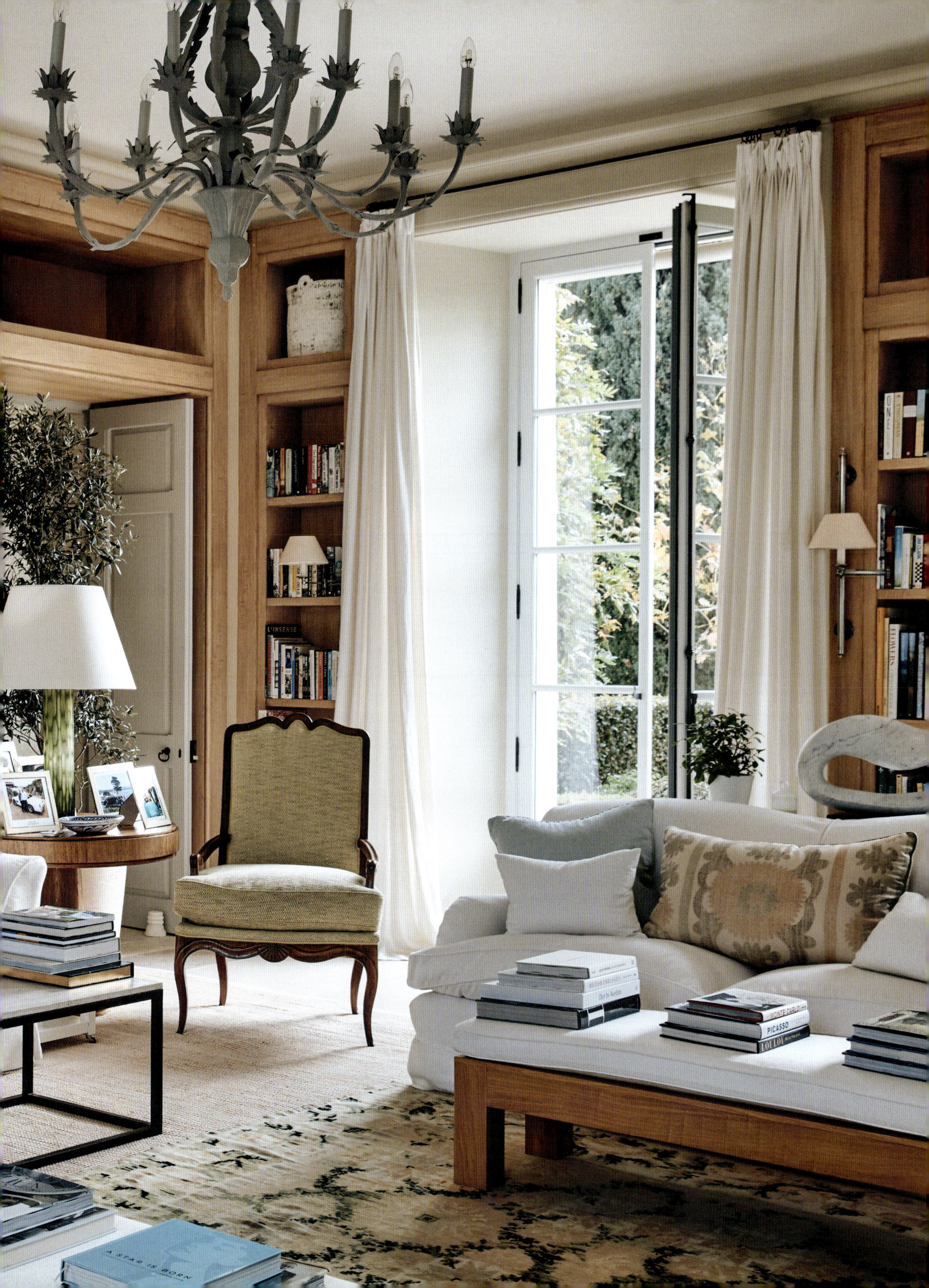
PICASSO
A STAR IS BORN

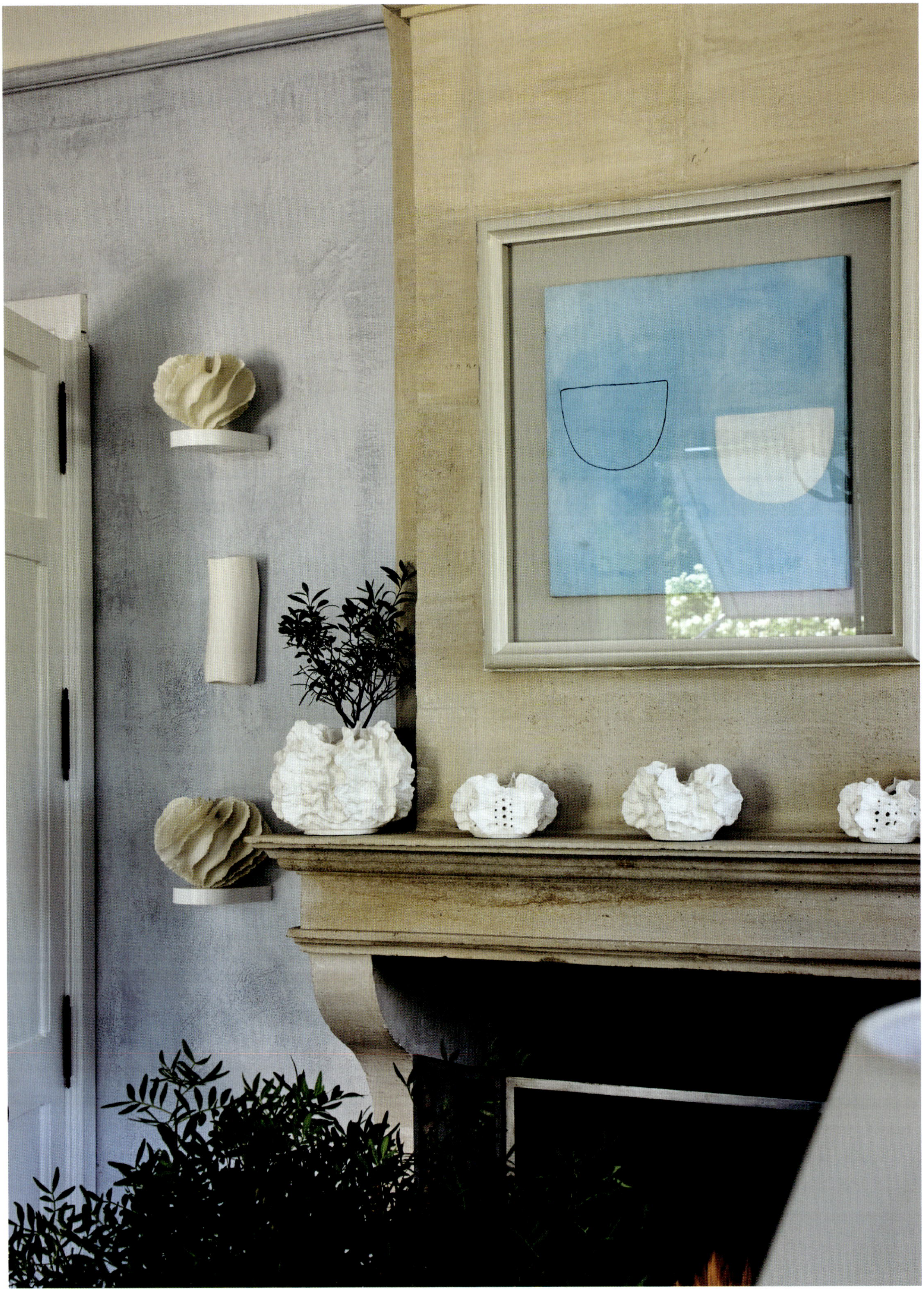

The morning room, which leads out onto the terrace where we usually have breakfast, is a peaceful, relaxed space. If art is the means of expressing your passions and interests in a home, then this room is a strong reflection of mine. There is a lot of work by artists I've discovered at Collect – the international art fair for contemporary craft and design – all of which reflect my appreciation of nature's artistry and my love of craftsmanship. Many of ceramicist Sandra Davolio's delicate white porcelain vessels with their rippled edges are inspired by the sea and made to resemble coral reefs or the unfurling of petals. Nic Webb's structural wooden sculptures and way of working align with what I am so drawn to in craft: he responds to the character of each piece of timber in an intuitive way, choosing to embrace the material's imperfections, encouraging cracks and splits and celebrating their beauty.

The consol table was designed by the British furniture maker John Makepeace, whose work and ethos I admire enormously. Entitled 'Perforation', it is carved from oak and was made by the carpenter who later so helped David Linley – a link that I like very much as he is somebody whose work has held a strong presence in my homes. Makepeace often spoke about his relationship with 'modern' design and his interpretation of it and this piece reflects his dual philosophy: using design to prioritise human needs while also upholding his environmental priorities – he used a range of indigenous timbers grown in Britain to try to encourage a diverse woodland ecology.

The cushions on the chairs are made by Nila, the not-for-profit organisation I founded, which is dedicated to supporting India's artisan communities and preserving its tradition of handcrafted textiles. The cloth itself is handwoven and dyed using natural indigo grown by farmers supported by the foundation.

Fireplaces throughout the house were quite a challenge. The scale of the rooms after Alain had opened them up meant that the original chimneypieces were too small for the new spaces, so we had to replace every single one. Even then, many of them had to be enlarged, which Alain did very cleverly by creating a style of secondary chimney breast. Wendy spent a lot of time patiently ringing suppliers all over France trying to source new pieces. A few of the fireplaces that are now in the bedrooms we were able to find at a local maker in L'Isle-sur-la-Sorgue, which made life a little simpler, but many had to come from much further afield.

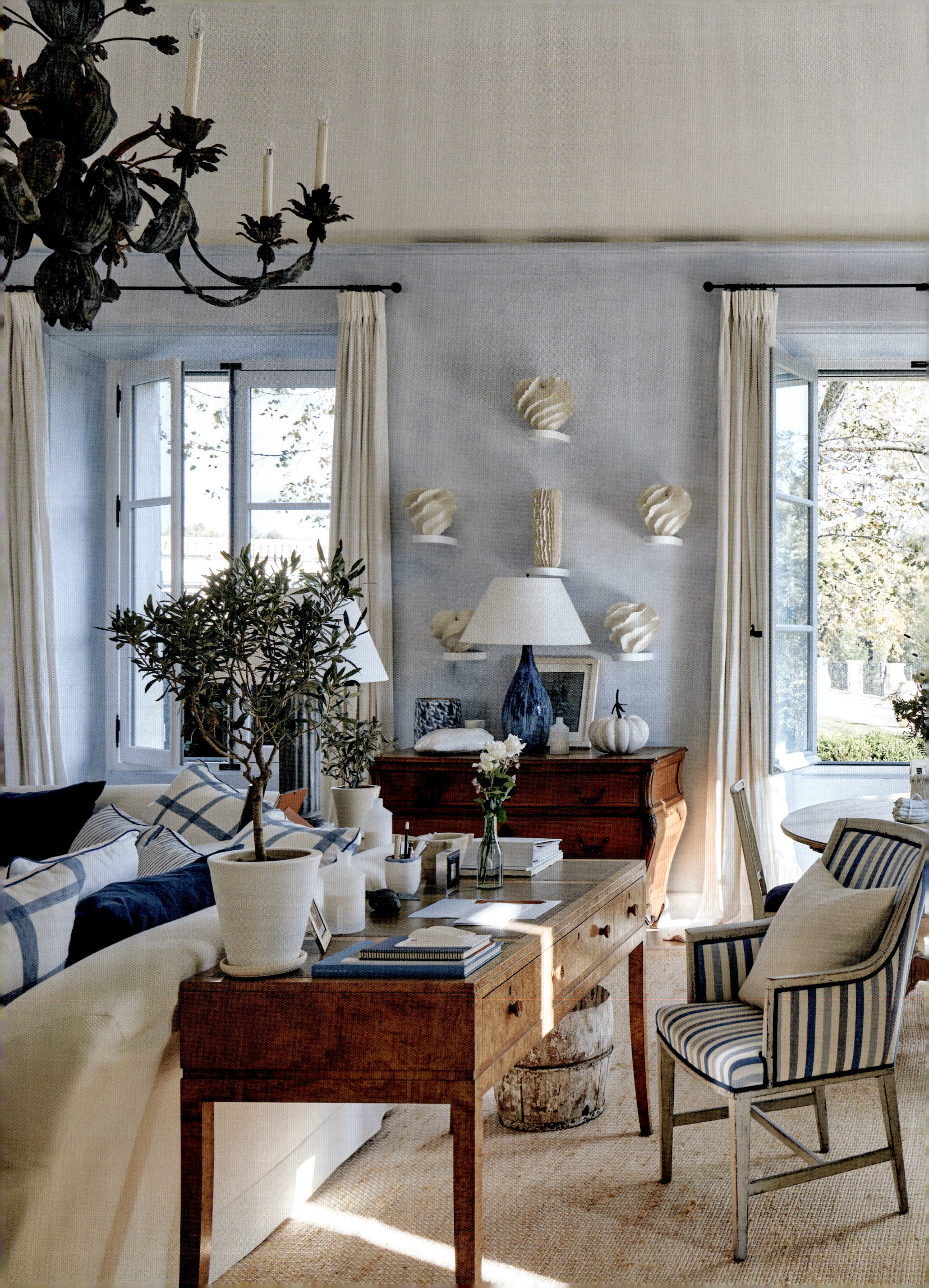

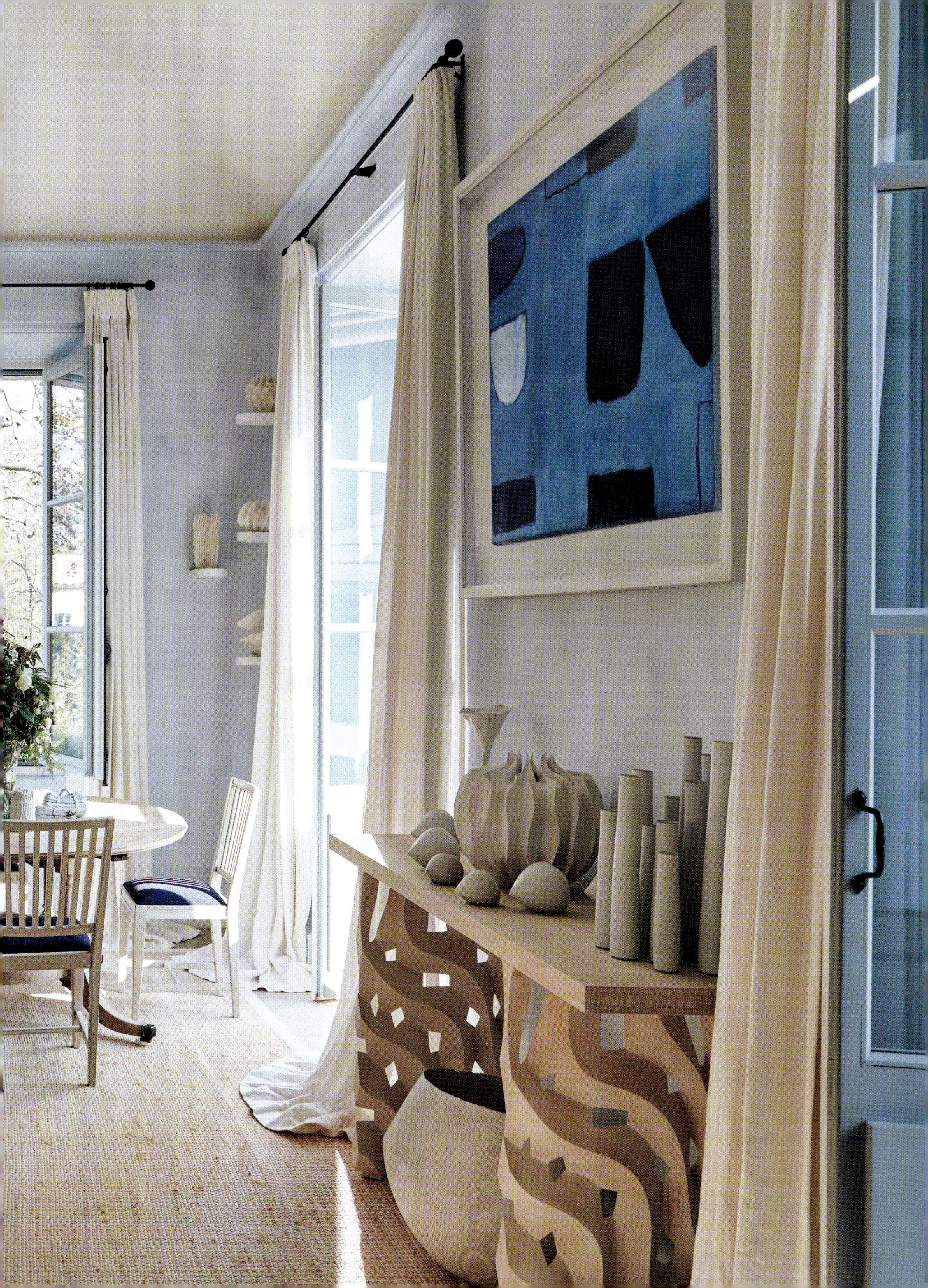

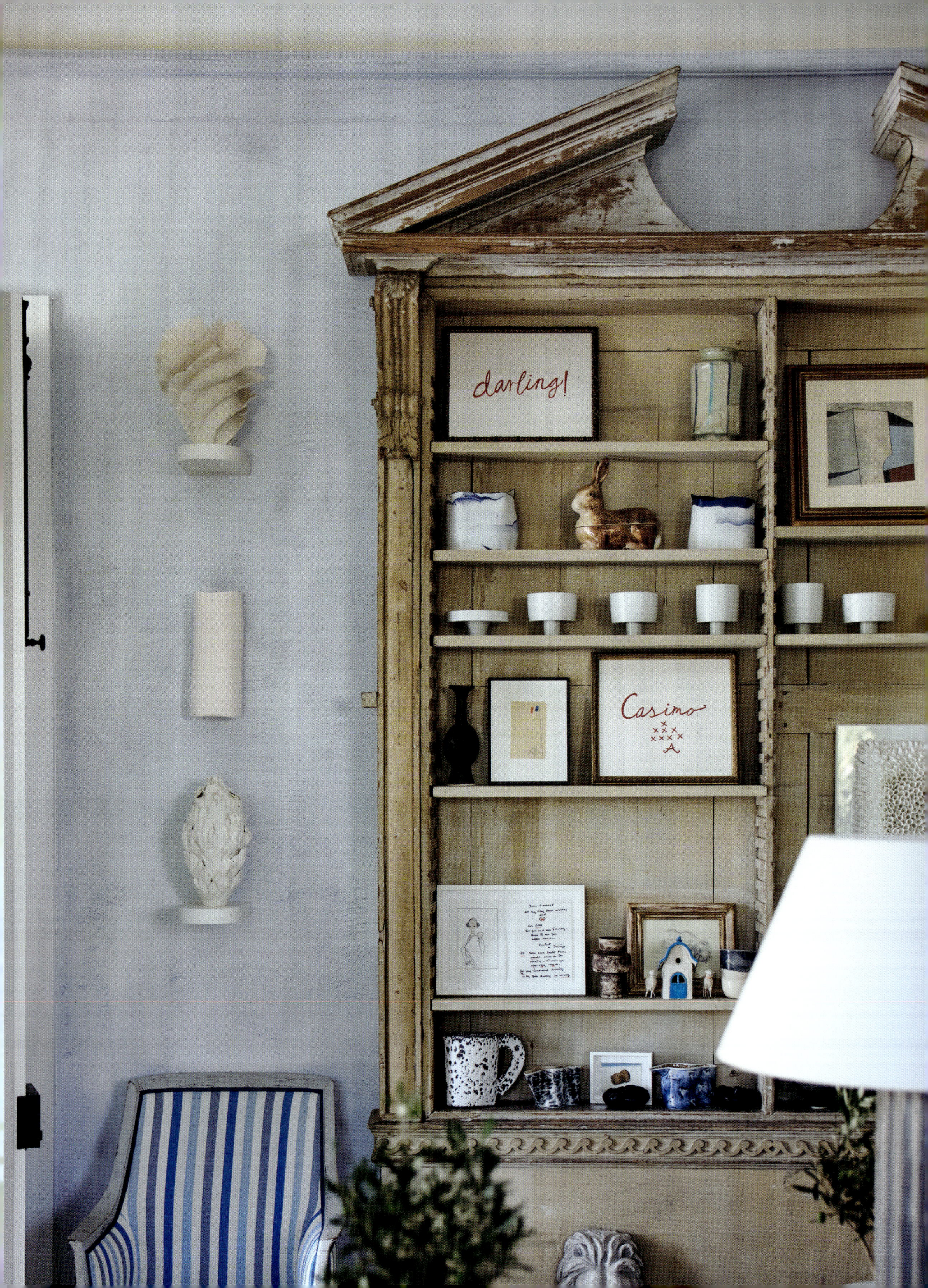
darling!
Casimo

ABOVE AND OPPOSITE Objects and trinkets collected or given to me by friends over the years, including the wonderful 'Darling!' and 'Casino' by my dear friend Hugo Guinness and a handwritten note and drawing of Audrey Hepburn by Hubert de Givenchy.

ABOVE Italian-born ceramicist Sandra Davolio's vessels draw from organic forms in nature such as the unfurling of petals.
OPPOSITE Nic Webb's structural wooden sculptures explore the natural curve and expression in the material.

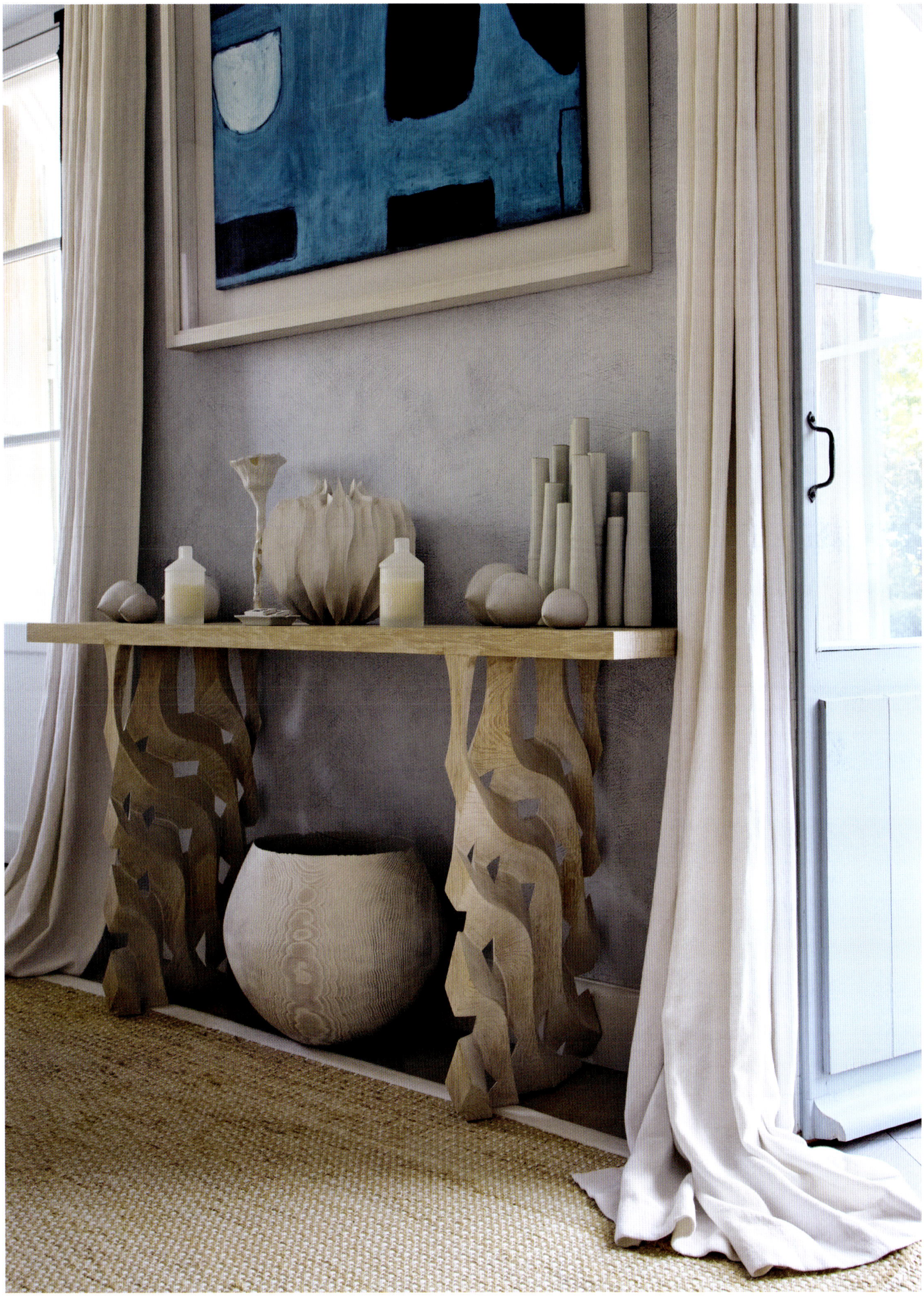

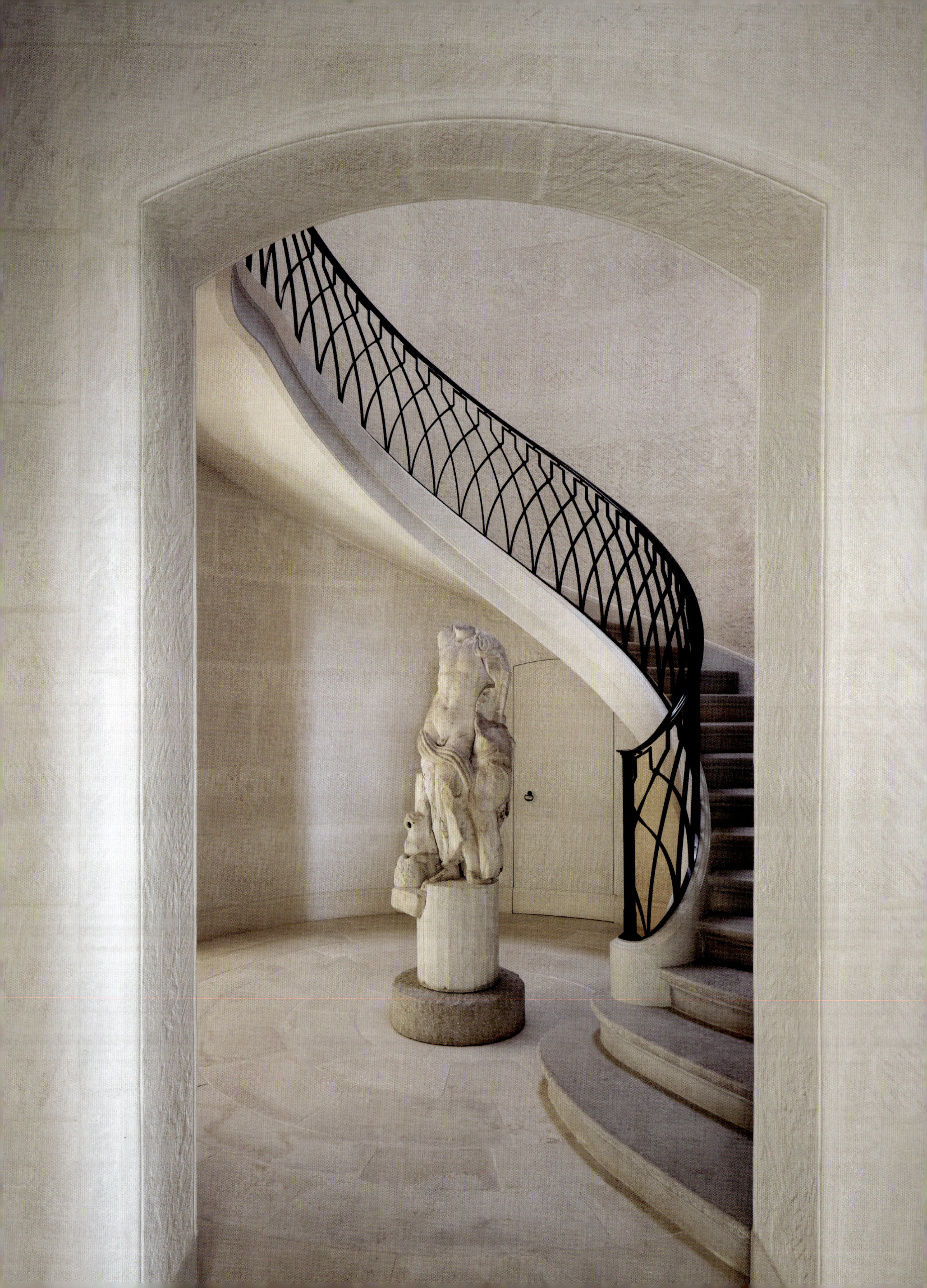

ABOVE The elegant winding staircase crafted by Alain reflects the typical style in a house of this period.
OPPOSITE A marble figure of Bacchus, Roman god of wine and the grape, 1st-2nd century AD.

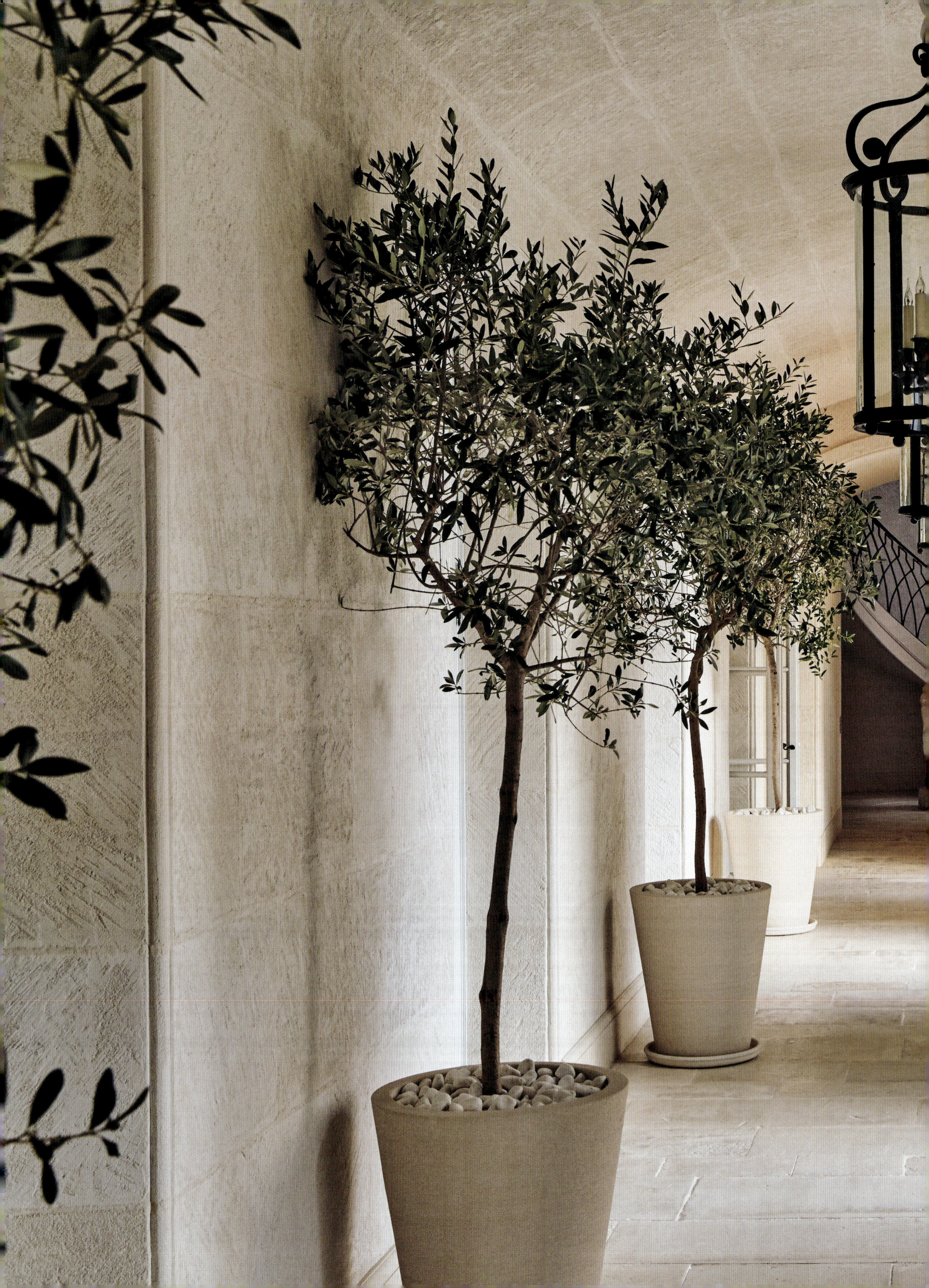

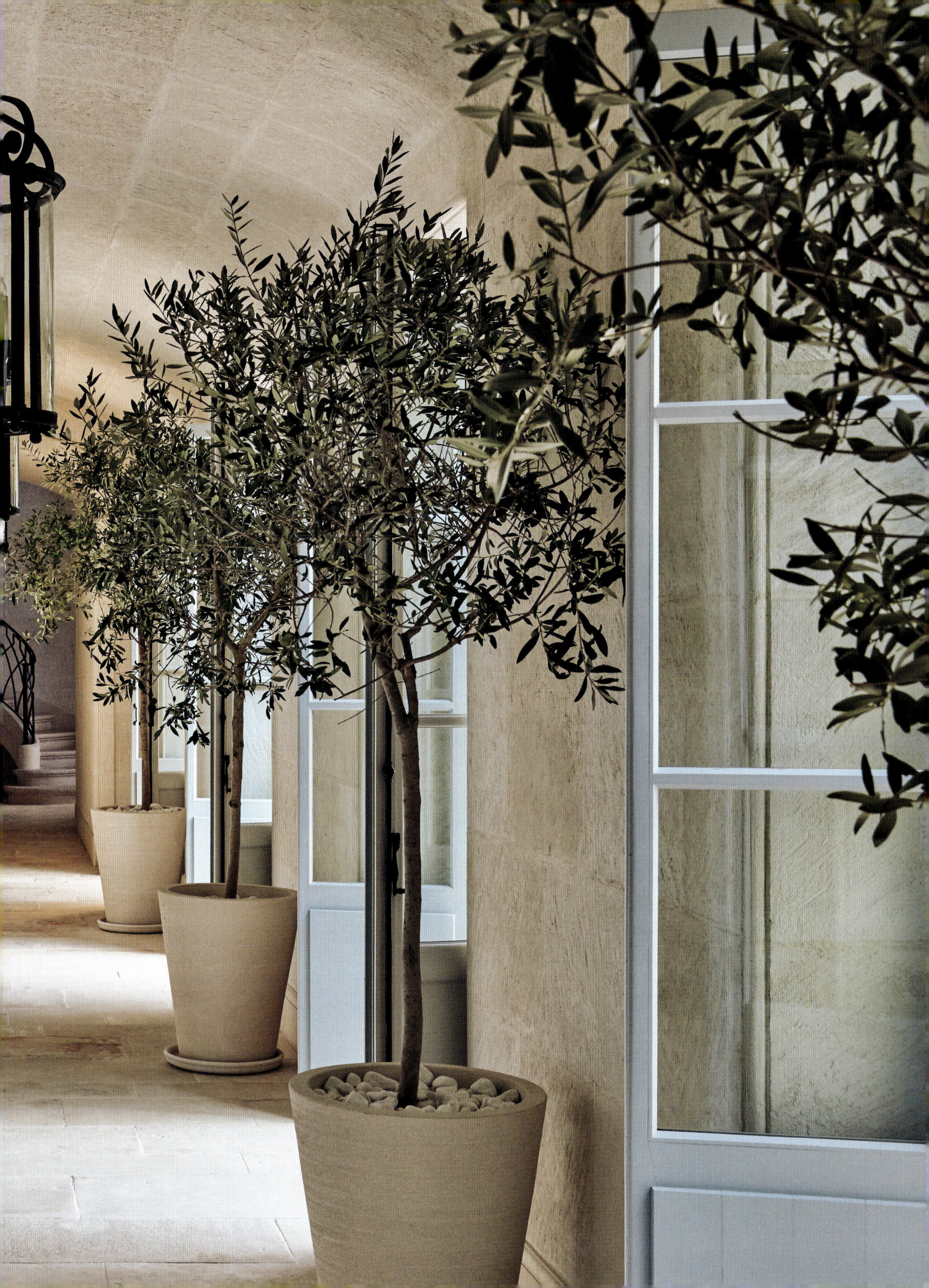

The gentle pace of life at Léoube means that it's somewhere I can take time to read and absorb the countless interior design books I adore yet so rarely have the time to enjoy at home in England. Books and what's on your bookshelves can tell you so much about a person – and the library does speak to my love of books but it also offers guests a chance to share in that interest and there's a huge array of books. Provence has captured the imagination of so many writers – from W. Somerset Maugham, the Scott Fitzgeralds, Hemingway and Camus to Peter Mayle and Elizabeth David – and the romantic in me loves the idea of honouring that past. All of them were captivated by the rhythm of life in the south of France and found inspiration in the scent of *garrigue* in the air and the quality of its light. I love looking at these shelves and being reminded of that connection. Somerset Maugham's *Up at the Villa* is a book I have been enchanted by for years and I've lost count of the numbers of times I've picked it up again when I'm here.

My sense with interior design is that if you've got a highly decorated room, it follows that you want a moment of calm. So, while the morning room and library are both full of art, objects and pieces that draw your eye, the dining room needed to be calm, uncluttered and restrained. The walnut table is from Axel Vervoordt and is made out of monks' benches. It is an exquisite piece that I feel very fortunate to have found. It is very long, necessary for a room of this size, and rich in a history that suits the peaceful tone of this room perfectly.

At some stage in its past the ballroom would have been a family chapel and we've honoured that in the way we chose to design it, which now echoes the style of a rustic Italian church. Once again we sought the talents of Lucinda, who created panelling made up of different shades of marbling using trompe l'oeil; it has given the walls a shape and grace befitting of the room's purpose. There's a slightly ethereal feel to the ballroom when shafts of light shine through the *œil-de-bœuf* windows onto the paint.

PREVIOUS PAGE Many of the lanterns were sourced but the ones in the hall had to be made because it wasn't possible to find any to fit the scale we needed.

OPPOSITE The 18th century dining room table is made of walnut monks' benches.

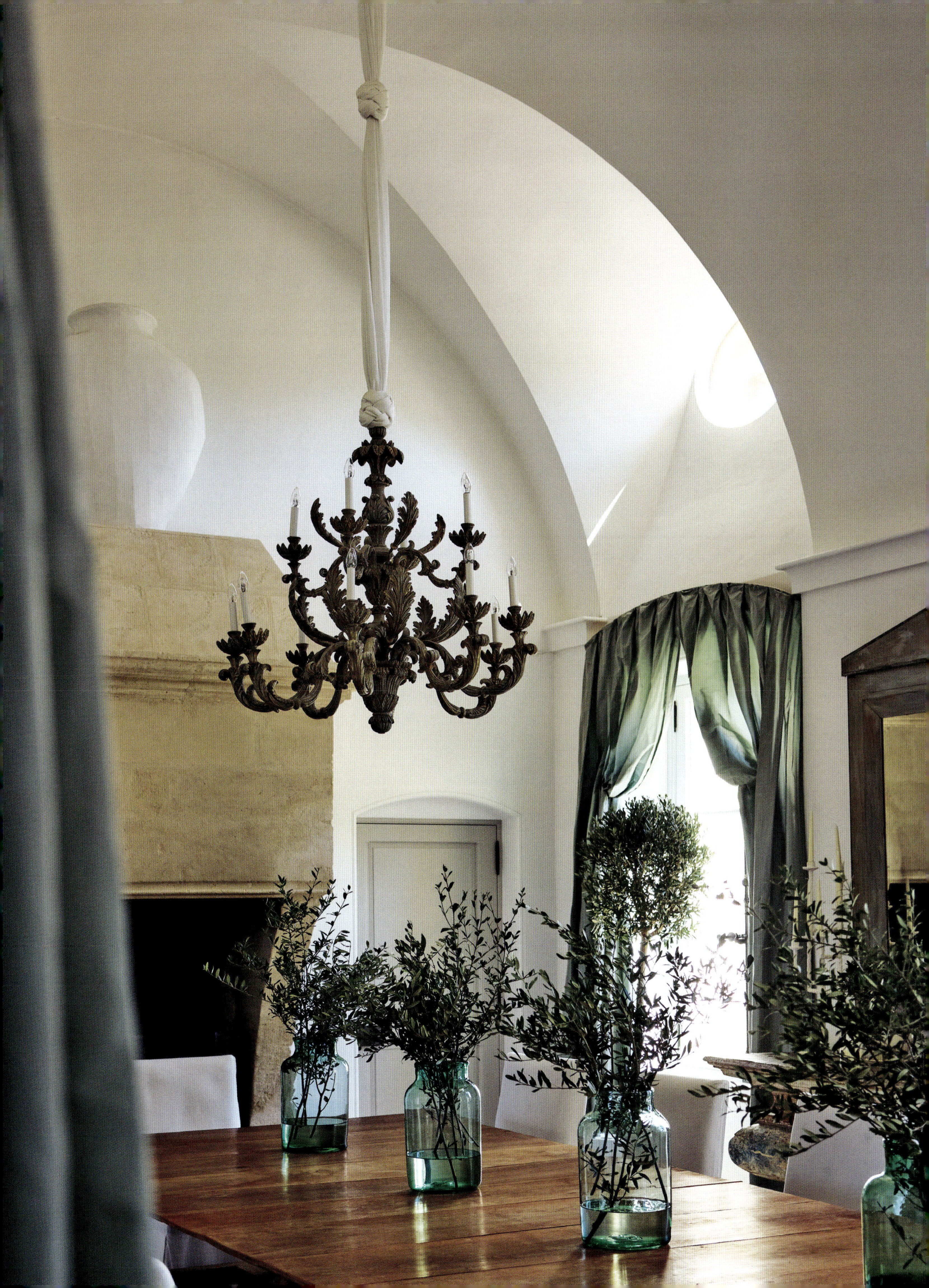

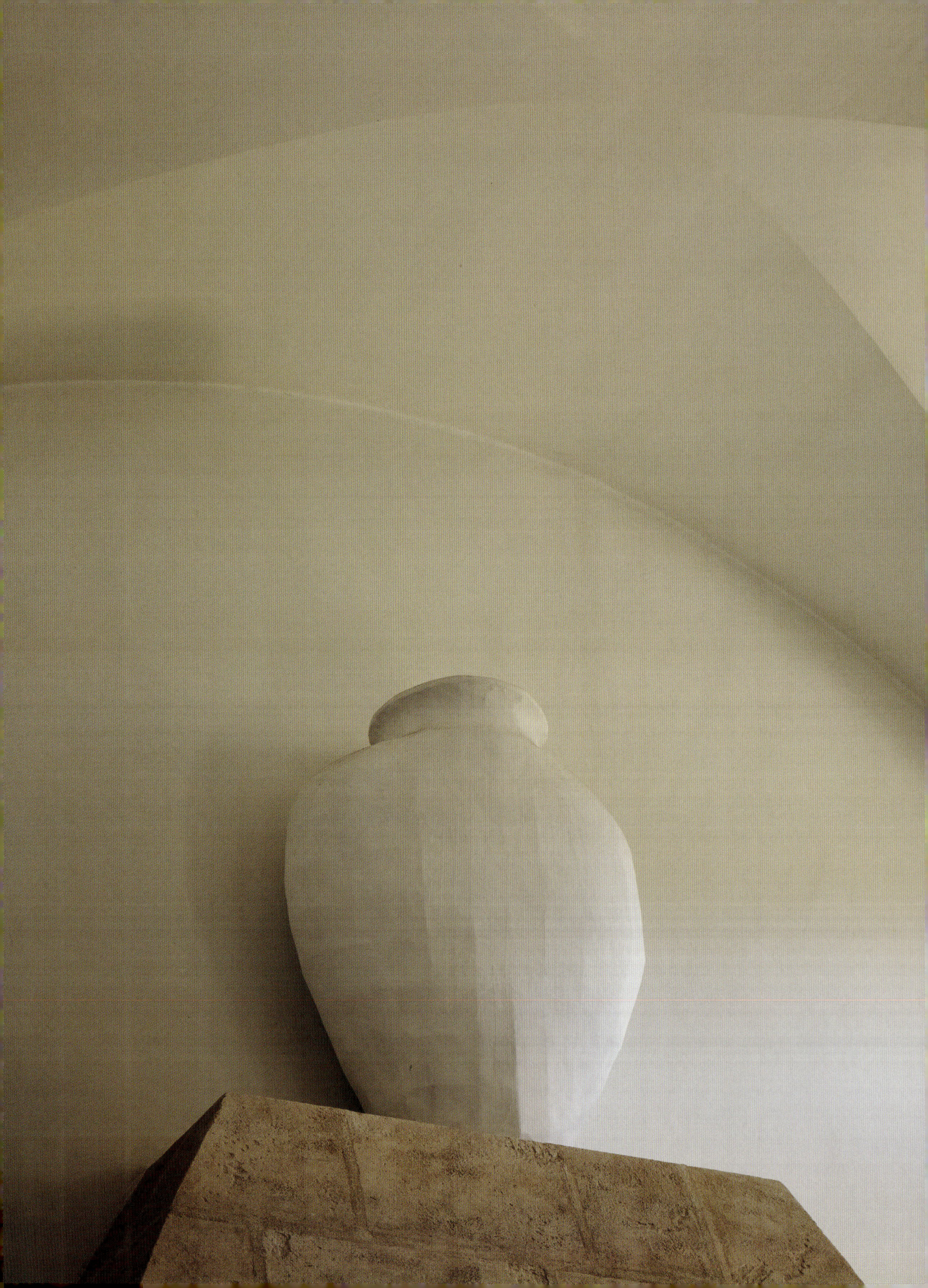

OPPOSITE AND OVERLEAF The space above the chimneybreast in the dining room felt a little bare and gaping so Alain had this papier mâché vessel made following a design Wendy had sketched.

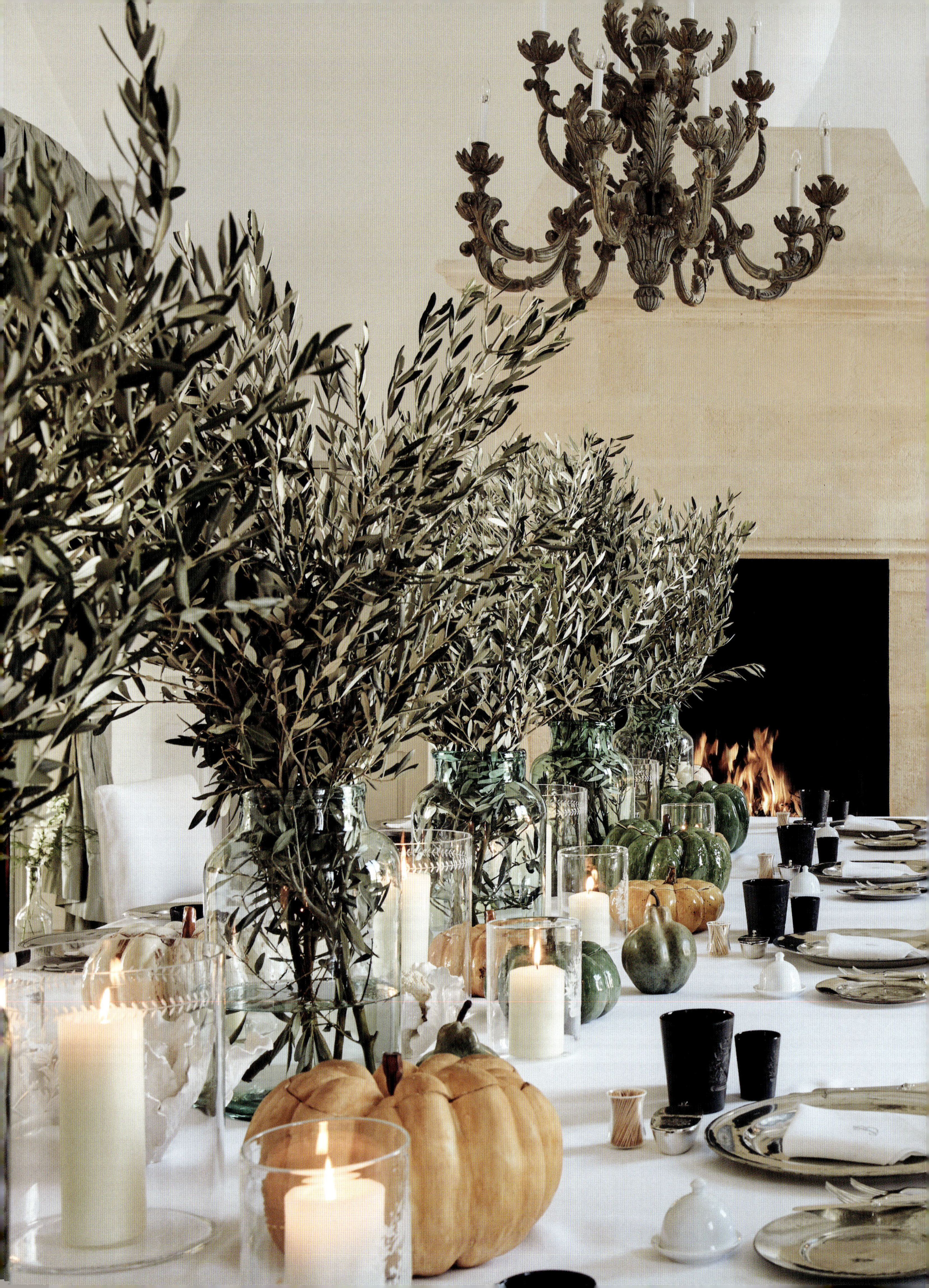

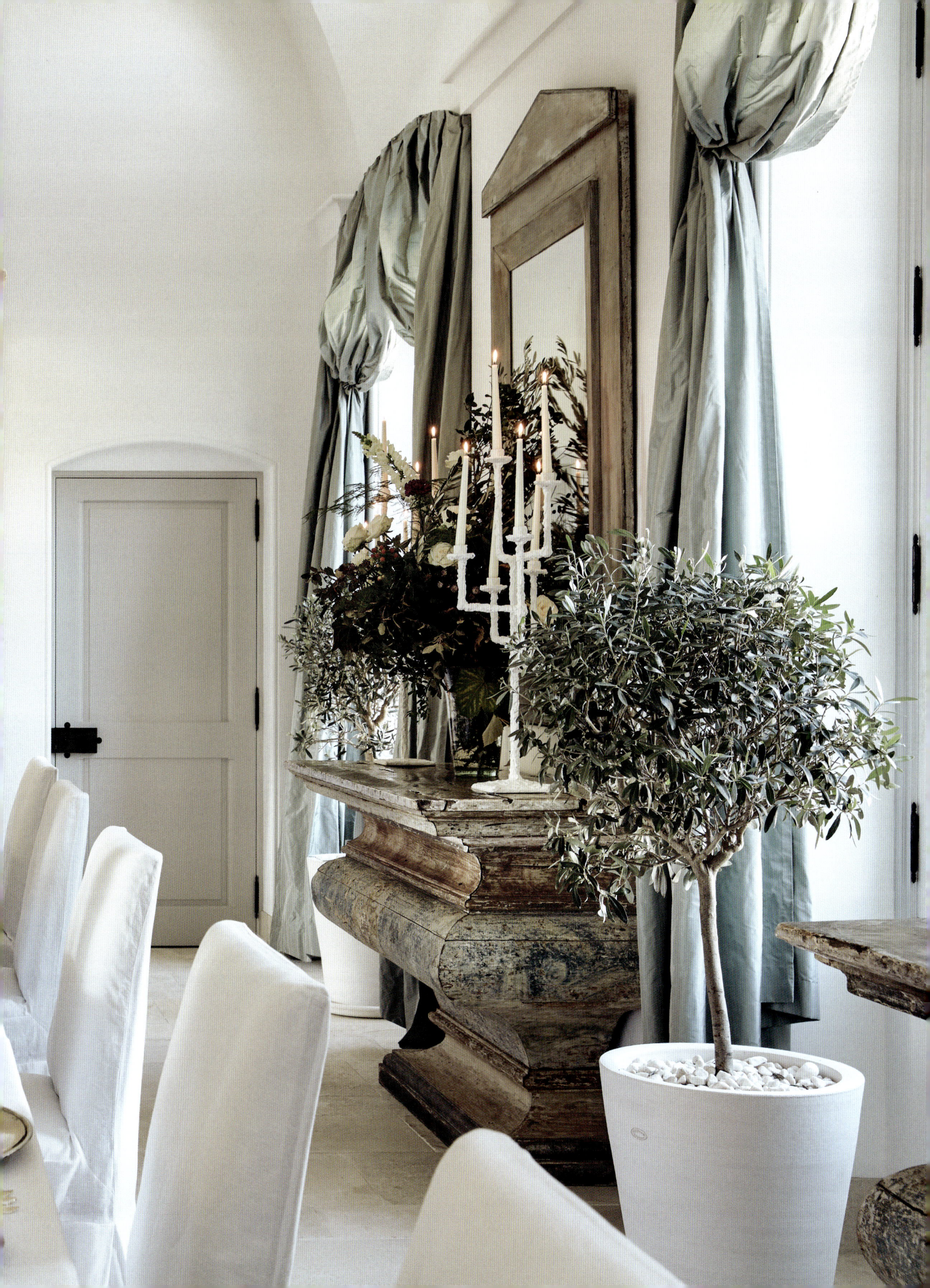

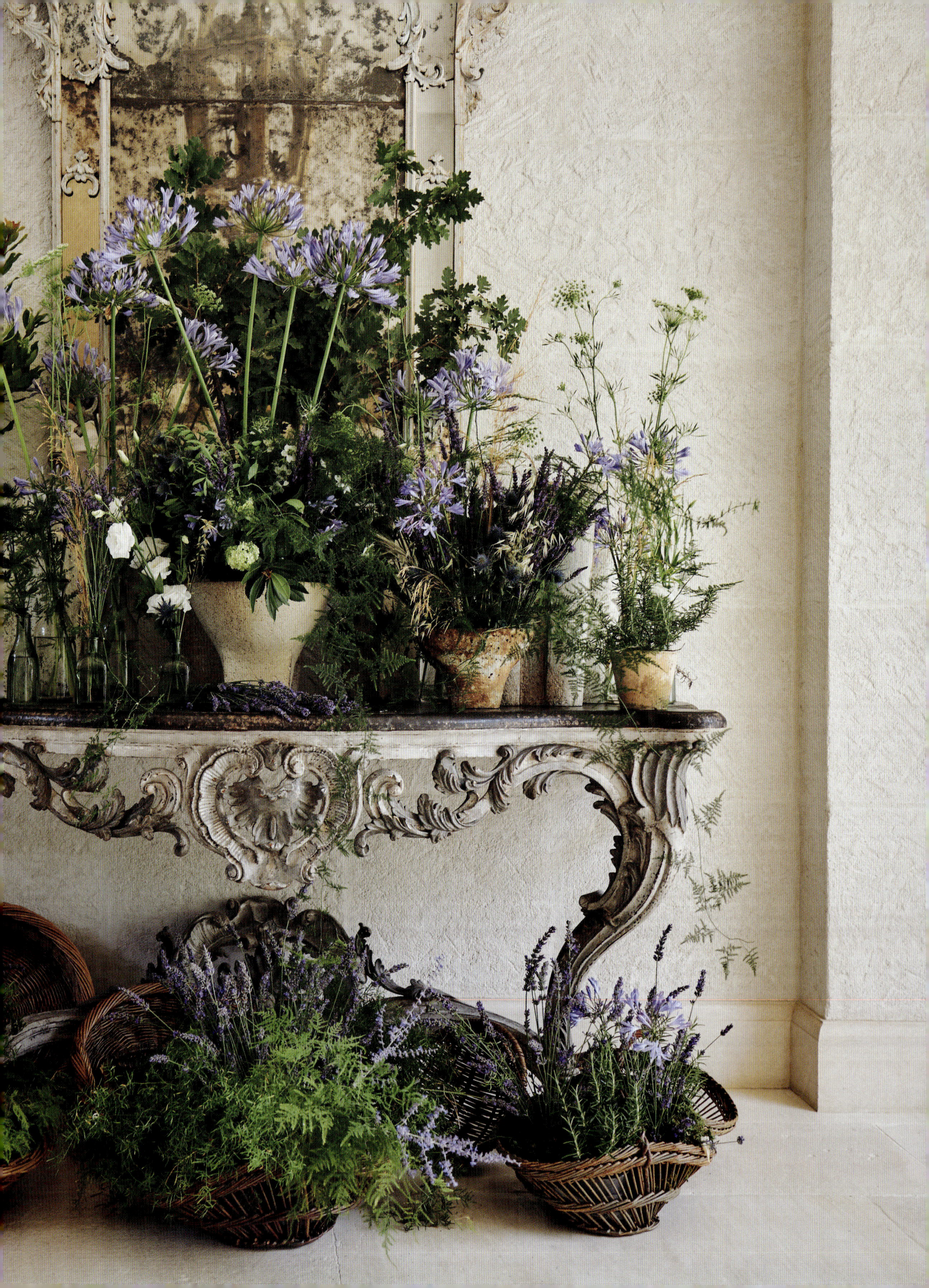

THE HOUSE: ENTERTAINING SPACES

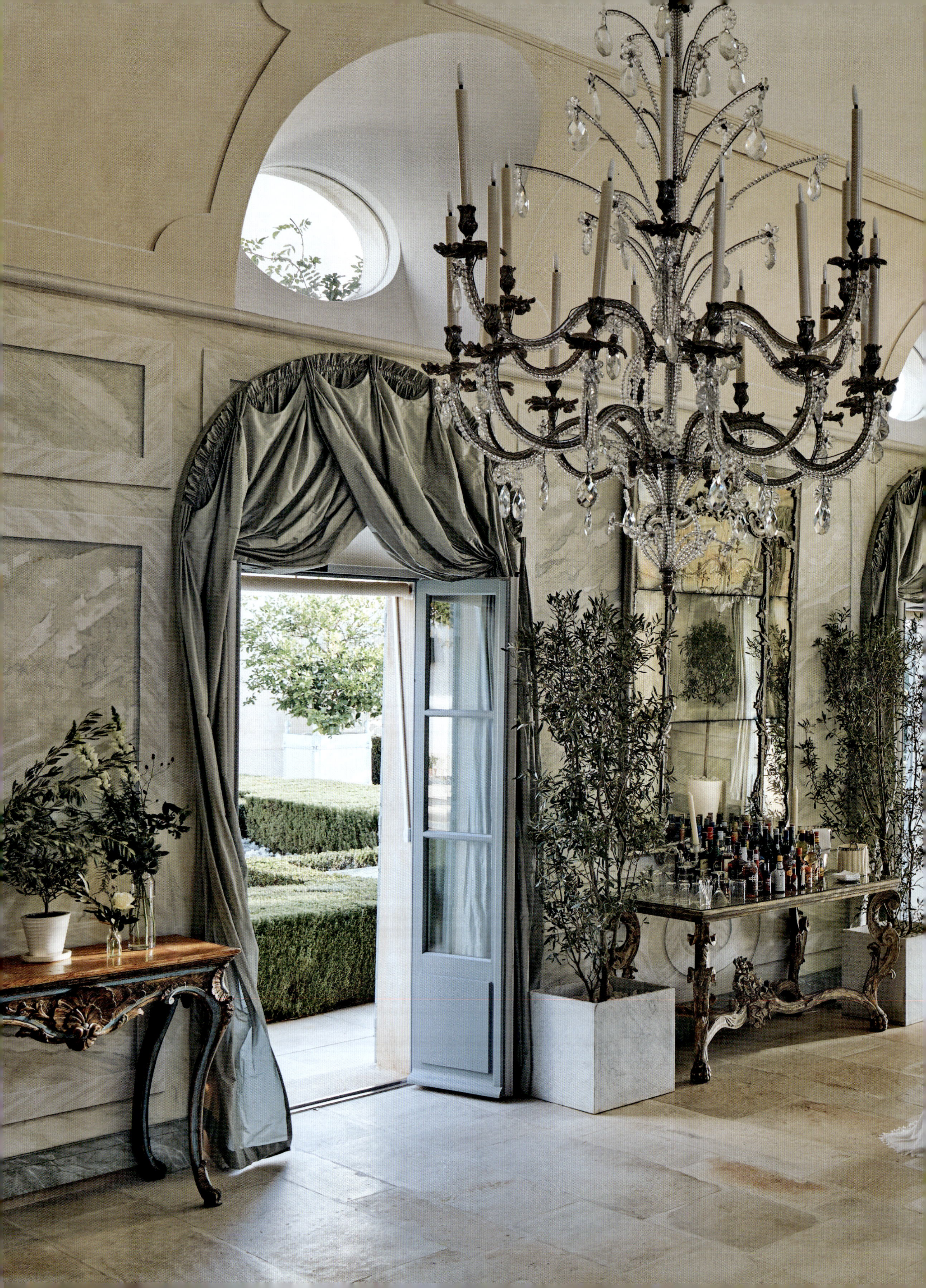

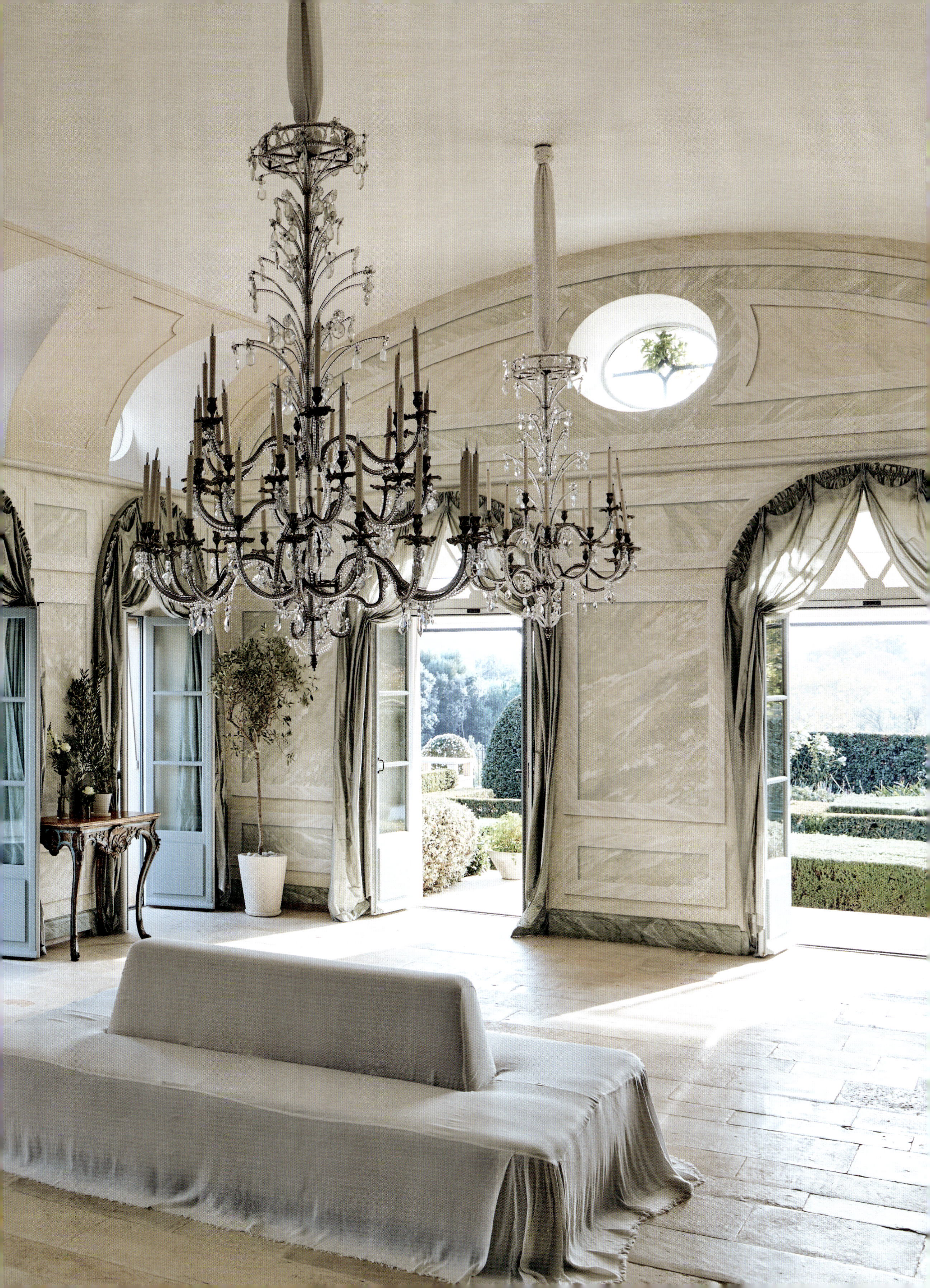

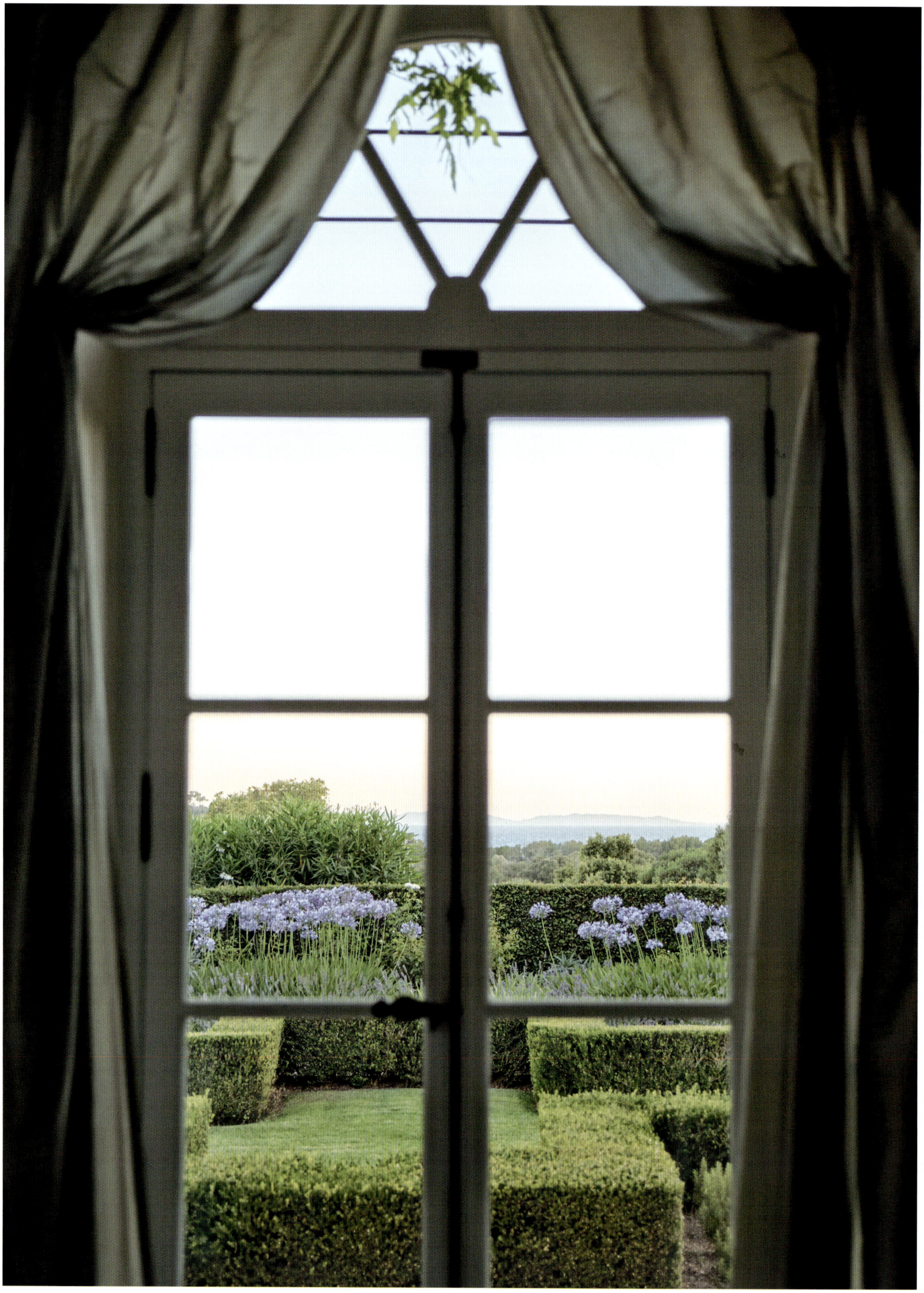

THE HOUSE: ENTERTAINING SPACES

ABOVE Fratelli Toso in Murano produce our glassware with the Bamford crest.

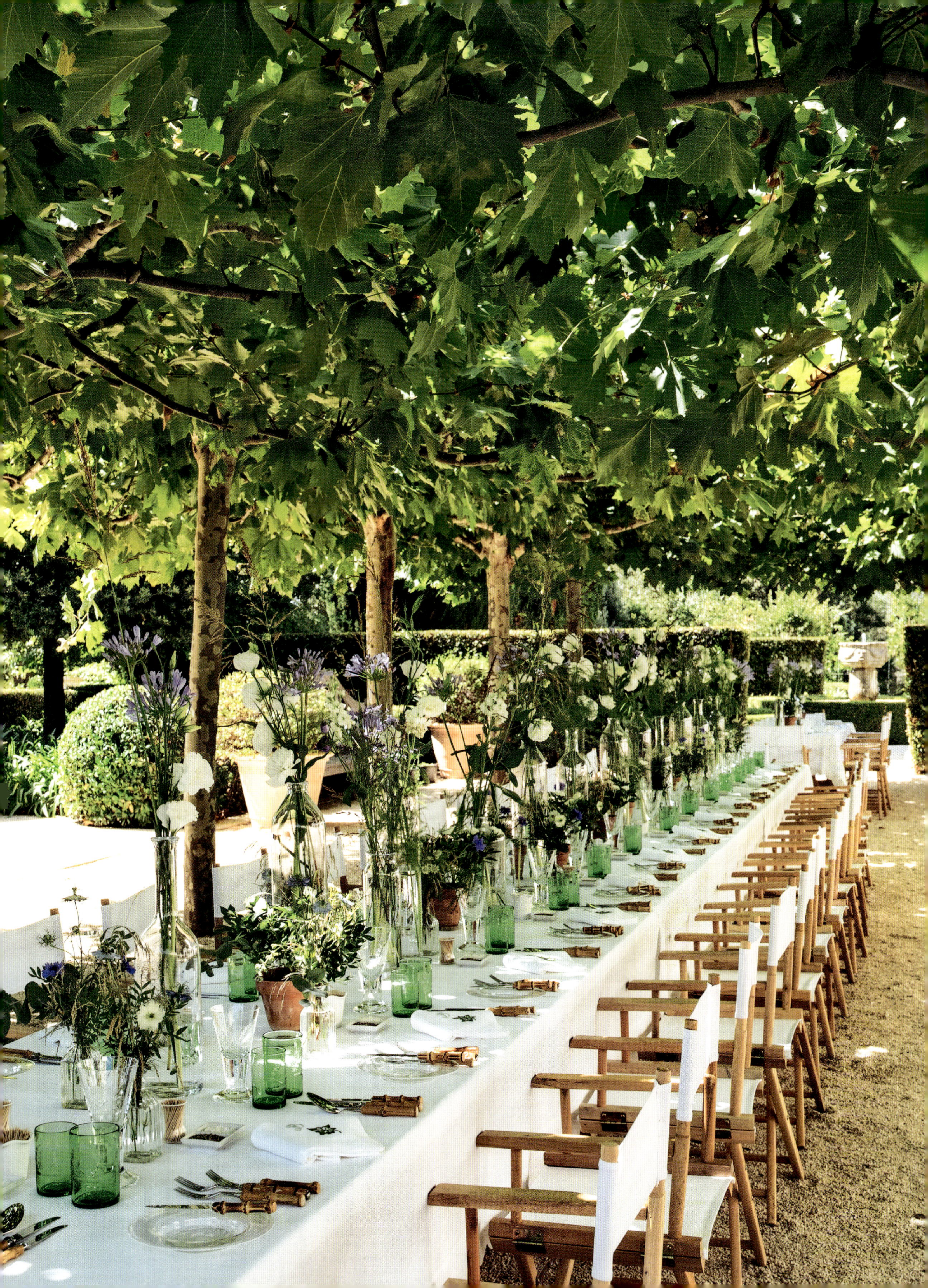

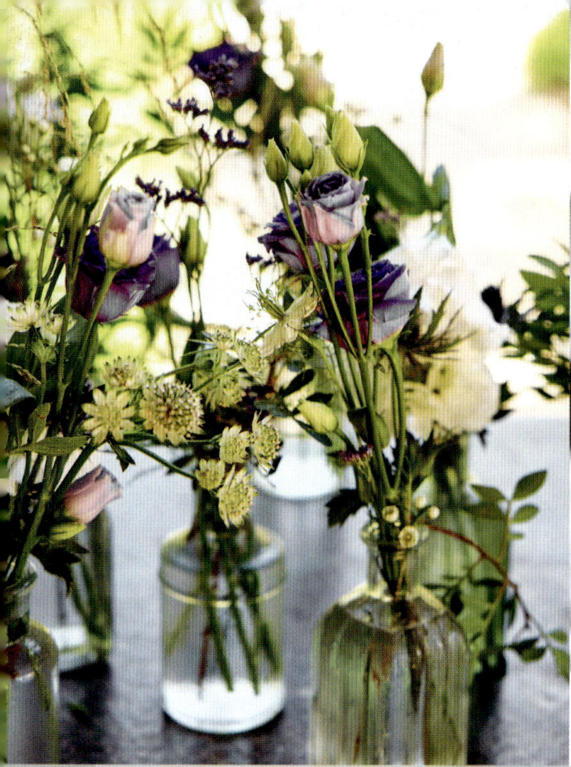
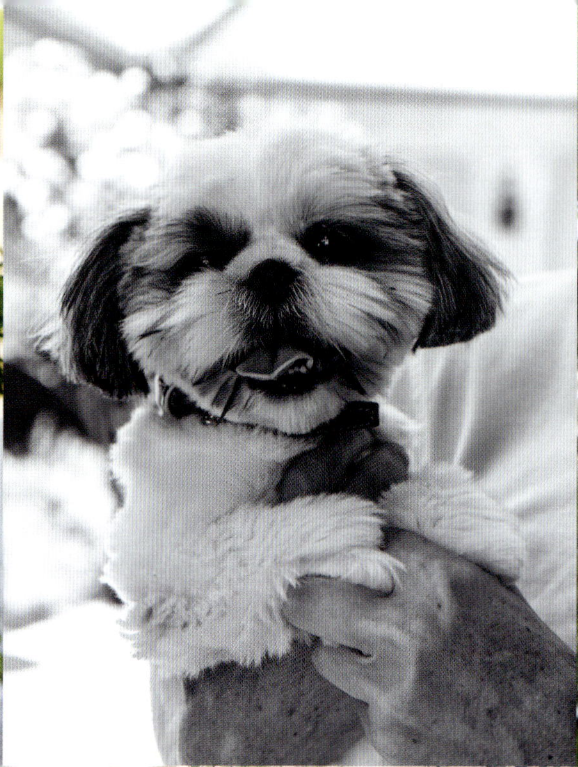
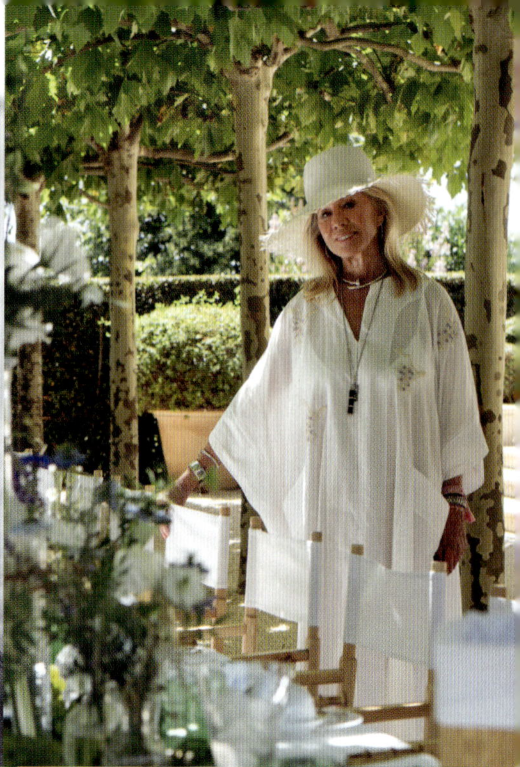

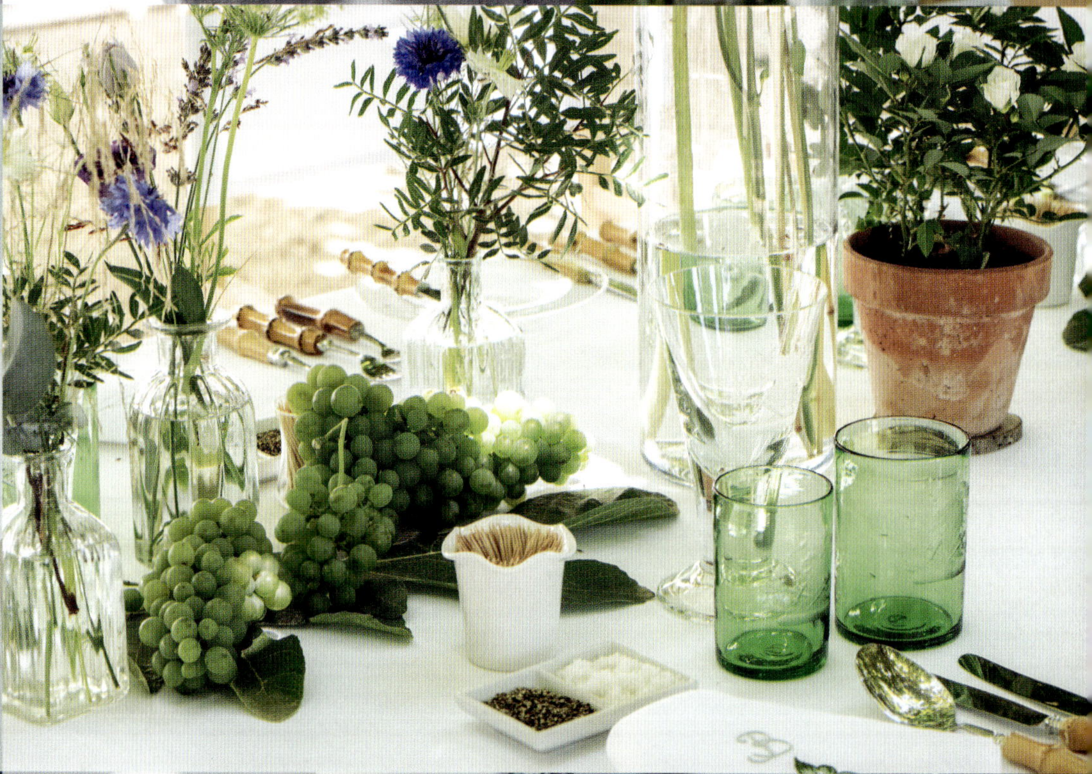
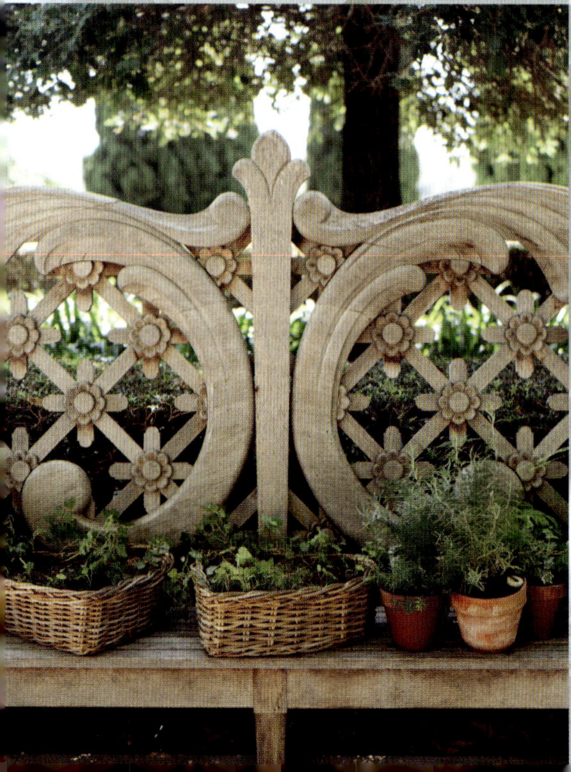
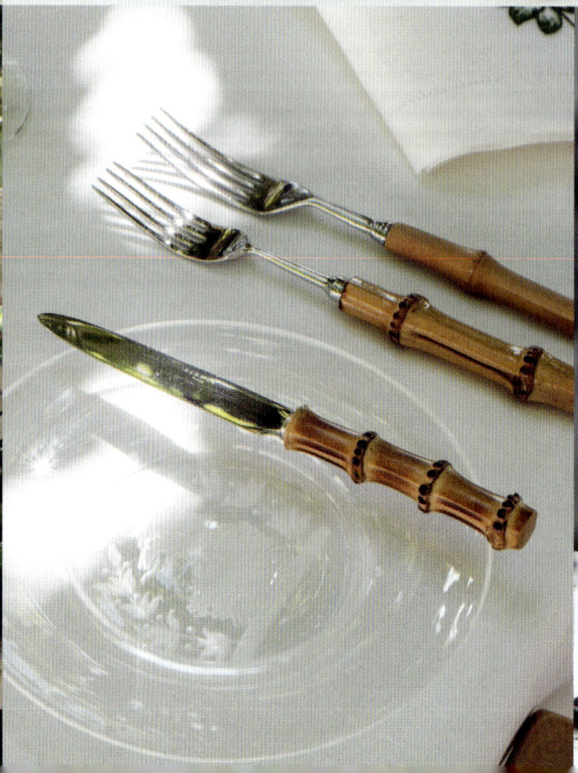
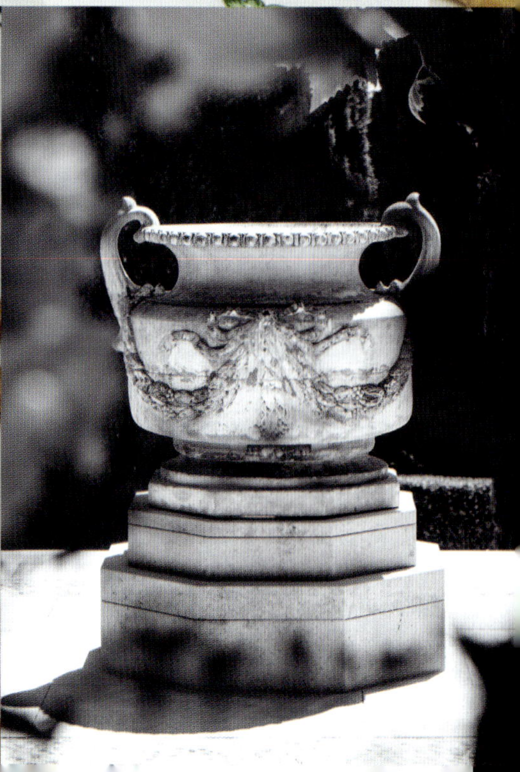

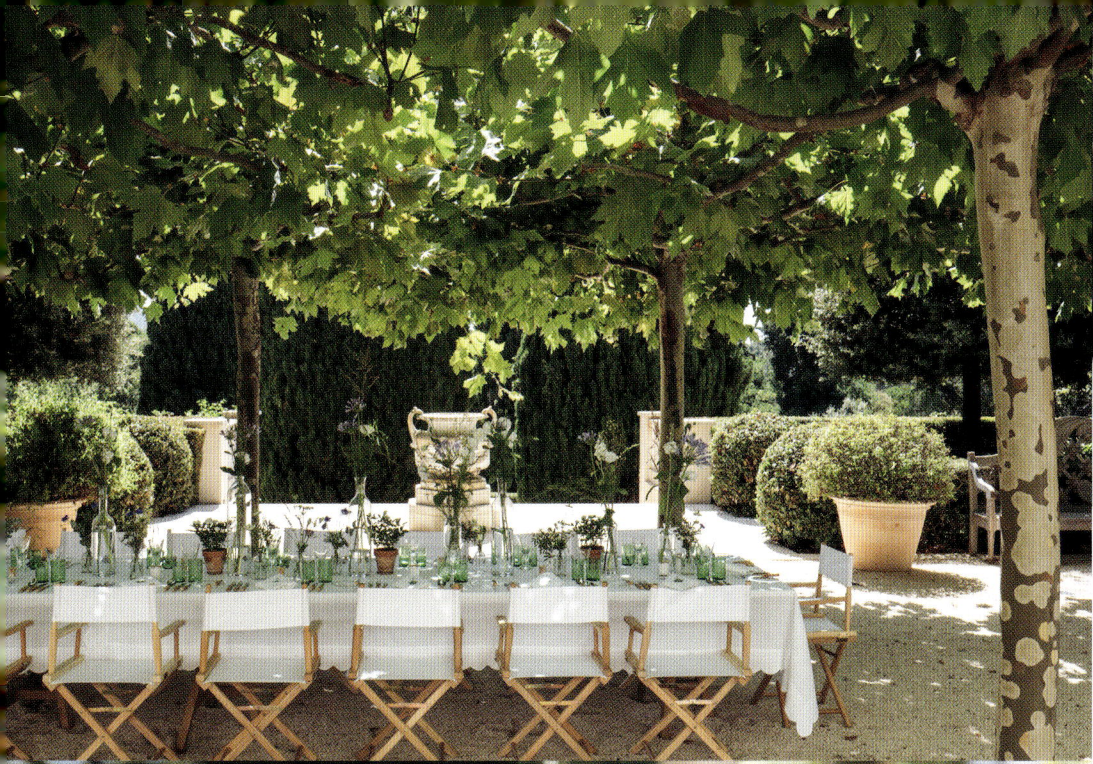
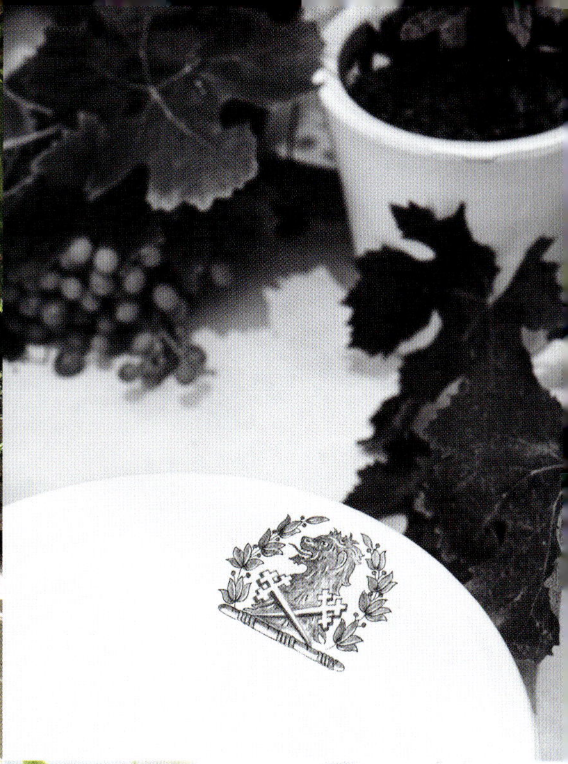
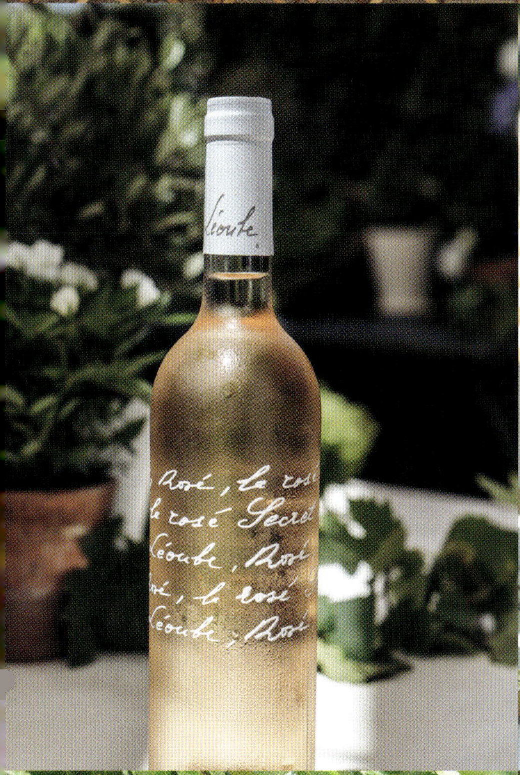
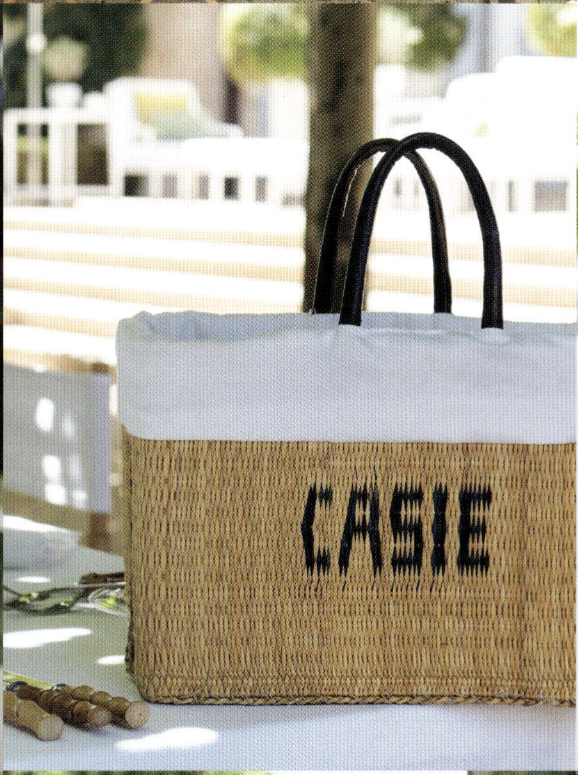
CASIE
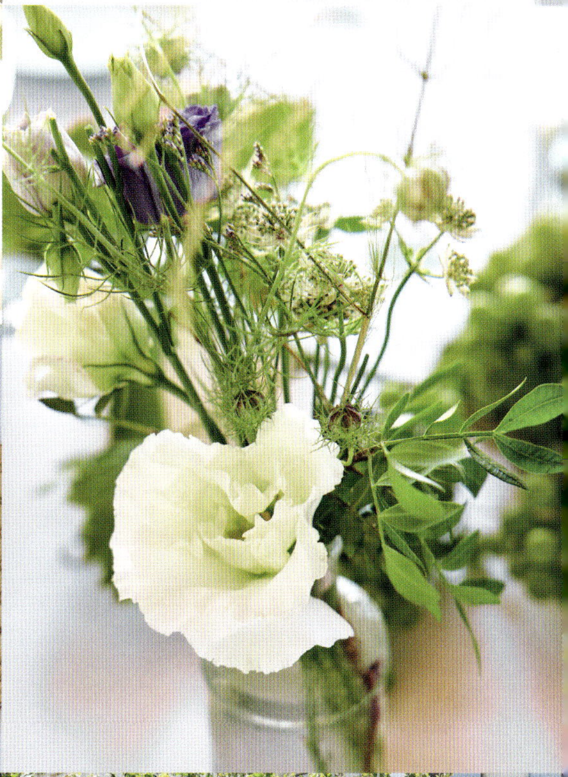
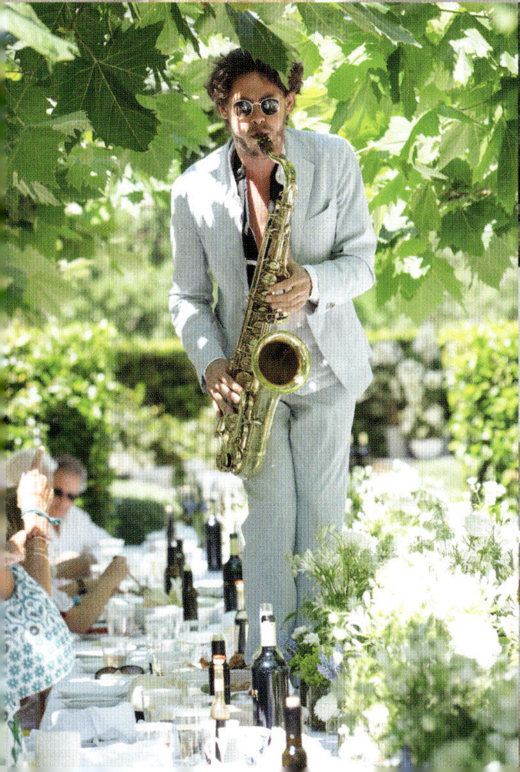
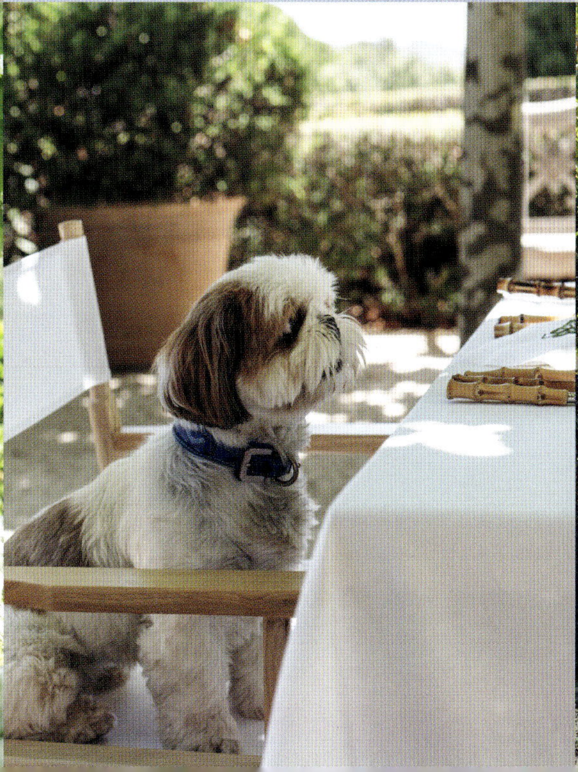
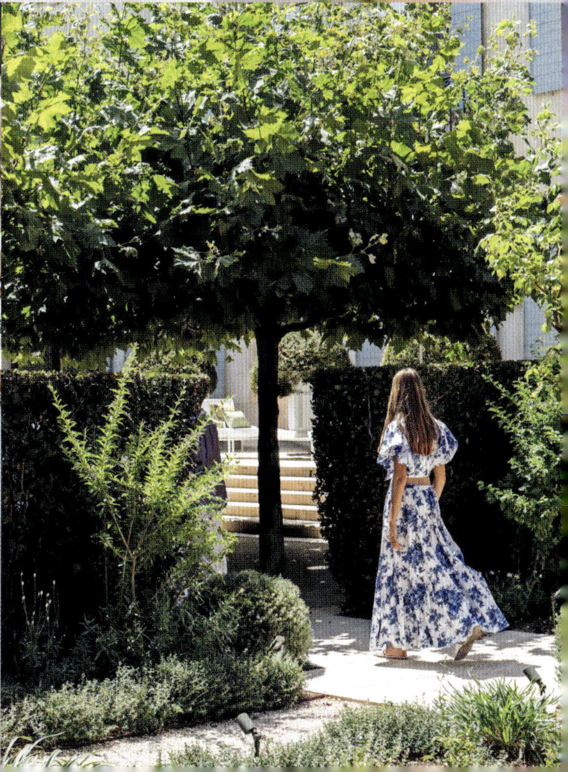

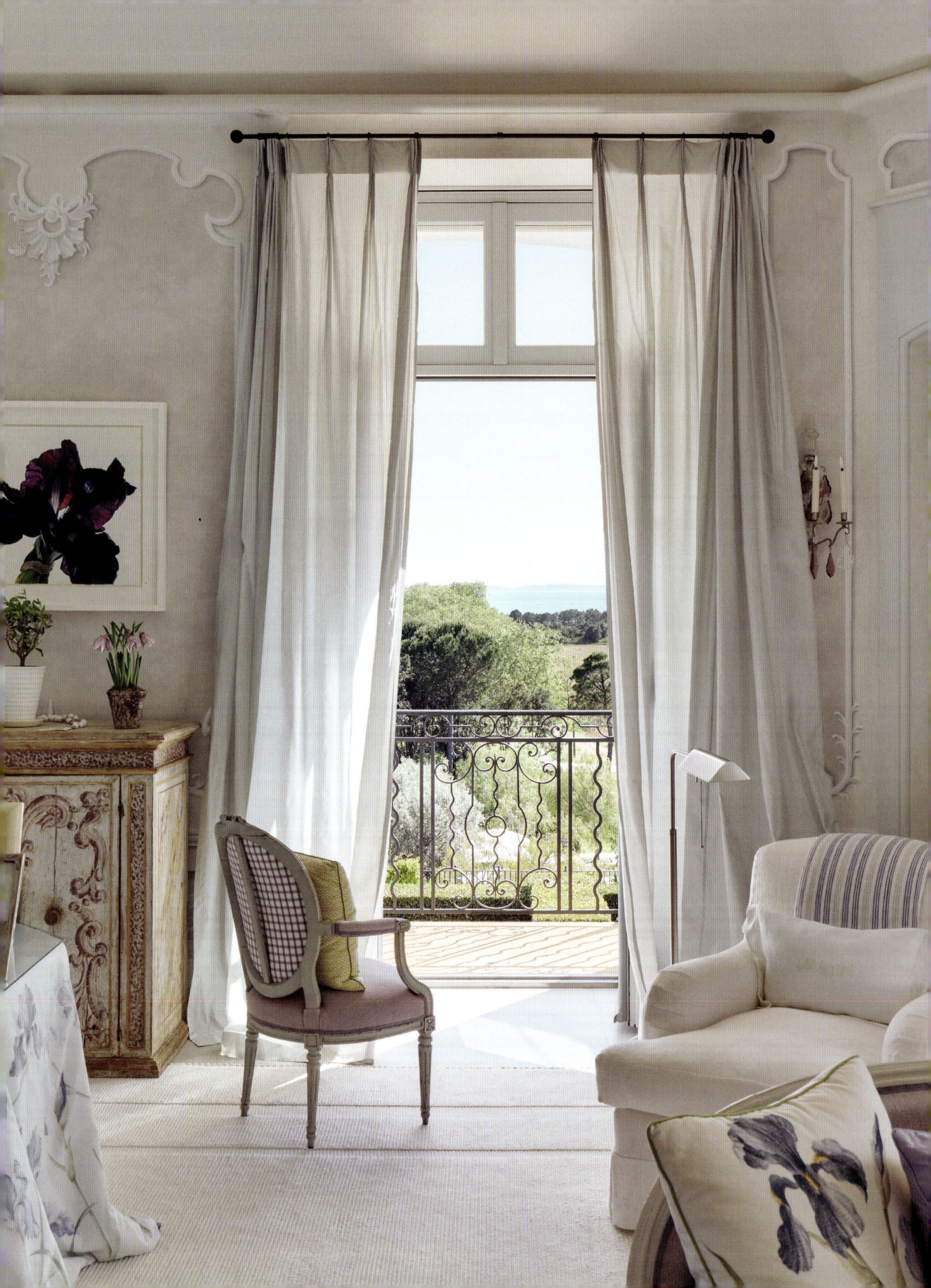

# THE HOUSE

LIVING SPACES

I rarely begin designing spaces simply by thinking about colours or how pieces of furniture might inhabit rooms – I'm led by something far more instinctive, something that sparks a feeling. Inspiration might come from a piece of fabric I've been drawn to, a painting or artwork that's moved me, or from nature, which inspires me in countless ways.

The connection to nature is inherent at Léoube but is perhaps most palpable in the design of the bedrooms, many of which were conceived by observing the flowers that flourish in the region and to which I am particularly drawn.

Irises have been cultivated in Provence since the time of the Romans. They have been an important feature of my gardens at Léoube and at home in England and I have always loved their fragrance and their deep violet and gentler sapphire tones – these were the starting point for my bedroom's decoration.

Wendy and I again asked Lucinda Oakes to come and interpret an iris, which she did beautifully, painting it on to a tablecloth, and the design of the room evolved from there. The proportions of the room are particularly large – it's a wide space, which needed to be broken up, so Lucinda also hand-painted the walls using a style of panelling in a very soft greyish mauve inspired by the tones of a traditional Italian palazzo.

OPPOSITE 'Still Life with Irises', 2006, watercolour, by Elizabeth Blackadder. Portraits of my grandchildren hang on the walls by my writing table.

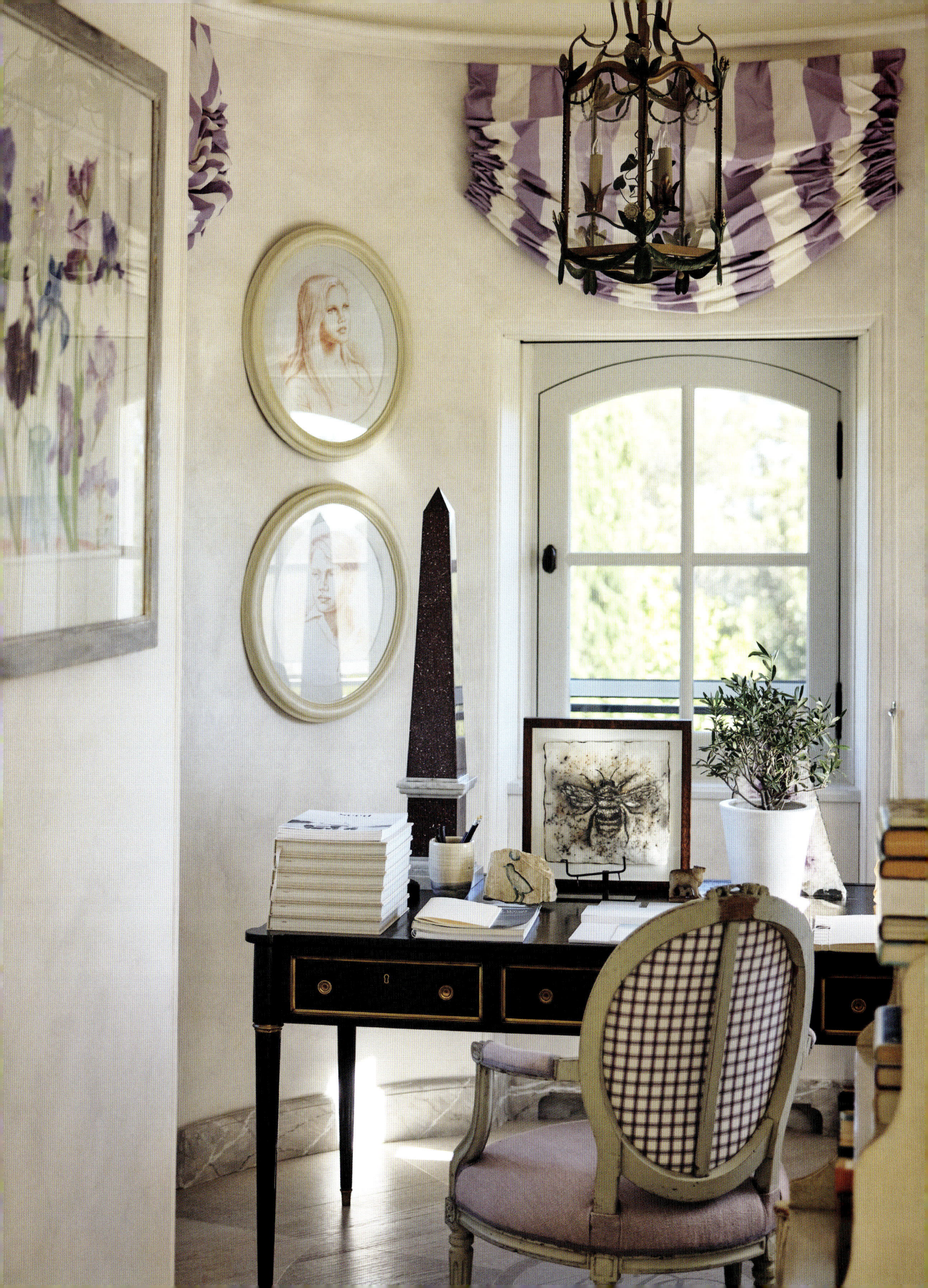

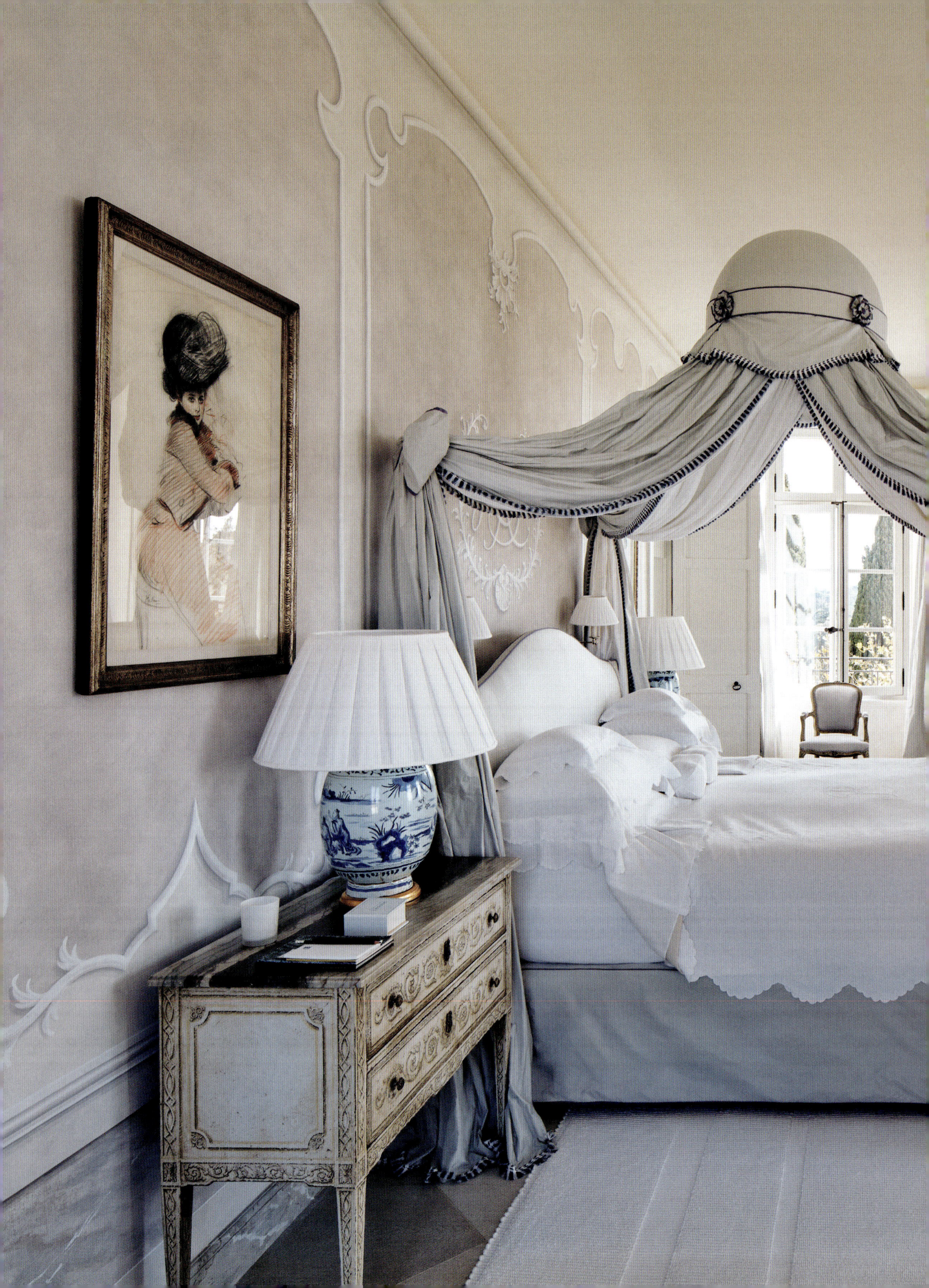

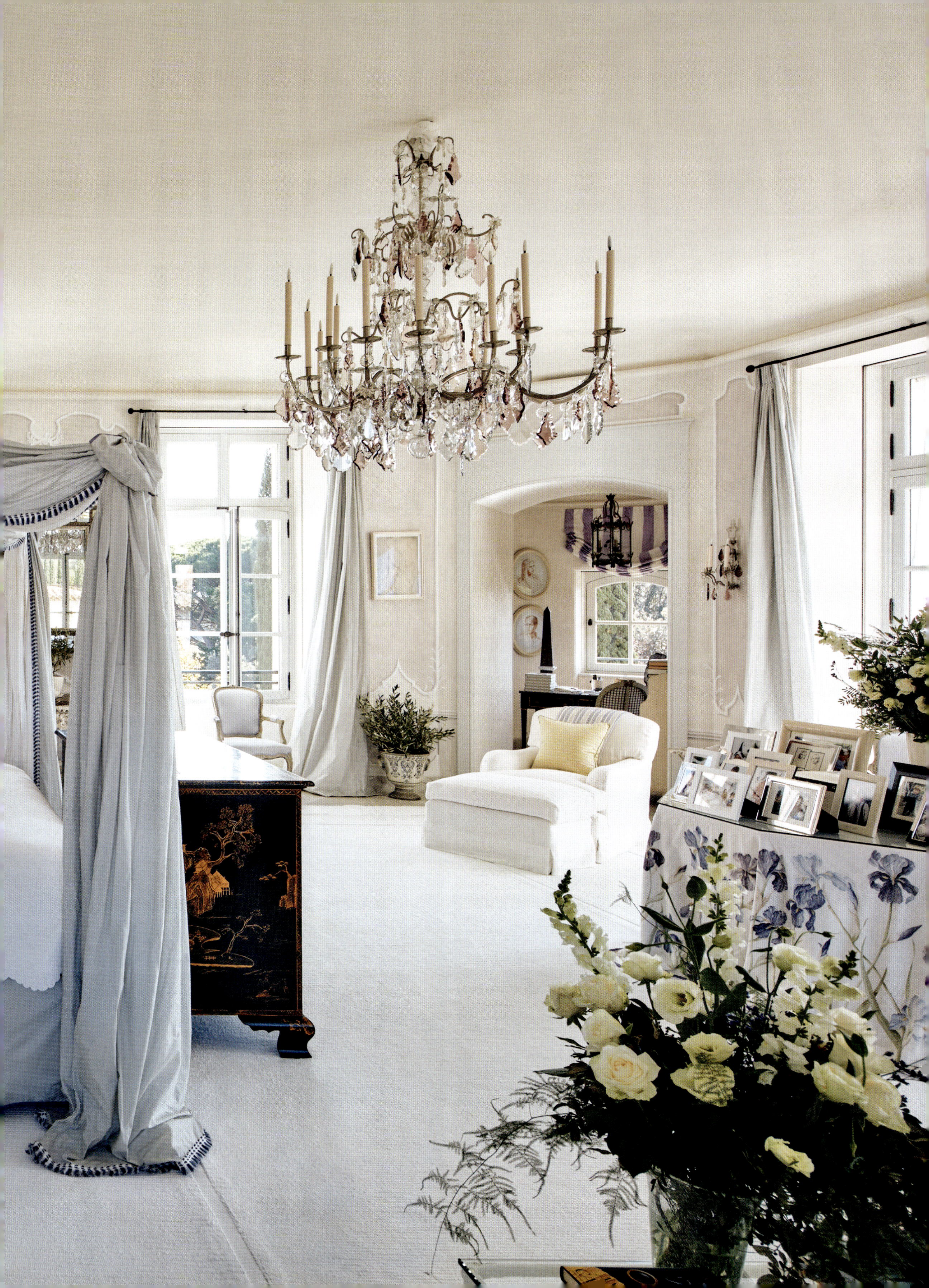

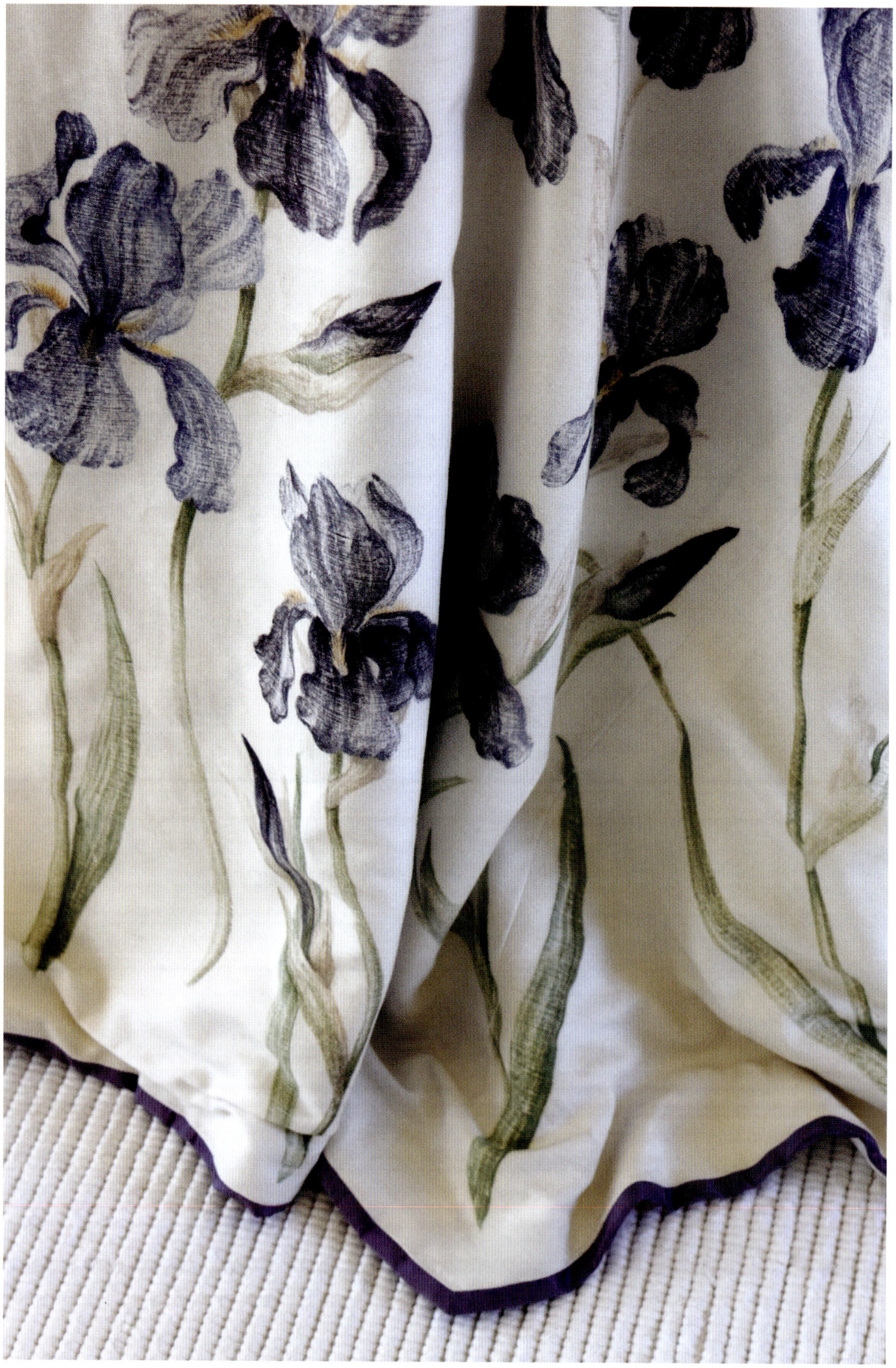

The towers at each end of the room frame the space and are cosy little nooks that add visual focal points while also enhancing the space and having function – in one is a beautiful French writing table, in the other my dressing table.

My bathroom is a sanctuary. The bath was carved from a piece of brèche violette marble, as was the arch framing the mirror above it, but the mauve marbling around the bath and on the fireplace is actually trompe l'œil. The violet and mauve tones add depth and softness to the room and the trompe l'œil's striking painted veins very deceptively echo the stone's natural beauty – most people are shocked when they discover it's not real. The terrazzo floor, made up of tiny inlays of stone in plaster, follows the very traditional Venetian style, adding warmth and giving it a very unique quality, no two floors being the same. I chose a pattern reflecting the motion of waves, a reference to our location by the sea, which is echoed by the shells on the walls which were cast in plaster and designed to house lights.

I have always held a deep reverence for handwoven textiles. The slub in their weave – the gentle irregularities where the yarn thickens and the presence of the human hand makes itself visible – reflects a quiet defiance of uniformity and an imperfection that I am inherently drawn to. Years of travelling to India has meant that I have a very deep-rooted appreciation of its traditional handwoven khadi cloth and own a collection of vintage fabrics, but France's own history is so closely interwined with linen-making and textiles that I wanted to reflect that in the house by using textiles made closer to home. There are table linens sourced from around France, but also from Portofino, in homage to the many Italian-inspired details in the house. There I found a company that has been designing and creating the most intricate and exquisitely crafted linens for 60 years. The hand embroidery and textiles have become such a defining, beautiful feature of the house and one that makes it very personal.

I was keen that hand-embroidery should also come forward in the design of some of the guest bedrooms– the lily of the valley room (another of my favourite flowers because of its association with spring's renewal, good fortune and the French tradition of offering posies of *muguet* to loved ones on May 1st) celebrates the delicate drooping blossom through hand-embroidered fabrics on the bed linens, curtains, blind and upholstery. The fabric was created by Chelsea Textiles in London and, while I fell instantly in love with their design for the lily of the valley, we spent a long time going back and forth over the tone of the green in the leaves, trying to get it to reflect what I believe is the colour true to the plants themselves.

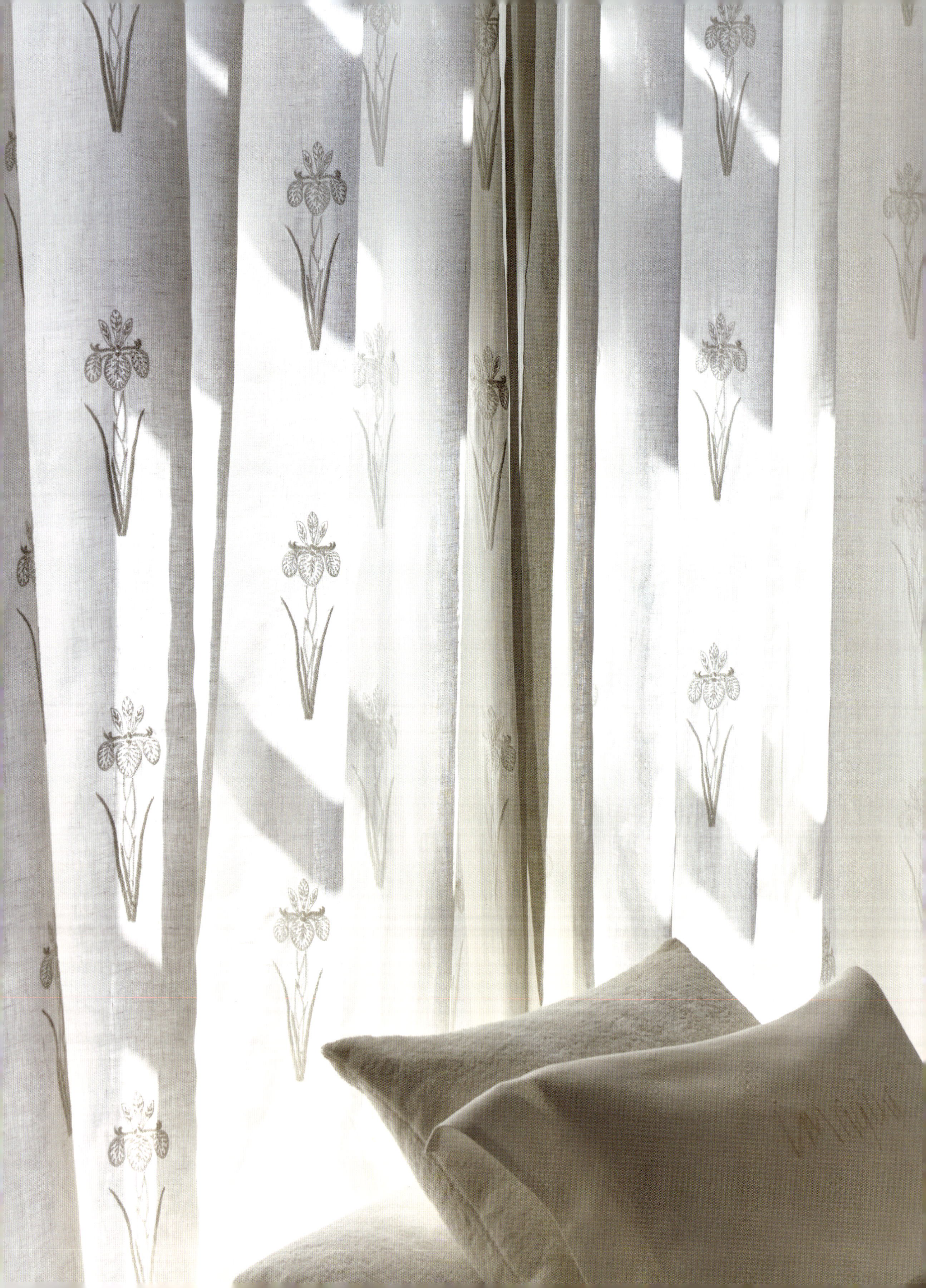

THE HOUSE: LIVING SPACES

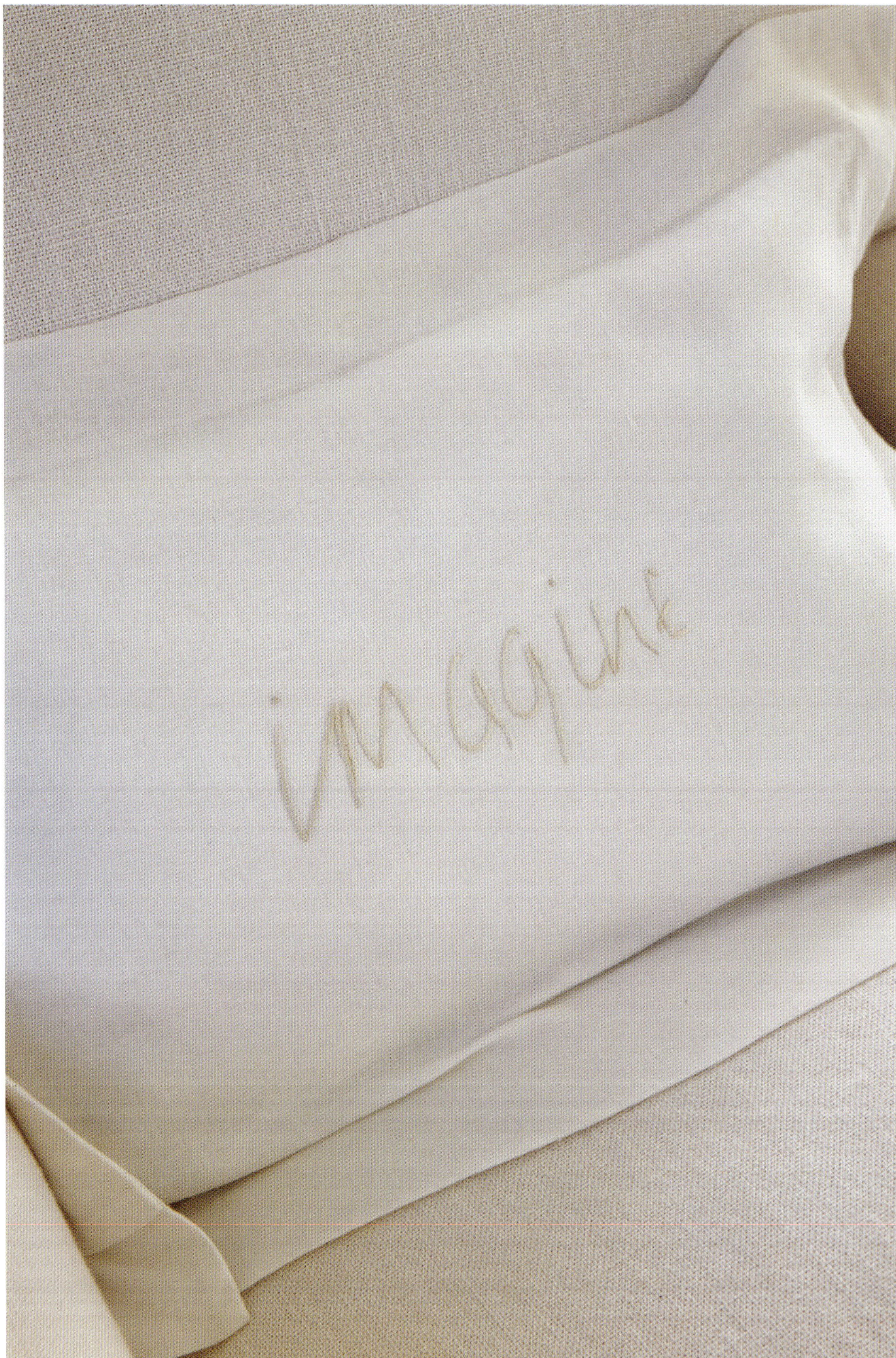
imagine

'We are all dreamers creating the next world, the next beautiful world for ourselves and for our children.'

– YOKO ONO

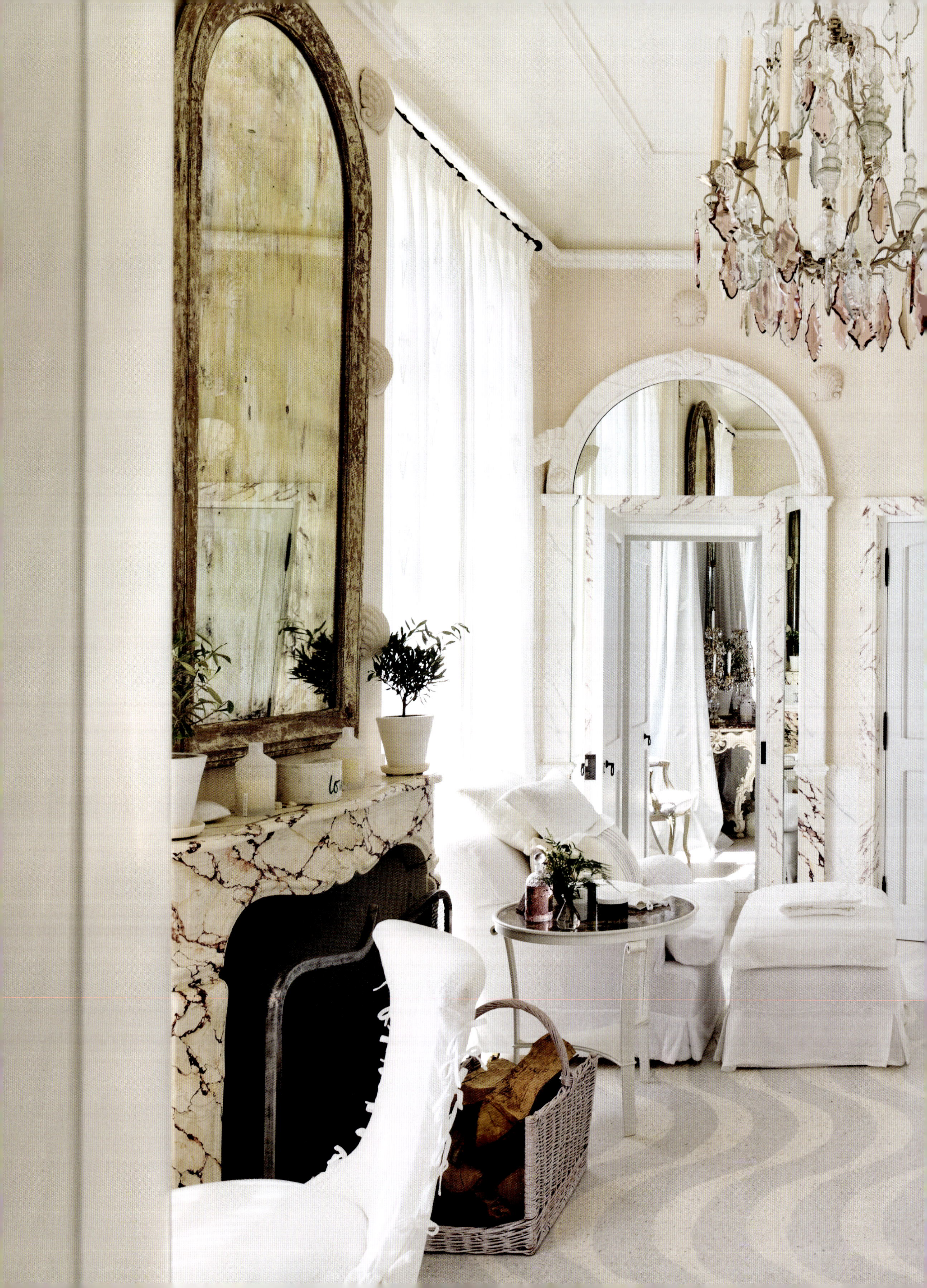

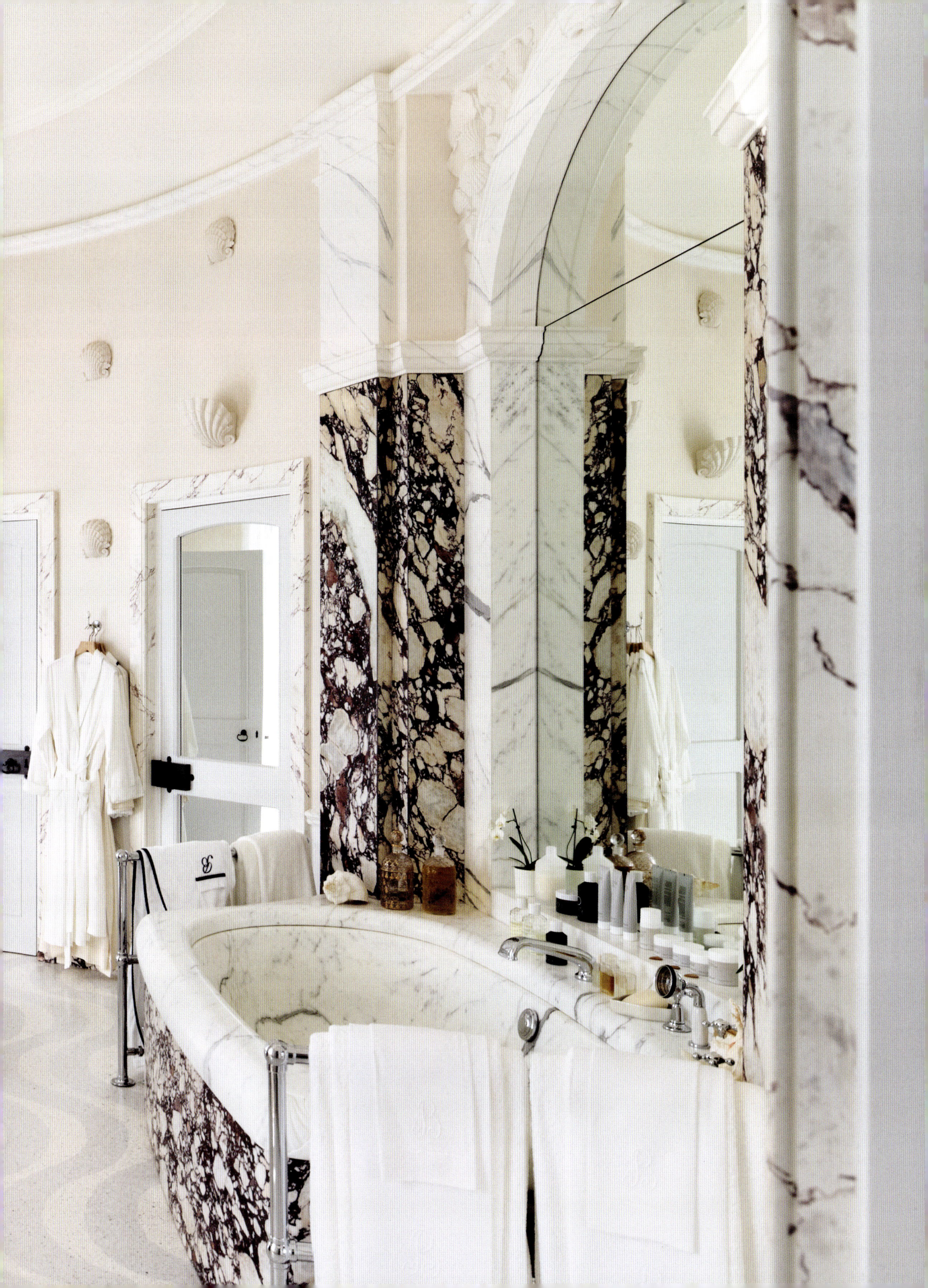

ABOVE Hand-embroidery is like poetry to me and transforms fabric into something deeply personal. The hand-embroidered linens at Léoube are made by a company in Portofino that has been crafting the most intricate linens for 60 years.

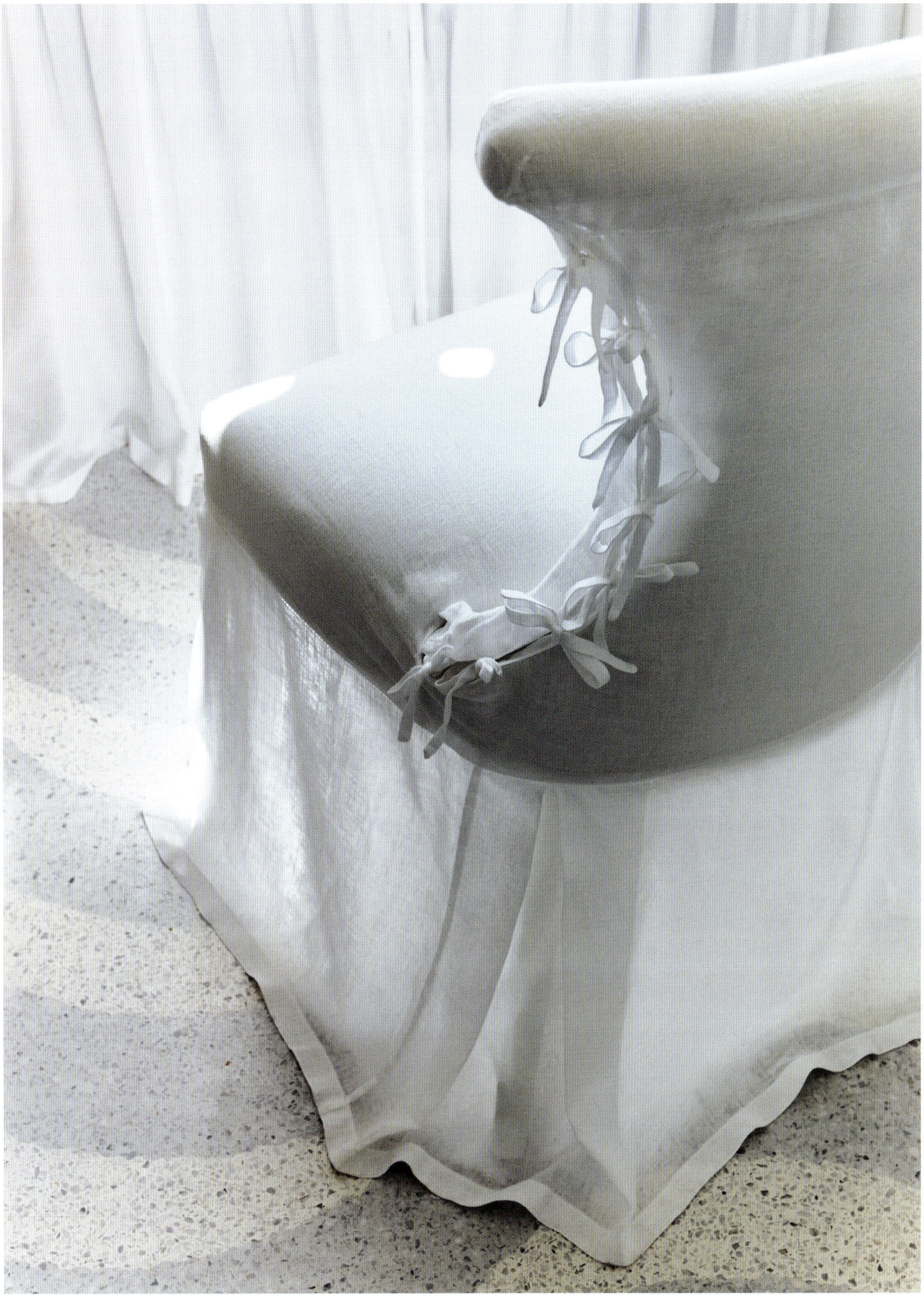

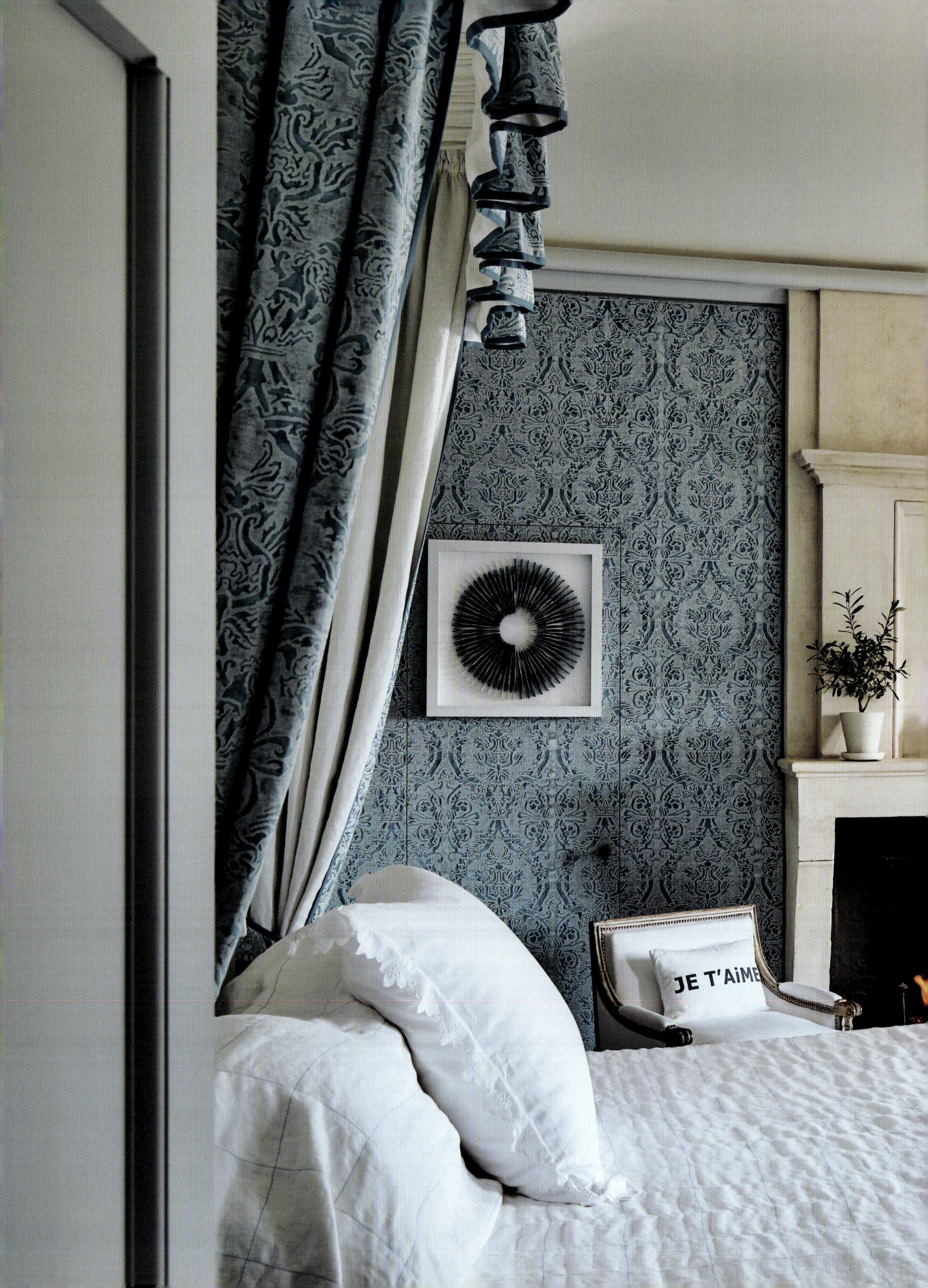
JE T'AiME

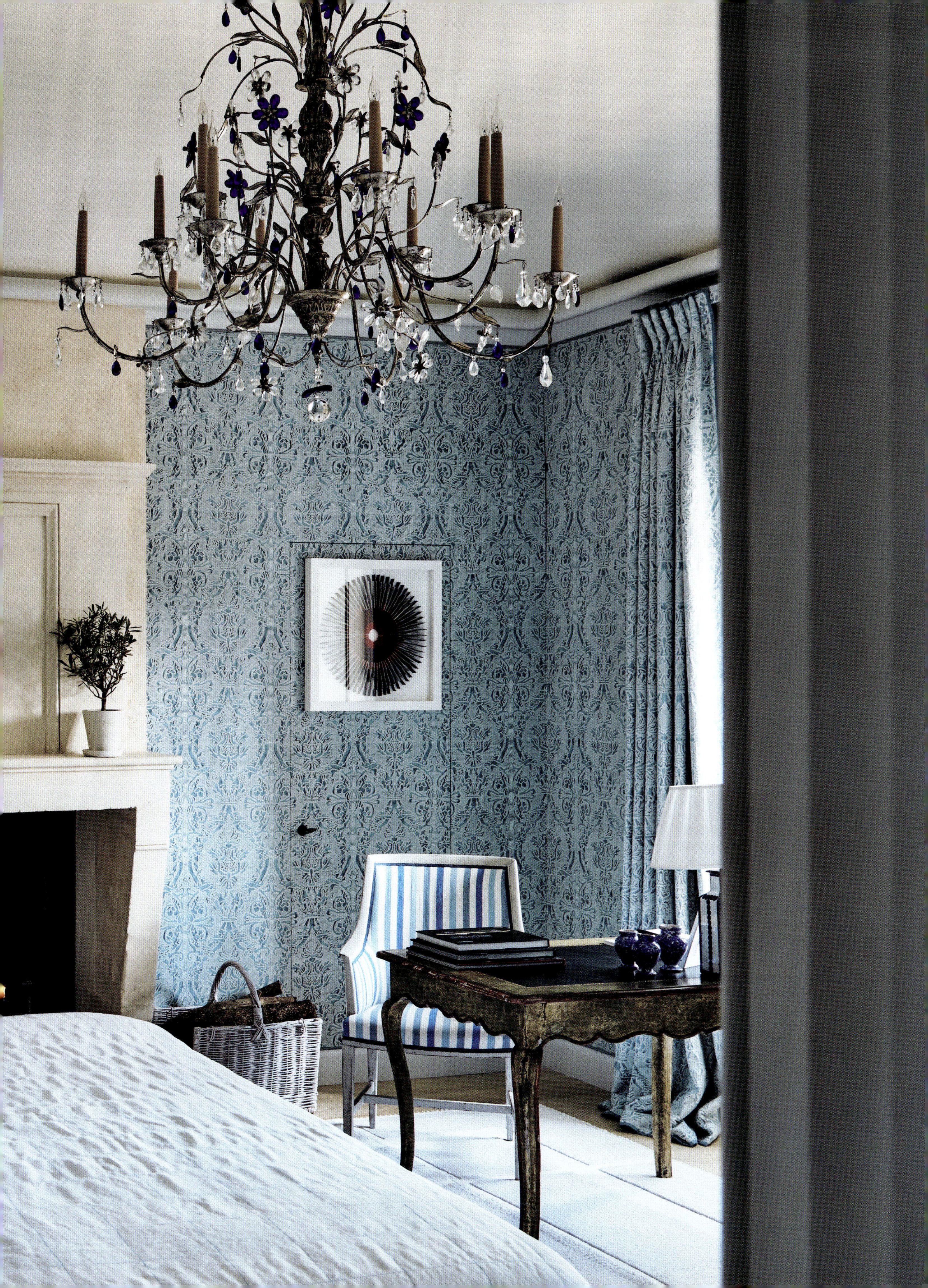

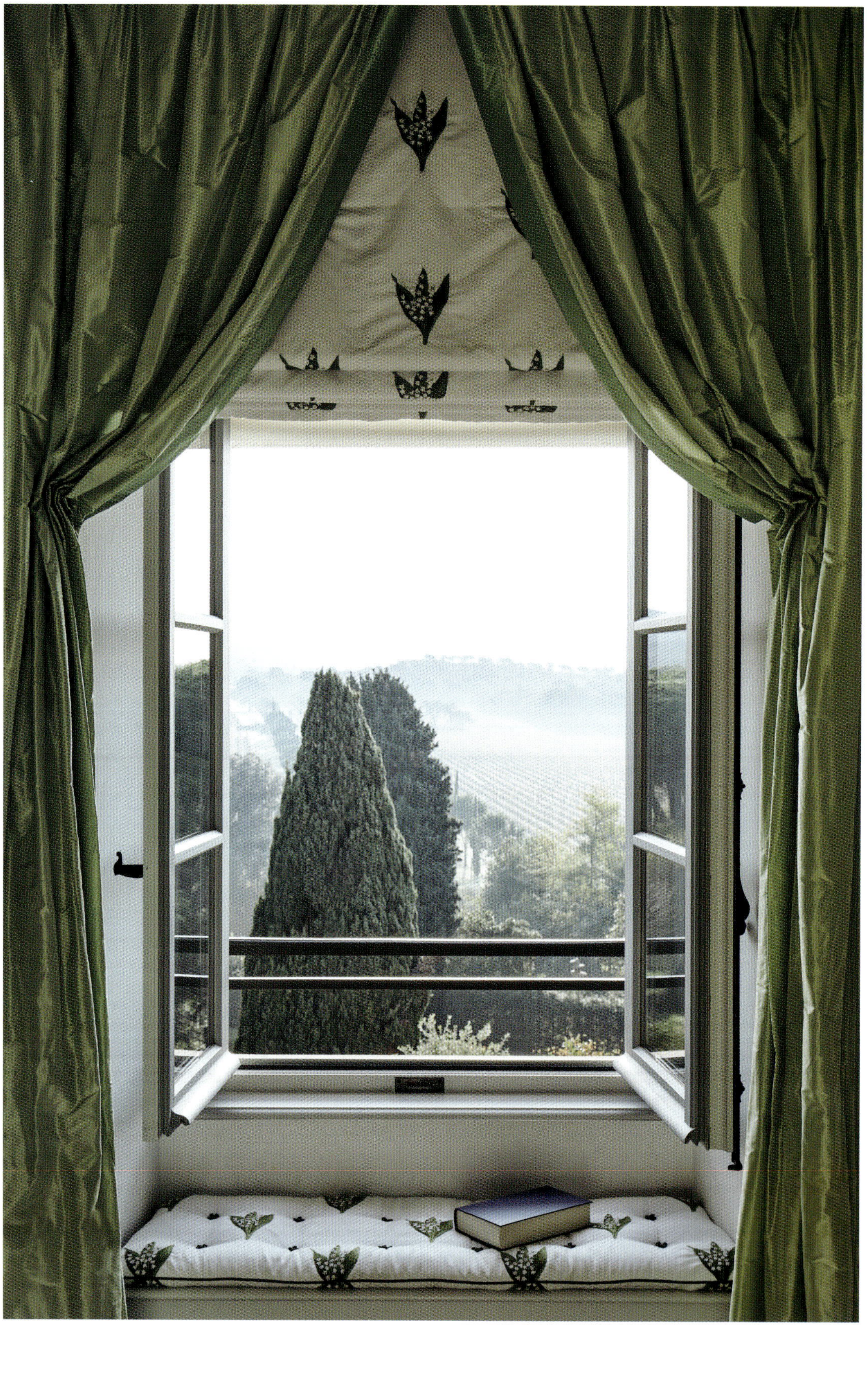

'Nothing in the world is permanent, and we're foolish when we ask anything to last, but surely we're still more foolish not to take delight in it while we have it.'

– W. SOMERSET MAUGHAM

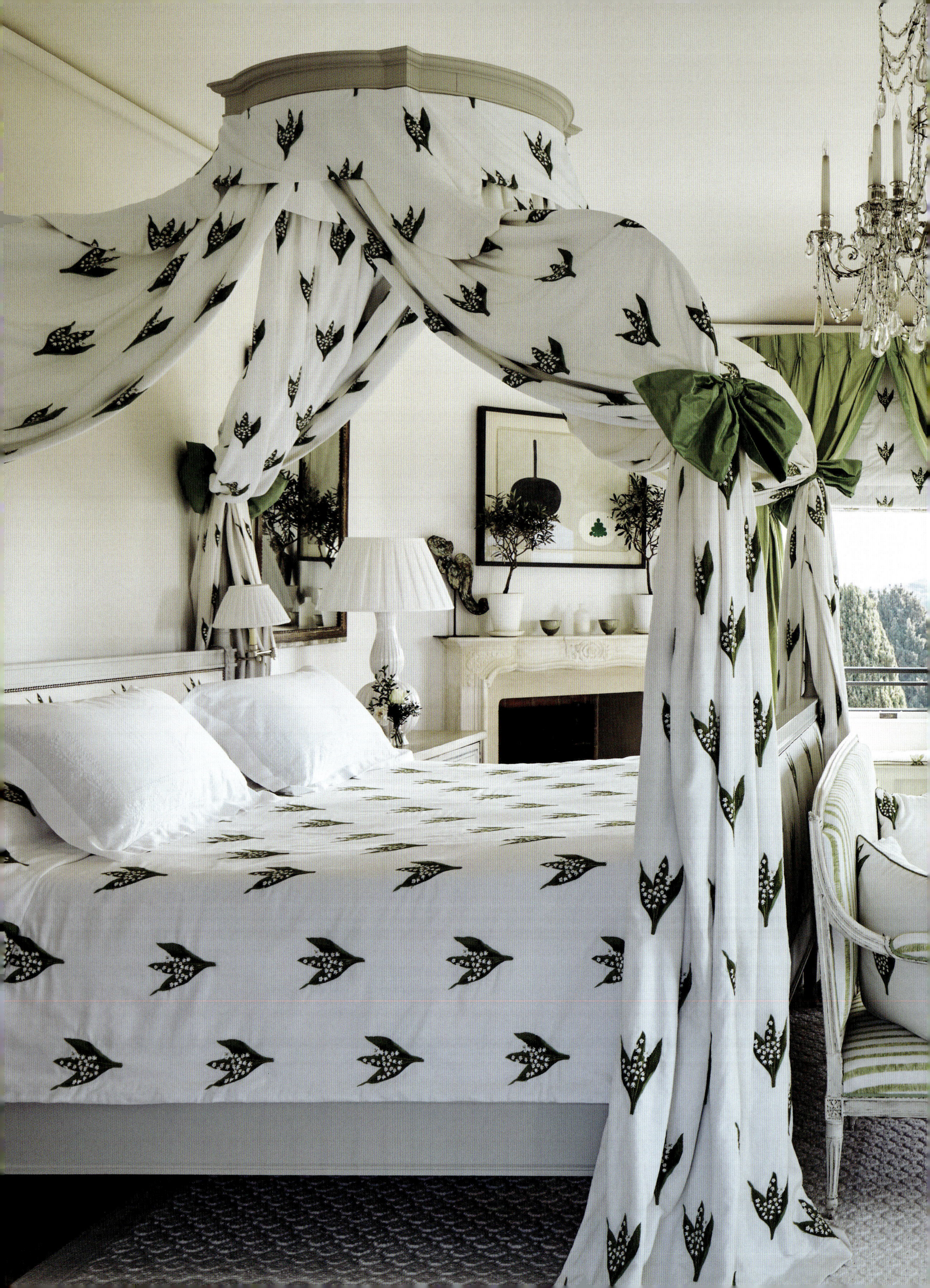

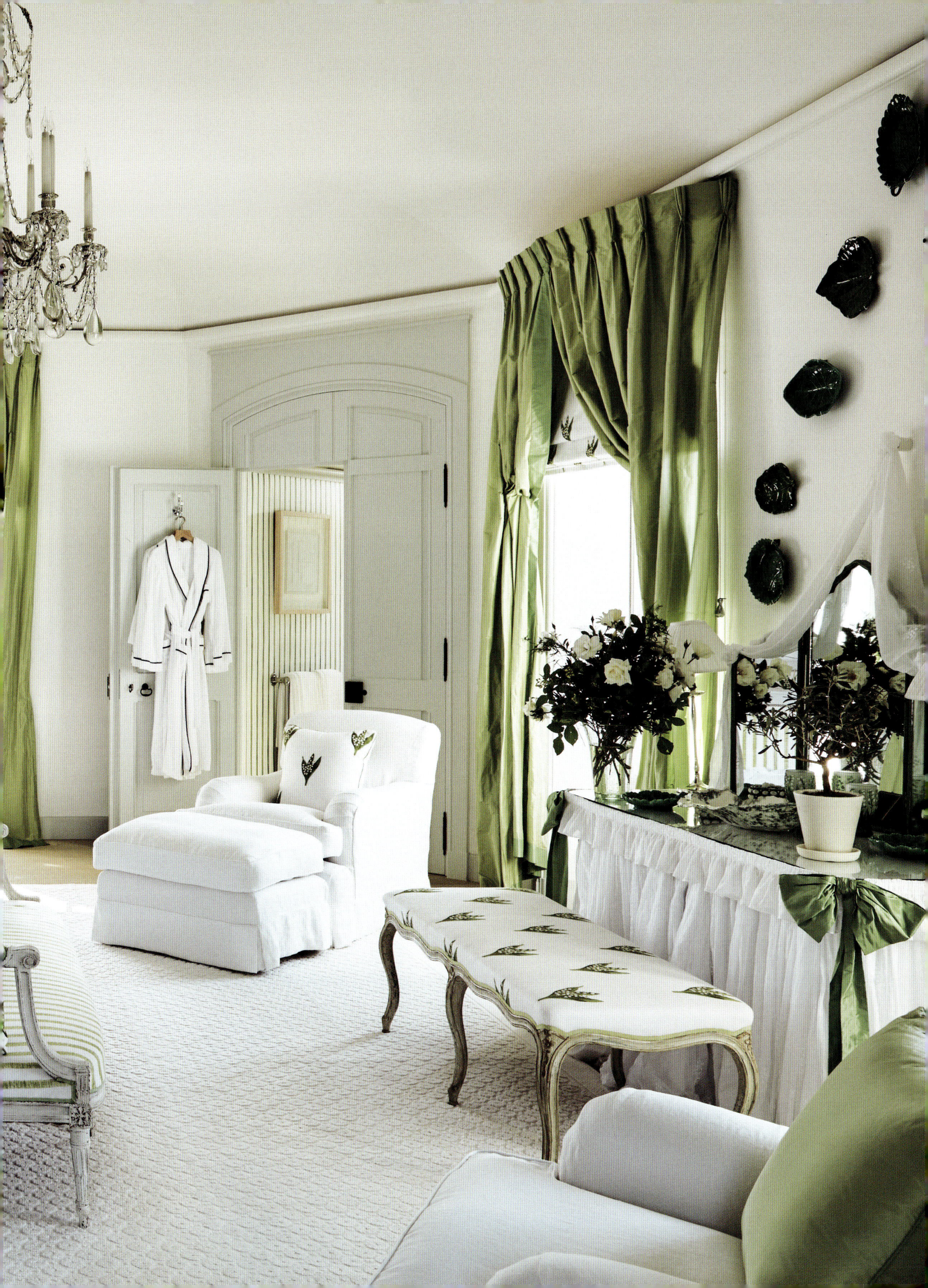

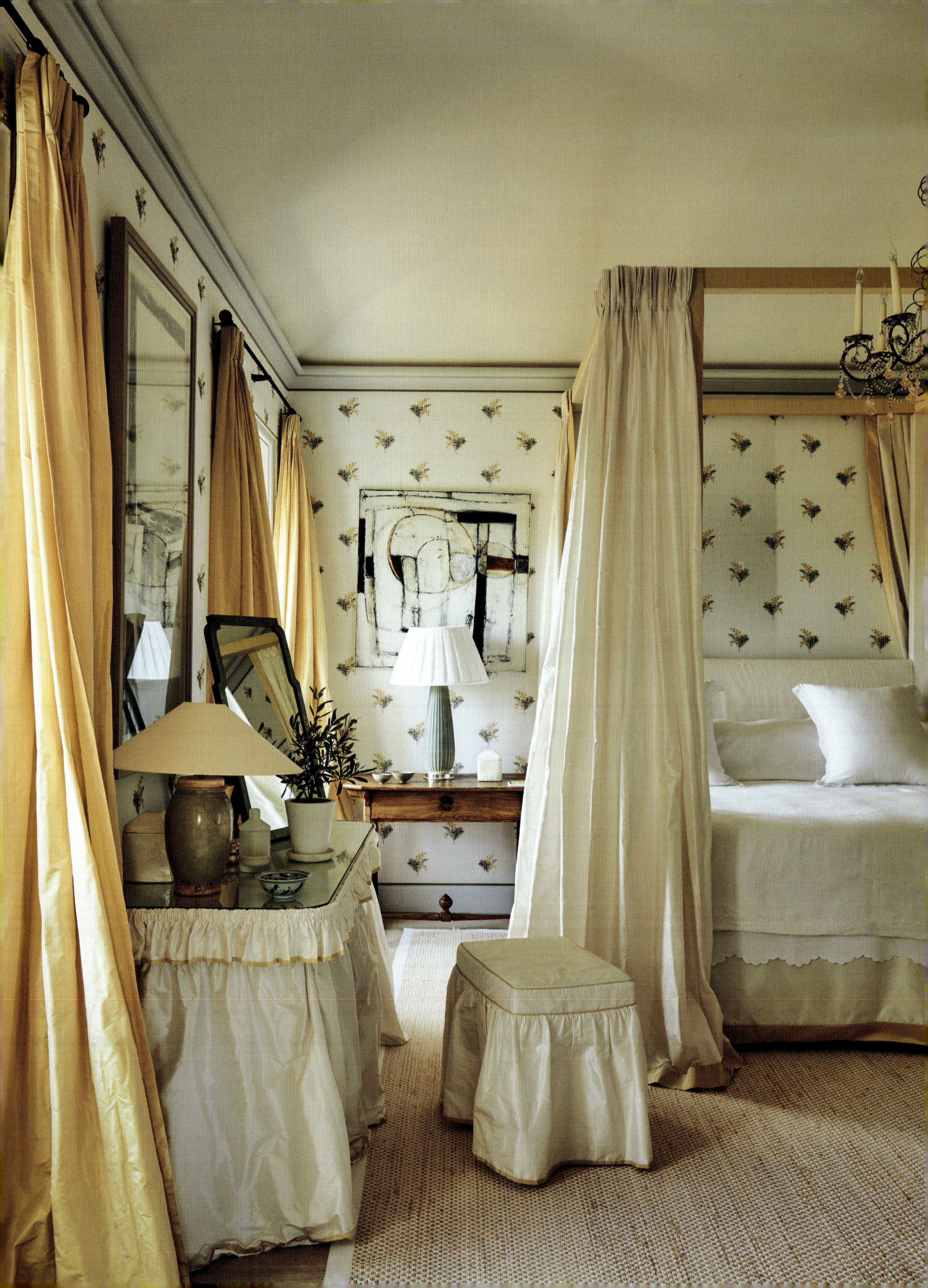

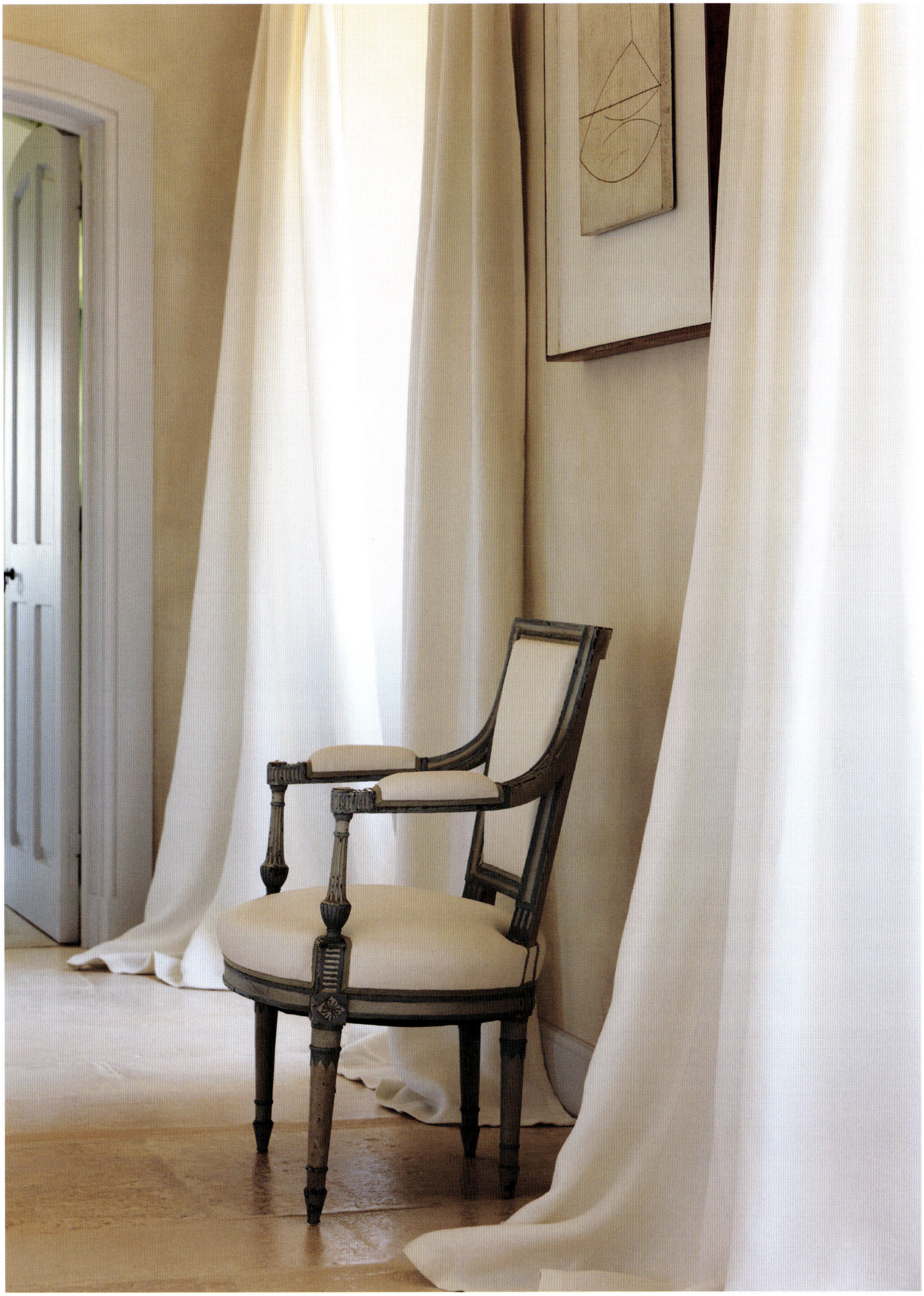

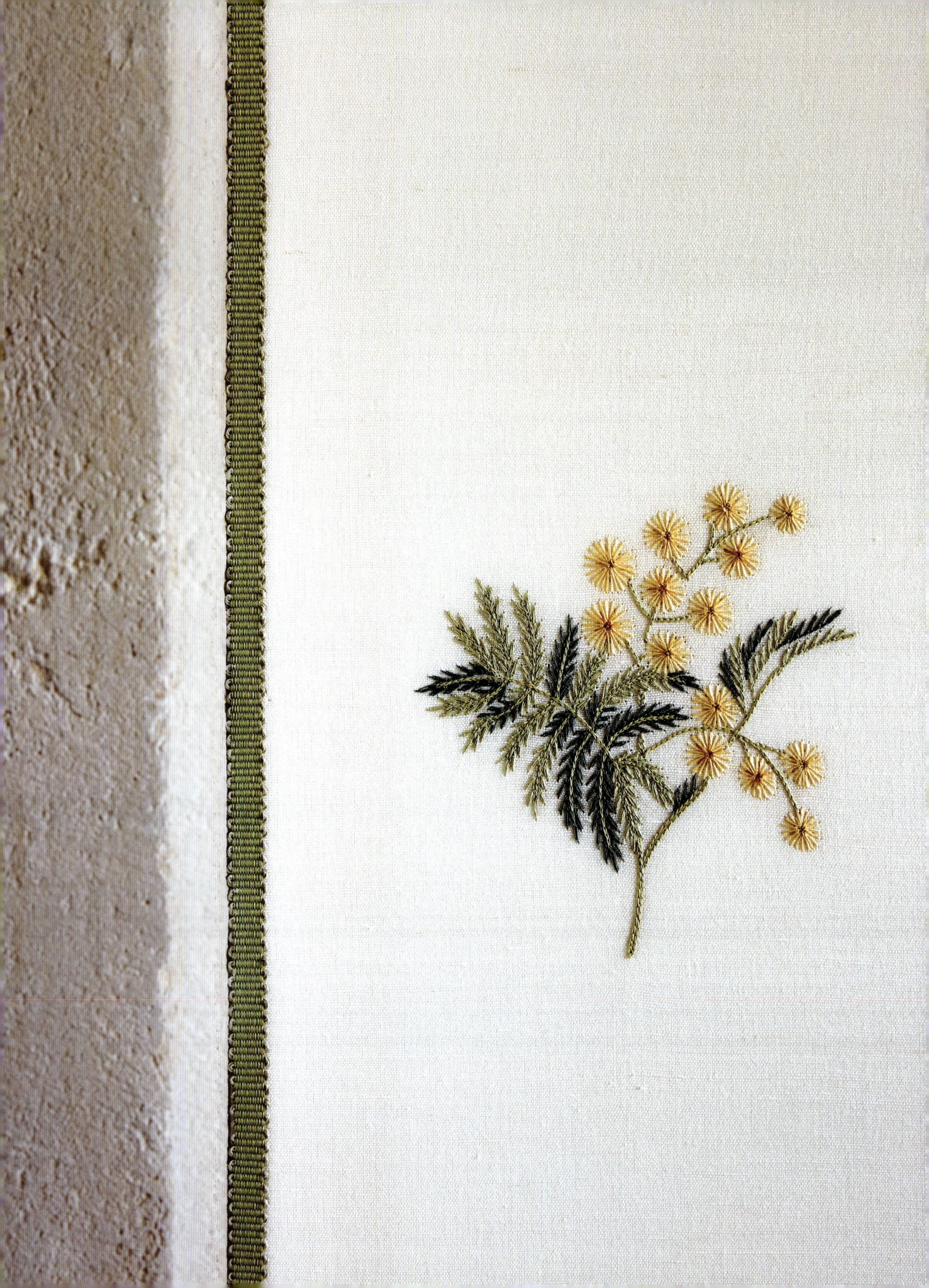

ABOVE AND OPPOSITE The mimosa bedroom's hand-embroidered fabric on the walls honours the significance of the vibrant yellow flowers to Provence.

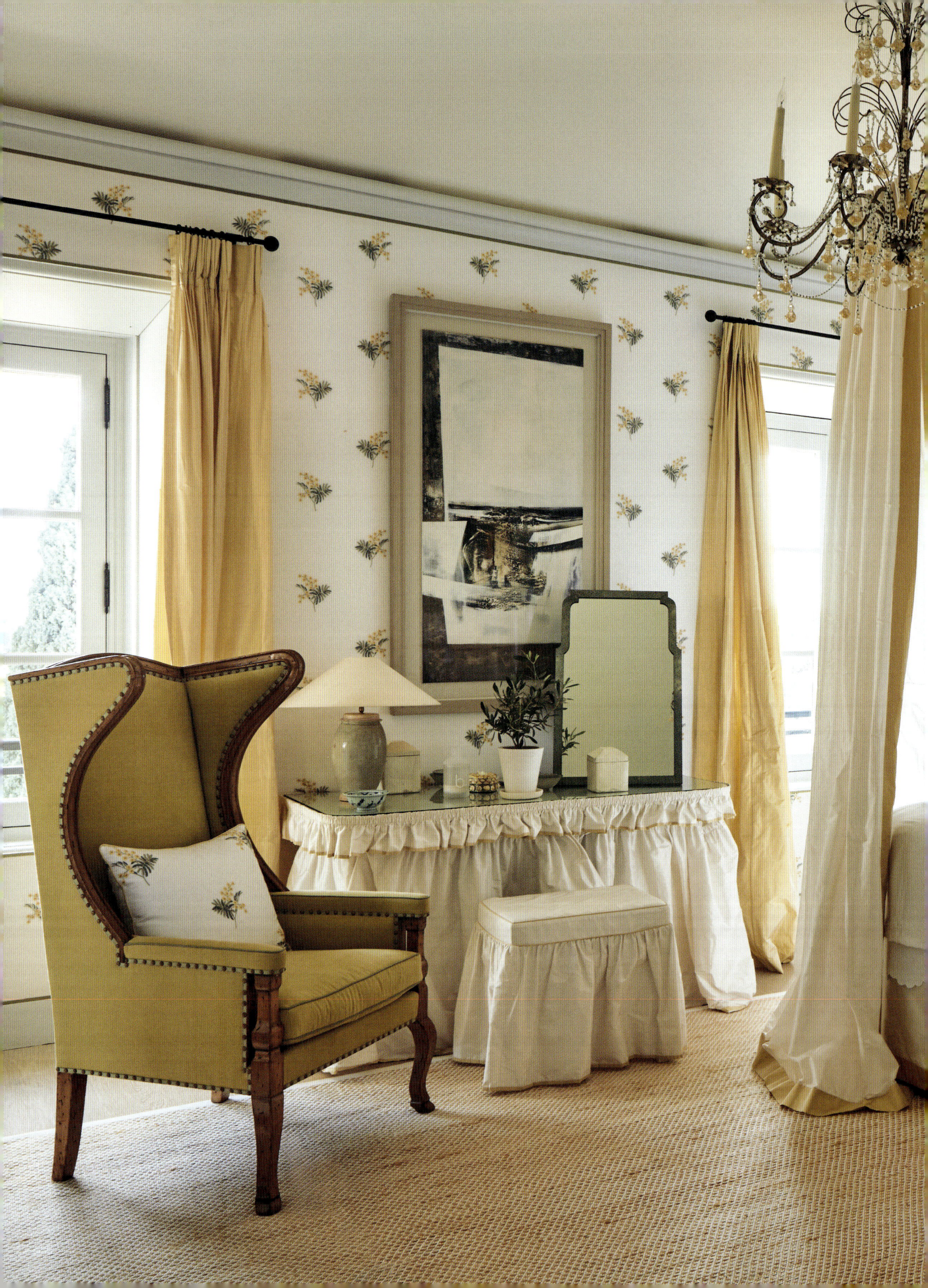

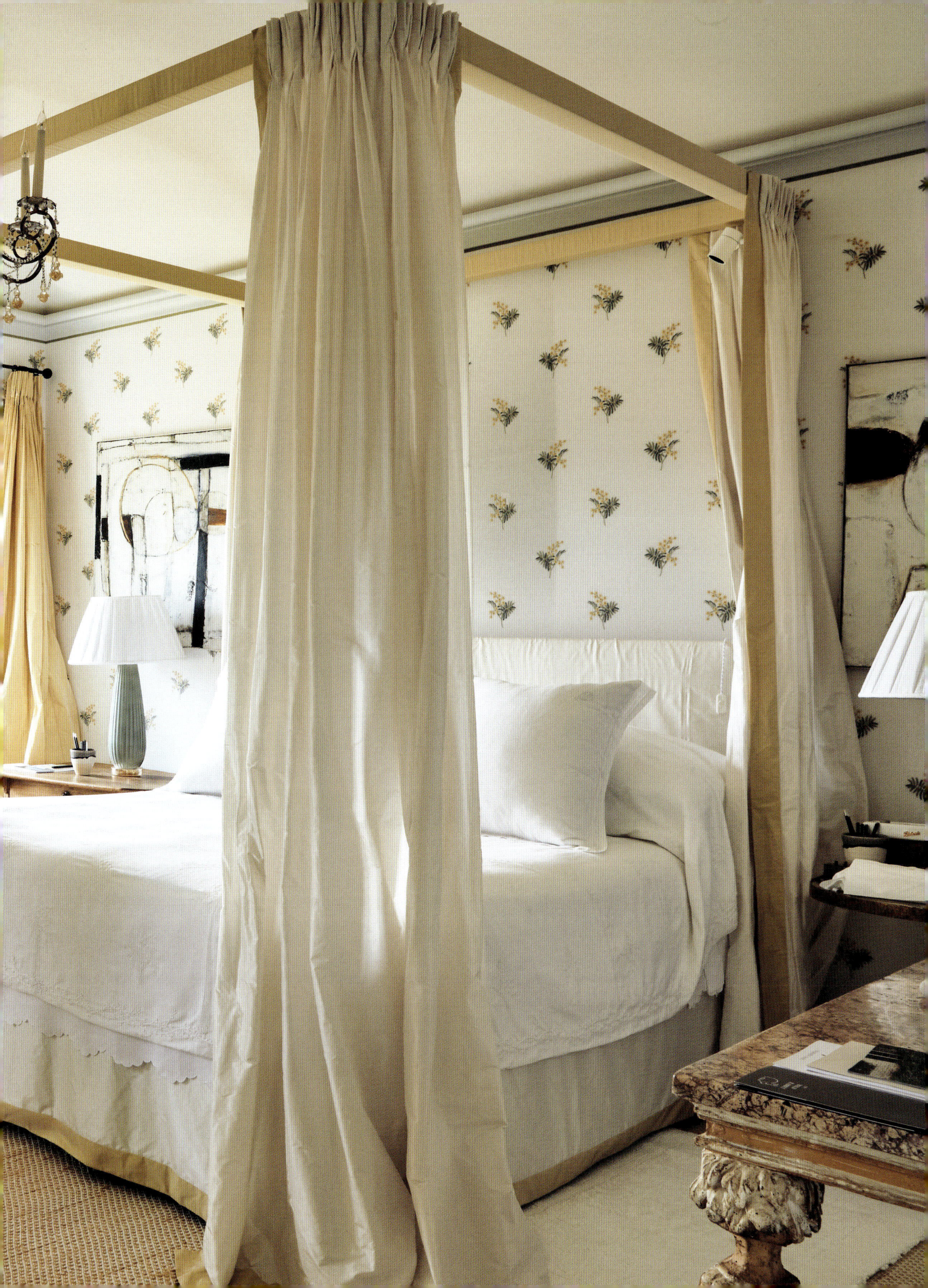

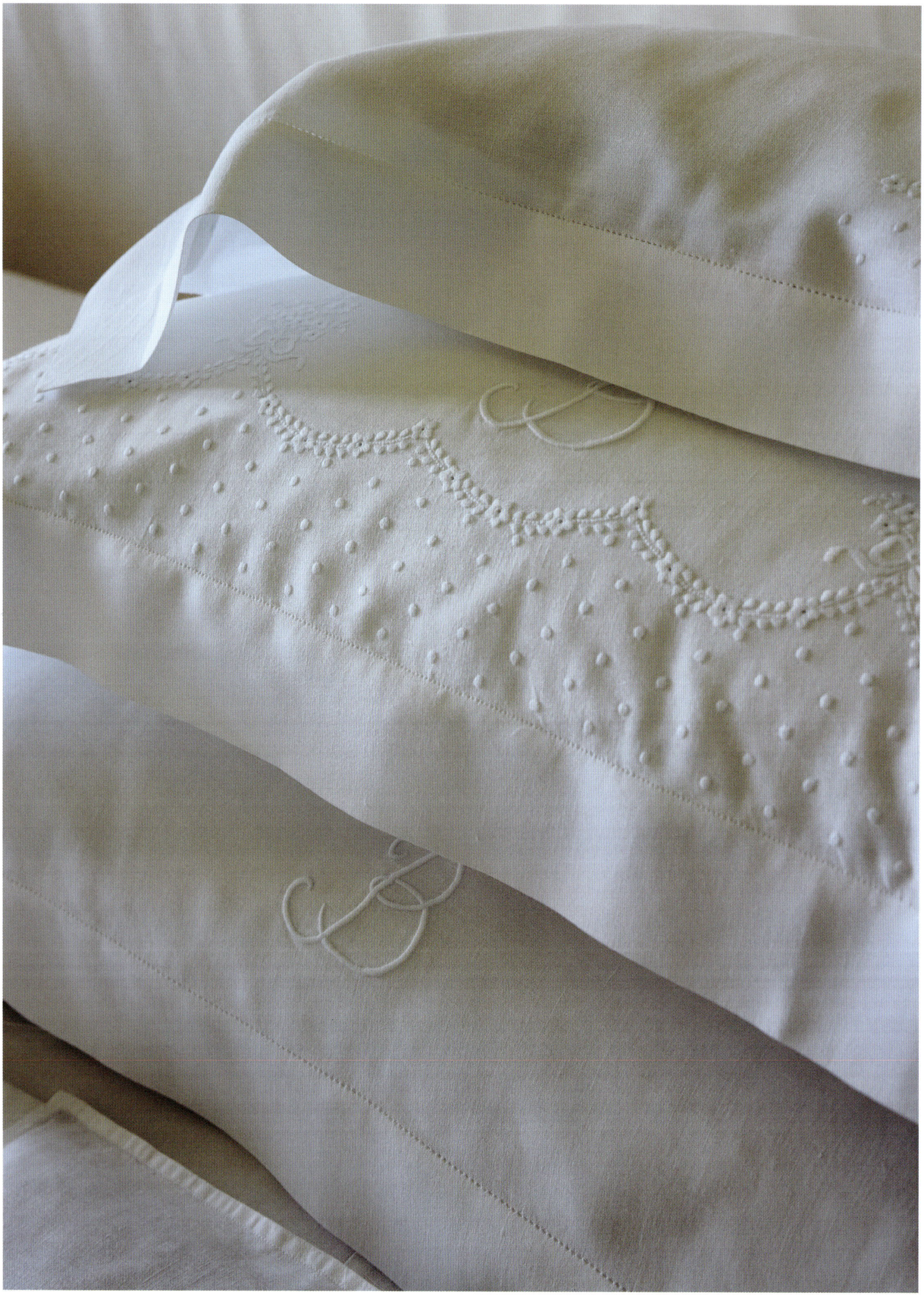

Mimosa season is a very special time across the whole of Provence but particularly in our local village, Bormes-les-Mimosas, with which the flower shares its name. Although it was originally imported from Australia, mimosa has become emblematic of Provence. Every winter, its landscapes are transformed into a golden spectacle as the delicate trees come alive with clouds of tiny, fragrant saffron-coloured spheres. To me, it is one of nature's most arresting sights, an ephemeral abundance of vibrancy that heralds the earliest whispers of spring while January and February are still gripped by winter's chill. Every February, Bormes-les-Mimosas hosts its renowned Fête du Mimosa which welcomes thousands of visitors from across the region. The village becomes a riot of yellow, with elaborately decorated floats, processions and music, culminating with the crowning of the Mimosa Queen.

Mimosa's significance to the region meant that I had to honour it in the house and in the mimosa bedroom, we've achieved that through a hand-embroidered textile on the walls. We gave a bunch of mimosa to Chelsea Textiles and they showed us lots of different designs for the shape of the blossom: I chose these little pompom-like spheres. This room feels very special to me – a timeless but fitting homage to this fleeting flower and our corner of Provence.

Covering walls in fabric is a decorating choice that has come in and out of fashion over the years but it is something I've always loved. I think it immediately makes a room inviting but also adds a little bit of drama to it. The tangle of vines and leafy tendrils of a Fortuny fabric called 'Spagnolo' add richness, depth and tactility to the striking blue bedroom. The pattern includes a pomegranate motif – which also pays homage to the city of Mariano Fortuny's birthplace, Granada – the Spanish word for pomegranate, which adds another layer of poetry and storytelling for me.

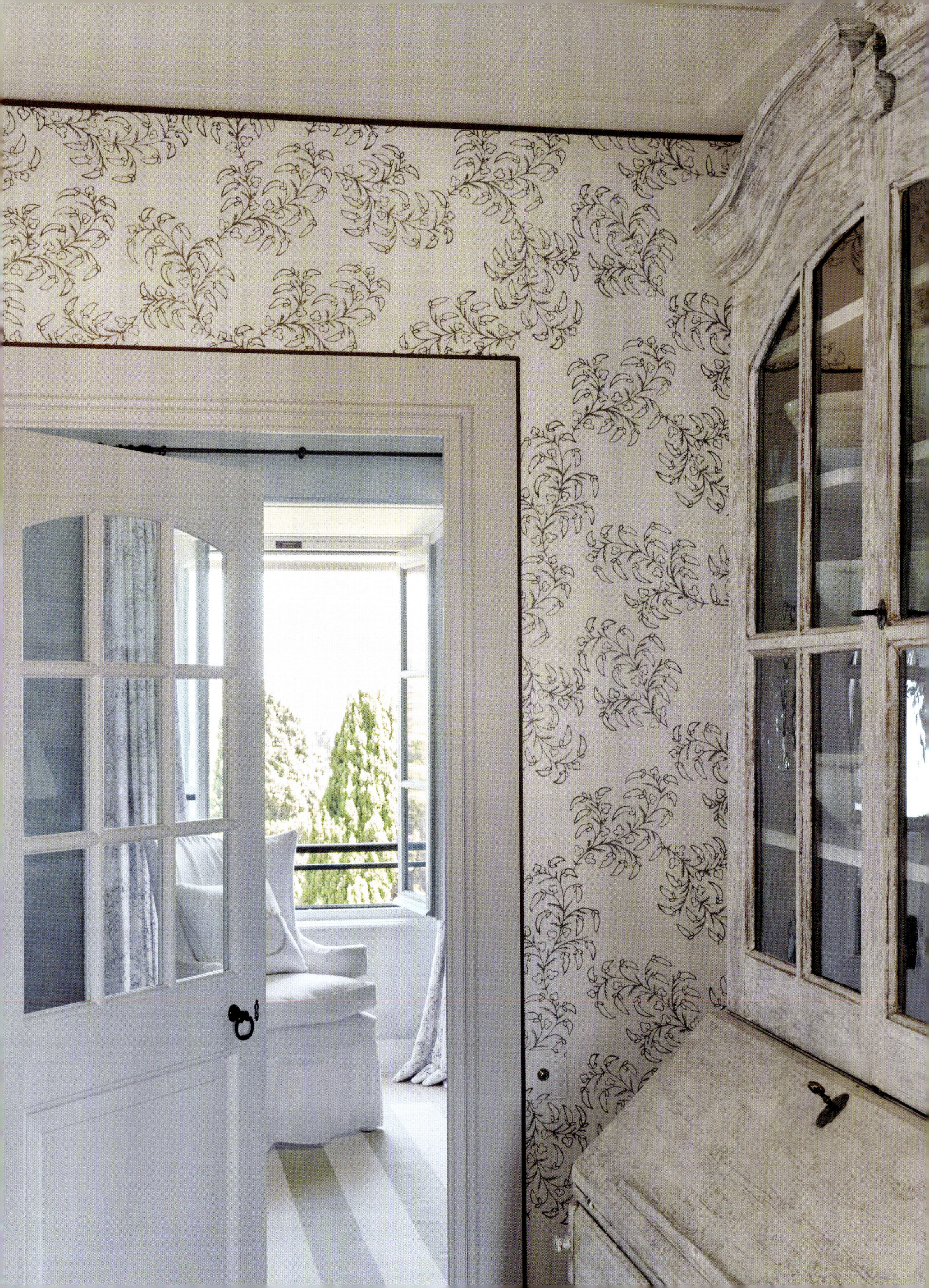

ABOVE, OPPOSITE AND OVERLEAF A Robert Kime Pea Pods fabric based on a woodblock print inspired the design of this bedroom.

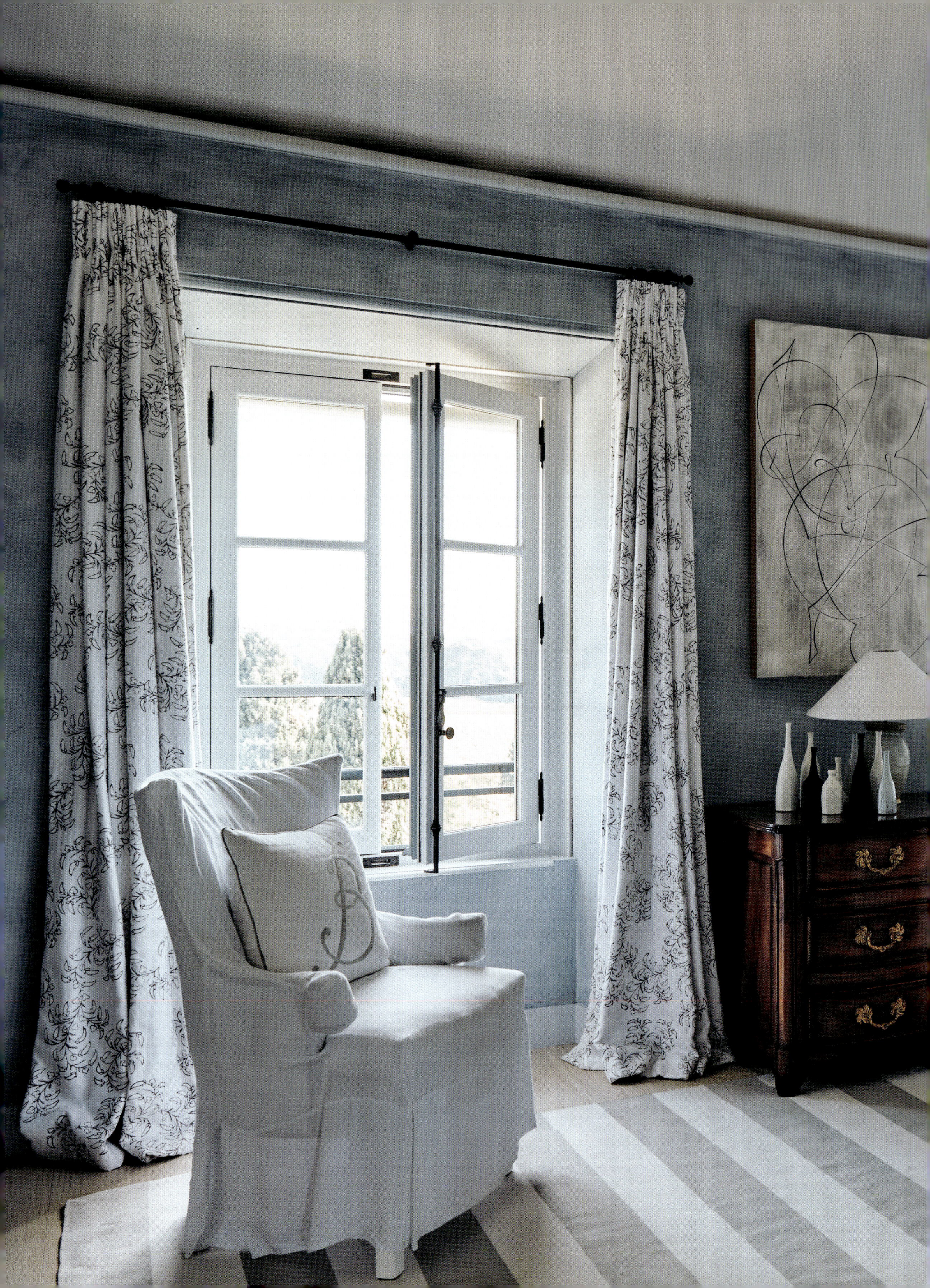

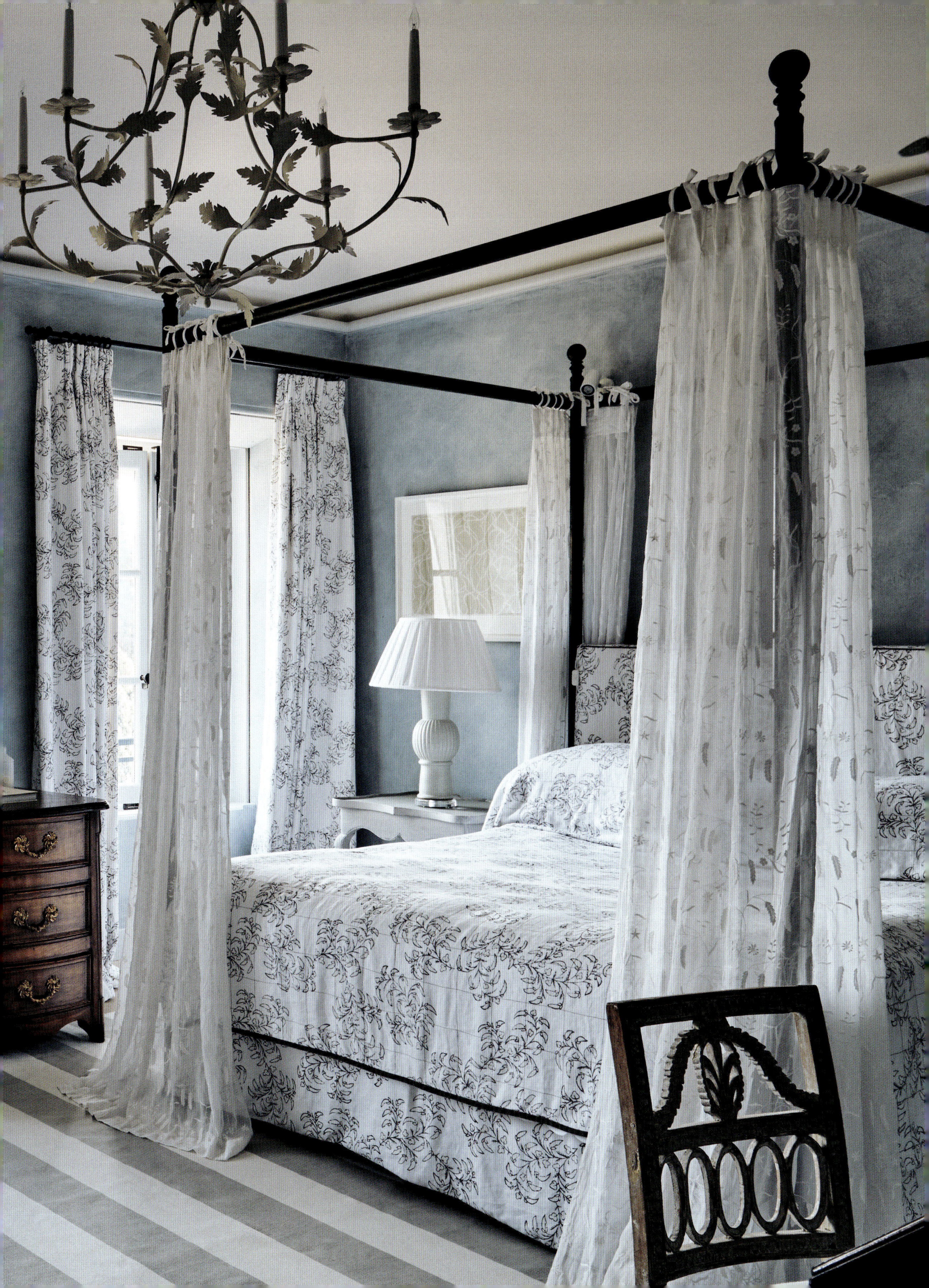

ABOVE The leaf design on the walls was created by Isabelle de Borchgrave, made from papier mâché transferred from the leaves and stuck on to the walls before it dried.

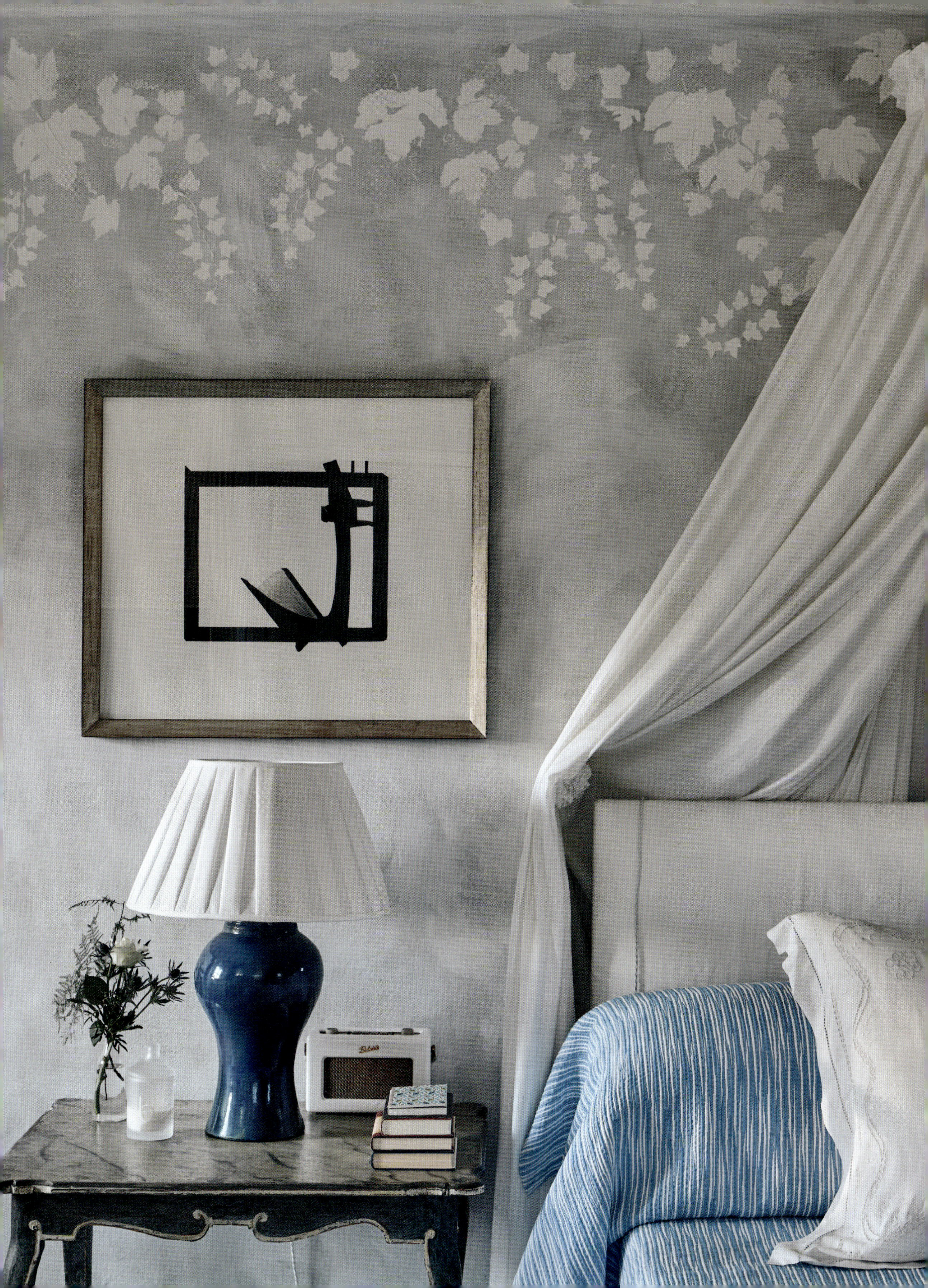

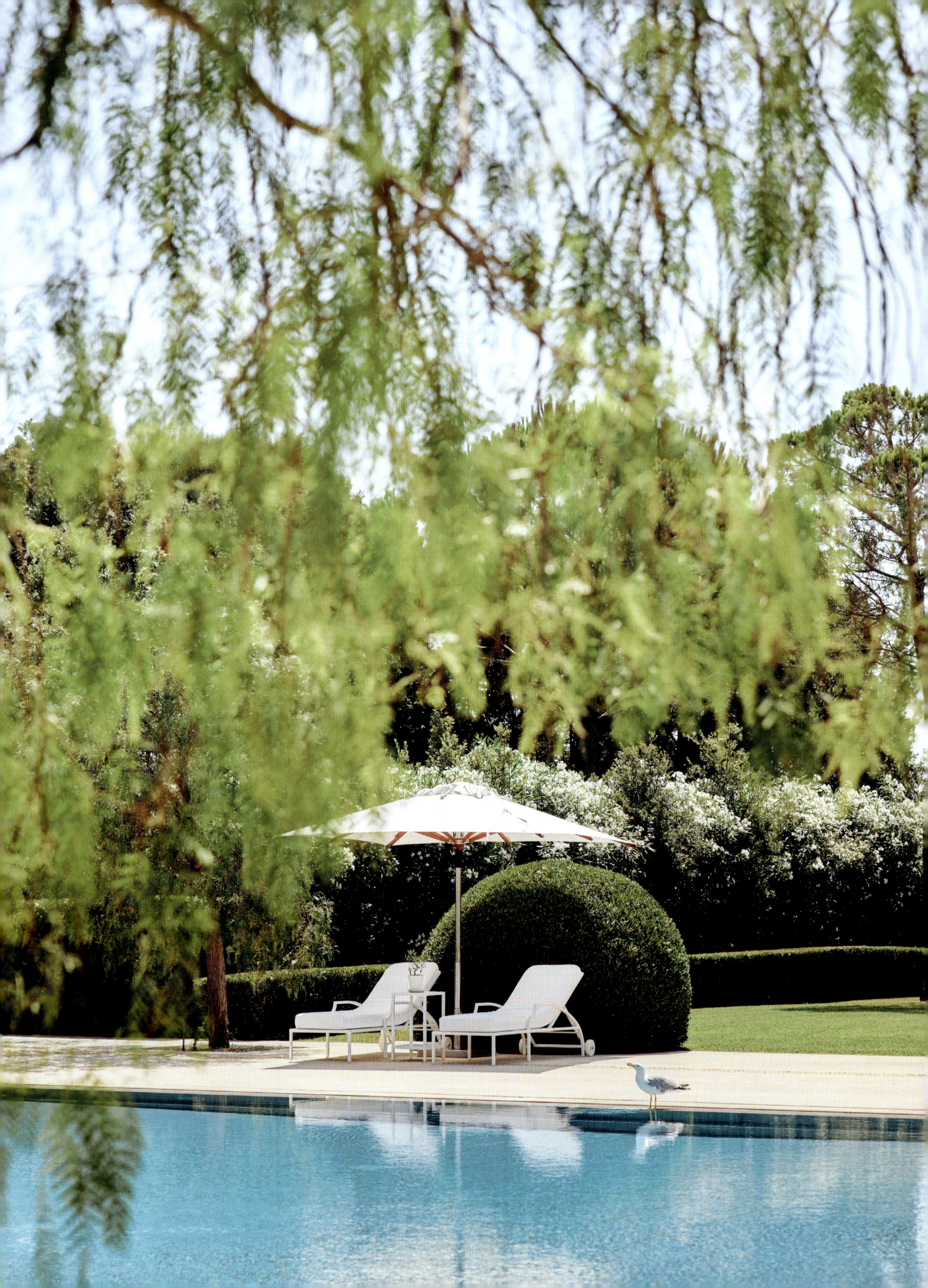

# THE POOL

AND POOLHOUSE

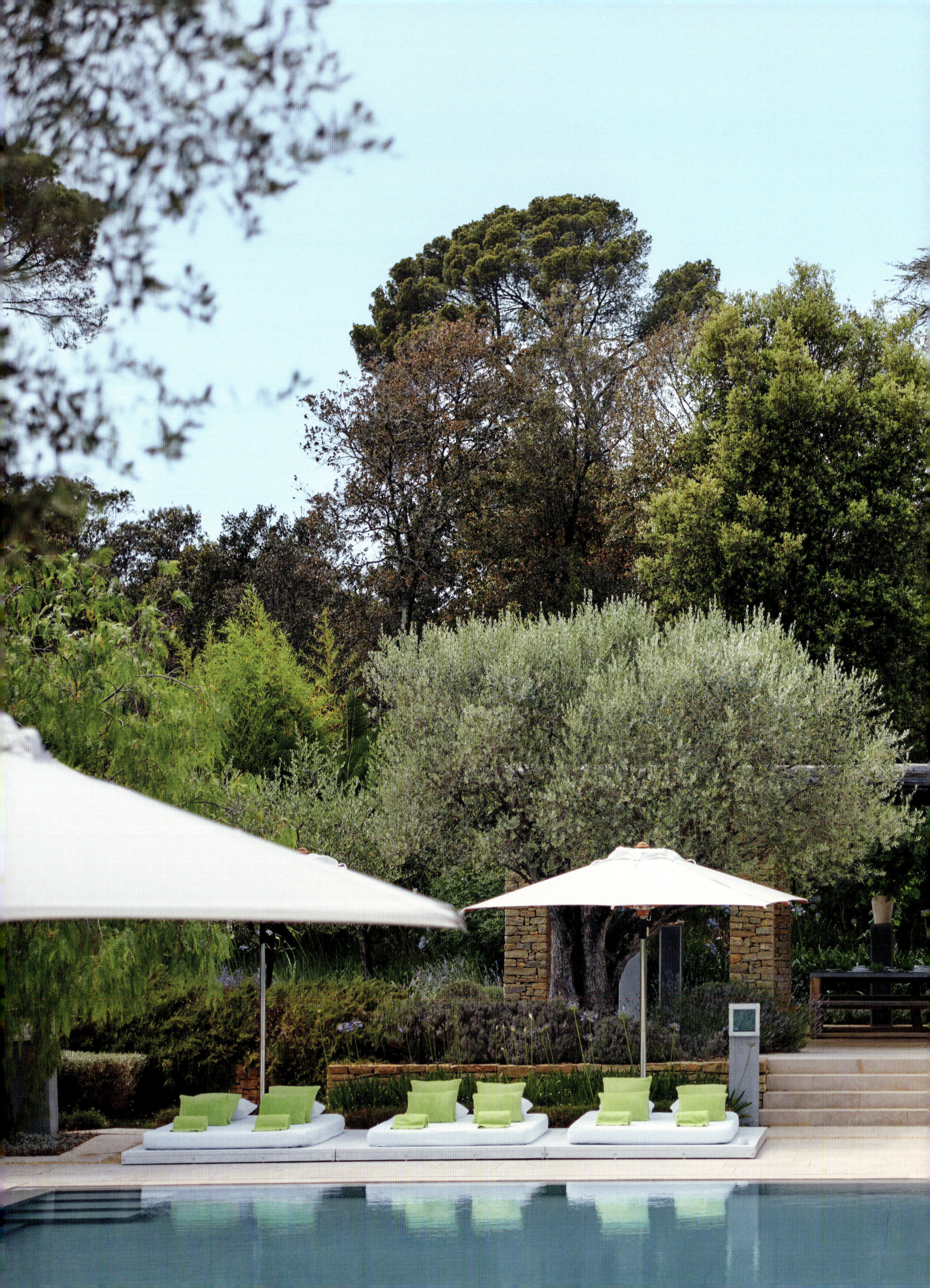

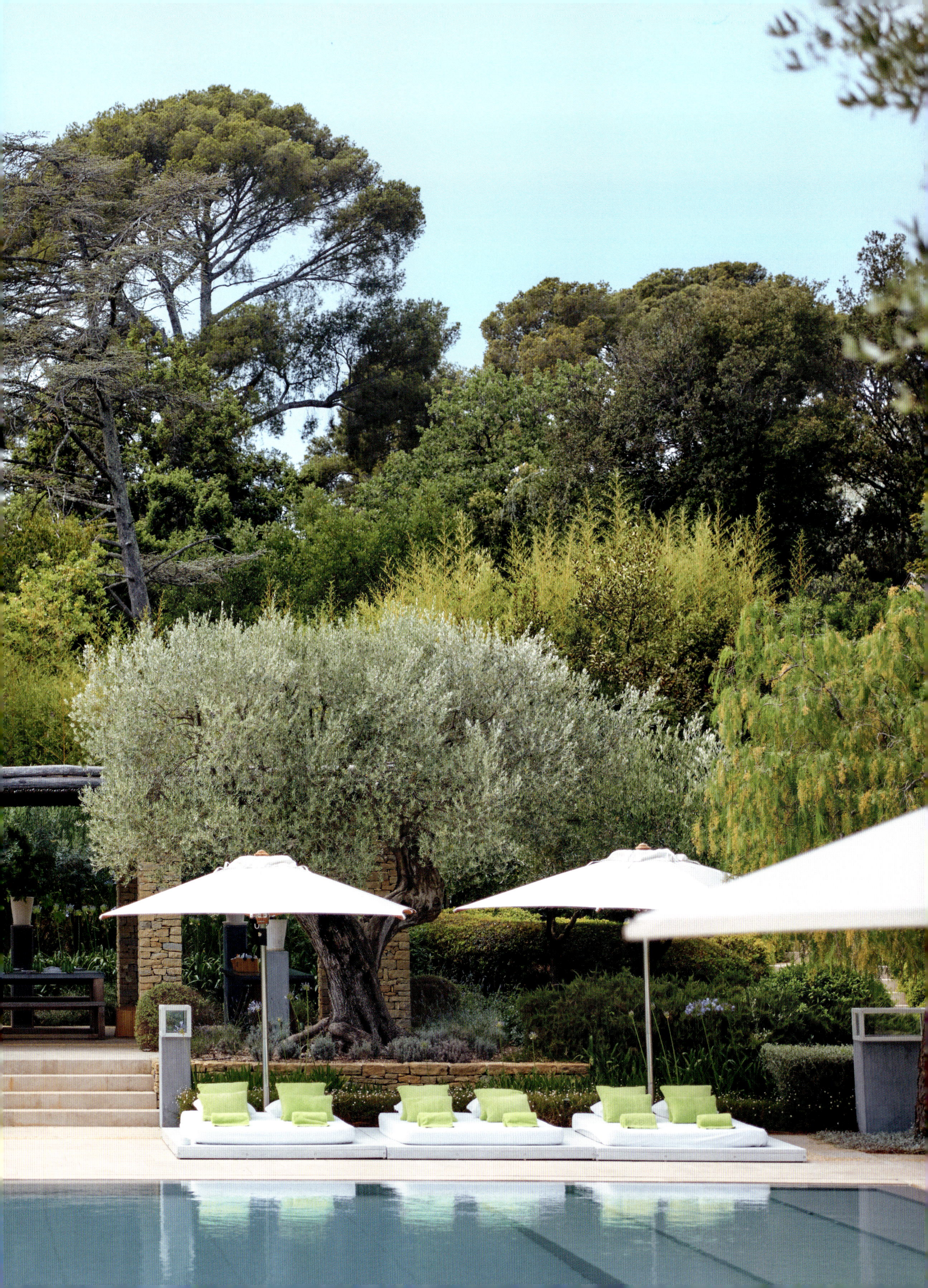

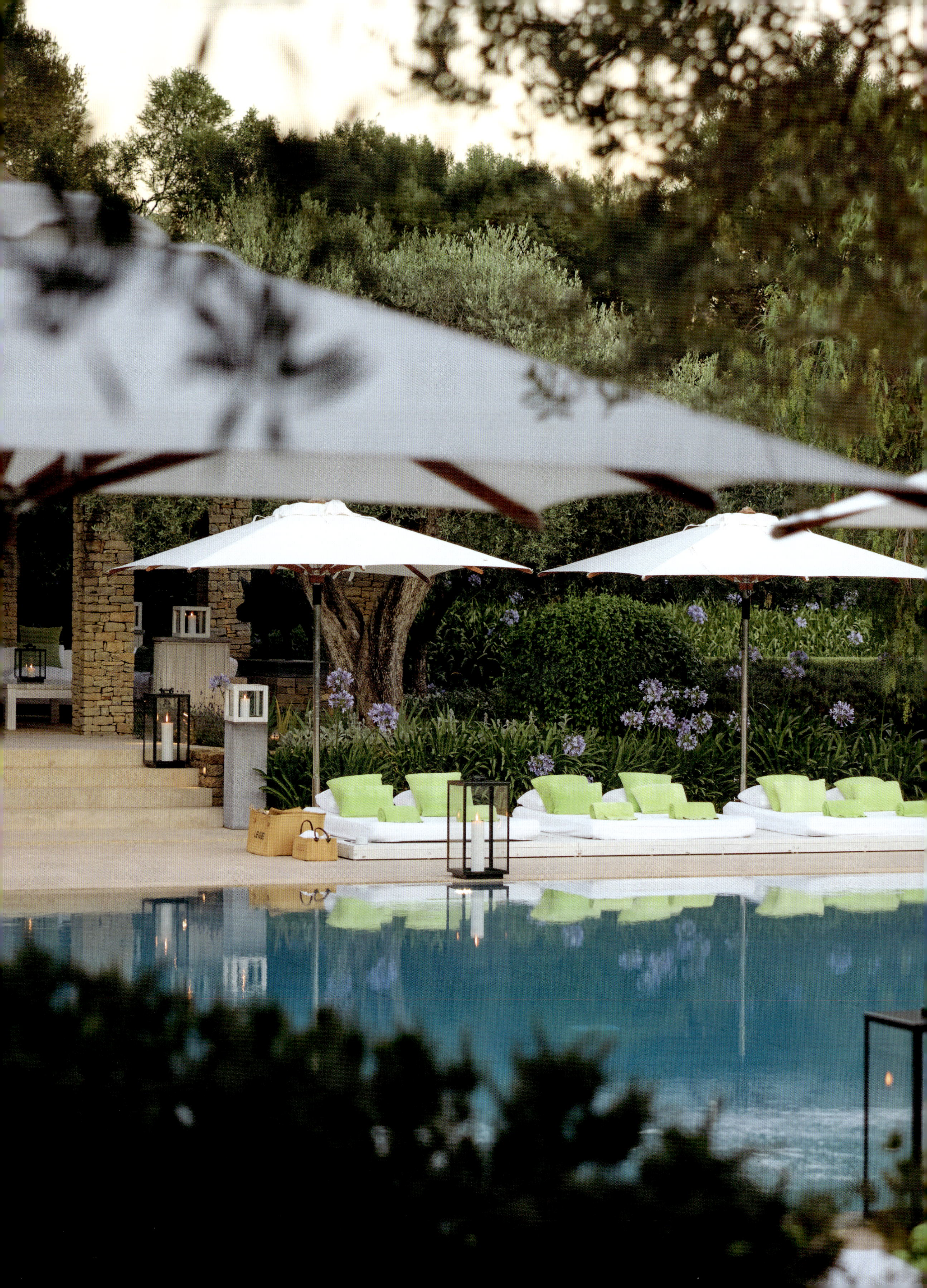

Building the pool house and its terrace transformed what was once a wild patch of overgrown grasses and brush in the garden into a part of the house that hums with life and gives form to our days.

Looking at the structure today, the pool house feels like a seamless confluence of architecture and nature. Olive and pepper trees cast dappled shadows over the terrace, beds of brilliant blue agapanthus frame stone pathways and plants and foliage mingle with pale stone walls providing a verdant backdrop to the patio. In their midst is the pool, a gleaming turquoise rectangle whose colour is intensified by the Provençal sunlight. While many traditional swimming pools in the region are designed to be discreet and blend into their surroundings, we wanted ours to be more of a focal point, drawing the eye and beckoning you in.

But the space hasn't always felt so harmonious. The pool was designed to be set low, hidden from the château, but when the basin was dug out, it looked vast – a gaping hole in the ground – and I thought I'd made a huge mistake. The pool house seemed to tower behind it and when Alain presented it to us, Anthony and I and the team just stood there staring at it all, not knowing what to say. It was Tommaso who came to our rescue, designing, planting and nurturing the sanctuary of greenery that now envelops the building so fluently, ensuring the pool is indeed hidden from view and that you don't really notice the scale of the pool house.

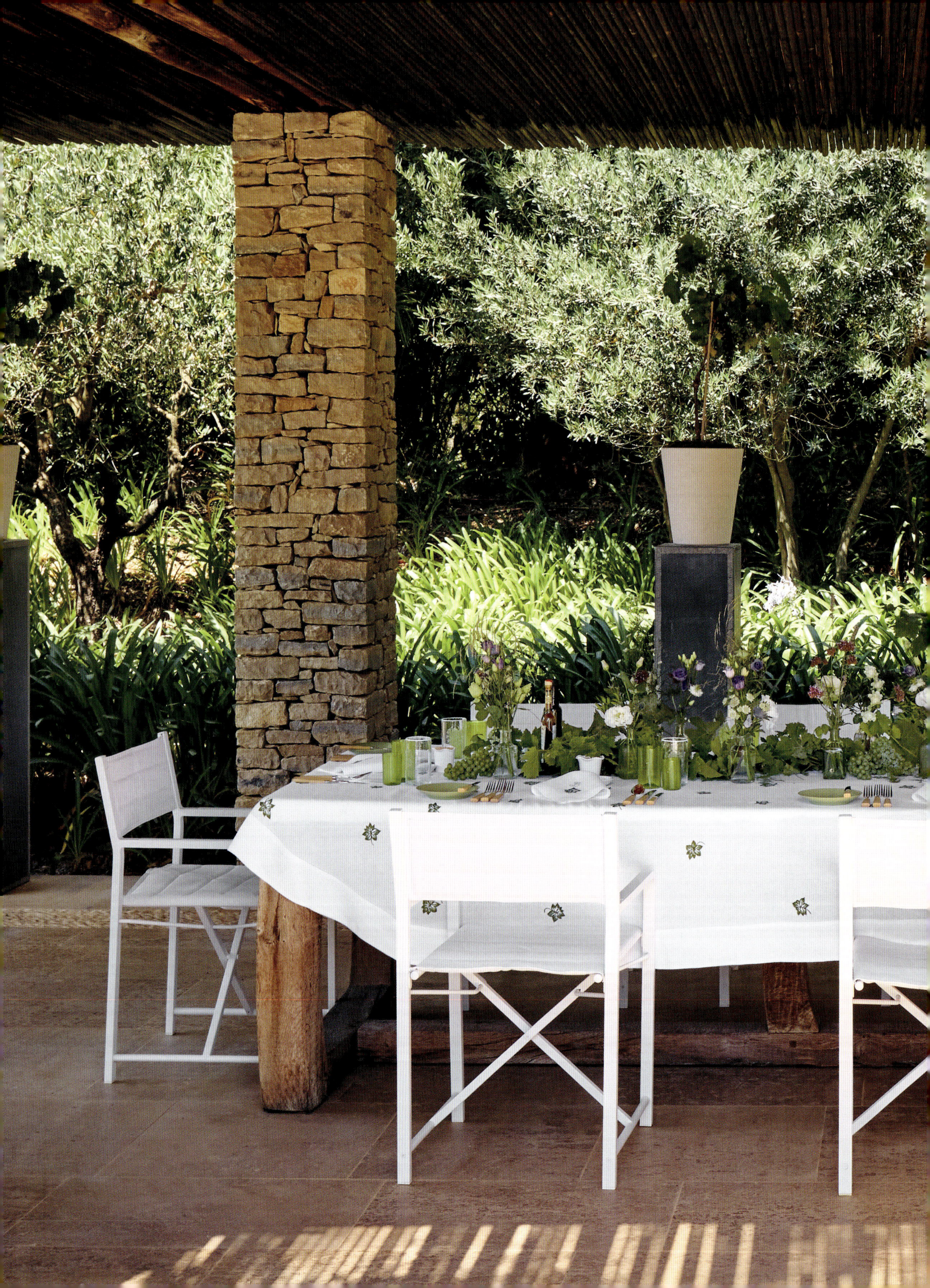

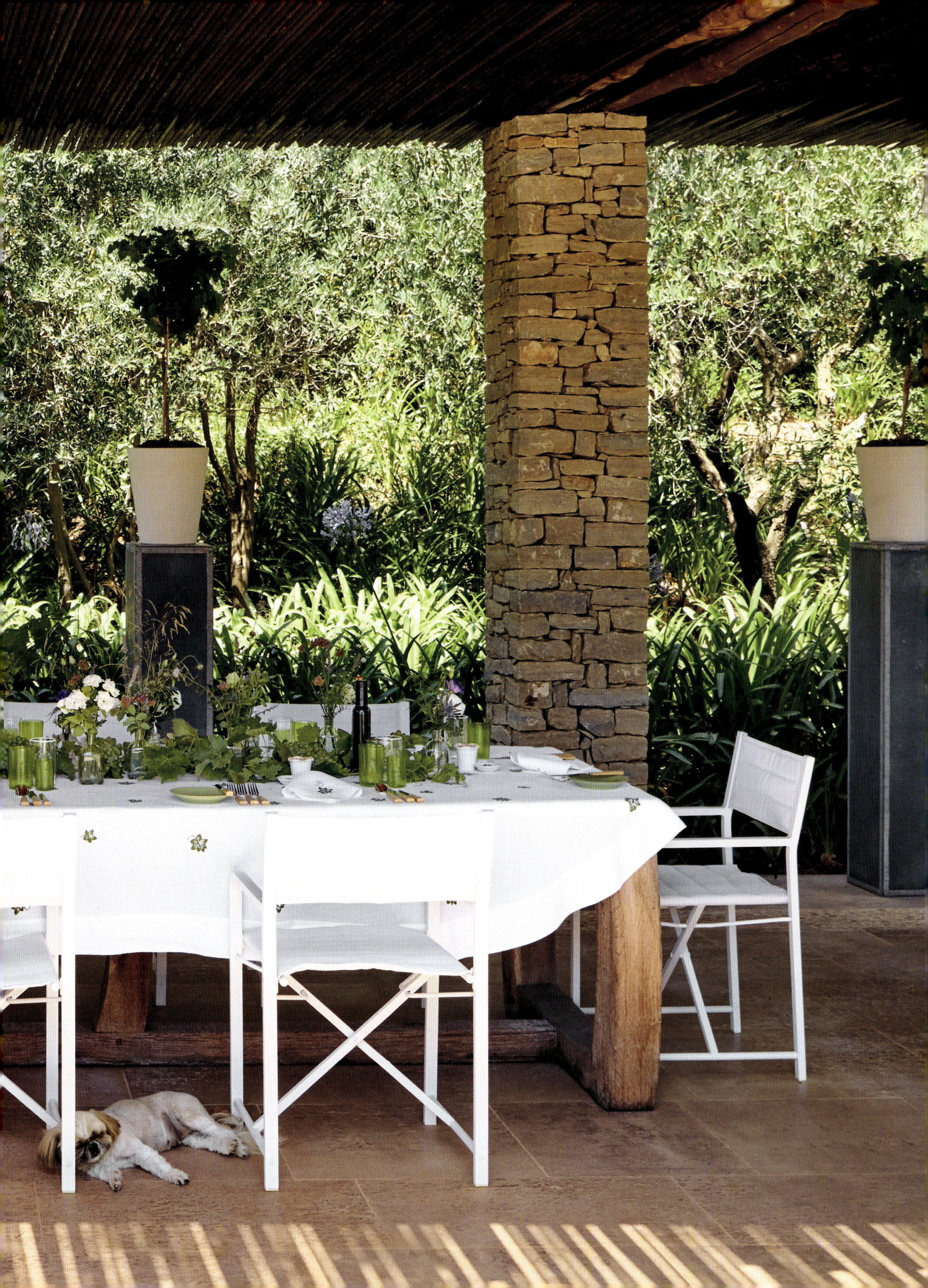

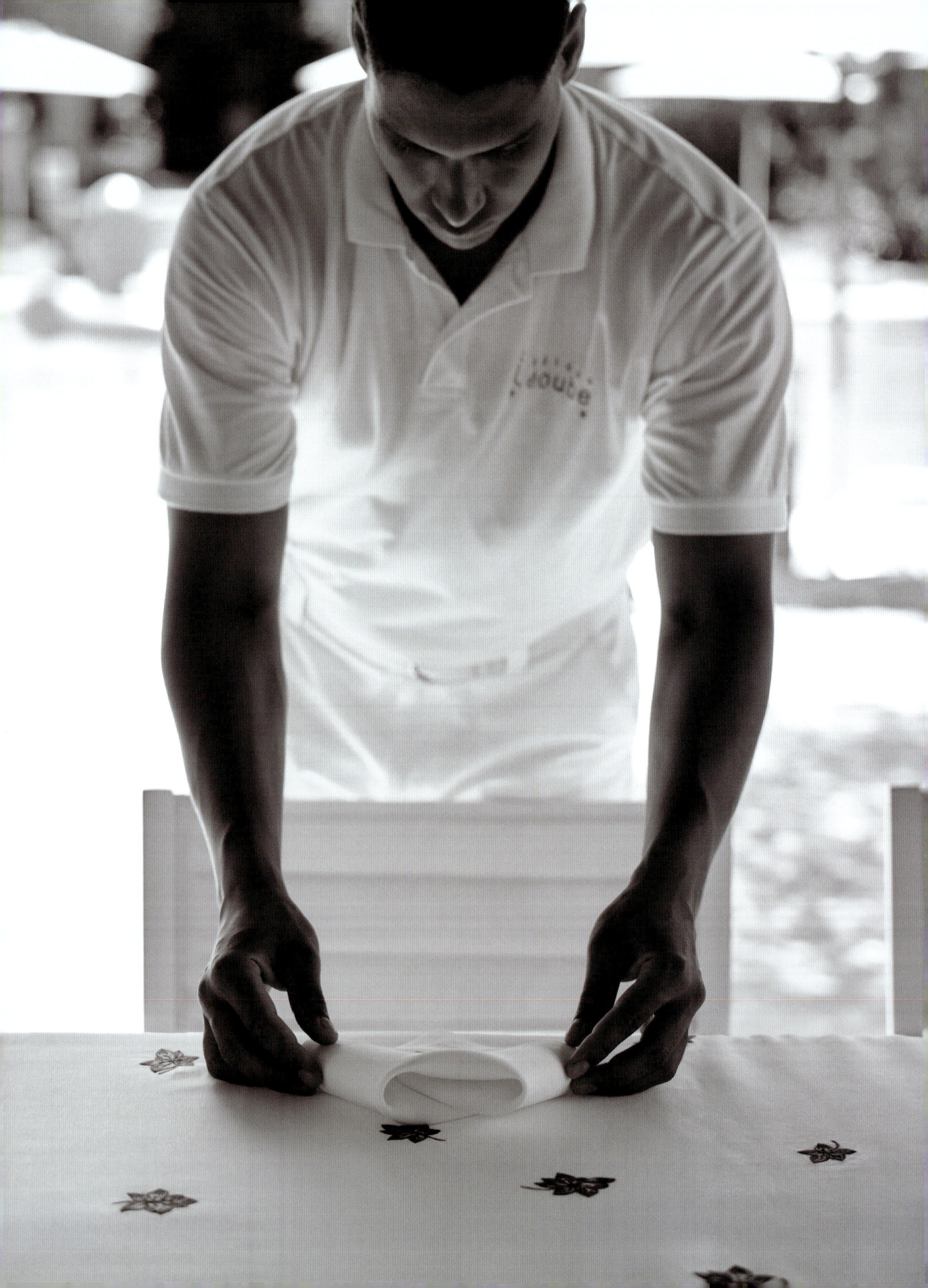

THE POOL AND POOLHOUSE

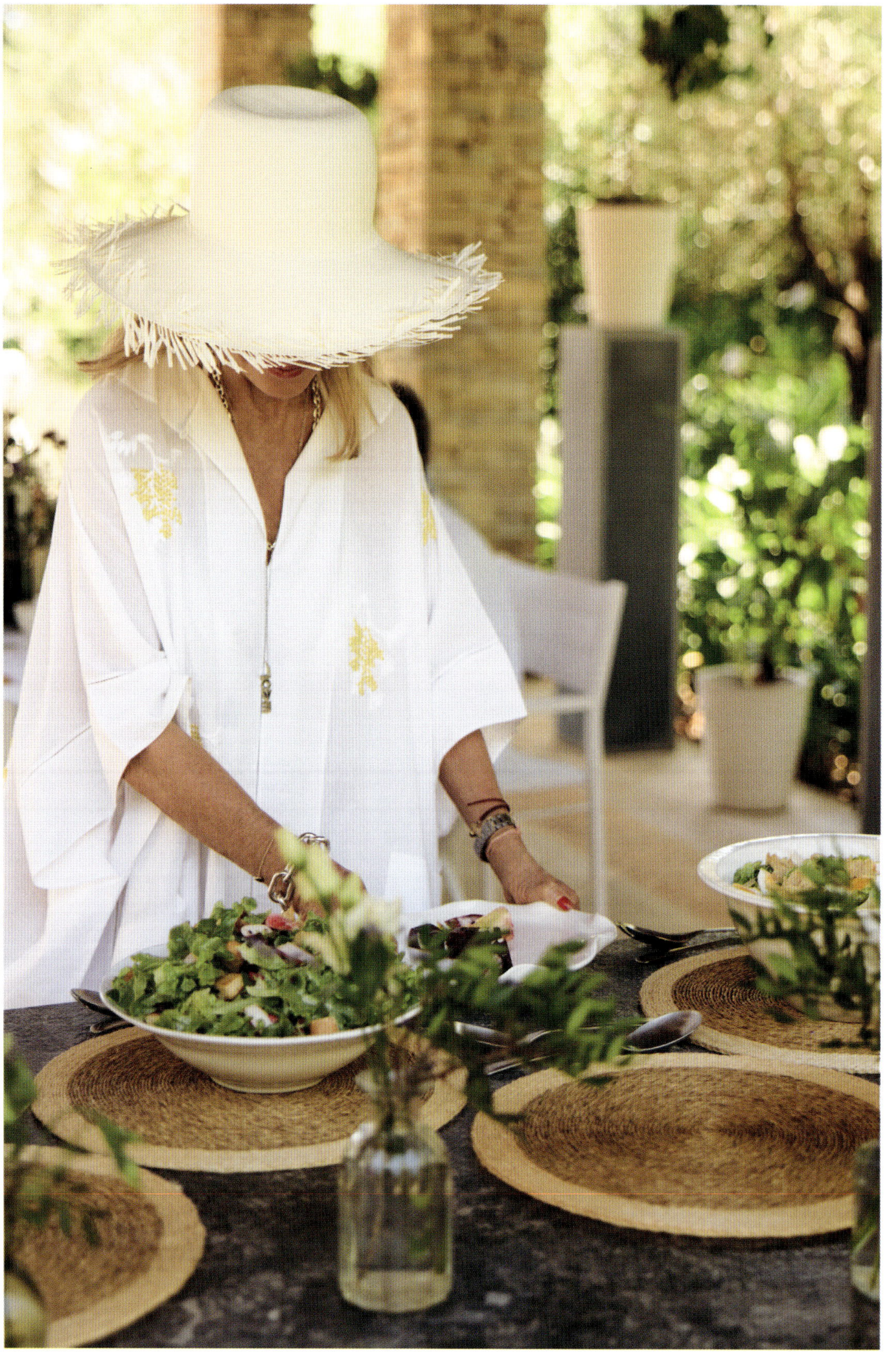

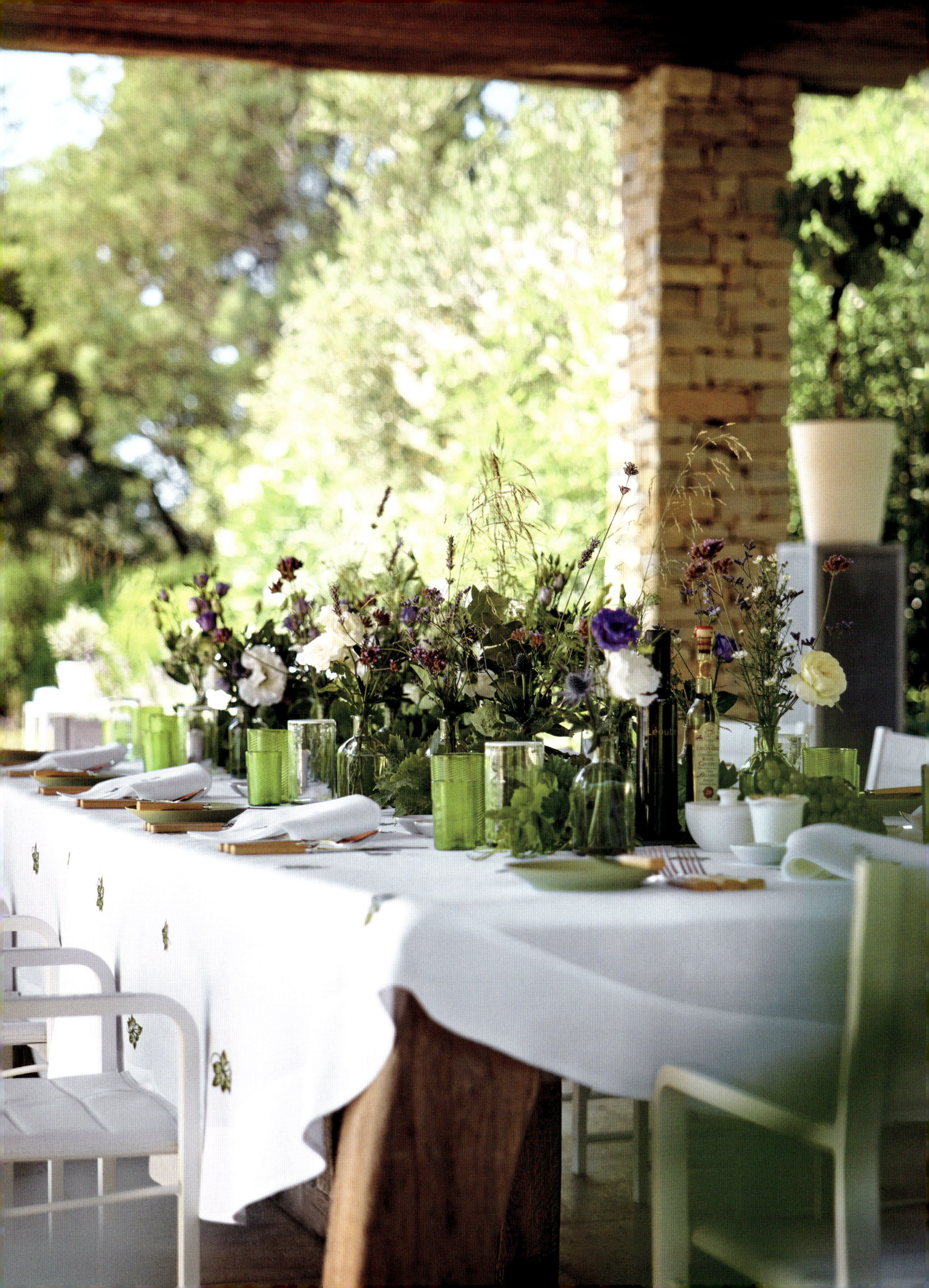

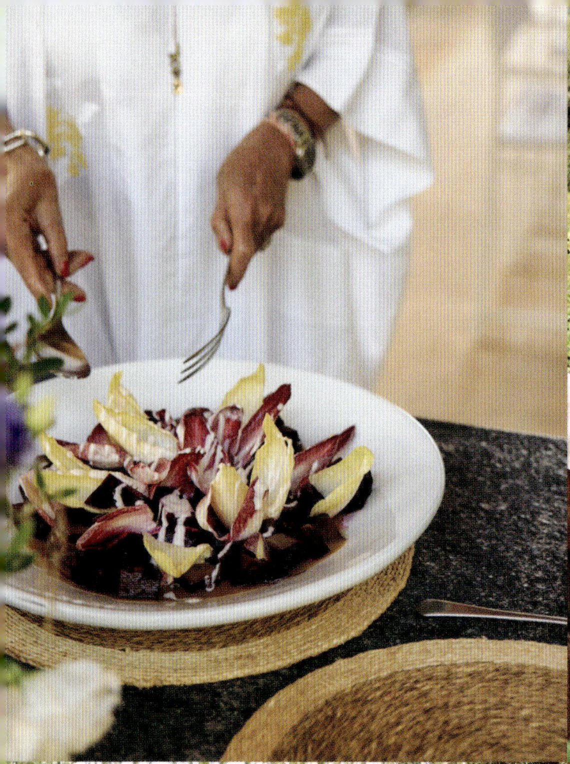
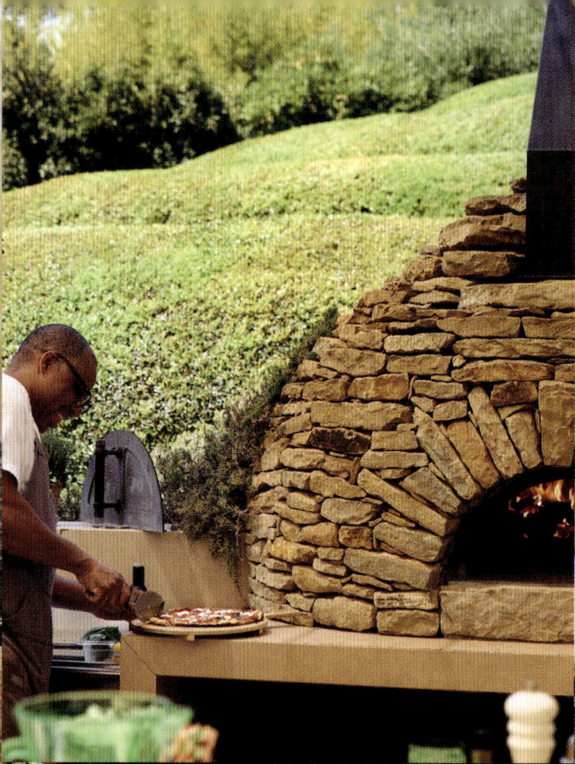
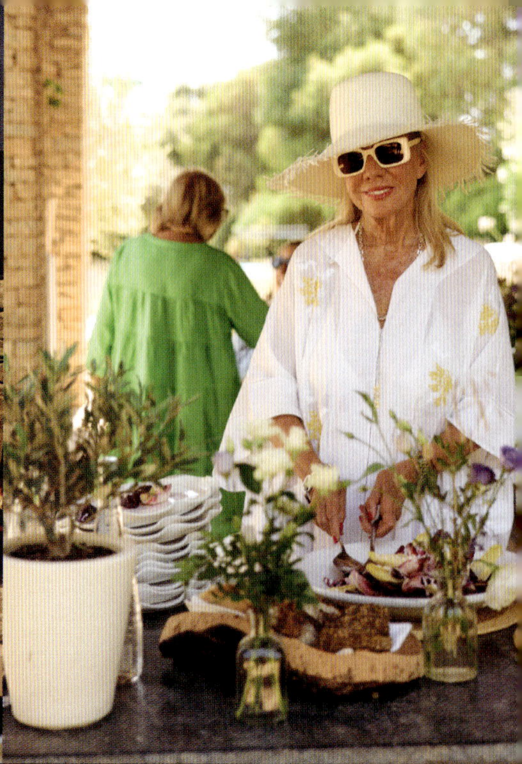
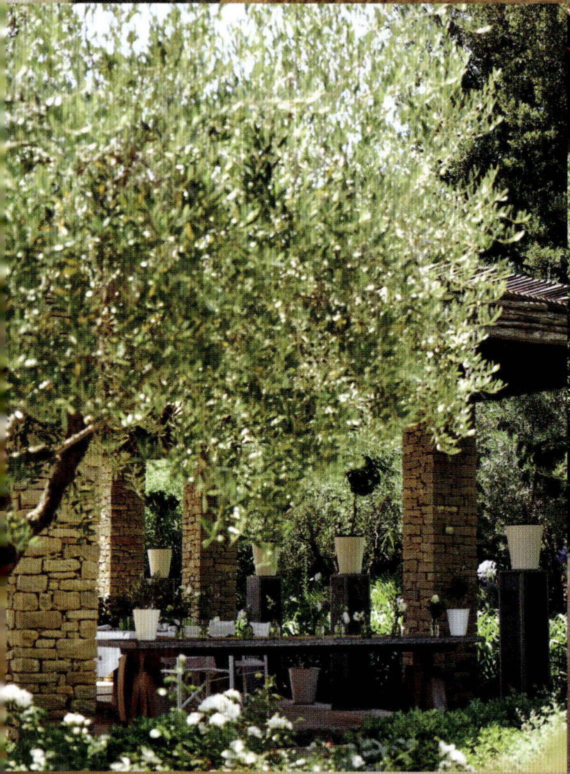
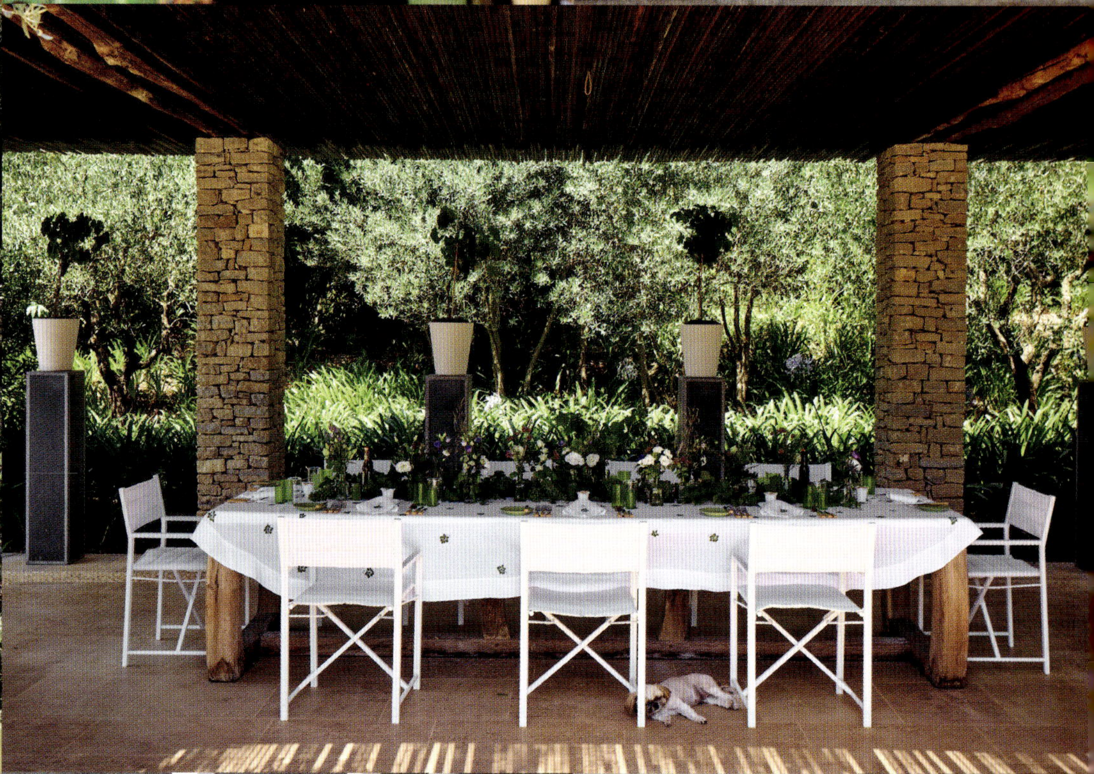
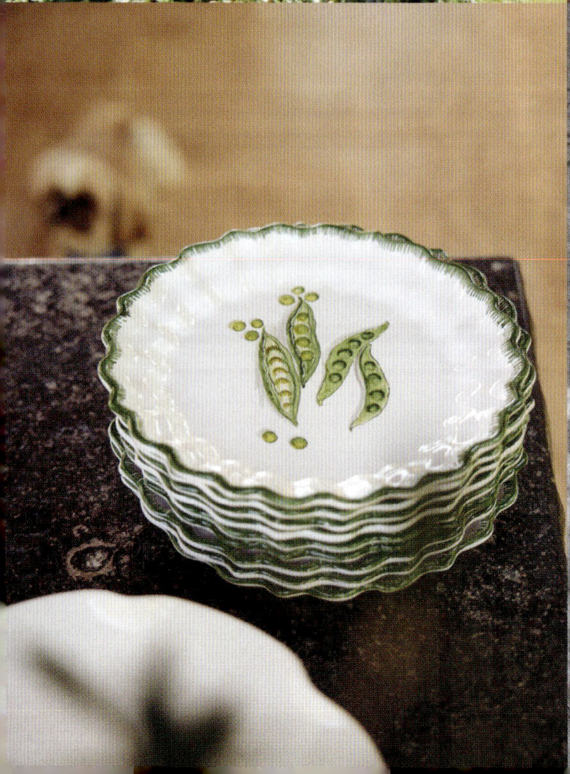
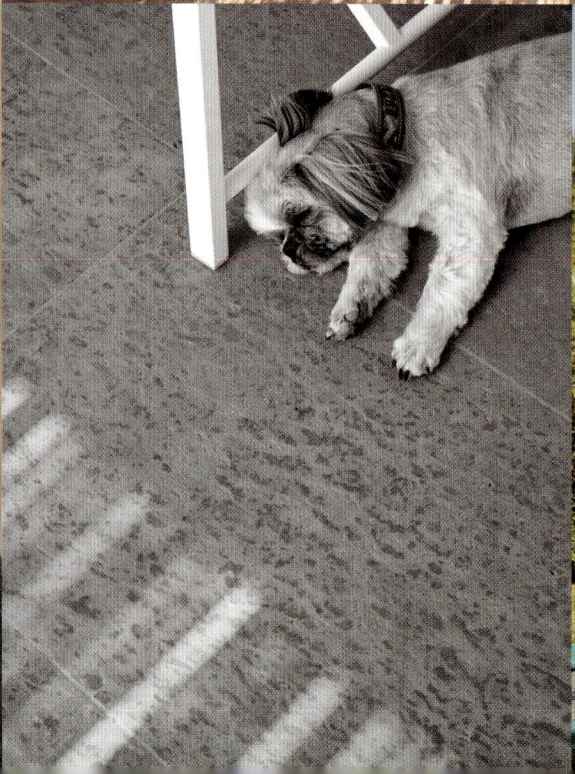
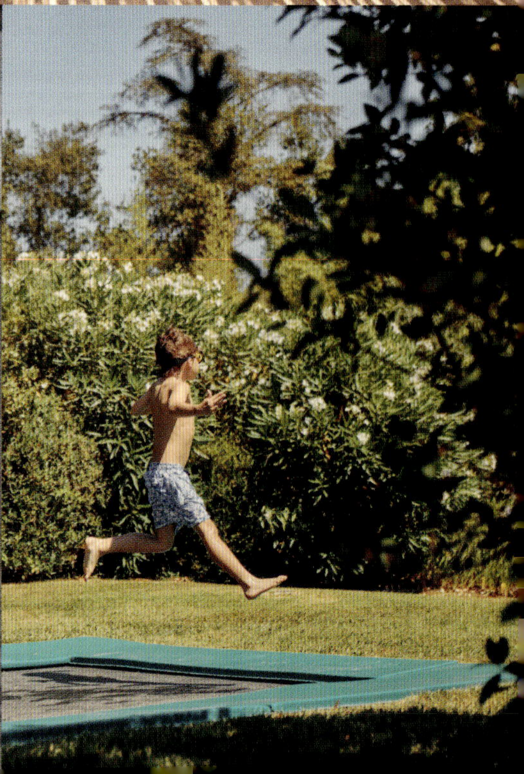

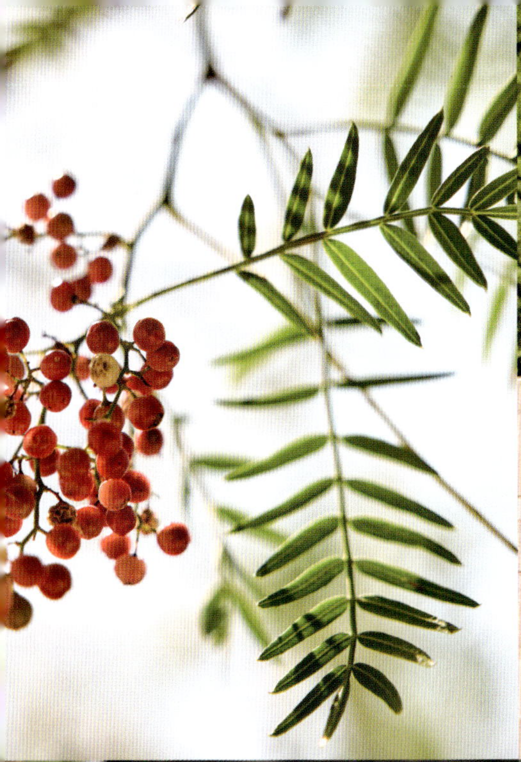
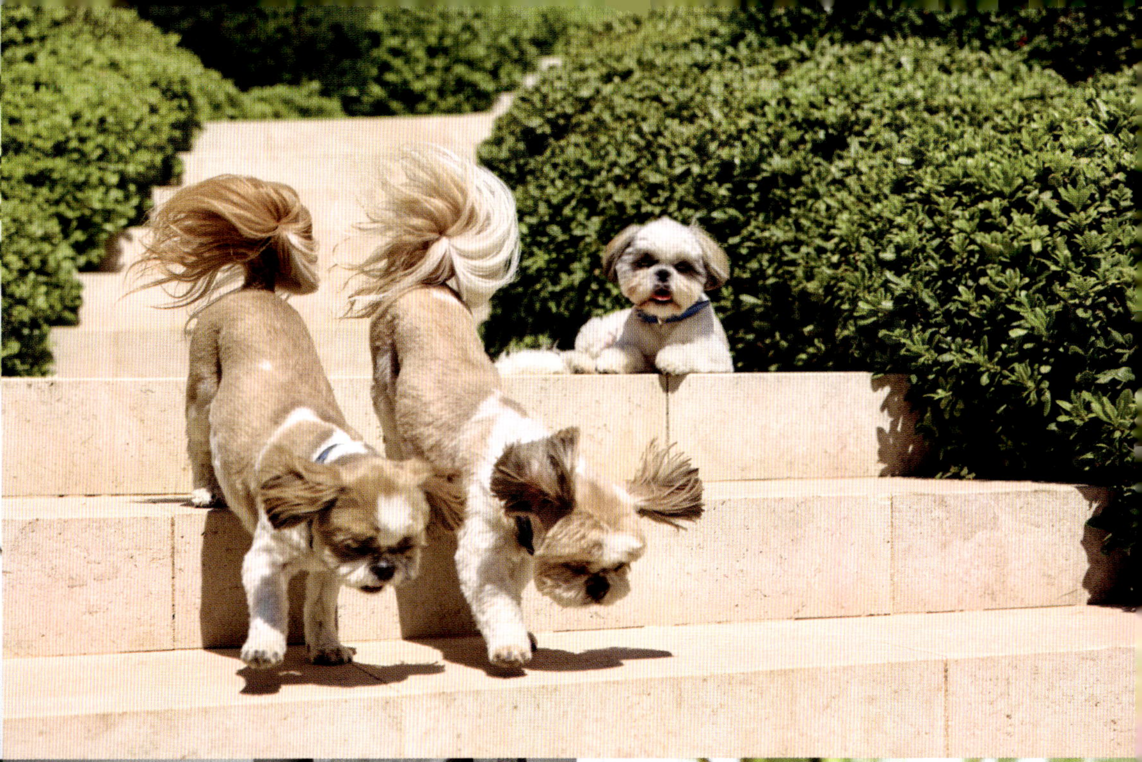
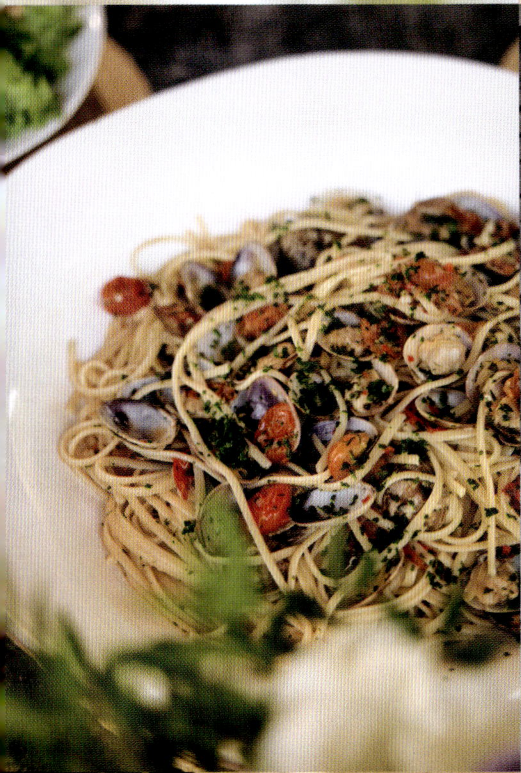
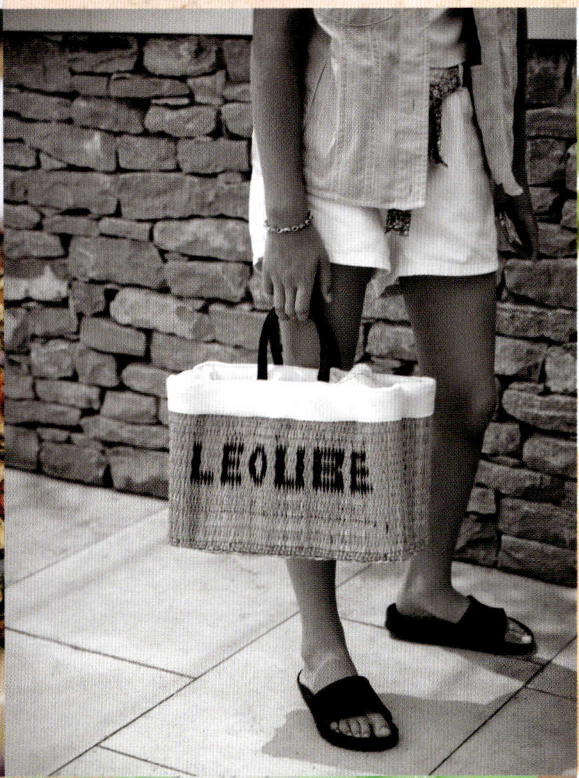
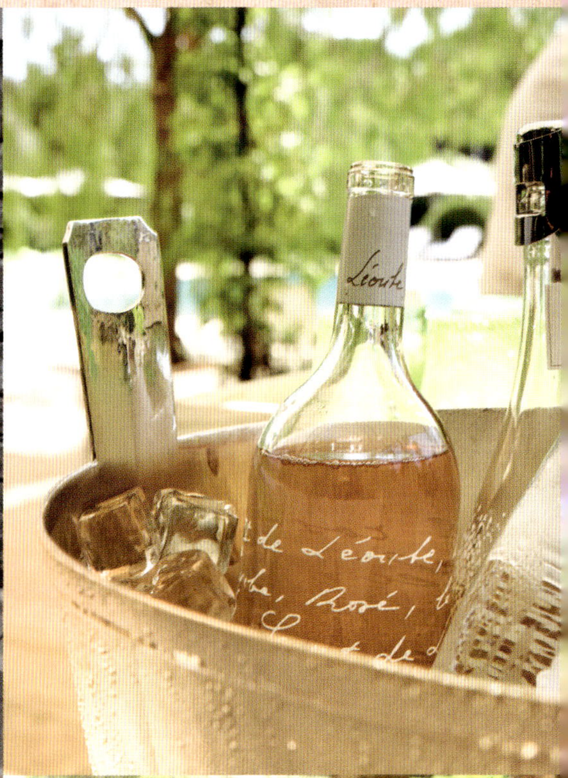
Léoube
de Léoube,
Rosé,
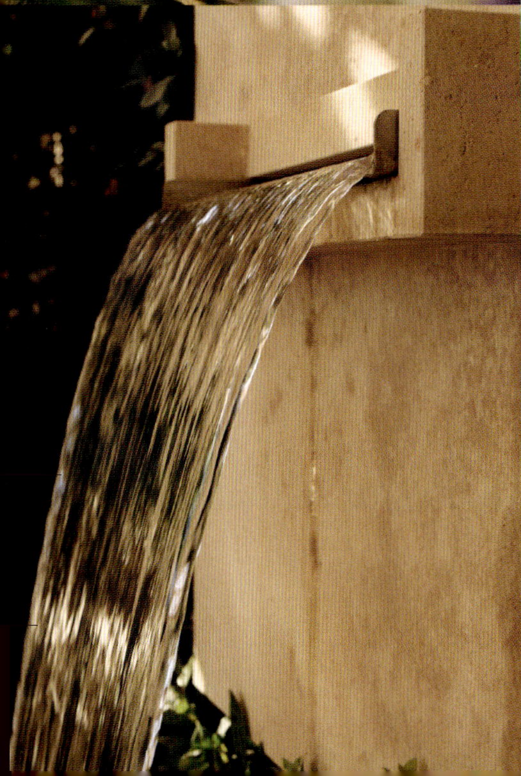
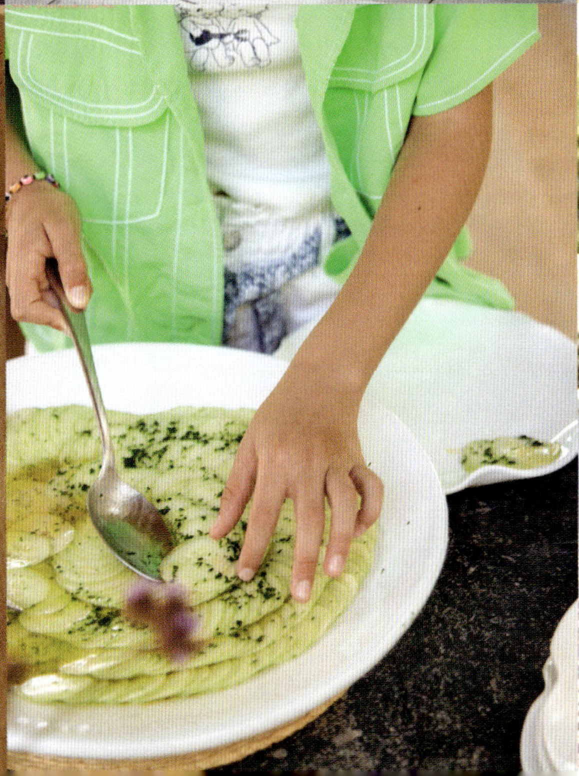
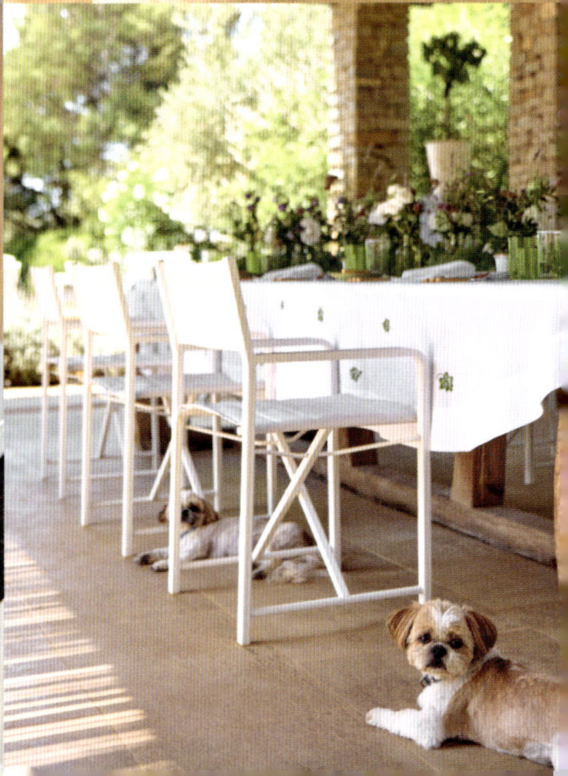

The pool area has become a space defined by different moods and rhythms but dominated by a strong sense of connection to nature and the elements.

Early in the morning, as Anthony and I sip our coffee on the shaded terrace, the pool is serene and the only sounds are the chatter of the cicadas and the cries of the occasional seagull or the rustle of the pepper trees as they sway in the breeze. Slowly, as friends and family and emerge, the energy of the space shifts. The loungers around the pool are quickly piled with towels and books and sunglasses, and the tranquil oasis becomes noisy and bustling.

At night, the atmosphere shifts gear again. Every evening, as the sun lowers in the sky, we set candles in tall hurricane lamps around the pool and up the steps back up to the house. It's a sight that never fails to take my breath away and I've watched countless guests stop in their tracks as they experience it for the first time.

Much of the way we chose to furnish and design Léoube was led by its situation on Provence's coastline and by my love of nature and craftsmanship but also by our desire to reflect the estate's function as a vineyard. We wanted the house to embrace and embody that sense of place. So we commissioned the British artist Jacob van der Beugel to create an installation that pays homage to our vines. His piece, 'Good Year, Bad Year', which is set in the back wall of our study in the pool house, is a thoughtful and reflective expression of the process of making wine.

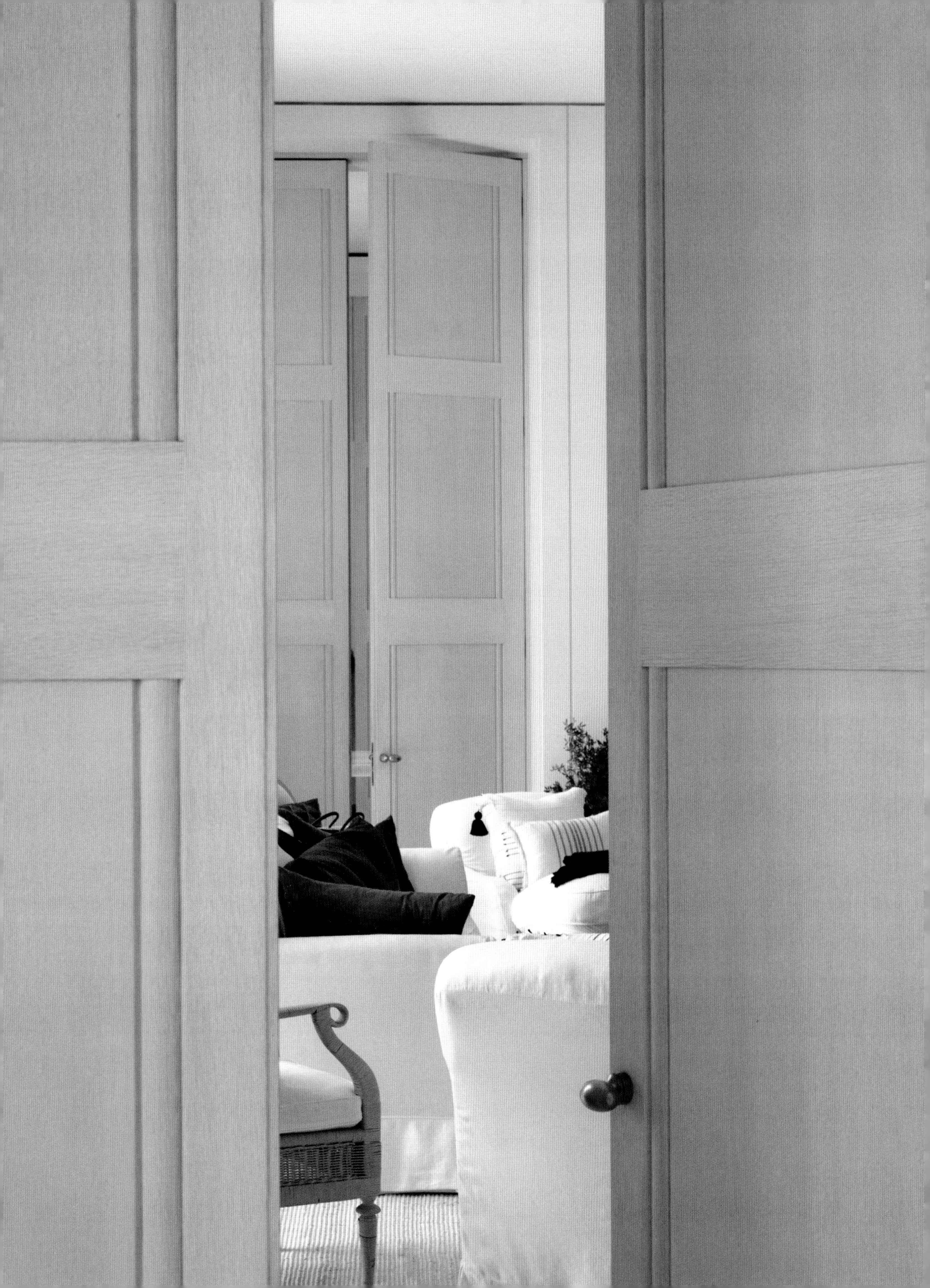

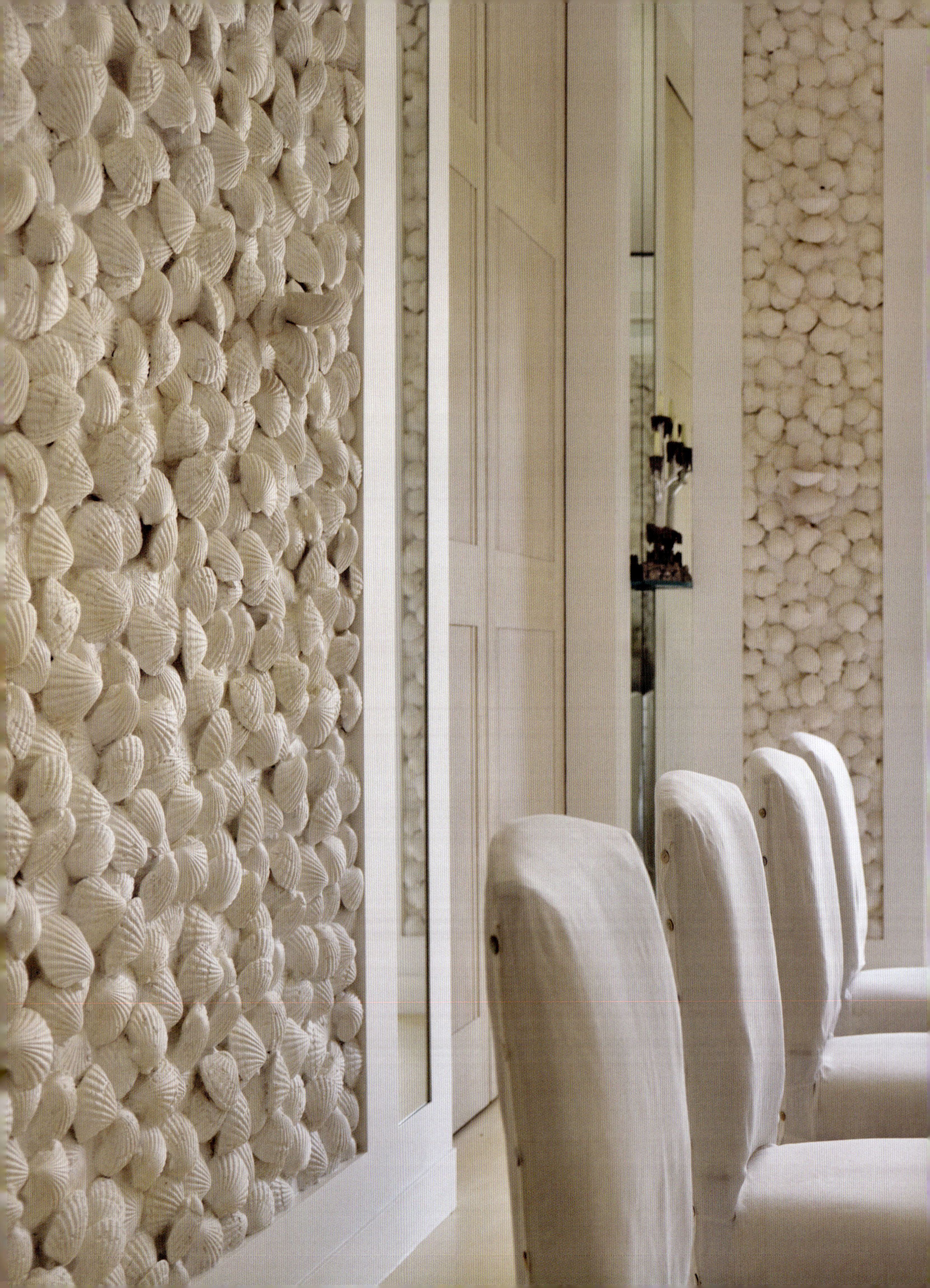

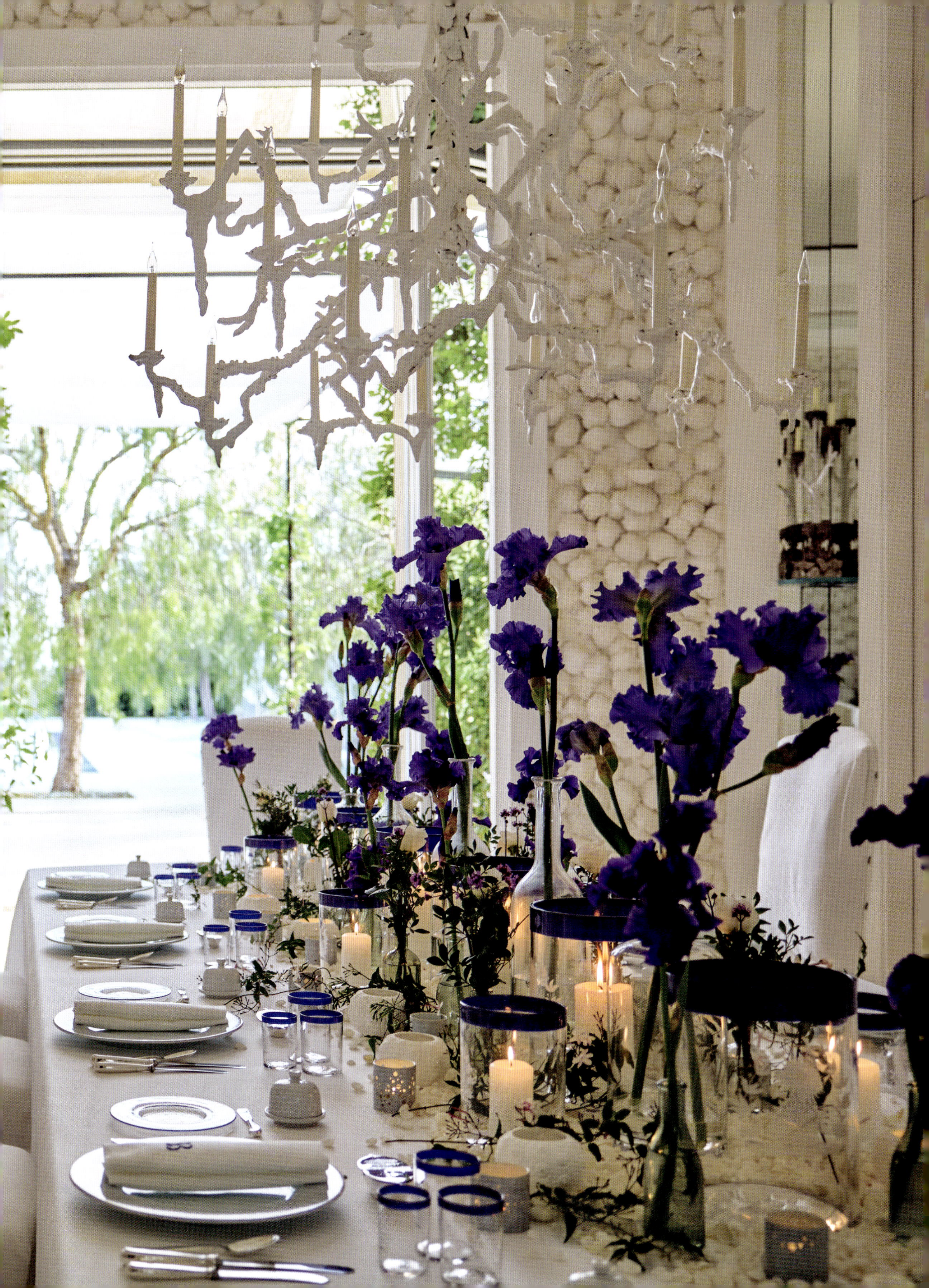

ABOVE The walls of the dining room were based on a slab of fossilised shells that Wendy found on sale at Christie's auction house.

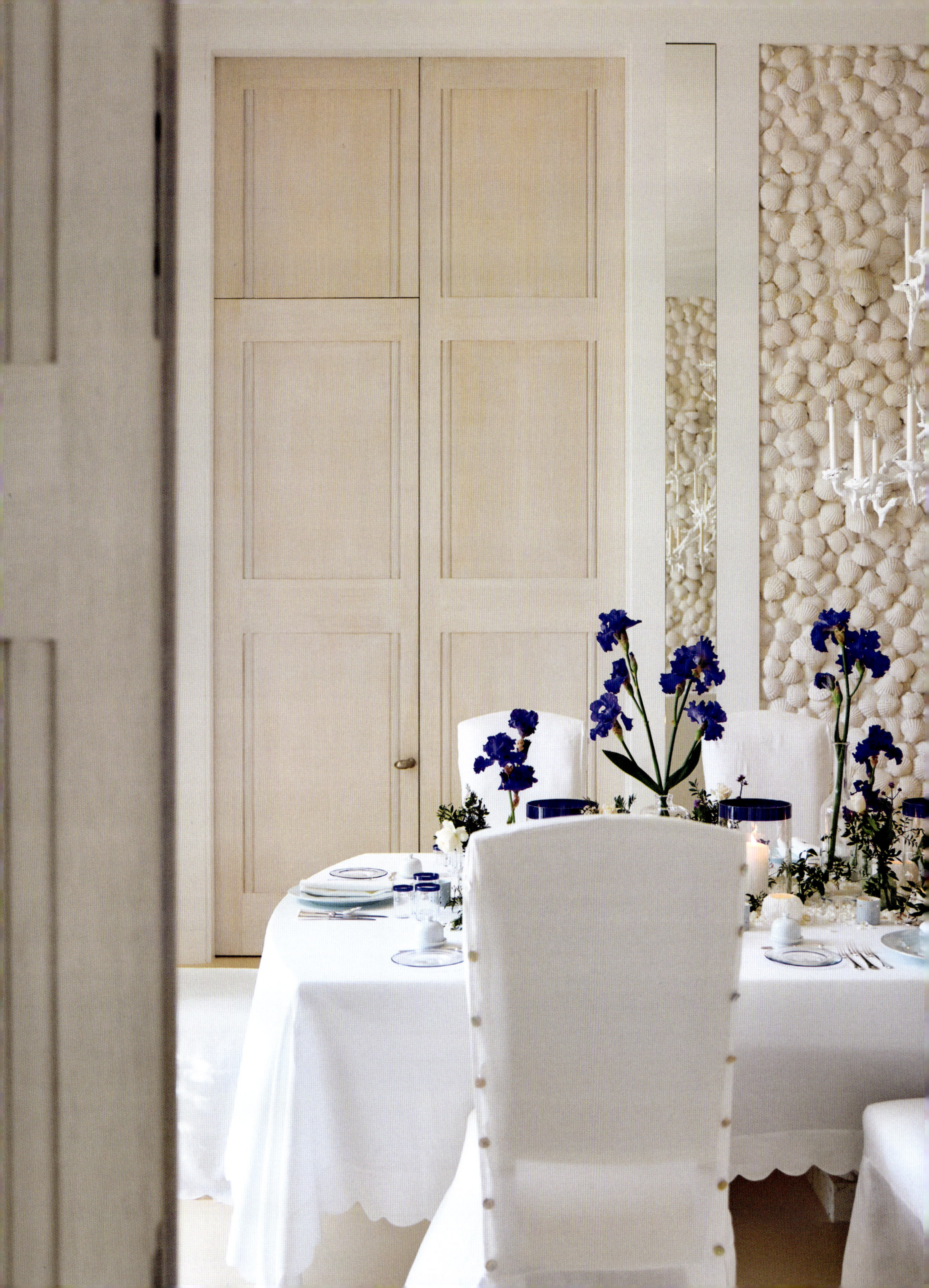

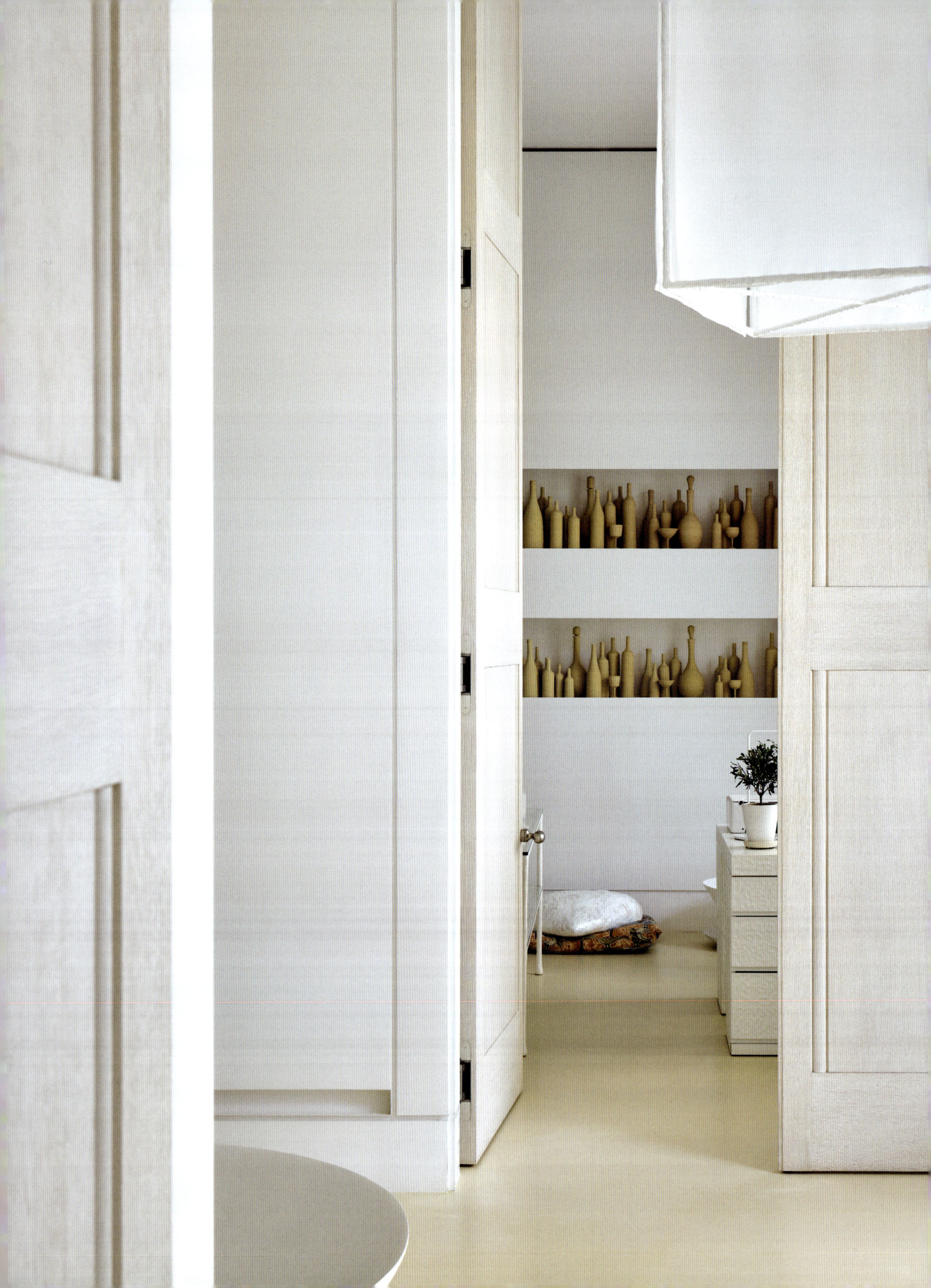

ABOVE AND OPPOSITE British artist Jacob van der Beugel's installation, 'Good Year Bad Year', a homage to Léoube's vines, is set in wide recesses along the back wall of our study.

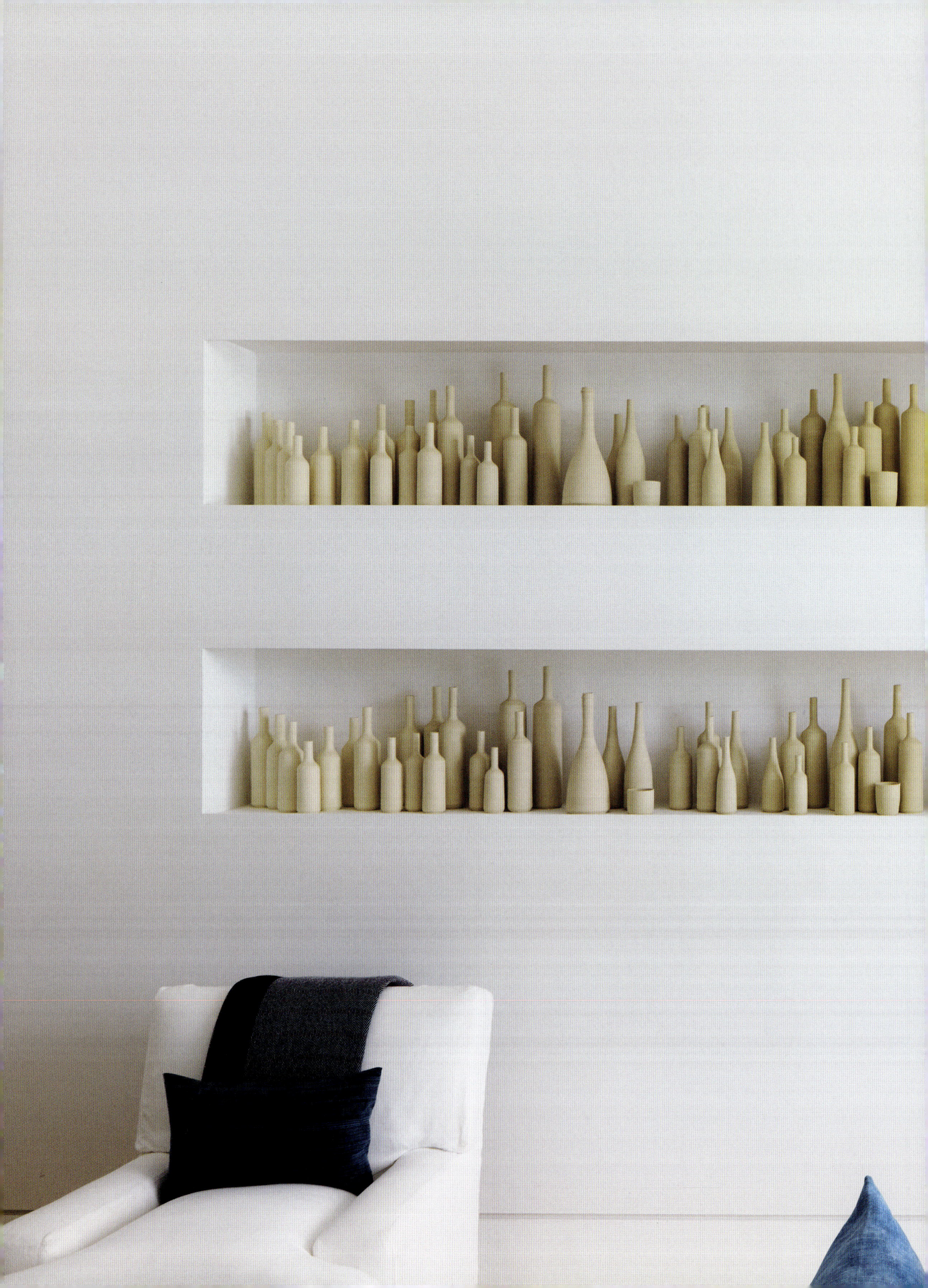

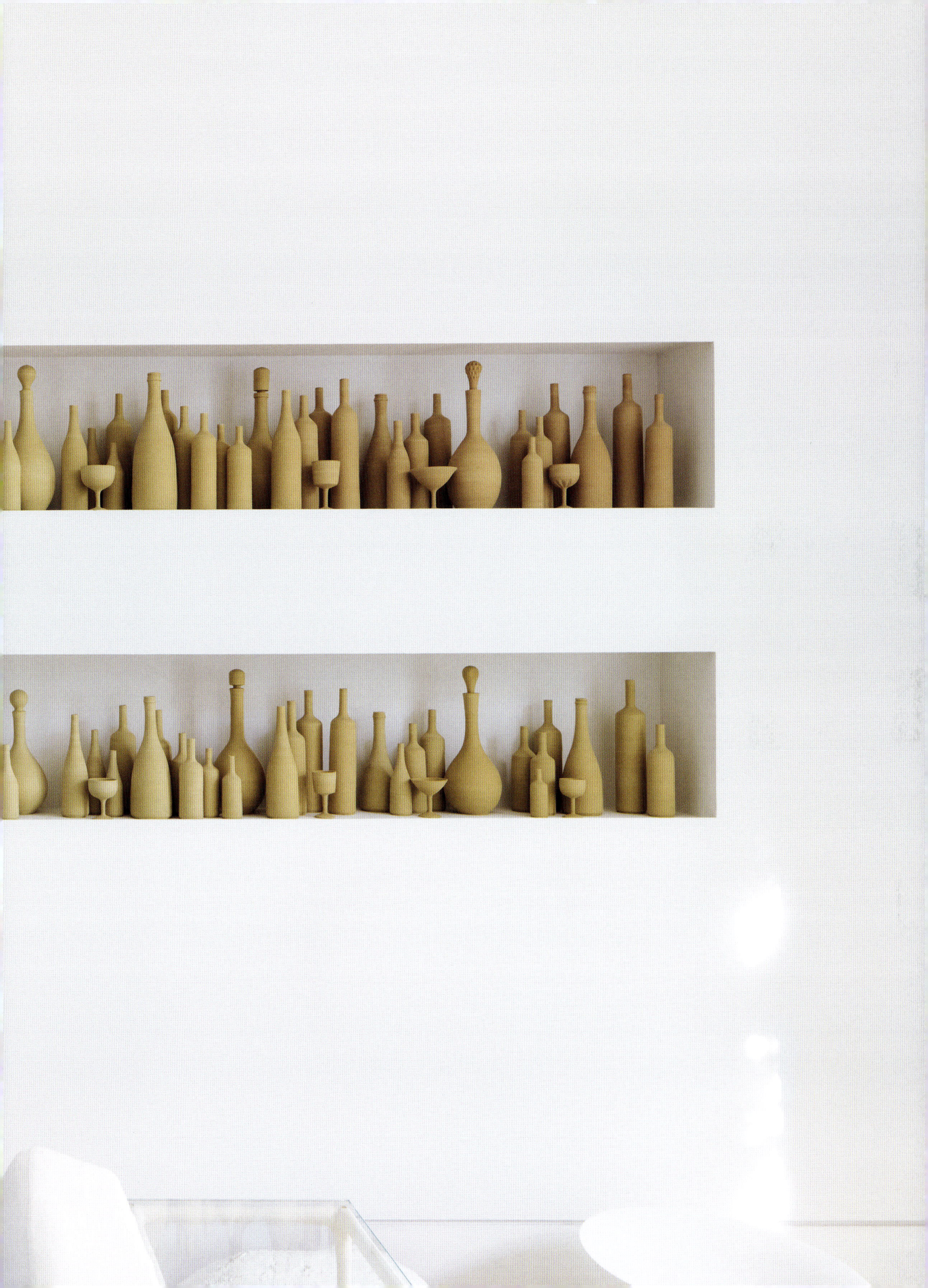

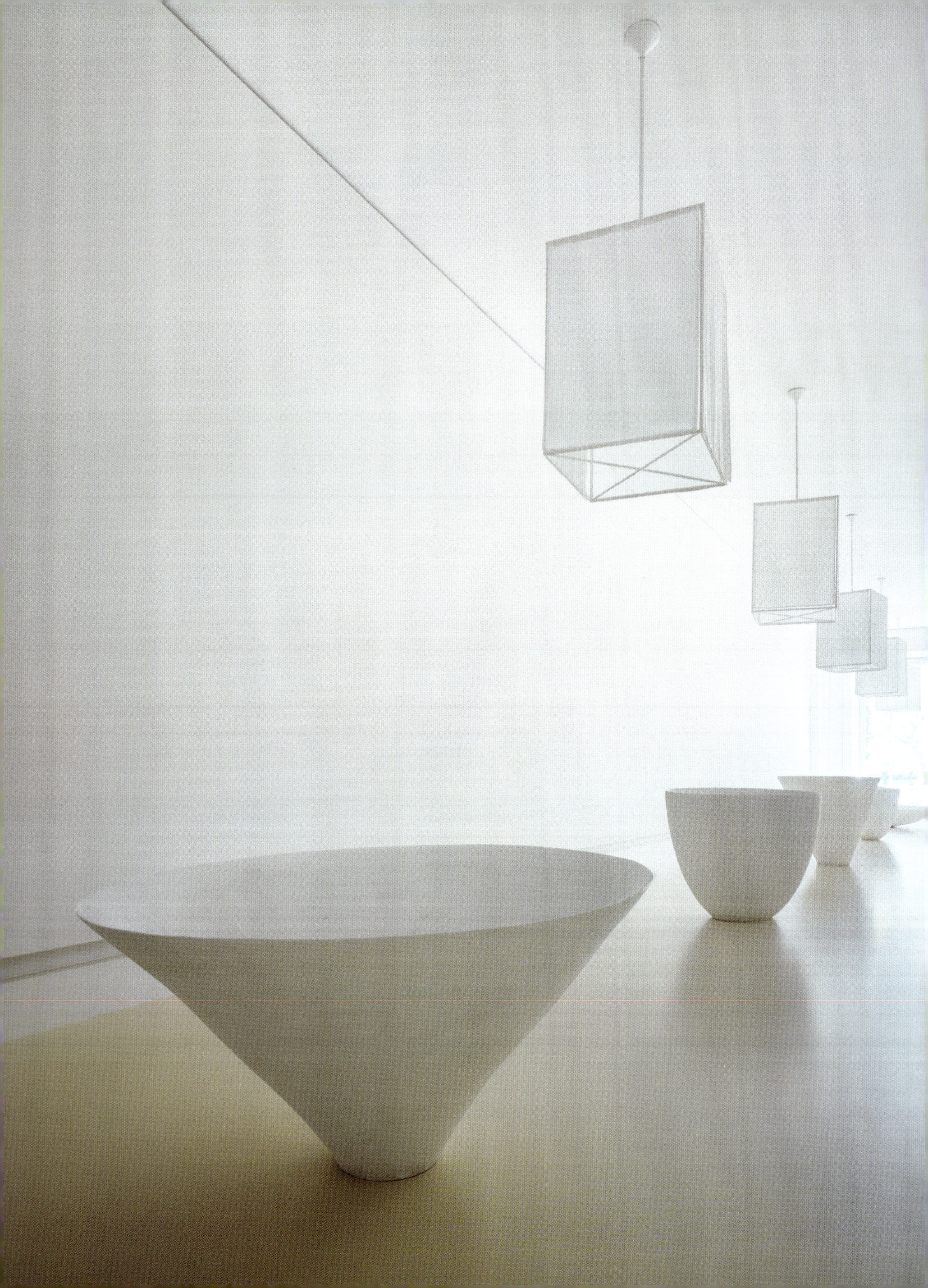

The work consists of a series of stoneware clay vessels – unglazed wine bottles and glasses in different forms – which gradually change in tone from light to dark. The effect is a sweep of colour that serves not only as a metaphor for the passing of time and the rhythm of the seasons, but acts as a commentary on the precariousness of producing wine, reflecting the nature of good and bad seasons. Jacob's approach to his craft is very much aligned with my own sensitivities, emphasising his appreciation of nature's ephemeral beauty and evoking the perfection one finds in its imperfection.

I've collected shells and pebbles since I was a little girl. I think of them as nature's treasures and I will always comb the beach in search of them wherever I am in the world. Shells have travelled – tumbled and rocked by the sea, they are a sign of nature's resilience – that I am fascinated by all that they represent. They've been a part of my life for so long and I wanted to bring that love of their form to the interiors in the house, which felt particularly fitting given its situation by the sea. The pool house offered a natural home and the walls of its dining room are crafted from a mosaic of overlapping plaster shells. It's a feature that feels extremely personal and is a poignant reminder that our homes can tell the stories of our lives and our design choices are not only an expression of emotion and memories but of who we are.

The chandelier above the dining table is very special. It was made in Paris in the style of Alberto Giacometti. Hand-carved from wood and covered in layers of plaster, its organic form and irregular texture is marked by the subtle imperfections that recall the motion of the artist's hands. The matte chalky finish softens the lights it holds and lends a beautiful intimacy to evening suppers under its glow.

The scale of the pool house building meant that we had a cavernous corridor to fill. I had found the sculpted porcelain vessels by the Swedish sculptor Eva Lange, which needed a setting large enough to allow them room to breathe, but when we set them down the space above them felt hollow and bare, so Wendy came up with the design for these lanterns and had them made so that they could be suspended in a line over the vessels. Simple linen shades hang from the rod frames and the lanterns blow in the breeze when it flows along the corridor. I love the quiet yet bold restraint of the space – it's a wonderfully peaceful juxtaposition to the energetic, sometimes frenetic, space outside.

OPPOSITE Eva Lange's statuesque porcelain vessels provide a calming but arresting focal point in this cavernous corridor in the Pool House.

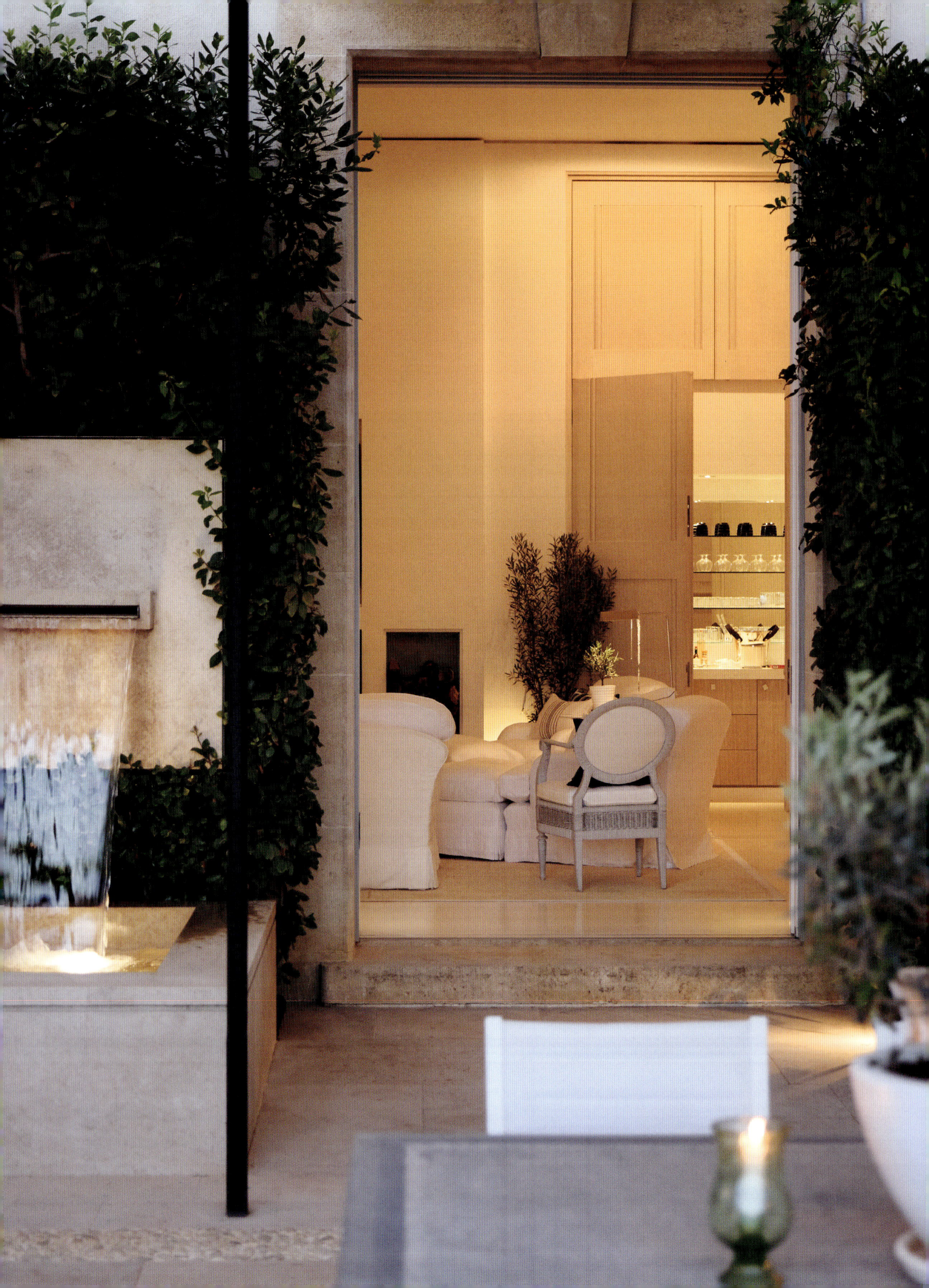

'There is a special kind of beauty
in the twilight hour, when the
sun begins to set and the world is
bathed in a soft, golden glow.'

– ERNEST HEMINGWAY

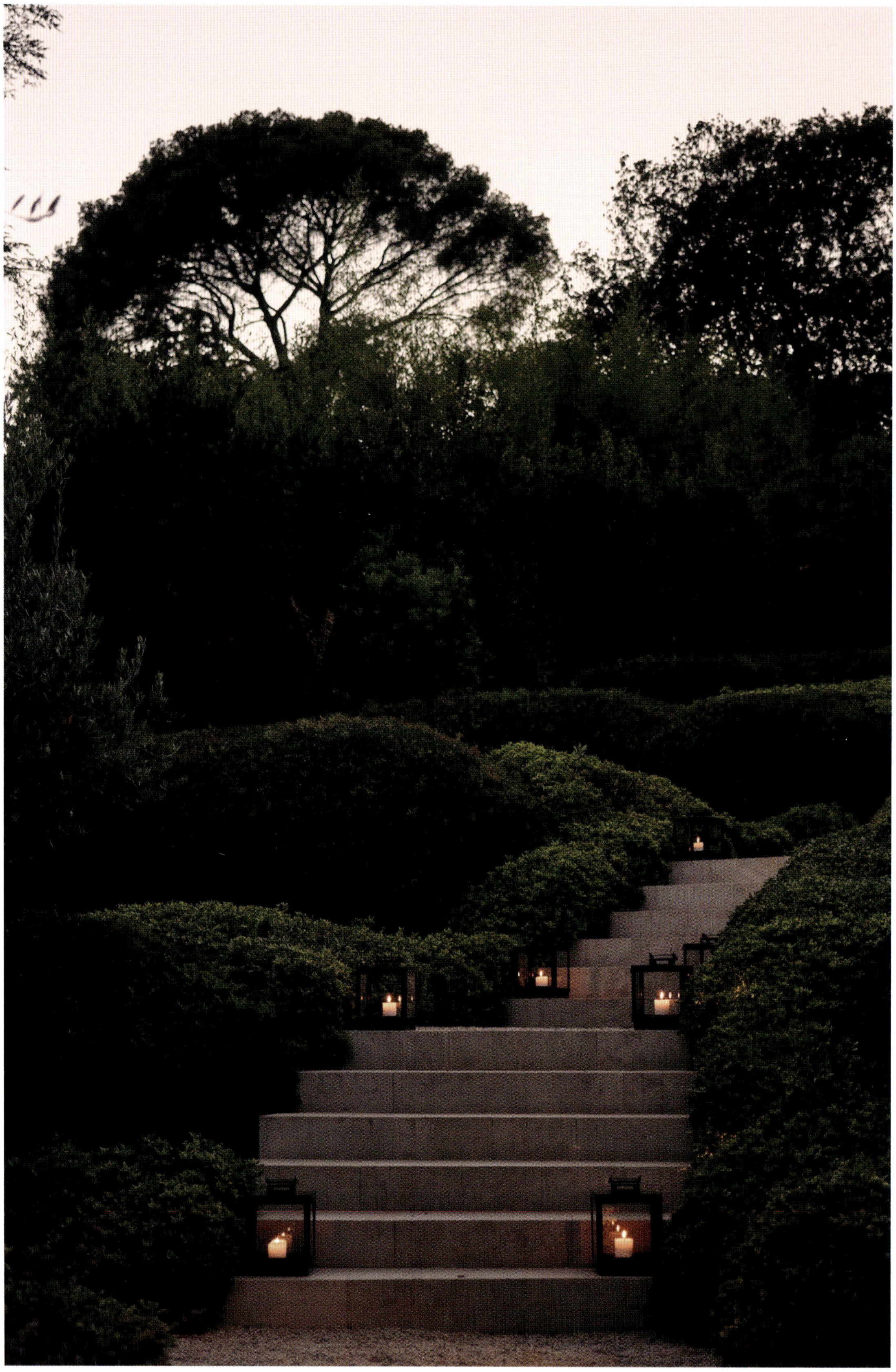

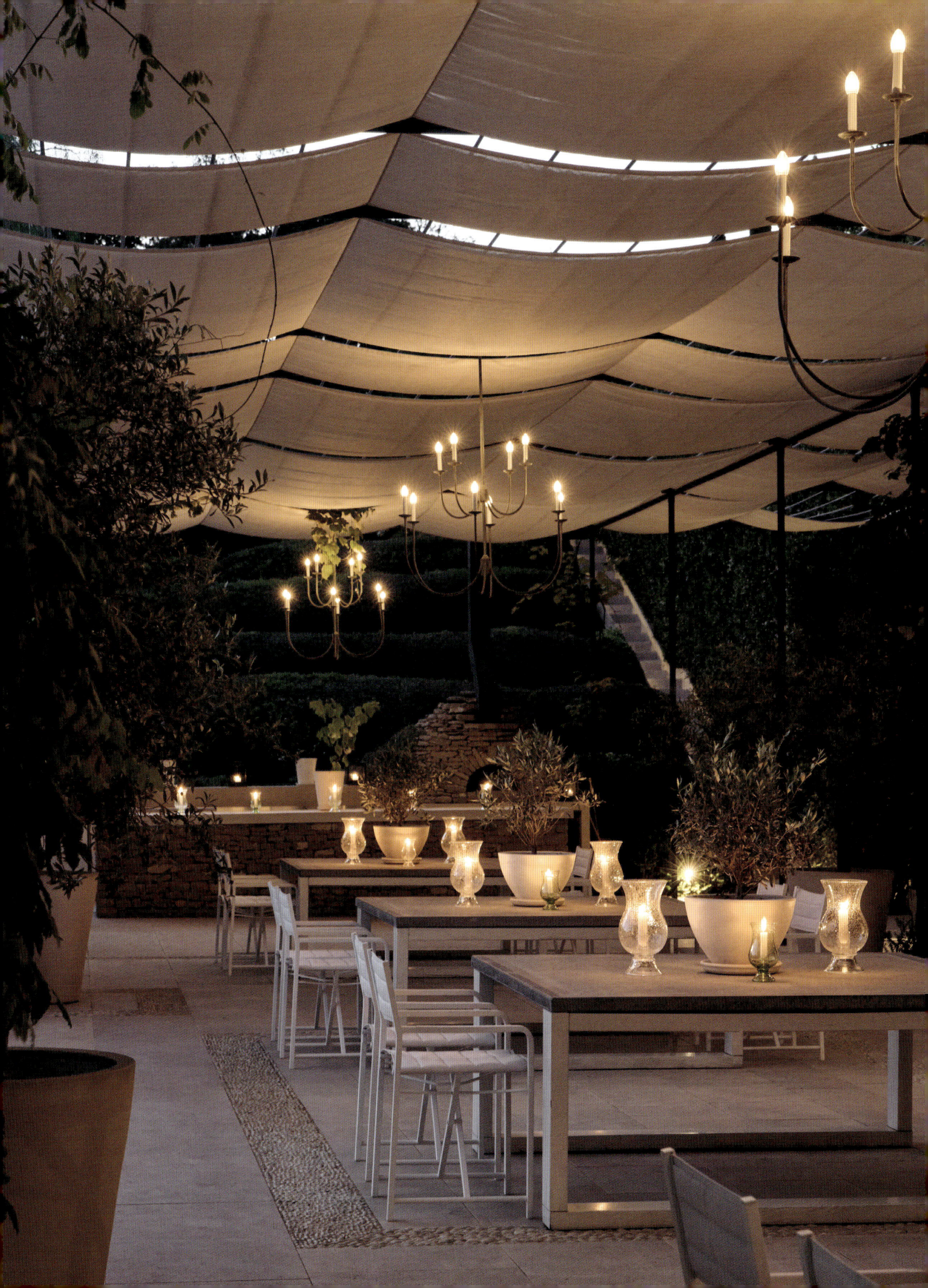

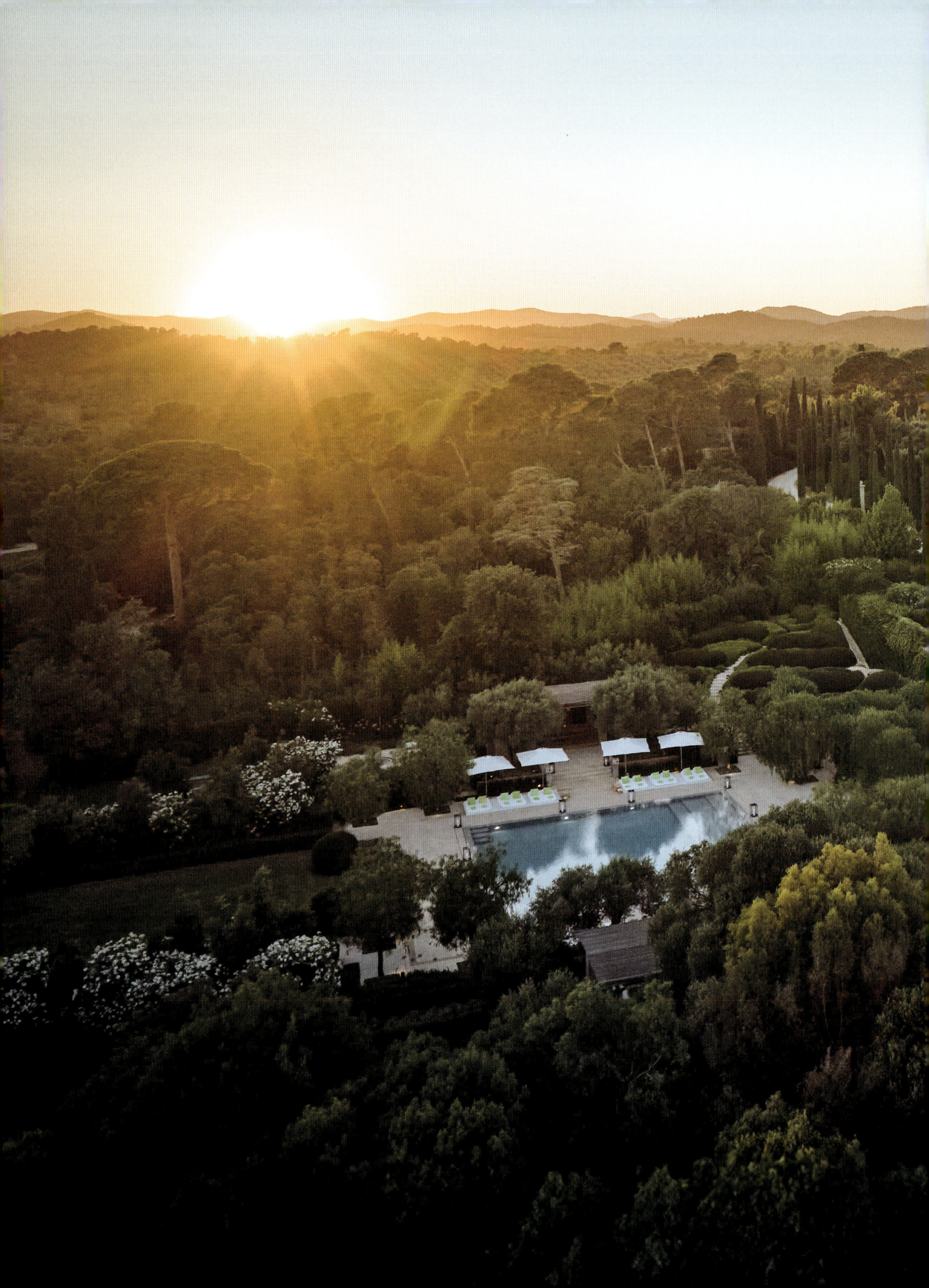

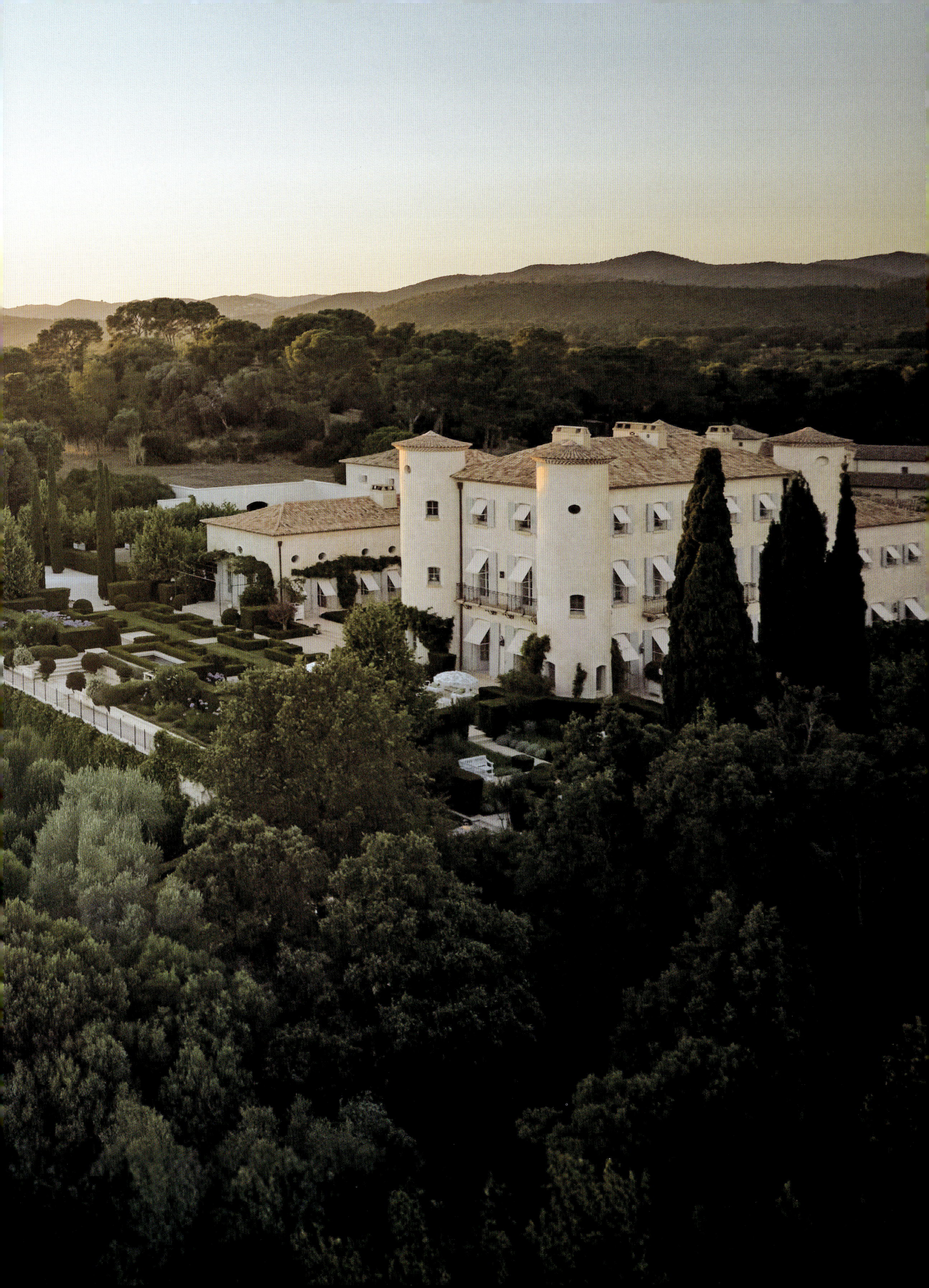

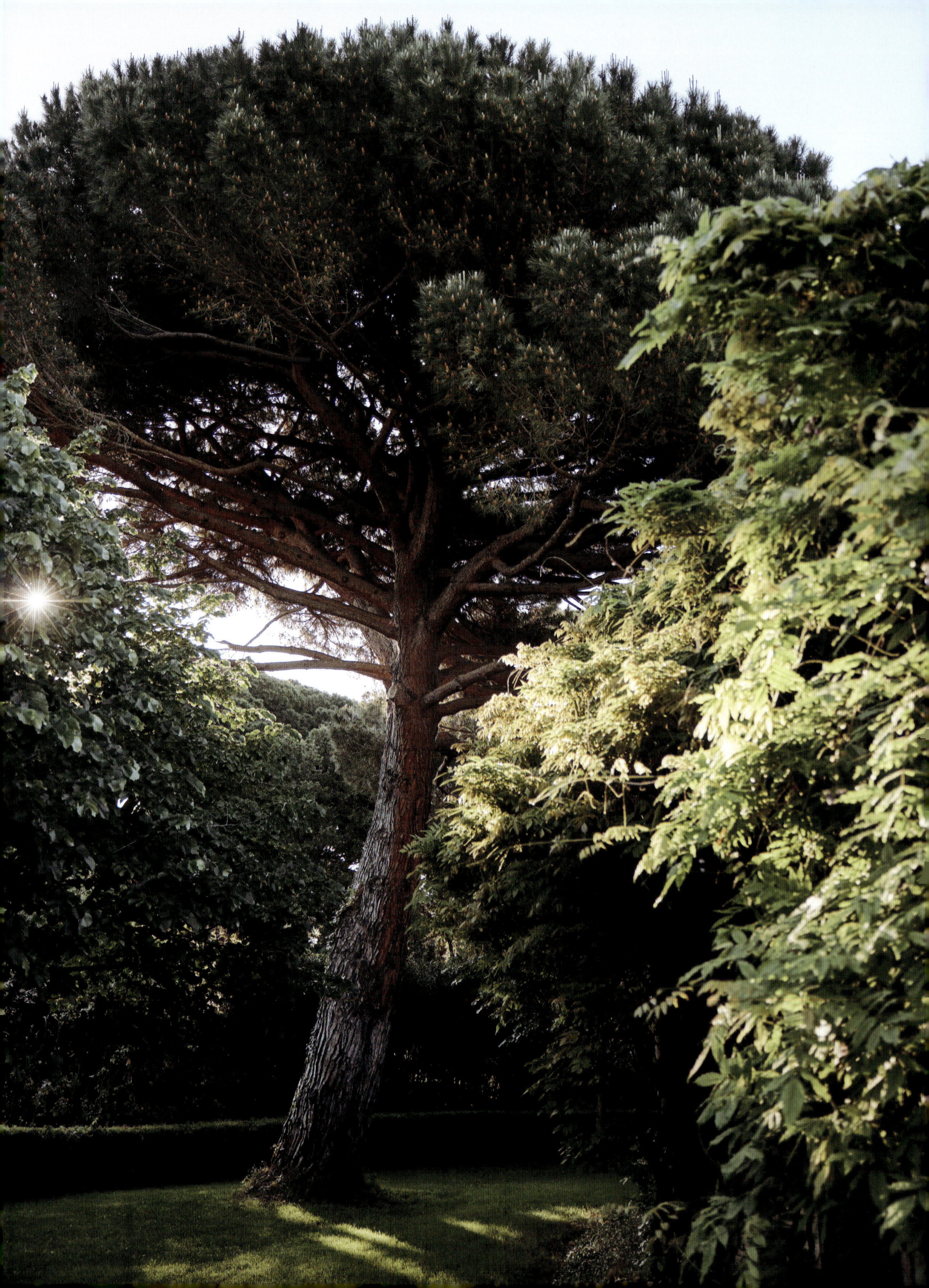

# THE GARDEN

The gardens at Léoube were first created and landscaped when the château was restored in 1920. When Tommaso came on board, we decided to preserve a lot of those original foundations in the gardens surrounding the château to honour the style of garden that would traditionally accompany a house such as this. We kept the formal French garden with its structured paths and symmetry, water features and fountains, as well as the cypress and pine trees. As is traditional, the gardens are laid out in broad parterres framed by a semicircle of umbrella pines and wisteria, the orderly beds enclosed in neatly trimmed hedges of laurel, boxwood and myrtle.

Early on I took two decisions which have endured in my approach to how we plan and organise the garden, which also acknowledge its heritage. I wanted the colours to be a harmonious partner to the château, so all the flowers are shades of blue, very deep purple and white. And it was important to me that all the plants were native and local. The only exception to that is the agapanthus, originally from South Africa but now grown widely all over the Mediterranean and thrives in the warm climate. The shape and colour of its slender, arching stems and globes of star-shaped flowers are so elegant, lending both structure and lightness to the landscape. Huge beds of agapanthus line pathways and soften the edges of terraces around the château and Villa Maria and every June the return of their delicate shades of blue brings me so much joy.

OPPOSITE Wisteria – *glycine* – is a defining feature of many Provençal gardens in the spring. Its climbing vines and cascading branches are often draped from pergolas providing shade and a wonderful spectacle of movement as they sway in the breeze.

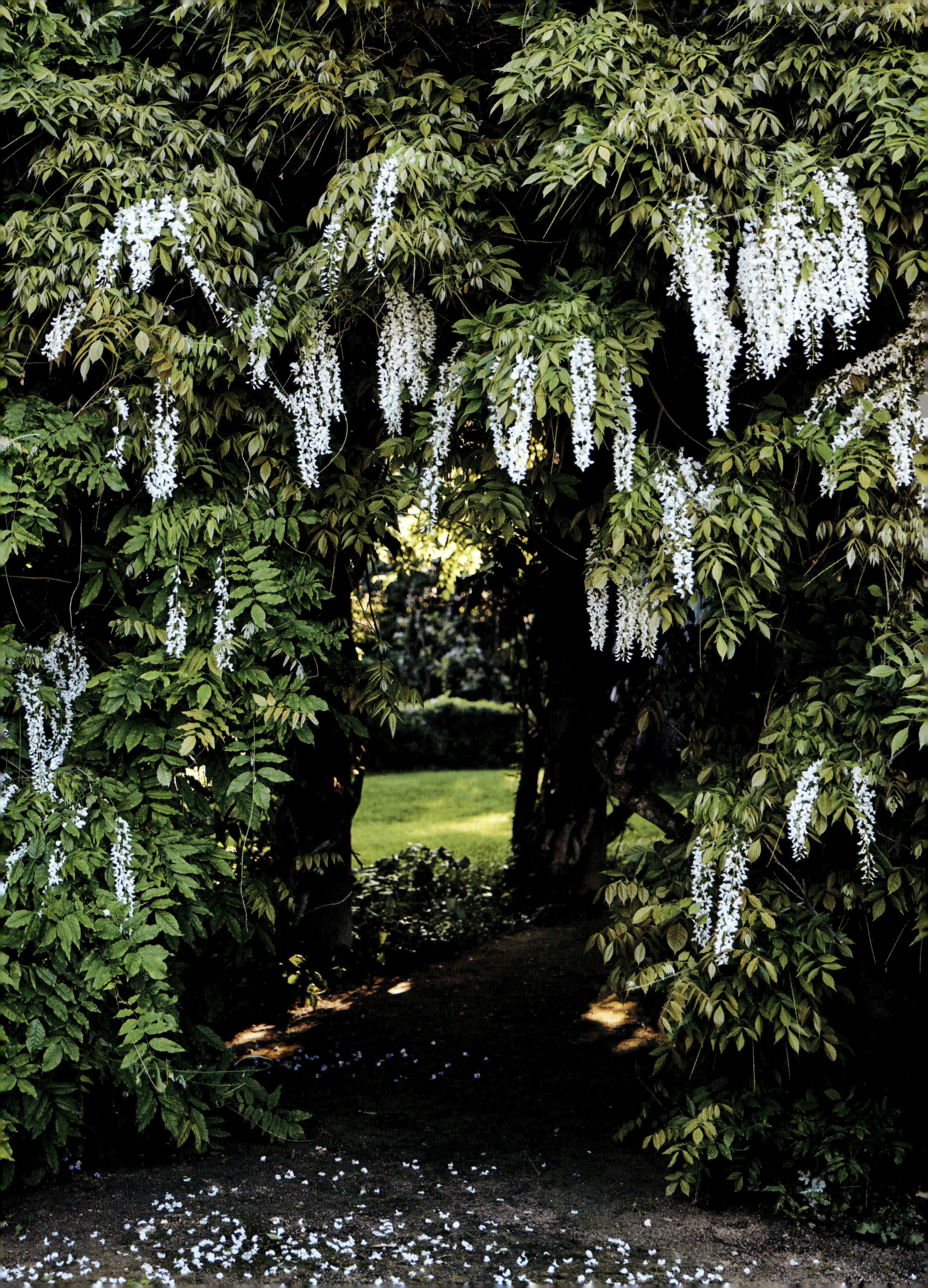

CHÂTEAU LÉOUBE

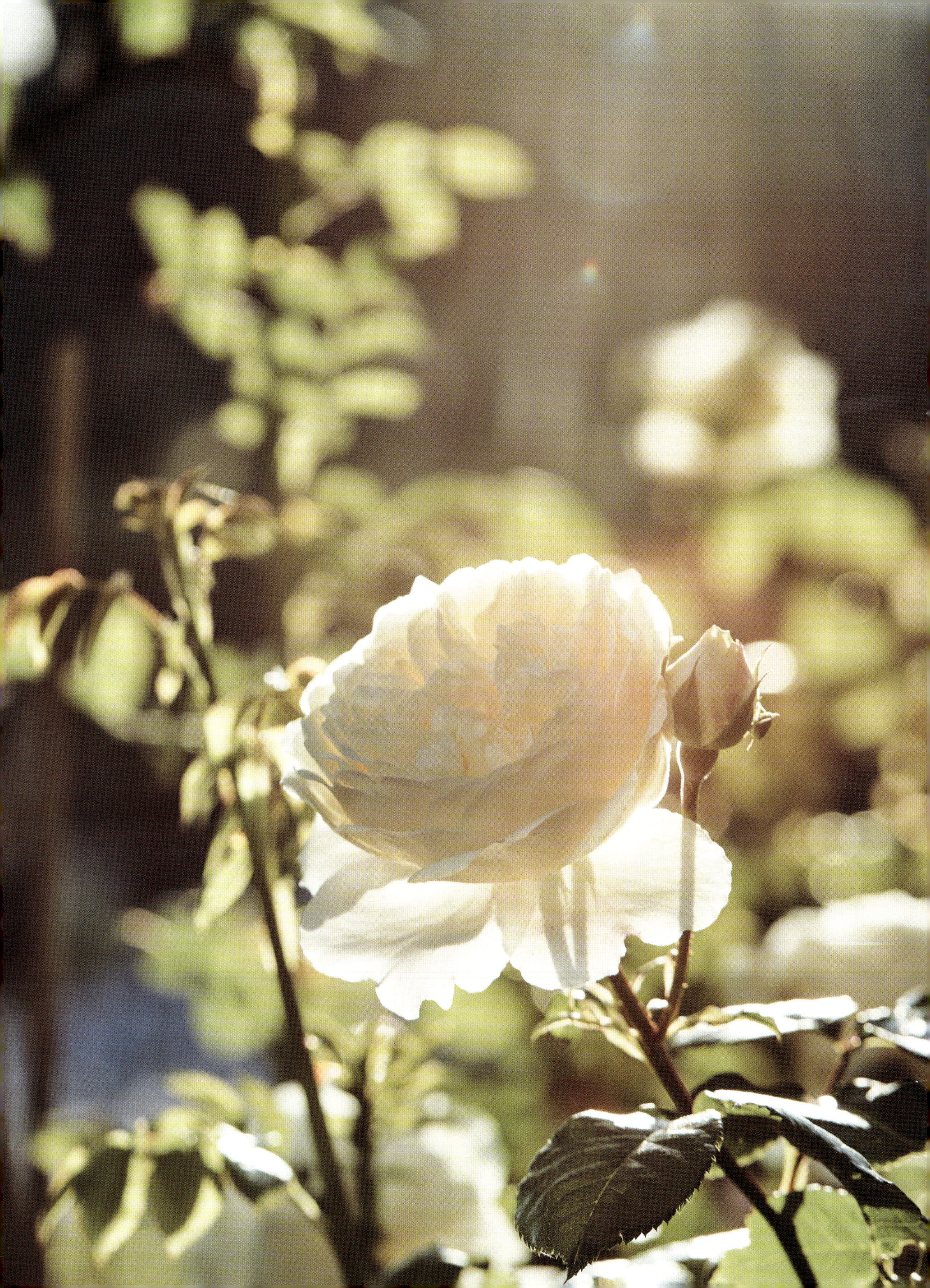

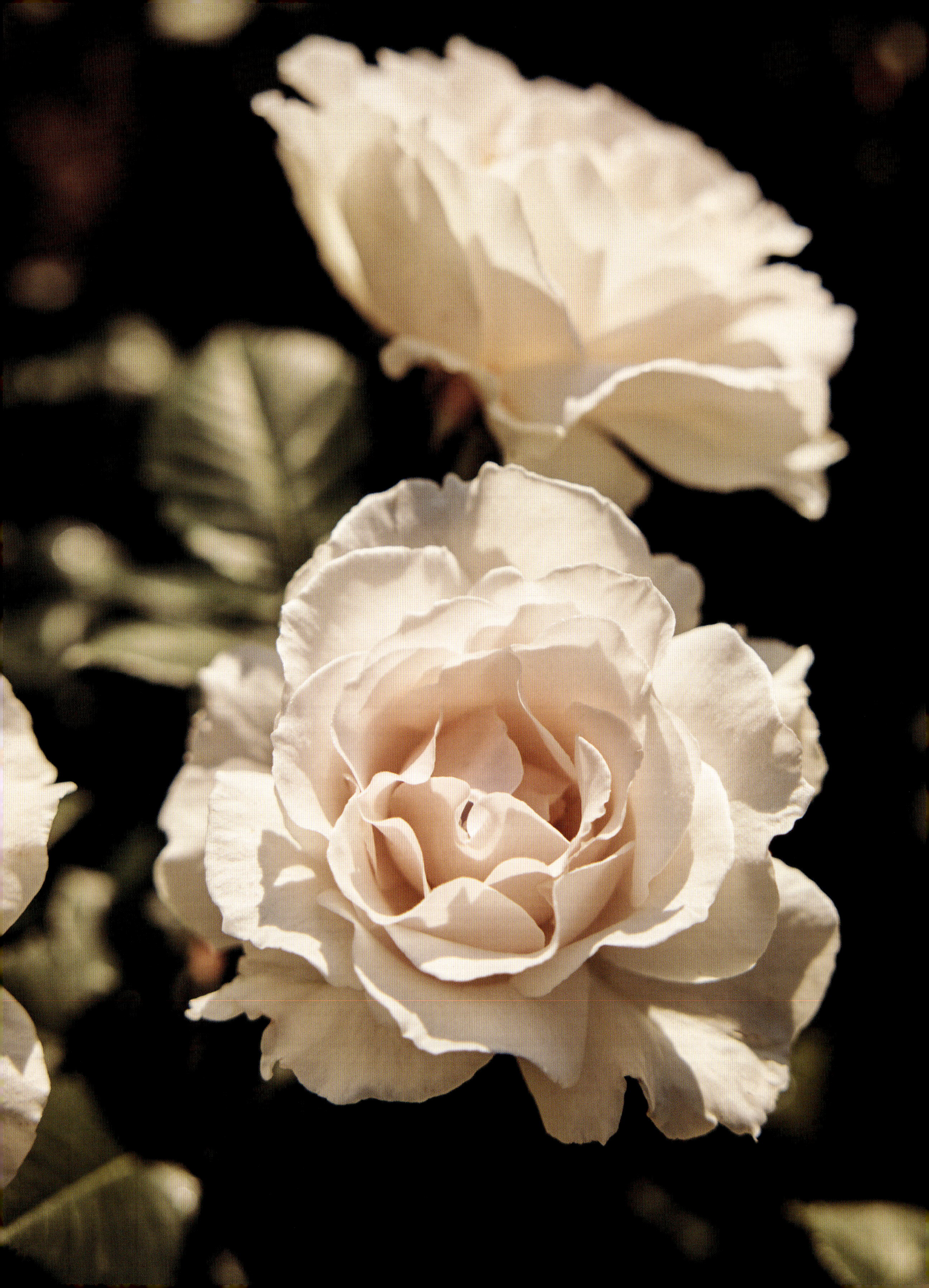

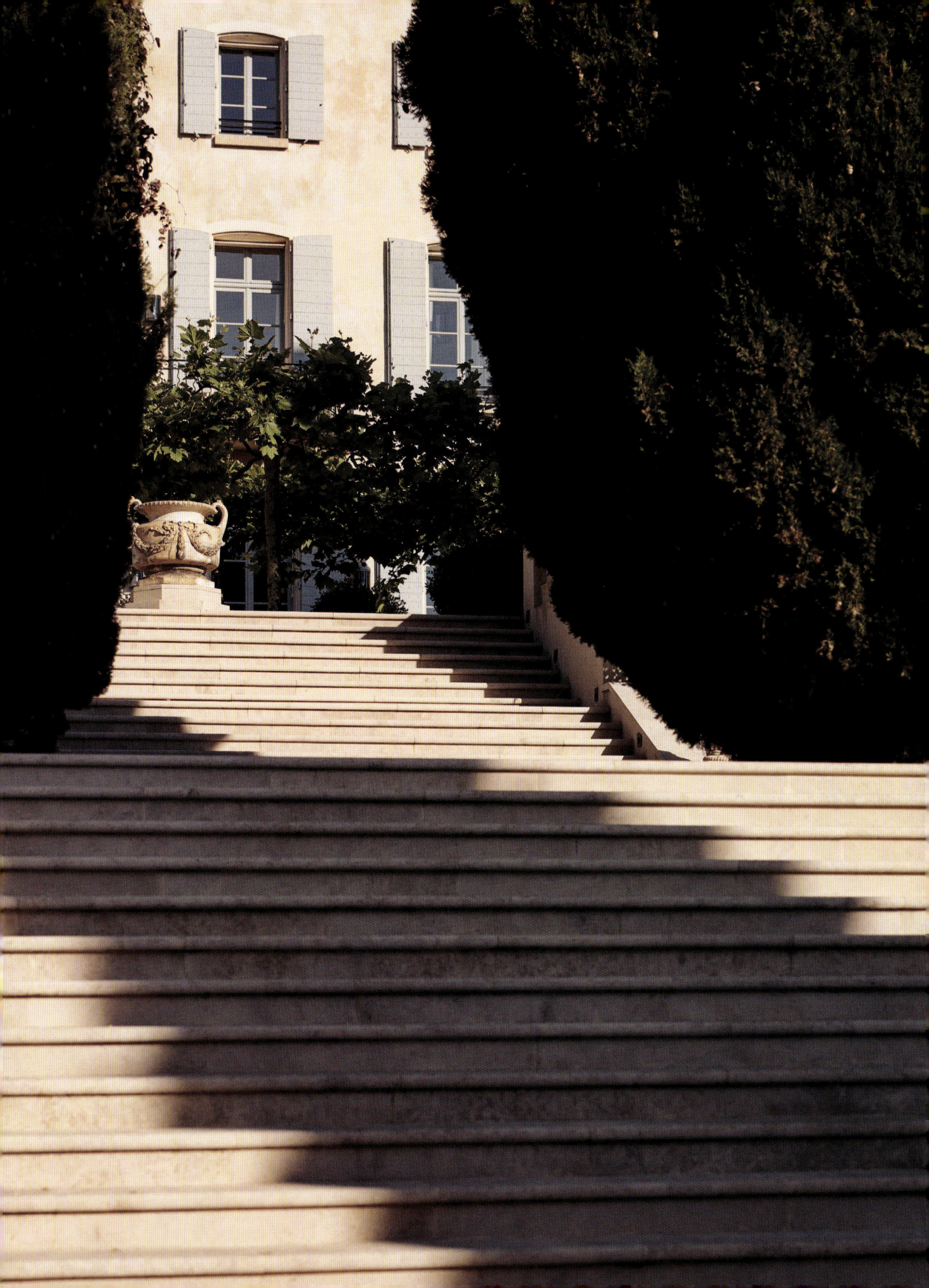

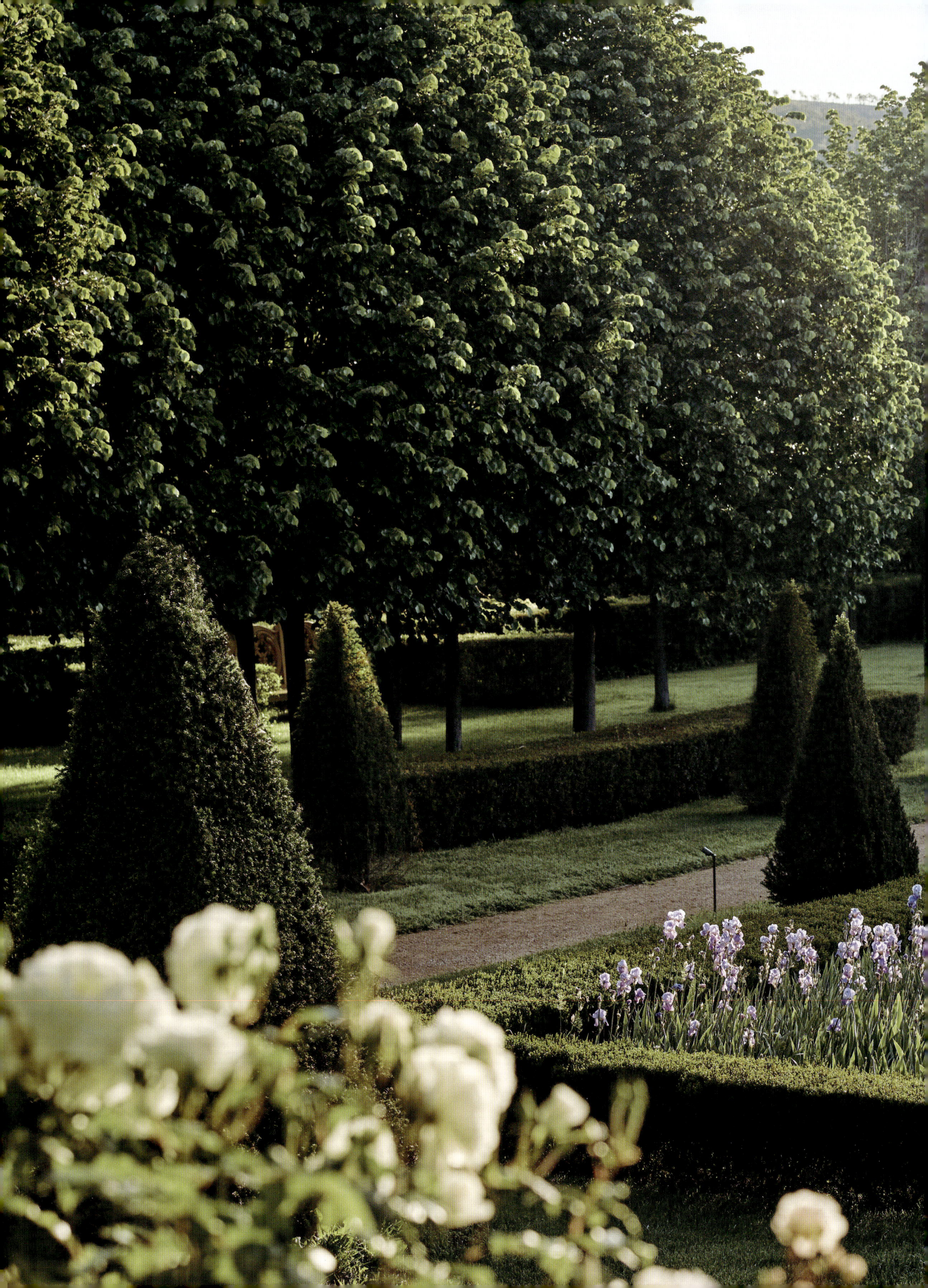

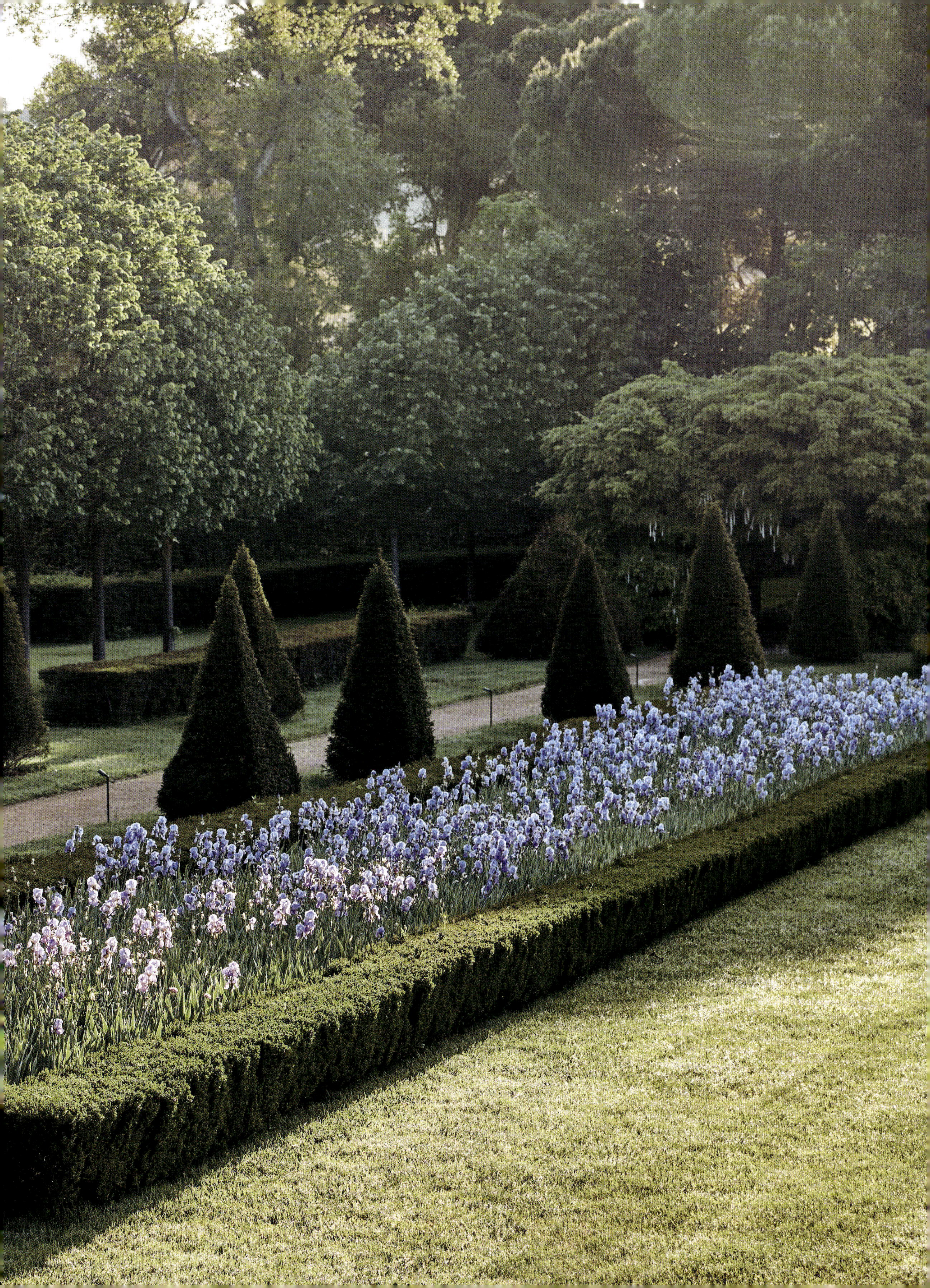

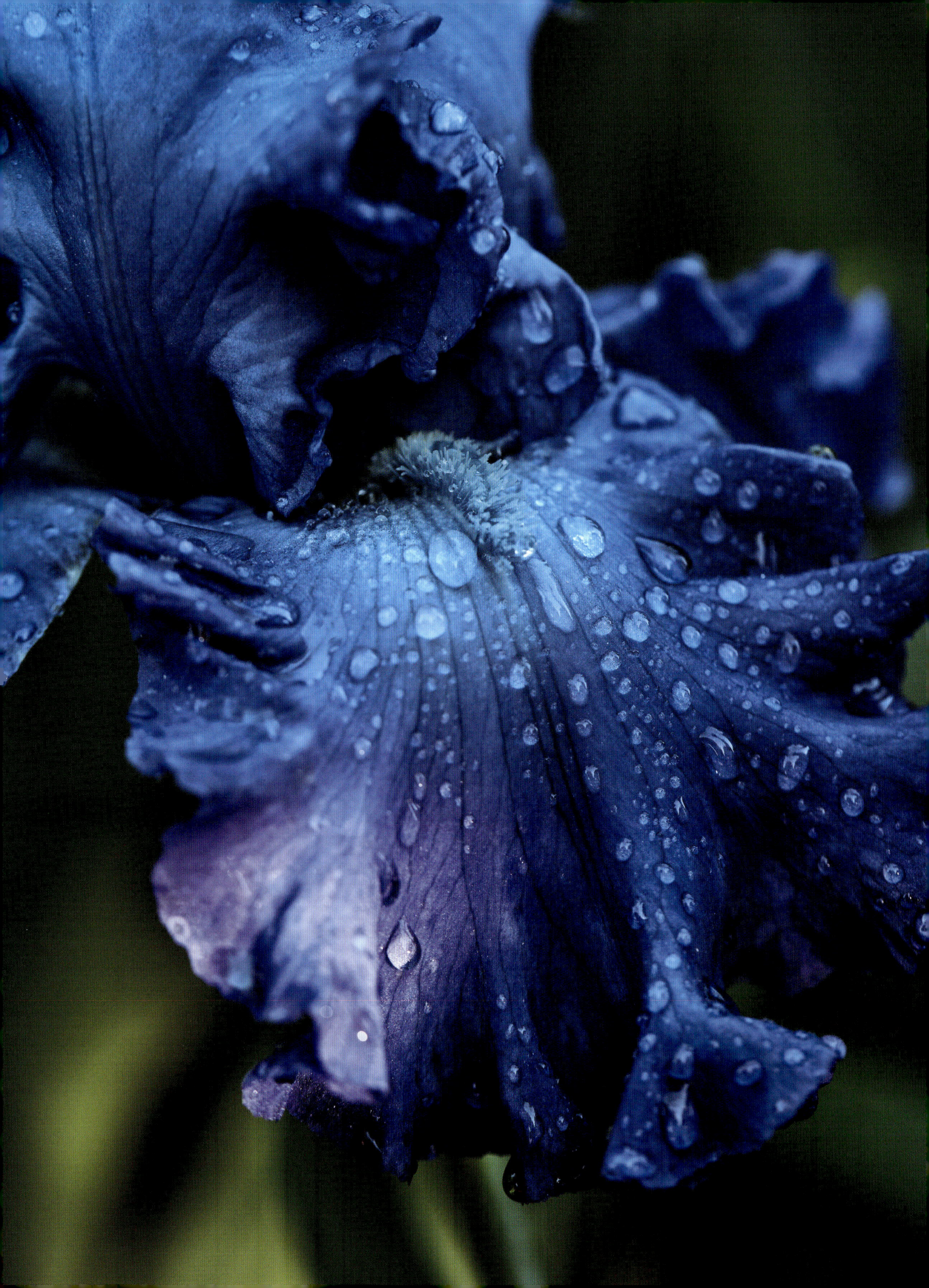

'Each year, you rediscover in a garden the magic of life. A flower arrives, and it is a miracle. The leaves fall in the autumn, and it looks fantastic. There is a tenderness about a garden, and you can't help but be sensitive to that.'

– HUBERT DE GIVENCHY

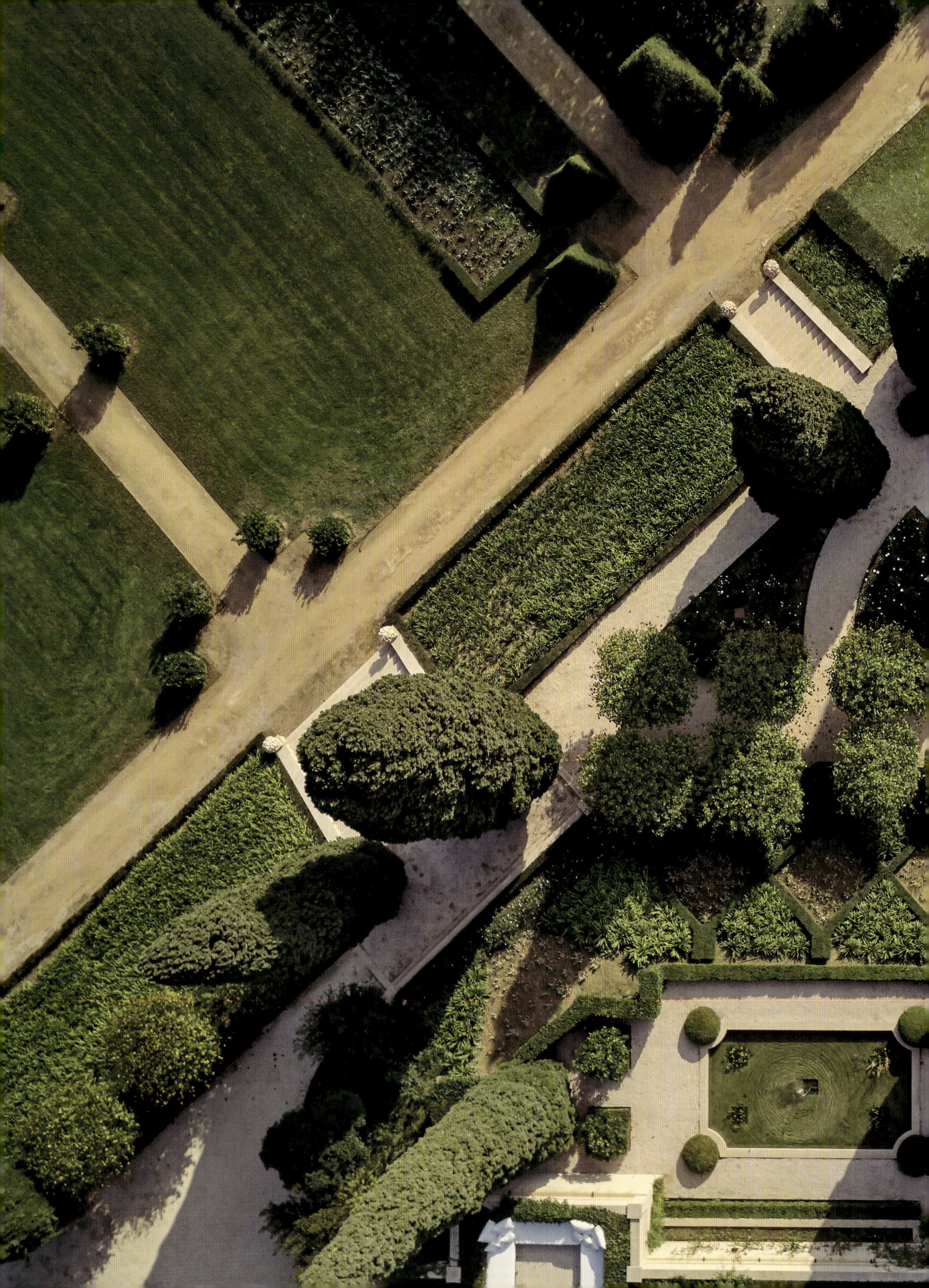

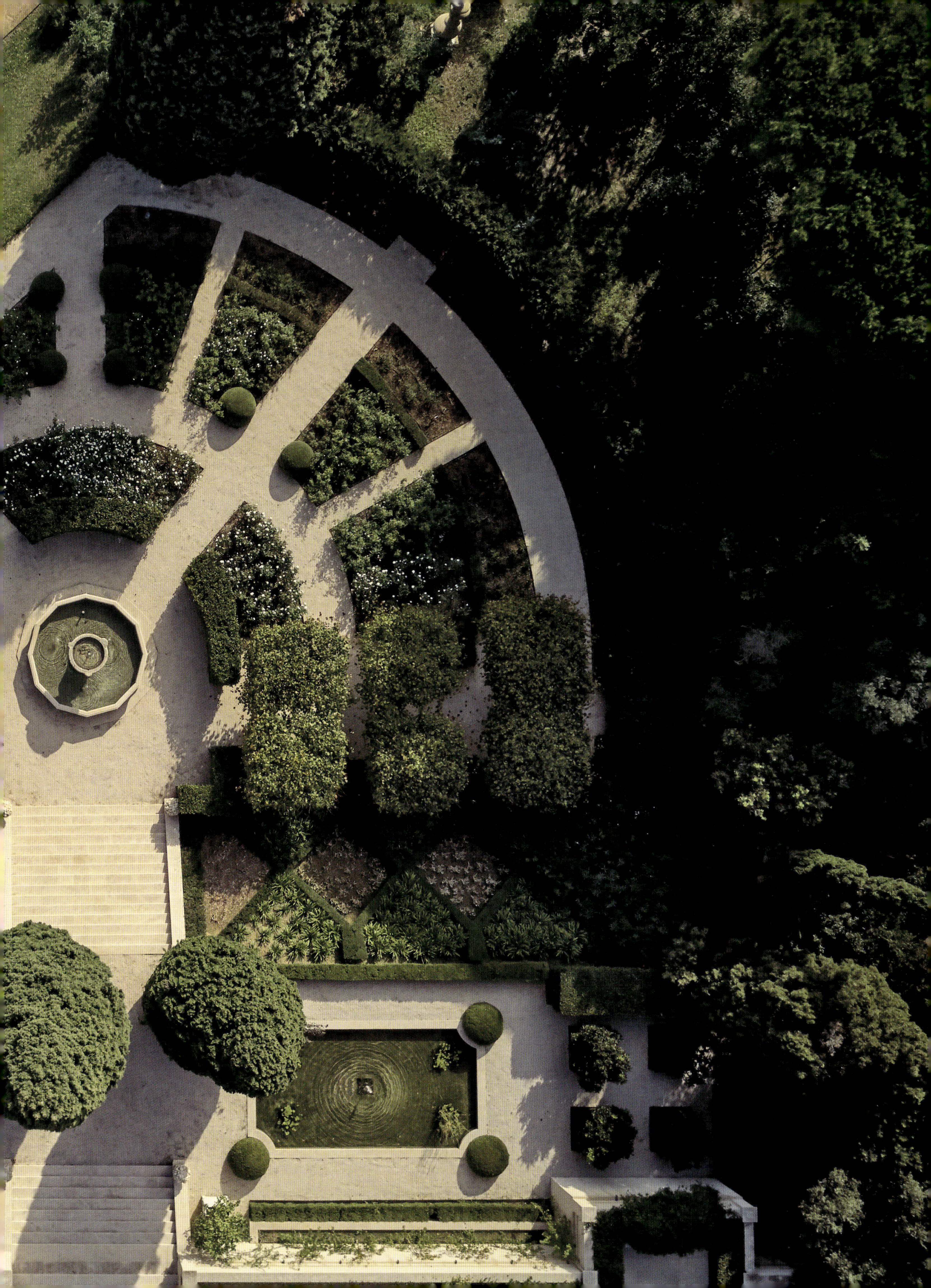

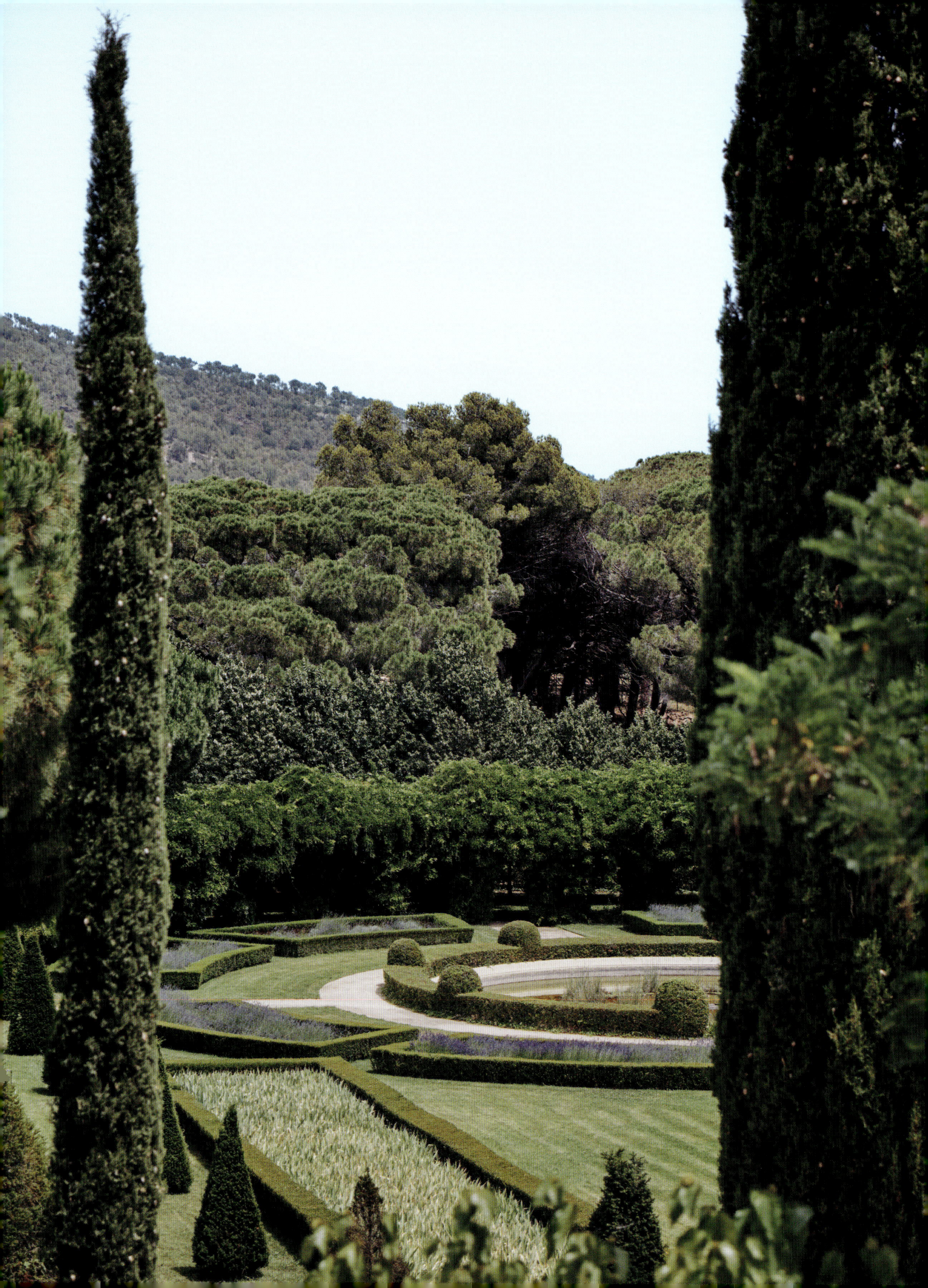

OPPOSITE AND PREVIOUS PAGE We kept the structure of the original formal French garden surrounding the château with its precisely configured paths and water features, as well as the cypress and pine trees. The beds of iris, lavender and other native flowers are enclosed in neatly trimmed hedges of laurel, boxwood and myrtle.

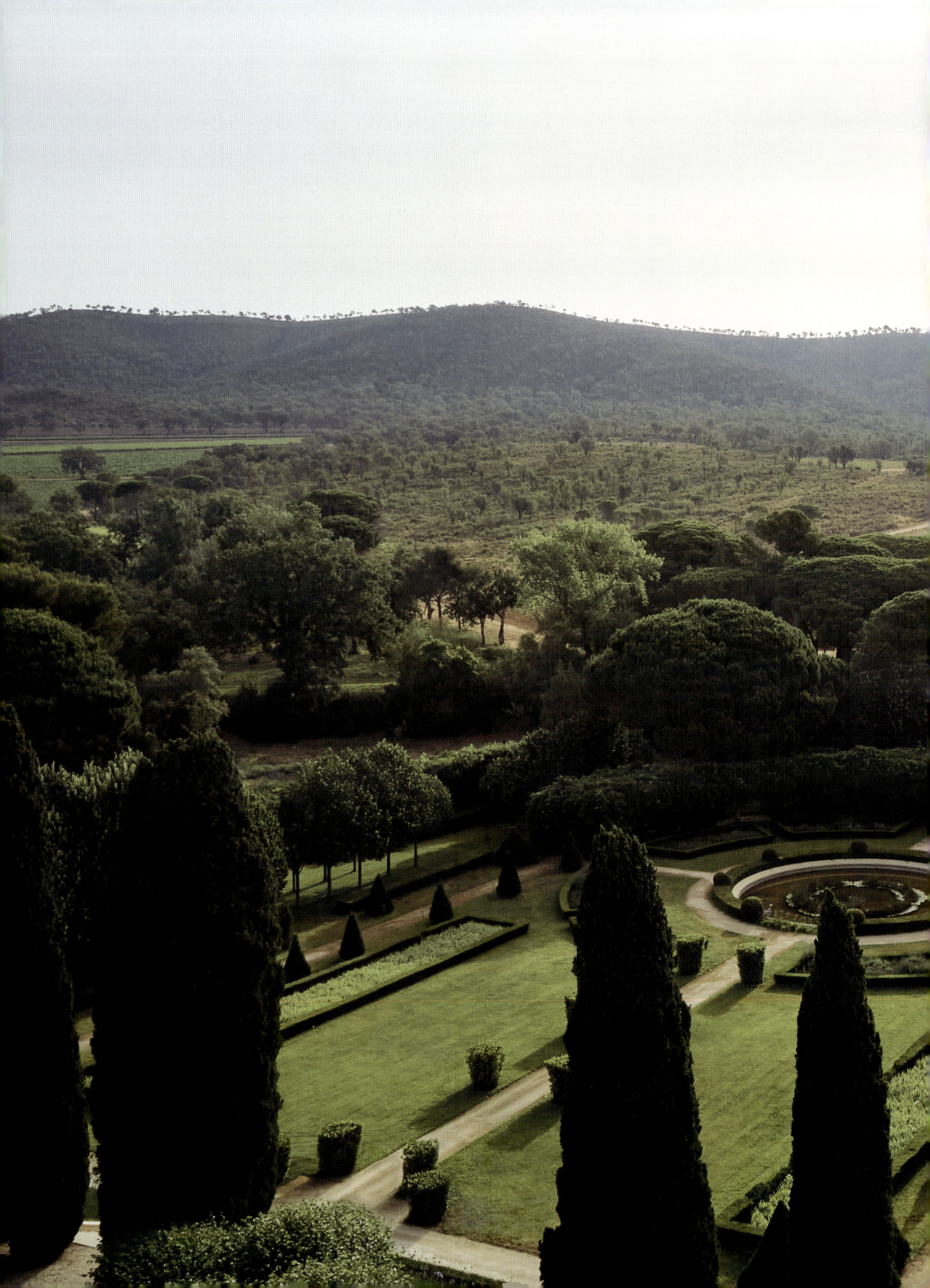

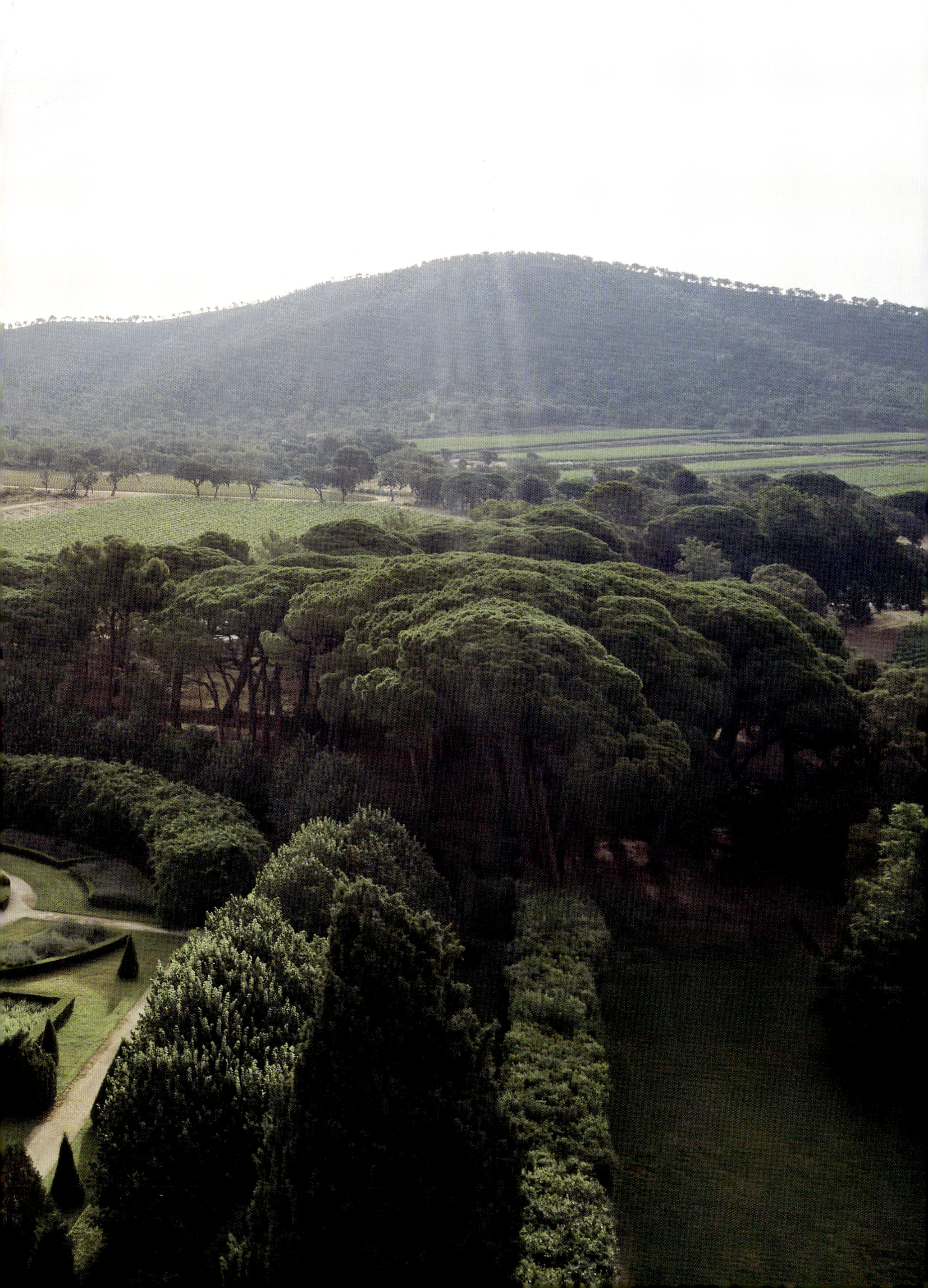

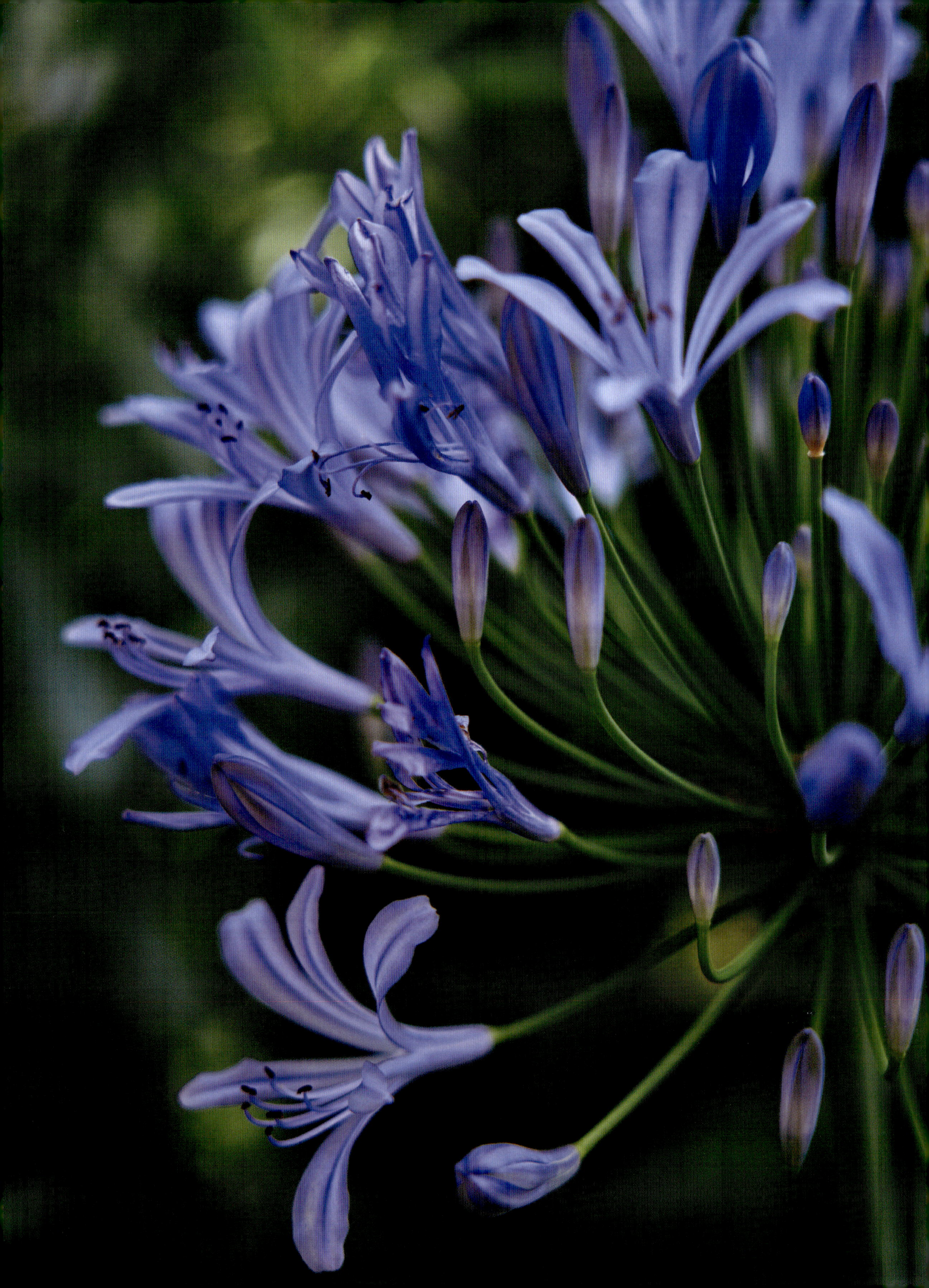

I've written about how irises influenced the interior design of the house but of course that love of the flowers finds its fullest expression in the garden, where a collection of irises covers over 1,500 square metres of ground. The varieties we grow – Blue Crusada, Java Bleu, En Profondeur and Devil's Lake – are planted in in long beds by the château and more loosely by Villa Maria, creating dramatic sweeps of colour that unfold in a spectrum of blues from the palest sky tones to rich azure and deep violet. Their appearance is fleeting, a brief spectacle in April, but for those precious weeks I bring as many as possible into the house, using them to decorate my tables and savouring their delicate beauty before they disappear.

No Provençal garden would be complete without lavender, which we've planted around the estate in expansive drifts and, along the driveway that runs up to the main entrance, intermingled with the cypress and plane trees. And to the east of the château, the rose garden is a haven of soft beauty devoted to perfumed varieties of rose. Roses bring quiet romance and grace to the garden and in the stillness of the early morning or the quiet of evening, the scent of their delicate fragrance lingering in the warm air is a reminder of the infinite sensory joys in nature. I'll often go down to the rose garden to seek a moment of quiet retreat, to admire the perfect unfurling of the petals and savour the stillness.

As the owner of an organic farm in England, it was essential to me that we grow fruit and vegetables on the estate. We've given over 2,000 square metres of land to a market garden and we also have a small kitchen garden right by the château. The market garden is planted following the principles of permaculture, which is a framework for growing grounded in ecological principles. Similar to the way we cultivate the vines and olive groves, it is designed to create growing spaces that are resilient, abundant and self-sustaining. We grow a vibrant mixture of typical Provençal produce – lots of heritage tomato varieties, as well as aubergines, fennel, courgettes, strawberries, lettuces and herbs – all of which supply the Café Léoube kitchen with fresh ingredients every day. We also have two hectares of orchard with around sixteen varieties of fruit trees, including peach, apricot and cherry, together with eleven varieties of figs and pistachios. Any fruit that isn't used in the kitchens will be turned into jams and preserves that we sell in the boutique.

OPPOSITE AND OVERLEAF Expansive drifts of blue and white agapanthus dominate the garden throughout June. While we've planted a few more, the cypress trees that line the driveway up to the château are the ones we inherited and are over a century old.

THE GARDEN

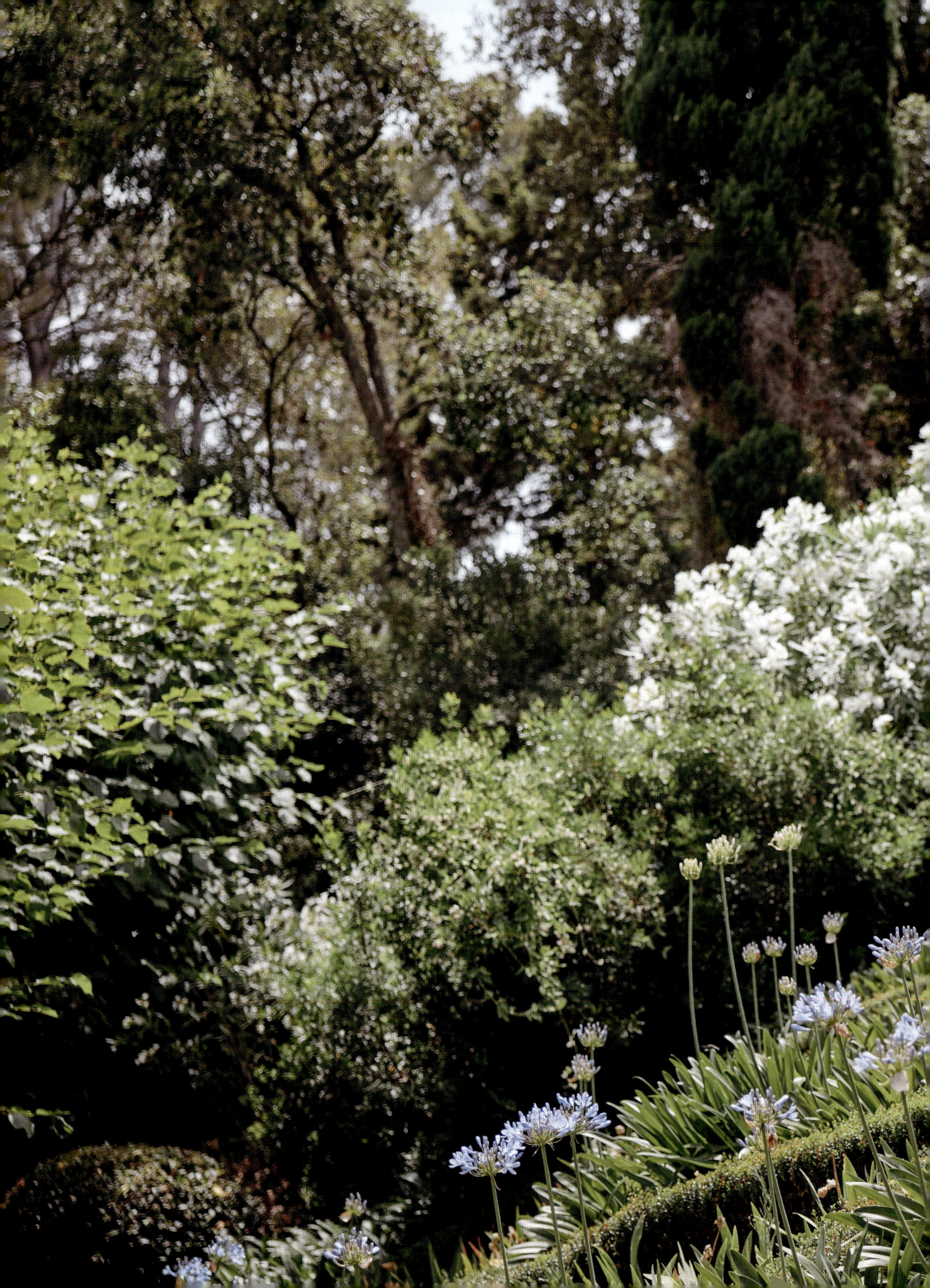

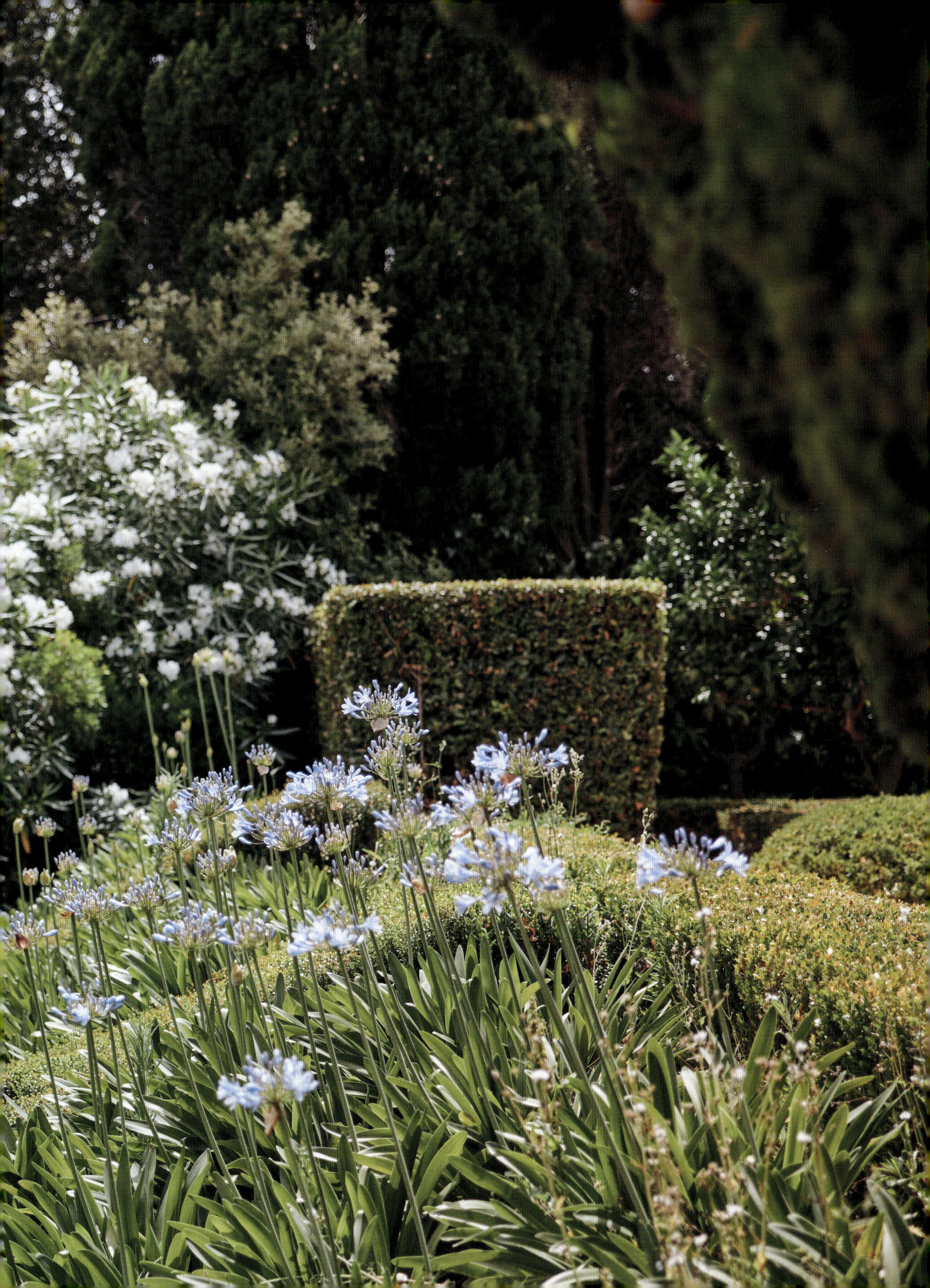

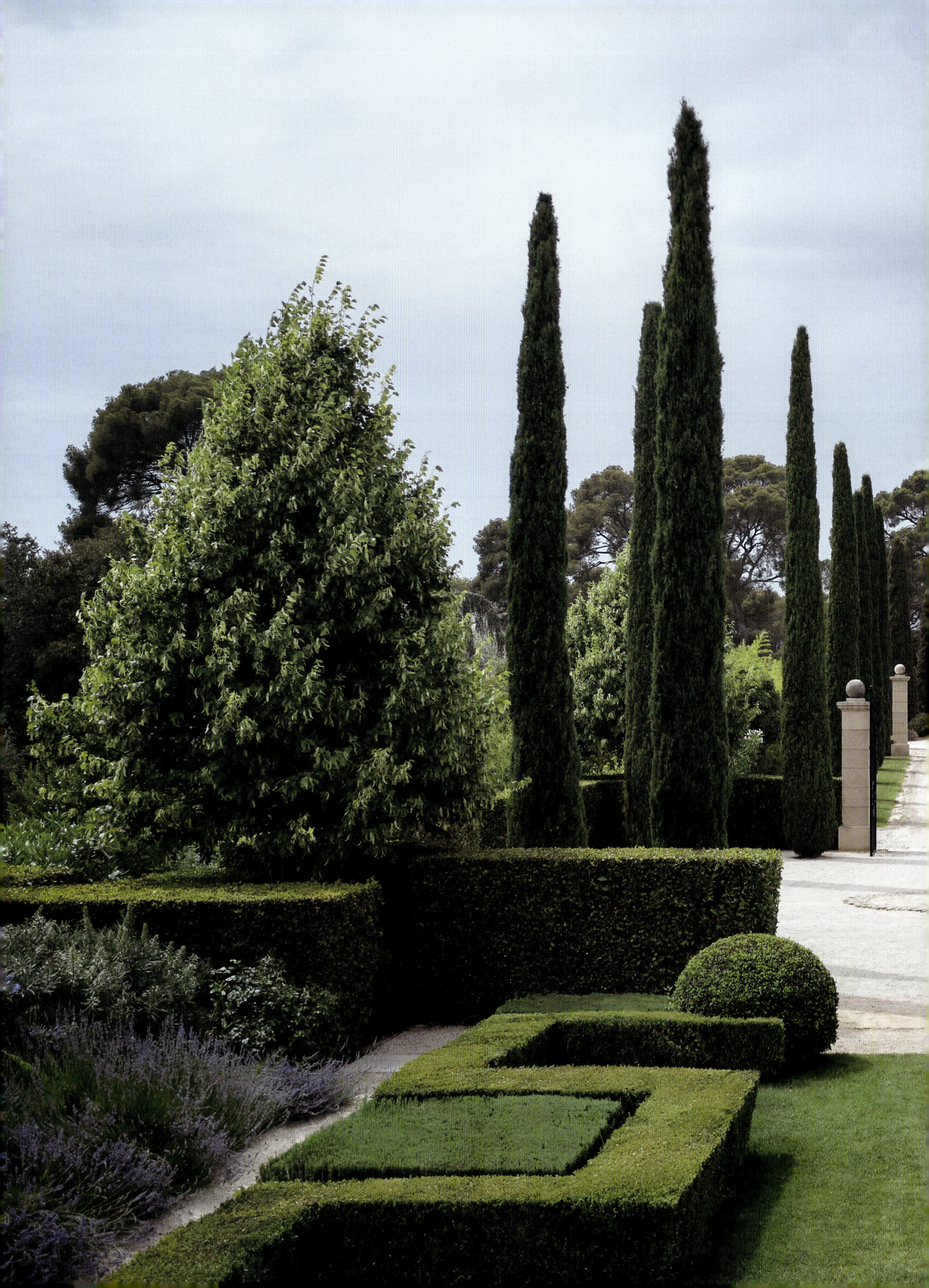

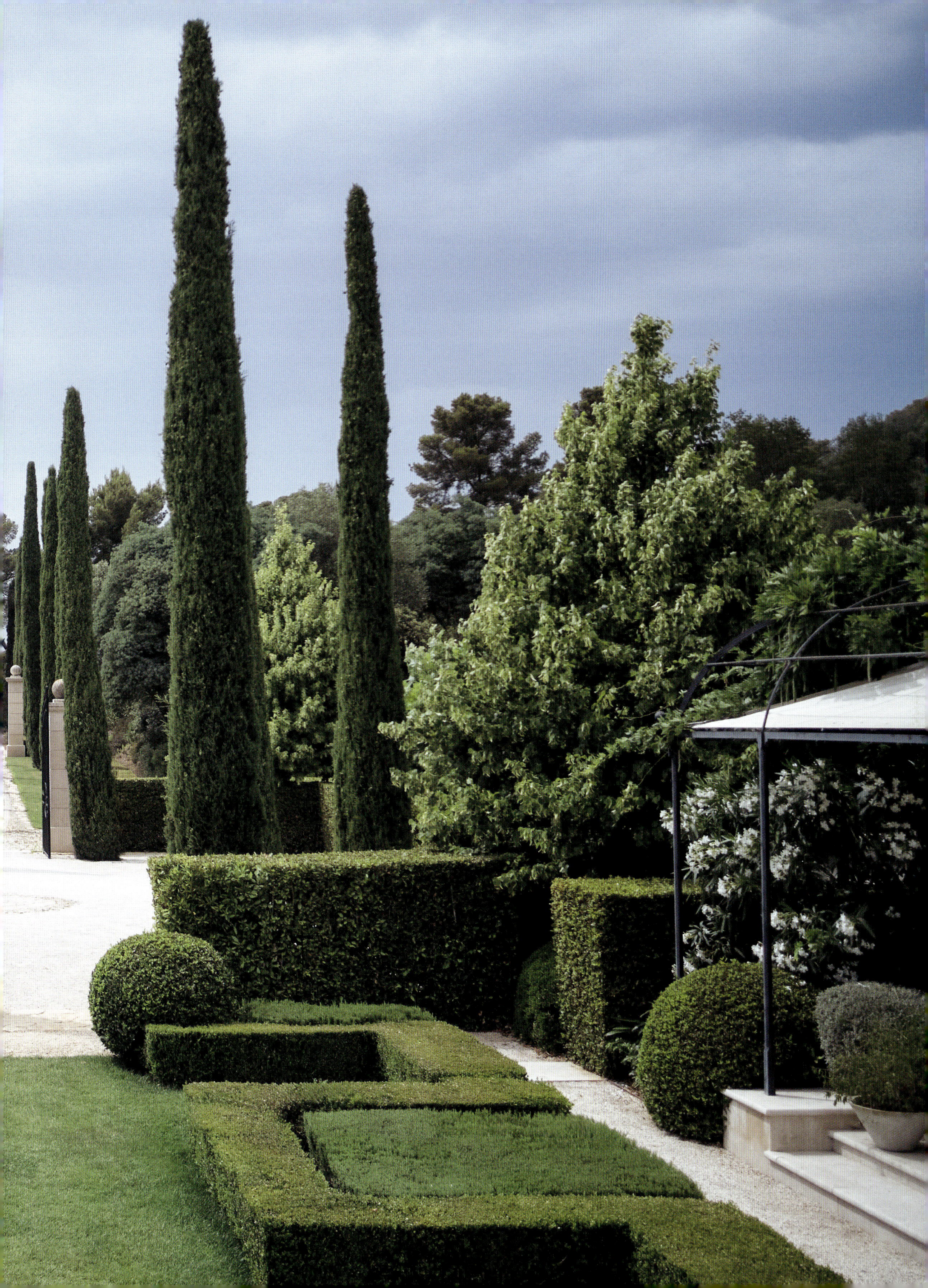

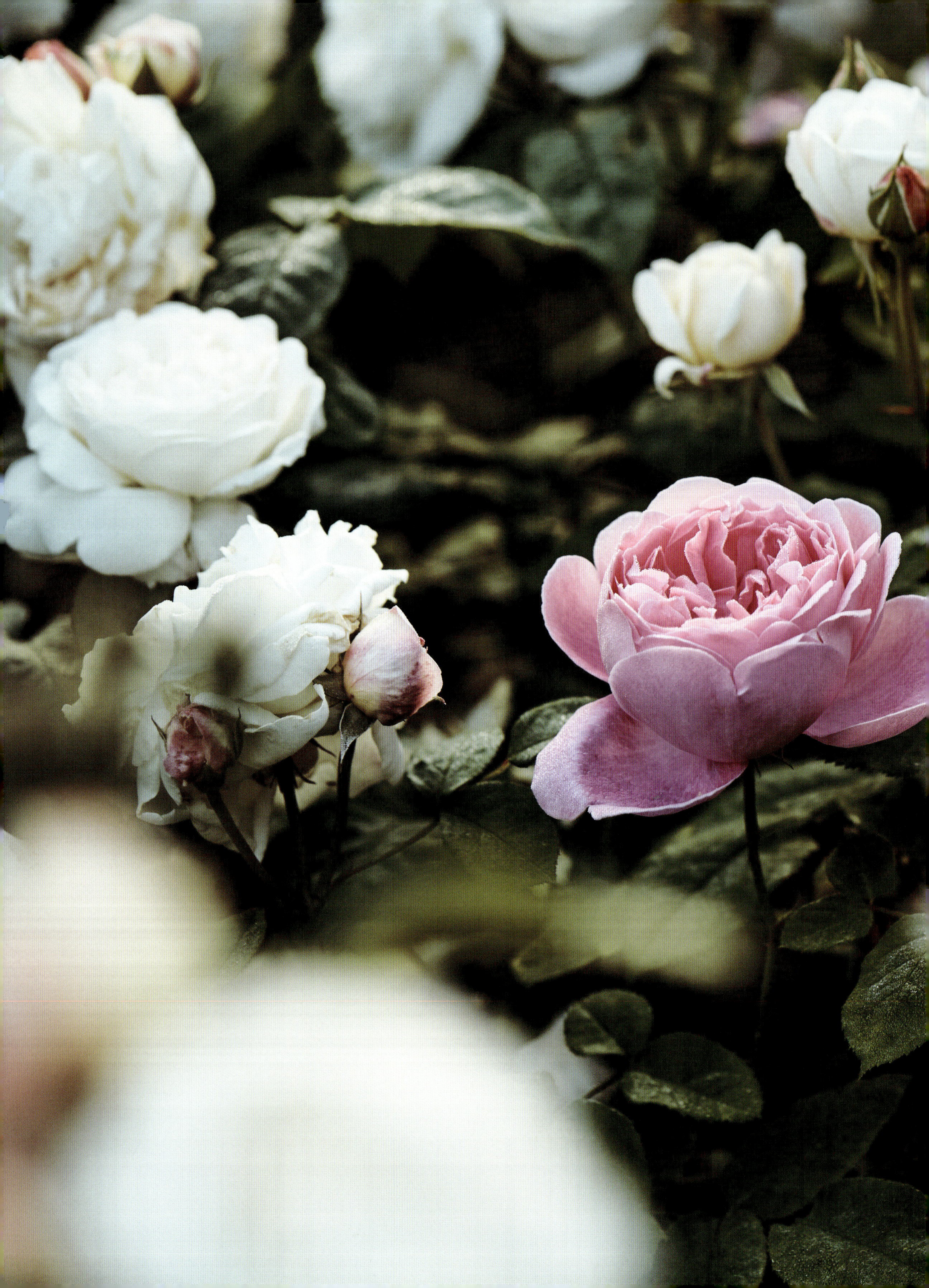

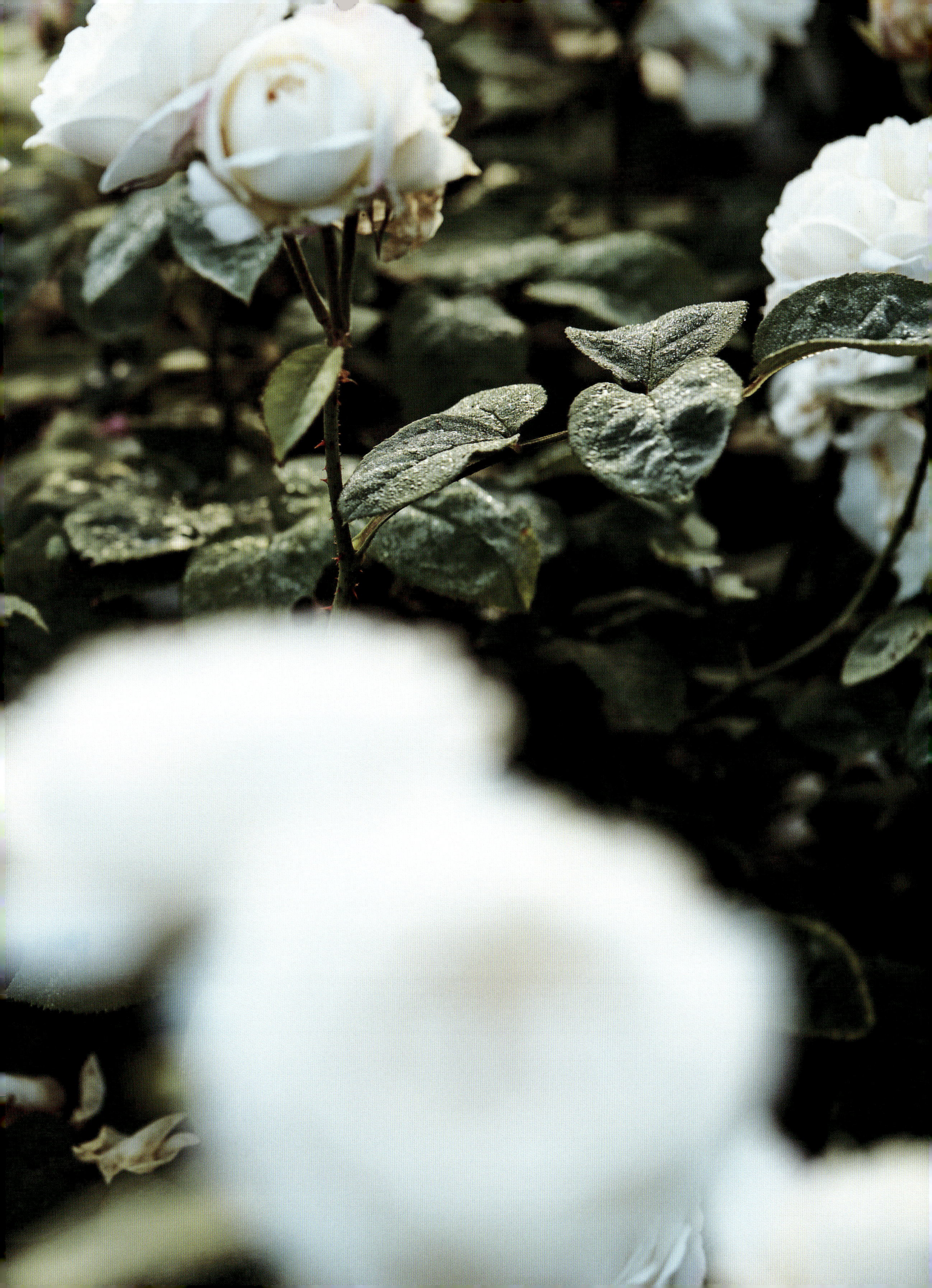

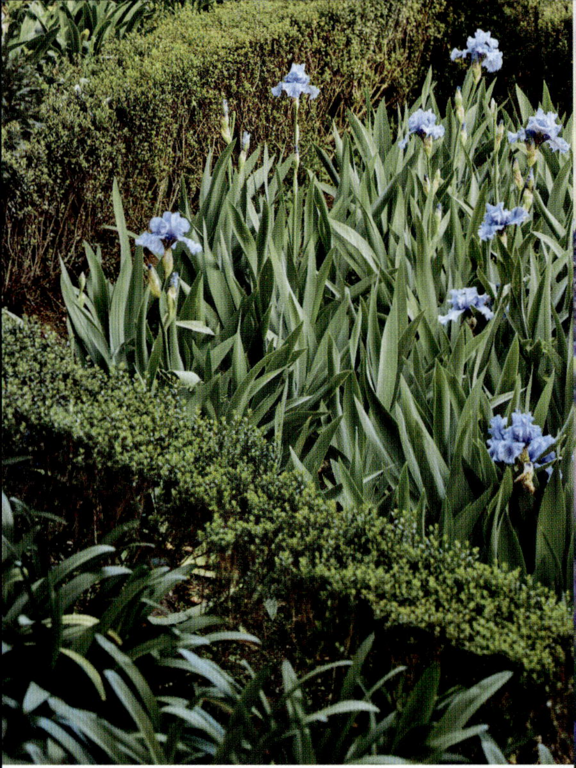
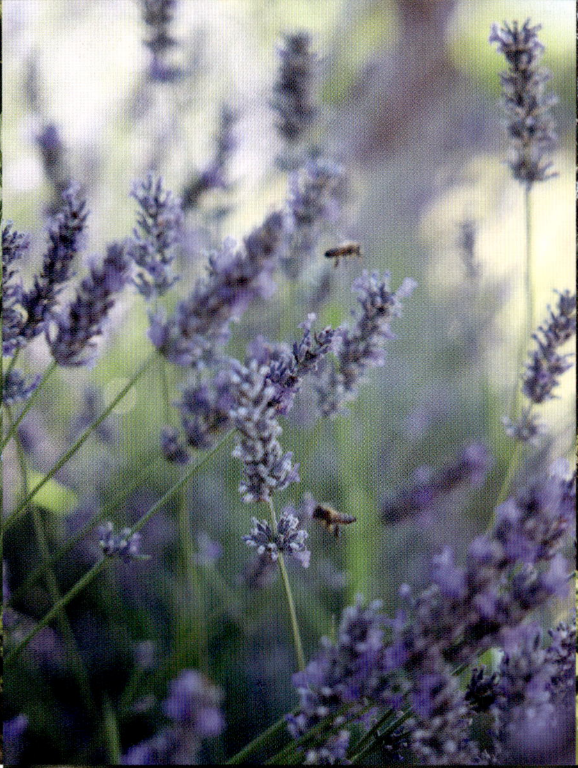
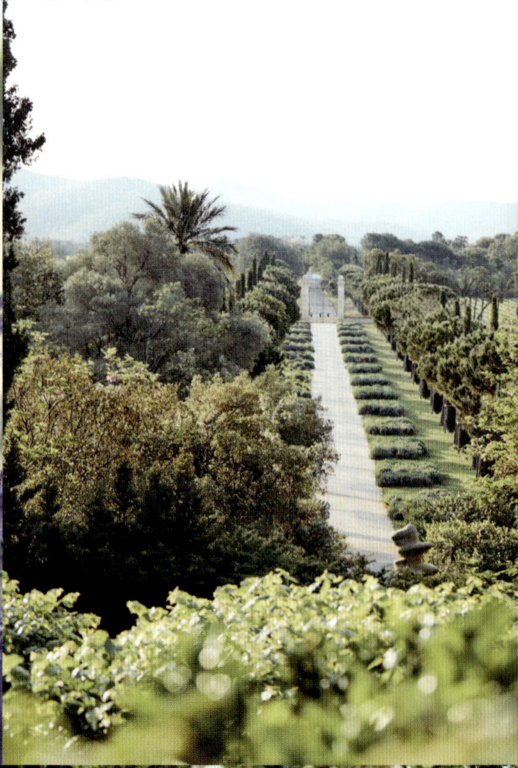
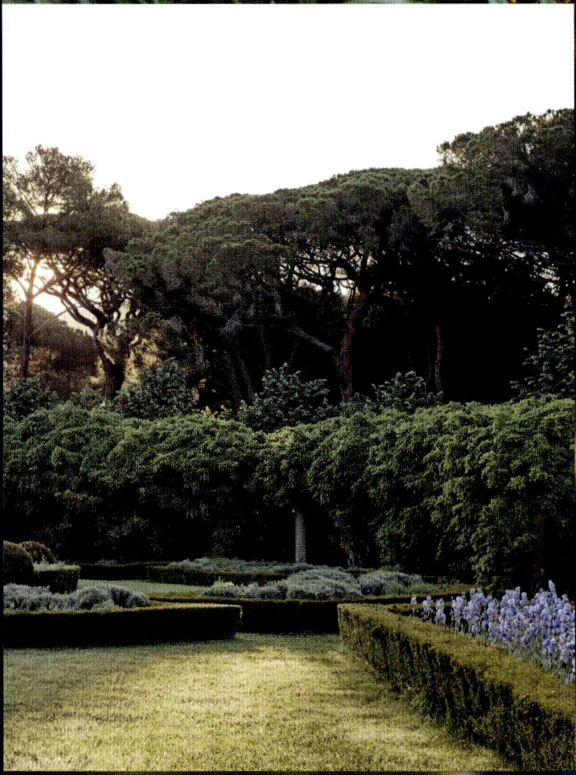
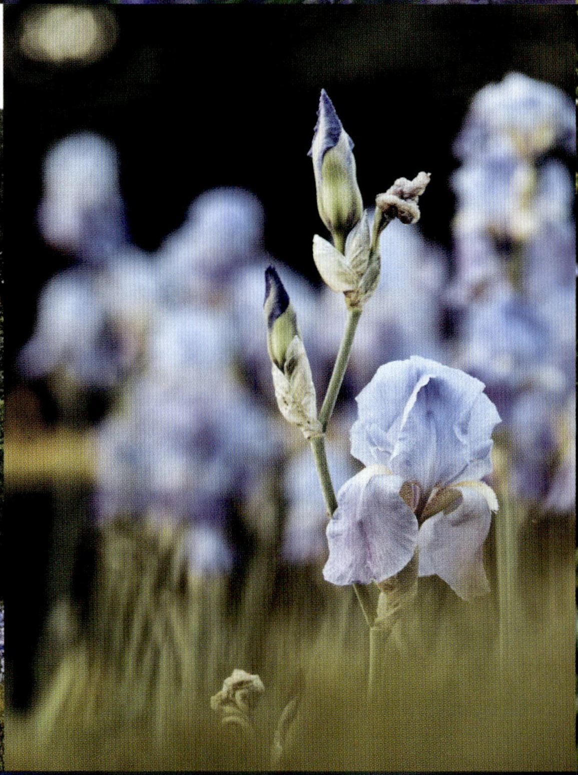
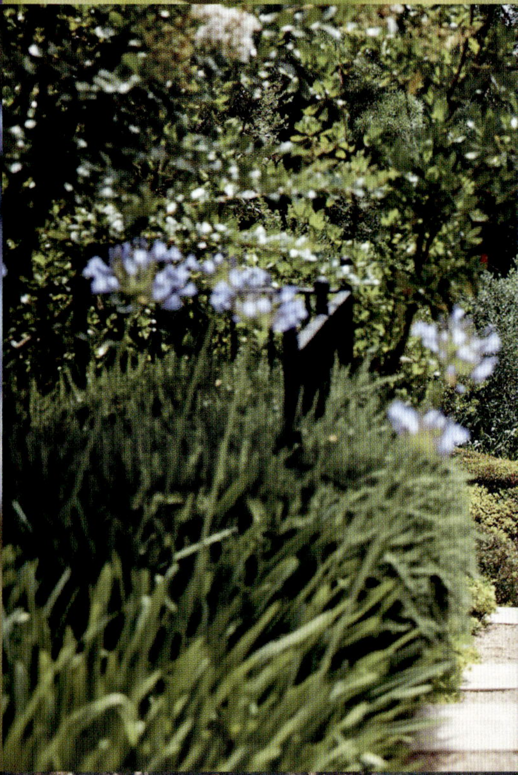
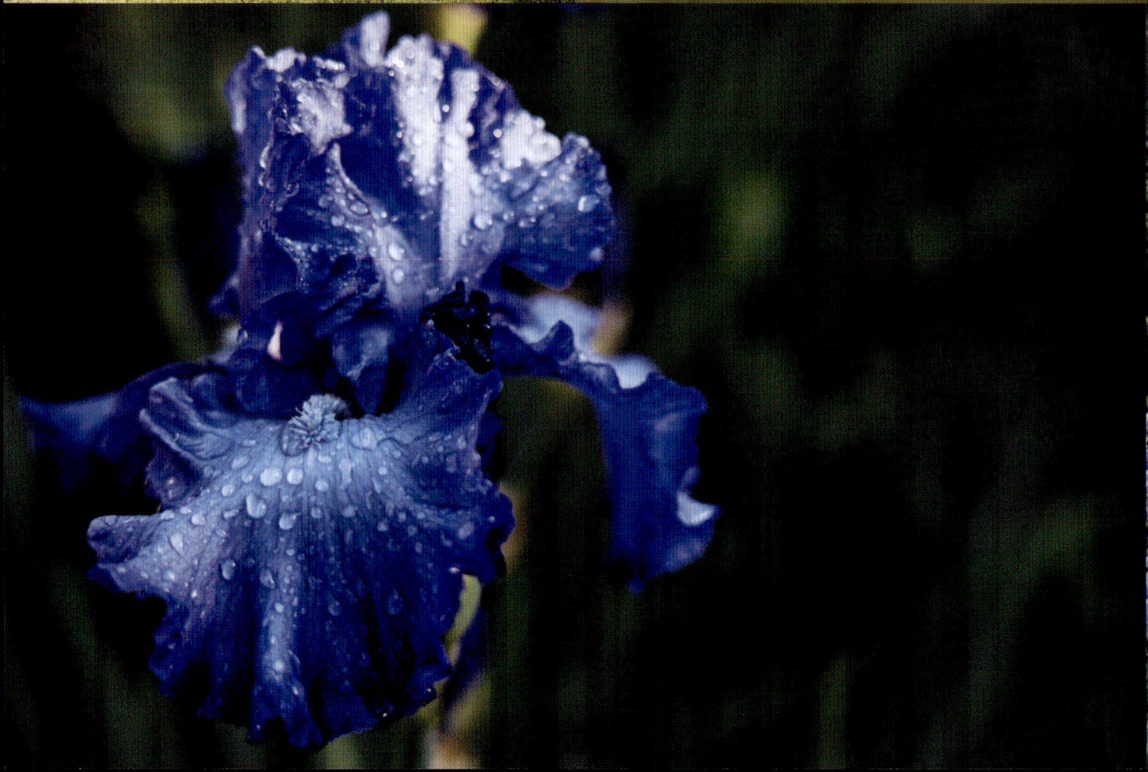
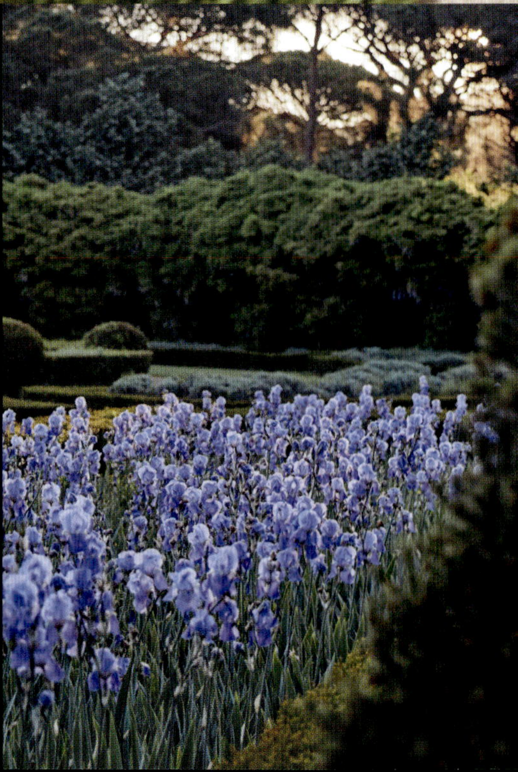

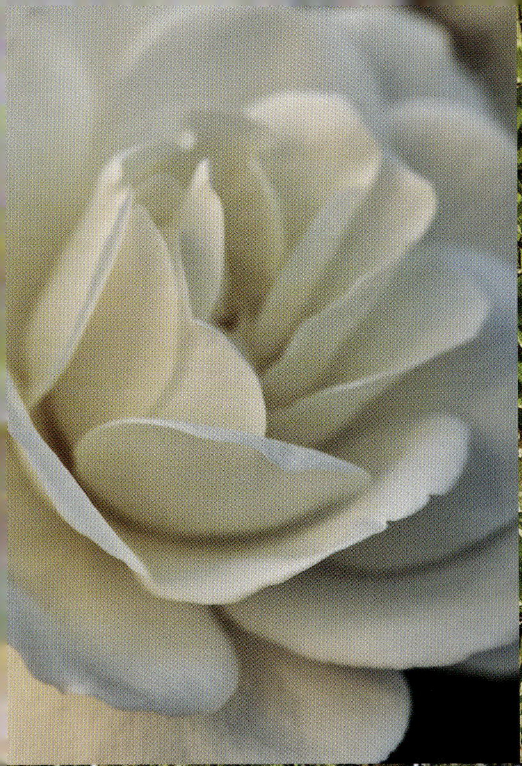
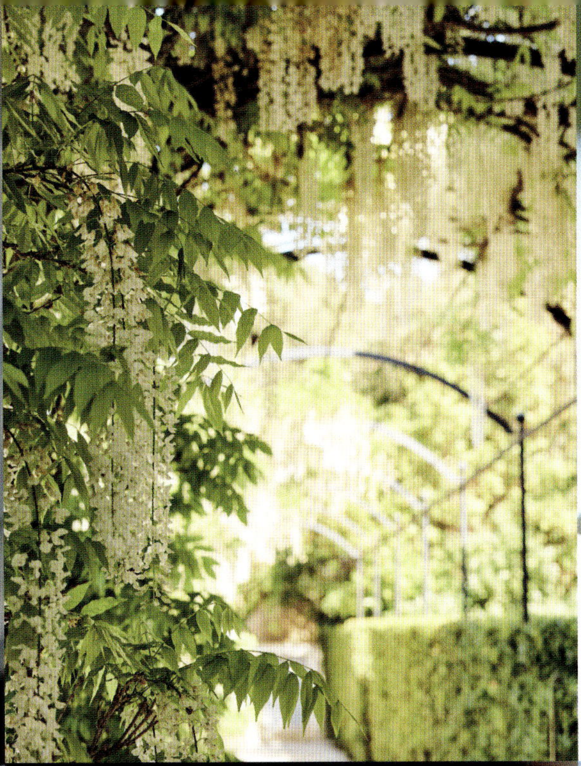
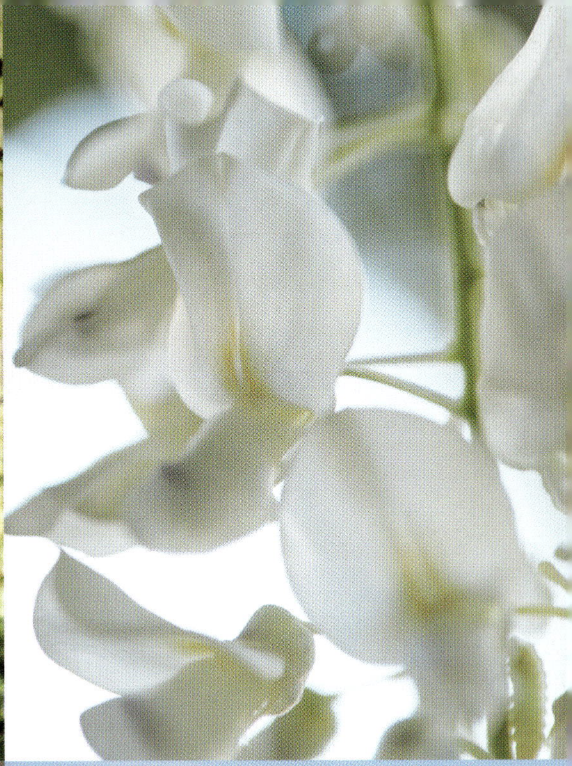
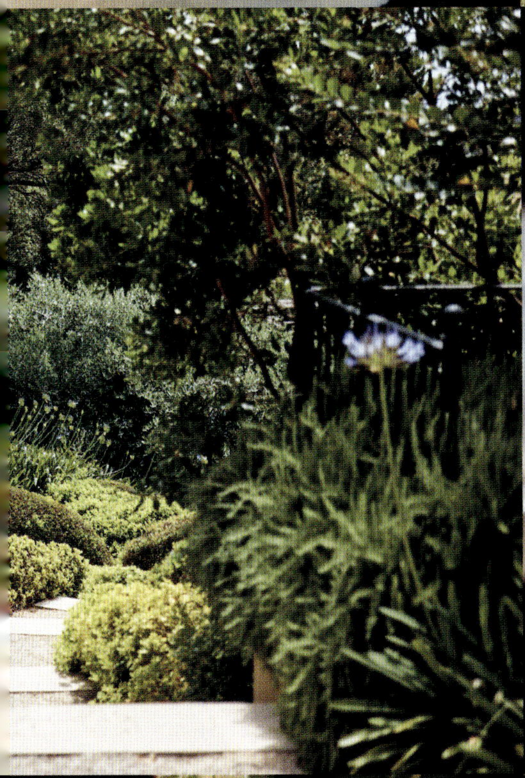
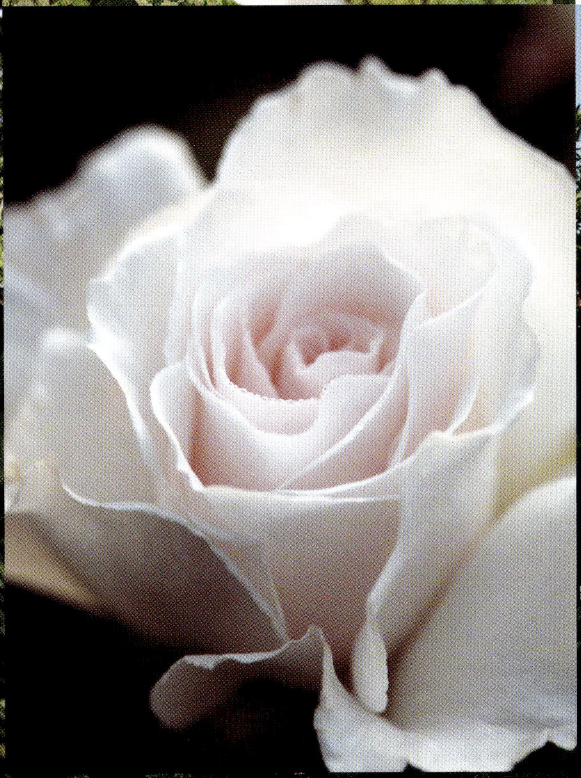
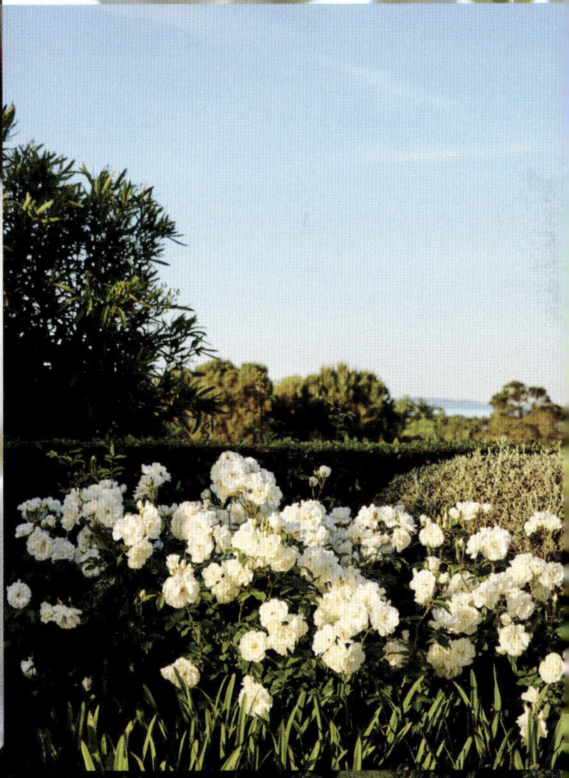
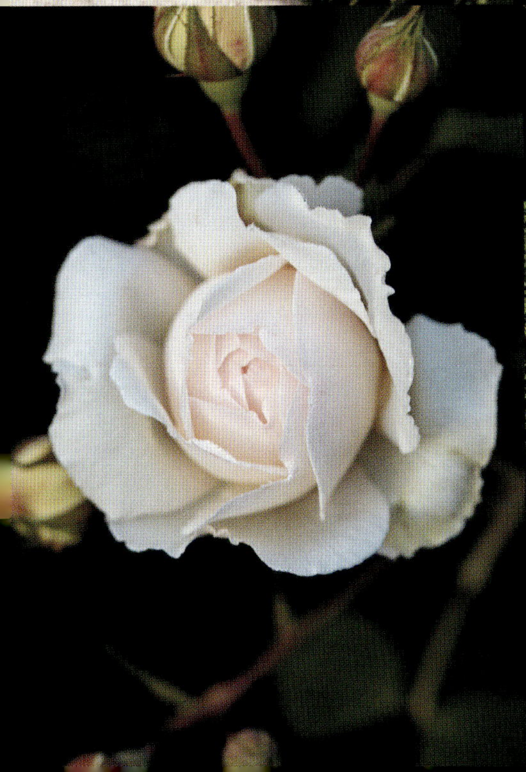
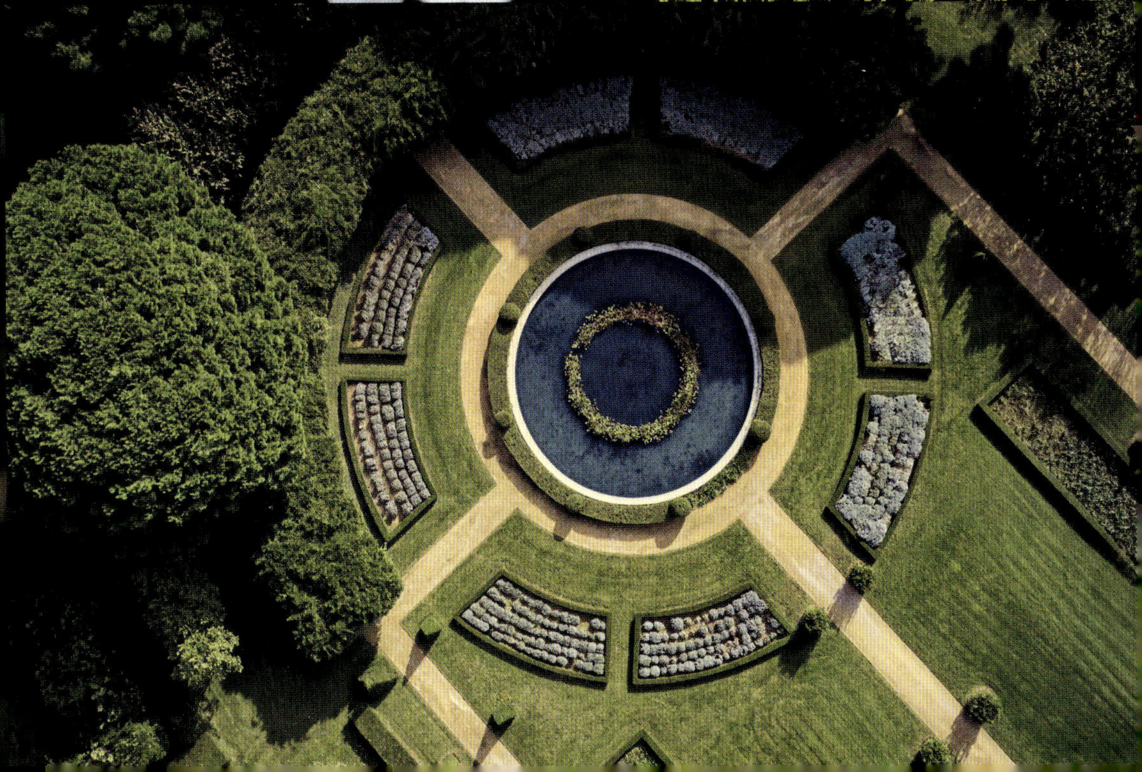

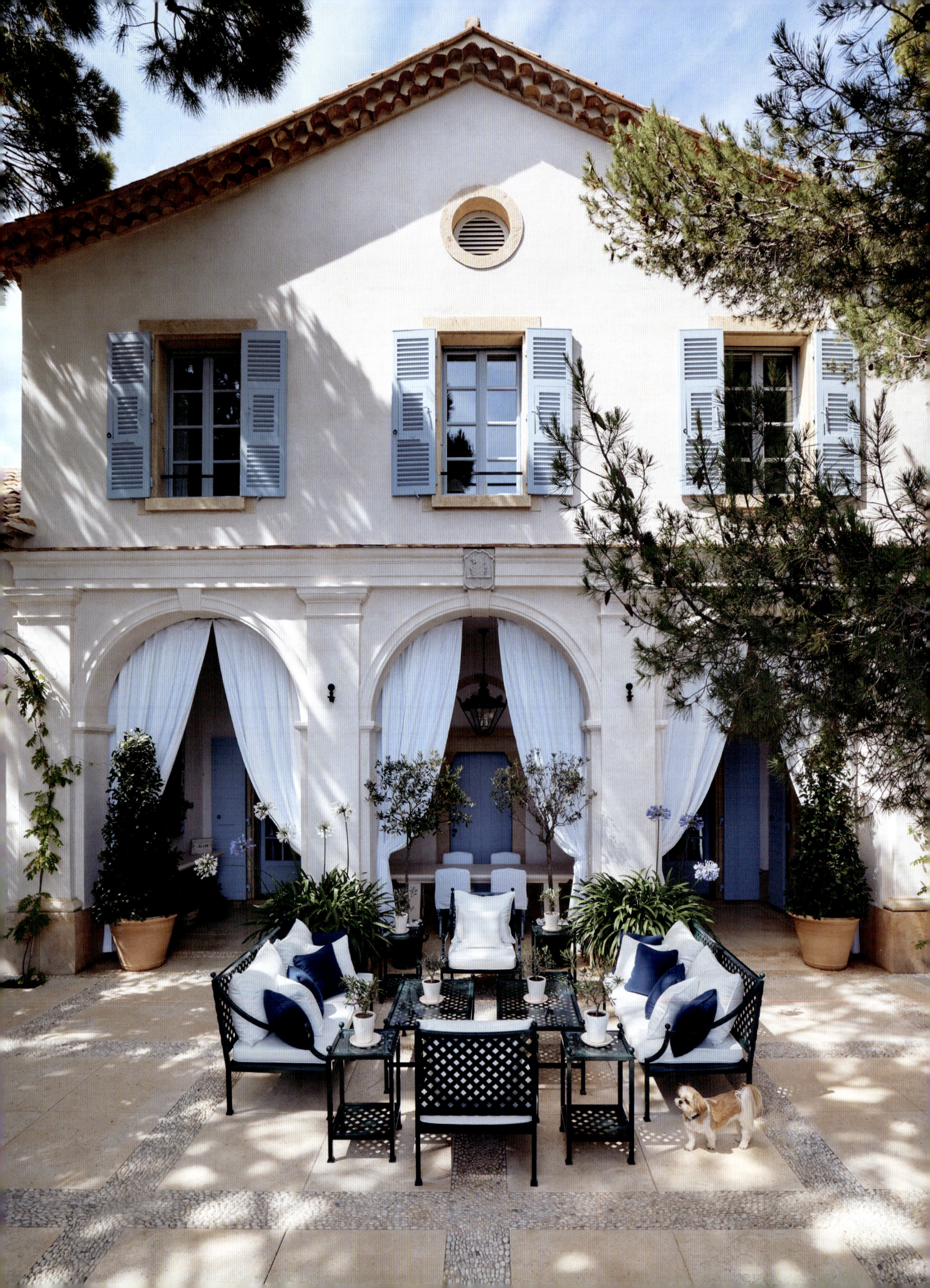

# VILLA MARIA

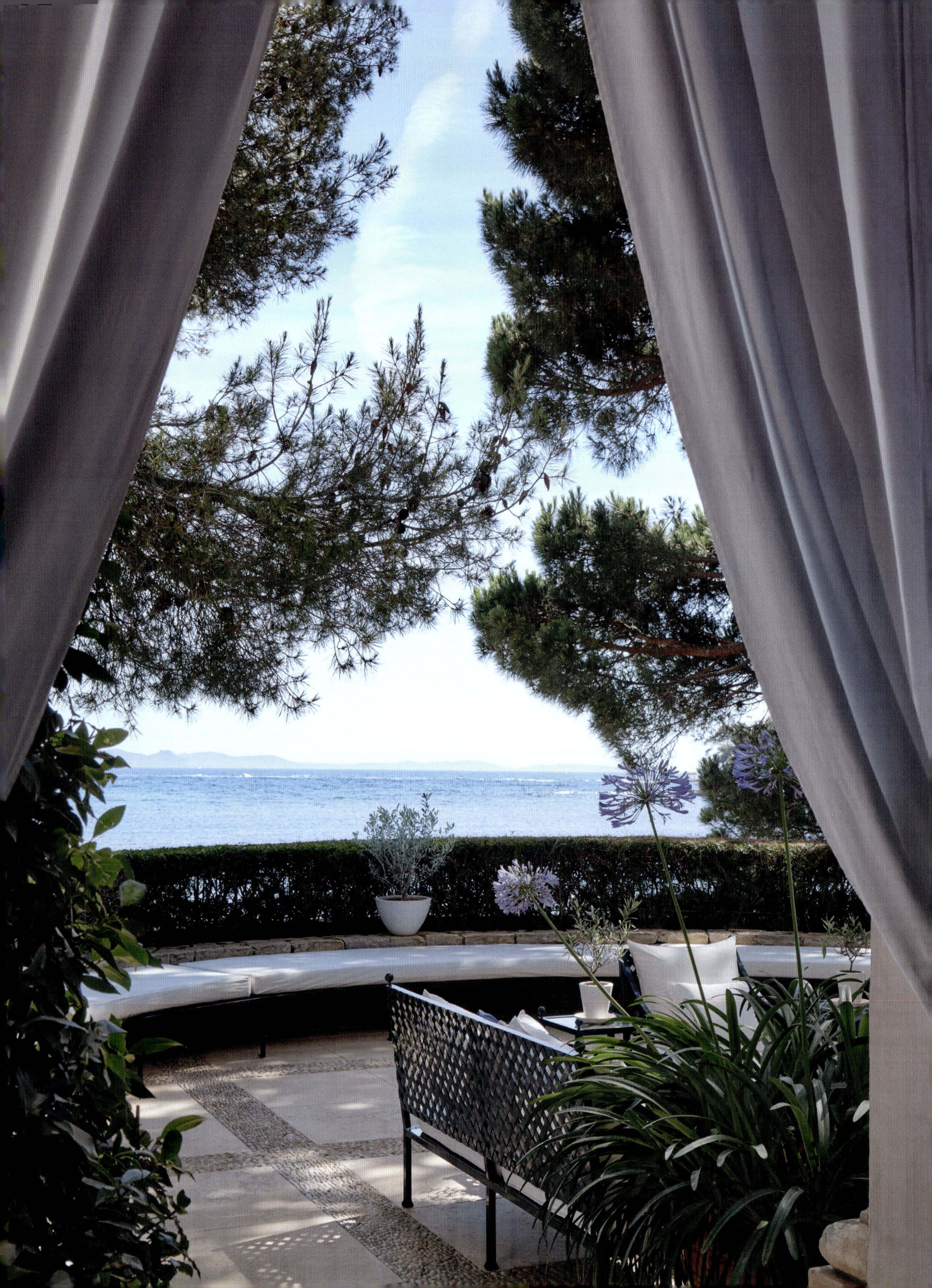

Villa Maria is our beachside *bijou* – the guesthouse – where the story of Léoube's restoration began. Formerly a military health post during the reign of Napoleon I, it became vacant after one of the previous owners of the château, Monsieur Bernardin Bremond de Léoube, died and it was then entrusted to the government in 1849 when it became a customs house.

Its position, a stone's throw from the sea, means that there is a meditative quality to the time we spend here. There's a musicality to the setting – a continuous melody from the lapping waves, the buzzing of cicadas and the cries of seagulls, the air imbued with the heavy scent of the pines. That setting also meant that when we took over the house, the building was weathered and worn and we had to take a number of practical decisions to allow us to protect it from the elements.

The beautiful blue shutters on the outside have been created to mimic the style of the doors typically found on rural houses and farmhouses in the region. In the traditional style, the *clous tordus* – the bent nails – were hand-forged from wrought iron and intentionally bent or curved into decorative patterns. However, instead of the sturdy wood doors, of oak or chestnut, we've created replicas made entirely of metal so that they can withstand the erosion of the salty air. The gentle slate blue that evokes the colours of the Mediterranean sky and the lavender fields is very typical of the region, in particular in the Luberon, and you can understand why: it creates an arresting contrast against the pale stone walls. It is a quintessential aesthetic that I was keen to reflect.

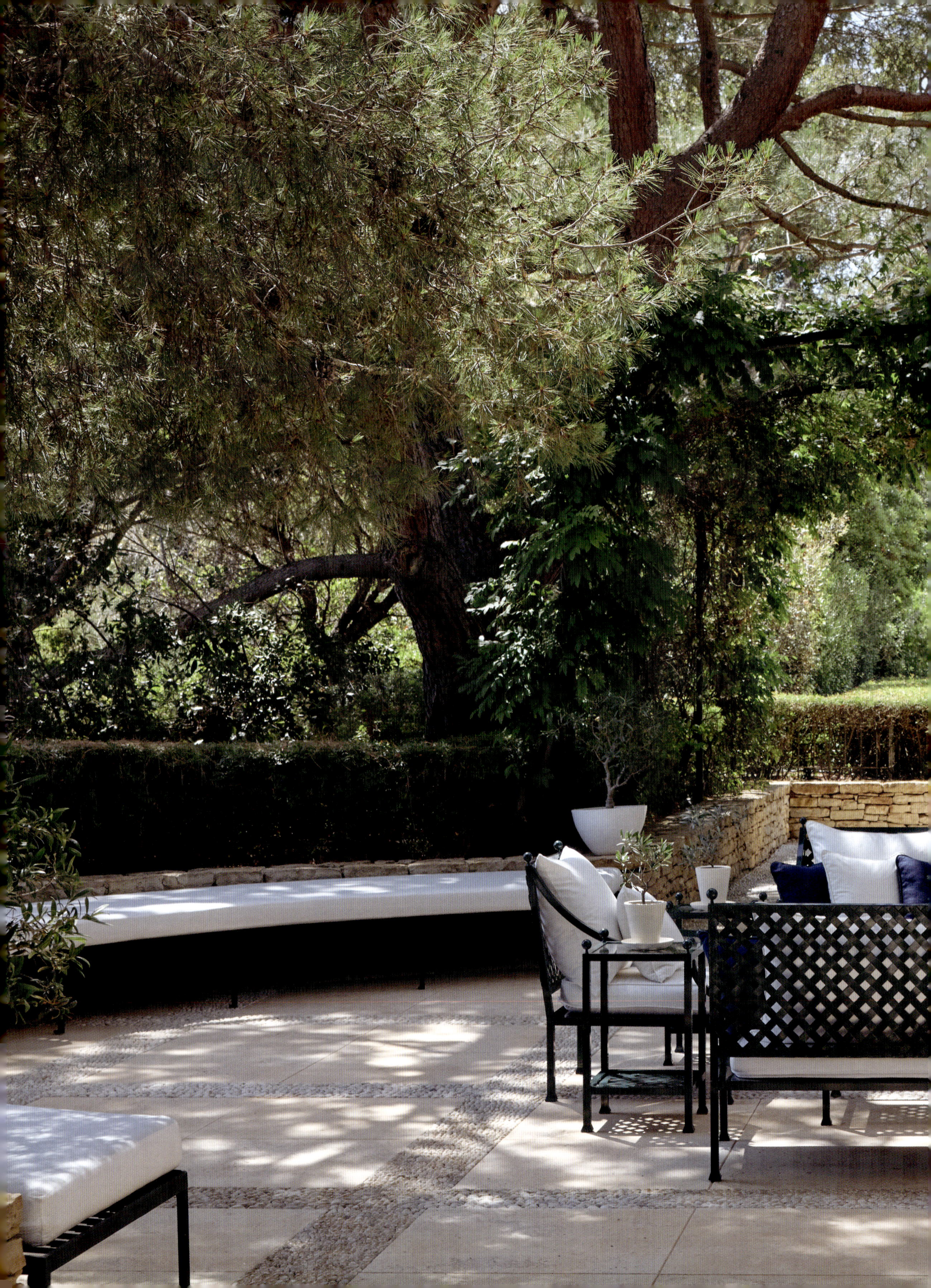

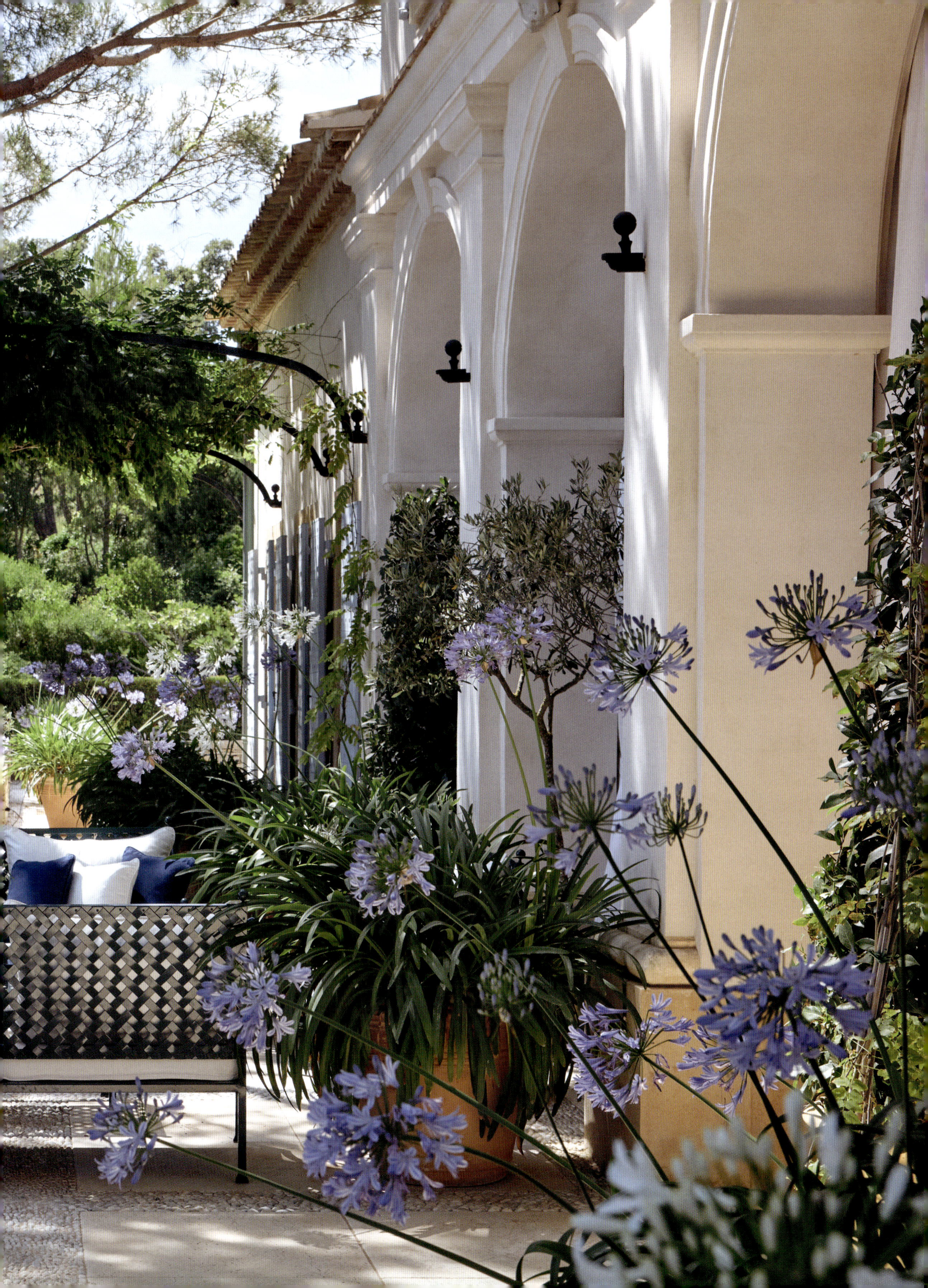

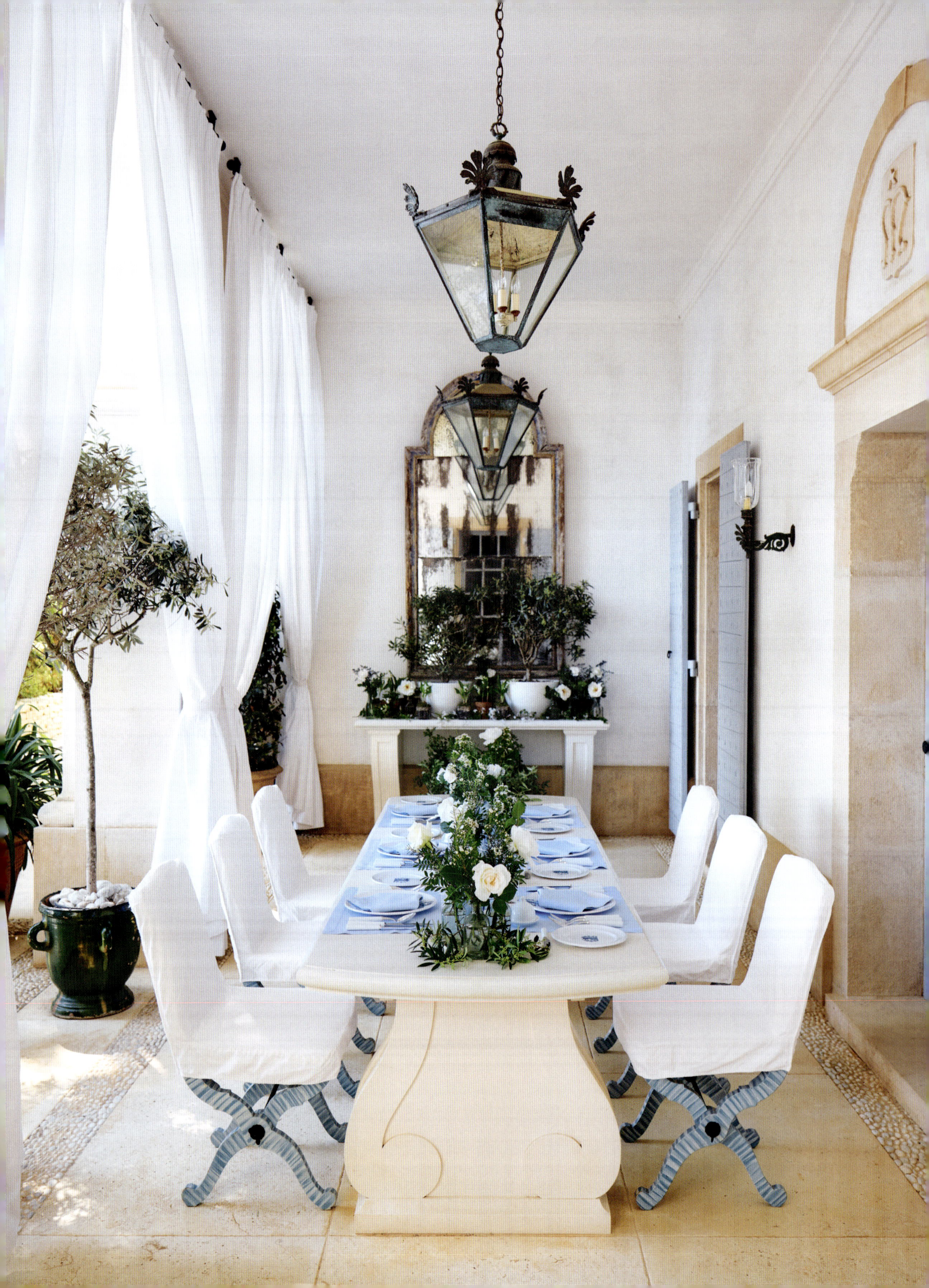

ABOVE AND OPPOSITE I've worked with several of the traditional *faïence* makers in Moustiers-Sainte-Marie to create many of the plates and tableware for Léoube, and will happily spend hours scouring the different workshops whenever I visit. These plates are from atelier Bondil.

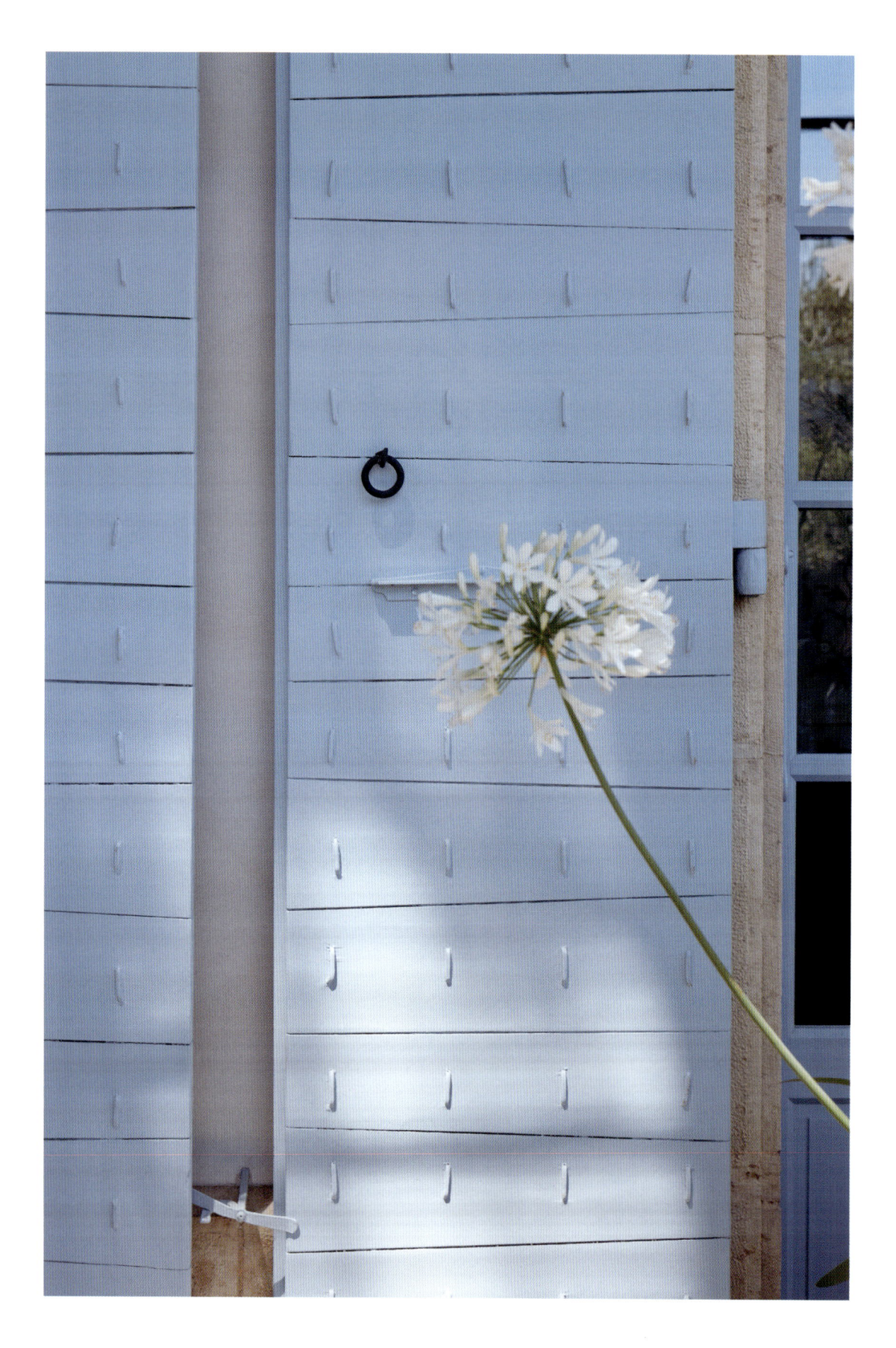

ABOVE We created metal replicas of the traditional style of wooden door typically found on rural houses and '*mas*' (farmhouses) in the region. Their '*clous tordus*' – bent nails – are lined up in different patterns and configurations.

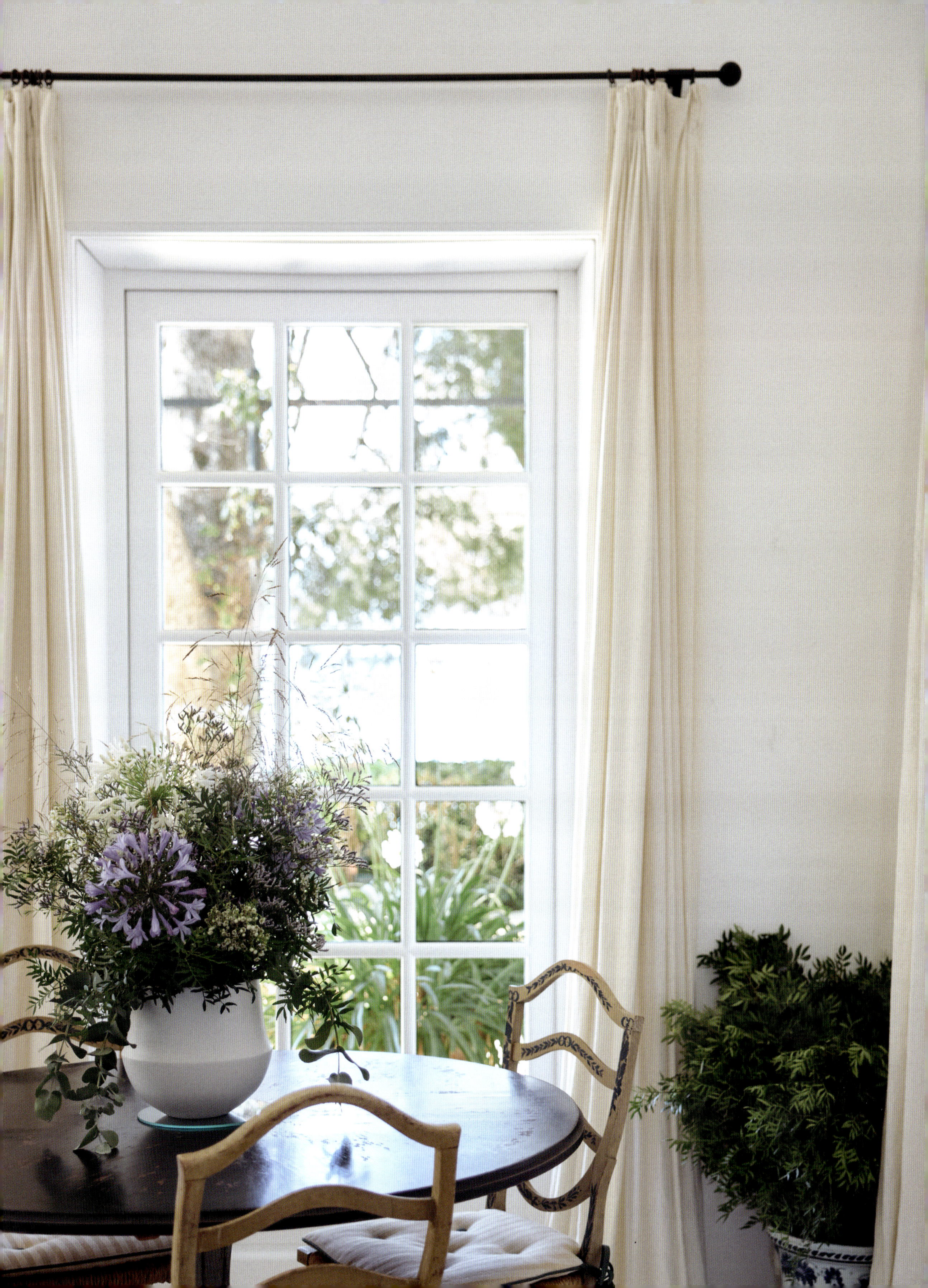

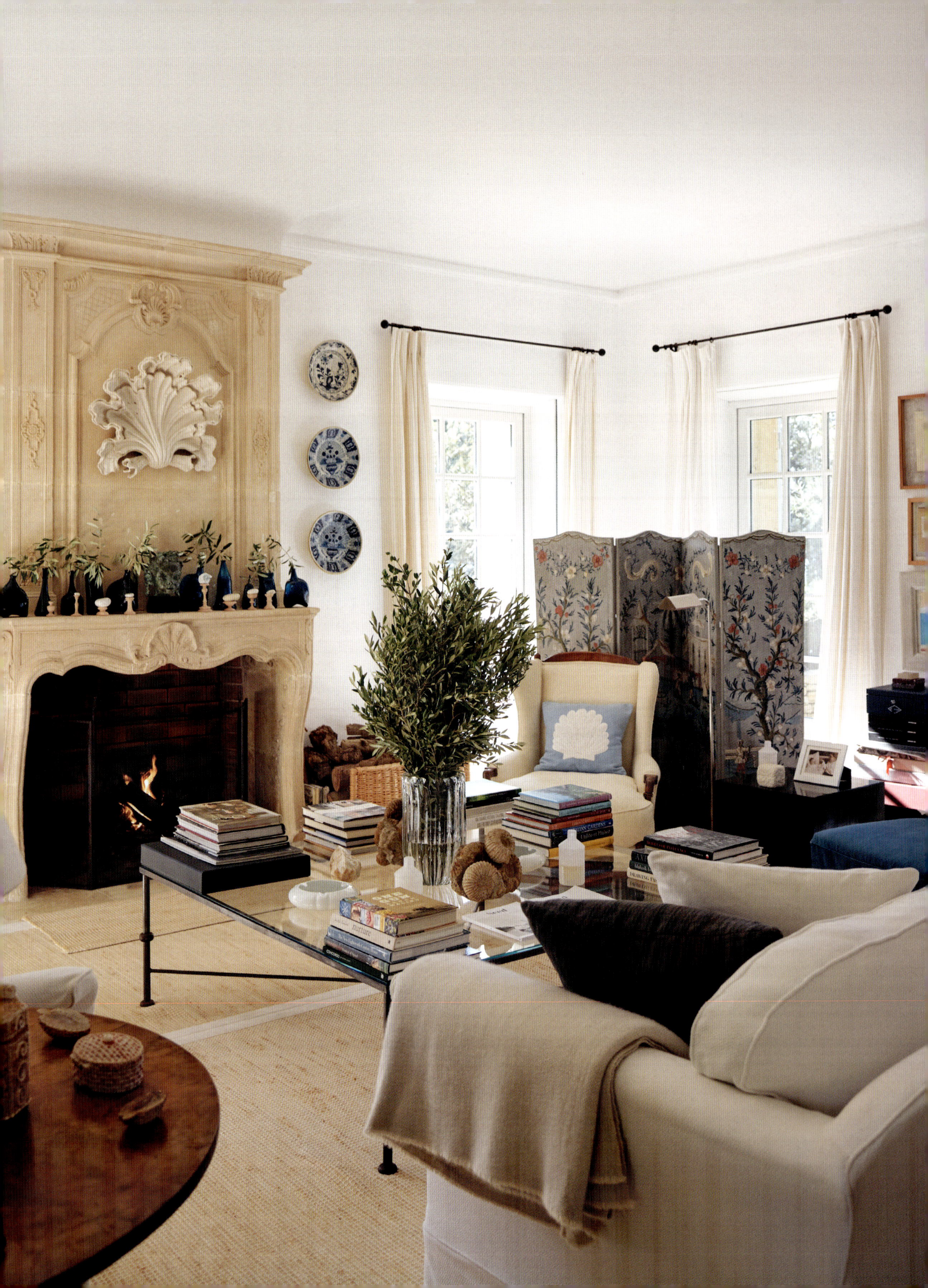

ABOVE My dear friend Hubert de Givenchy painted this set of pebbles for me – the paint is fading now but the sentiment and meaning behind them is just as strong.

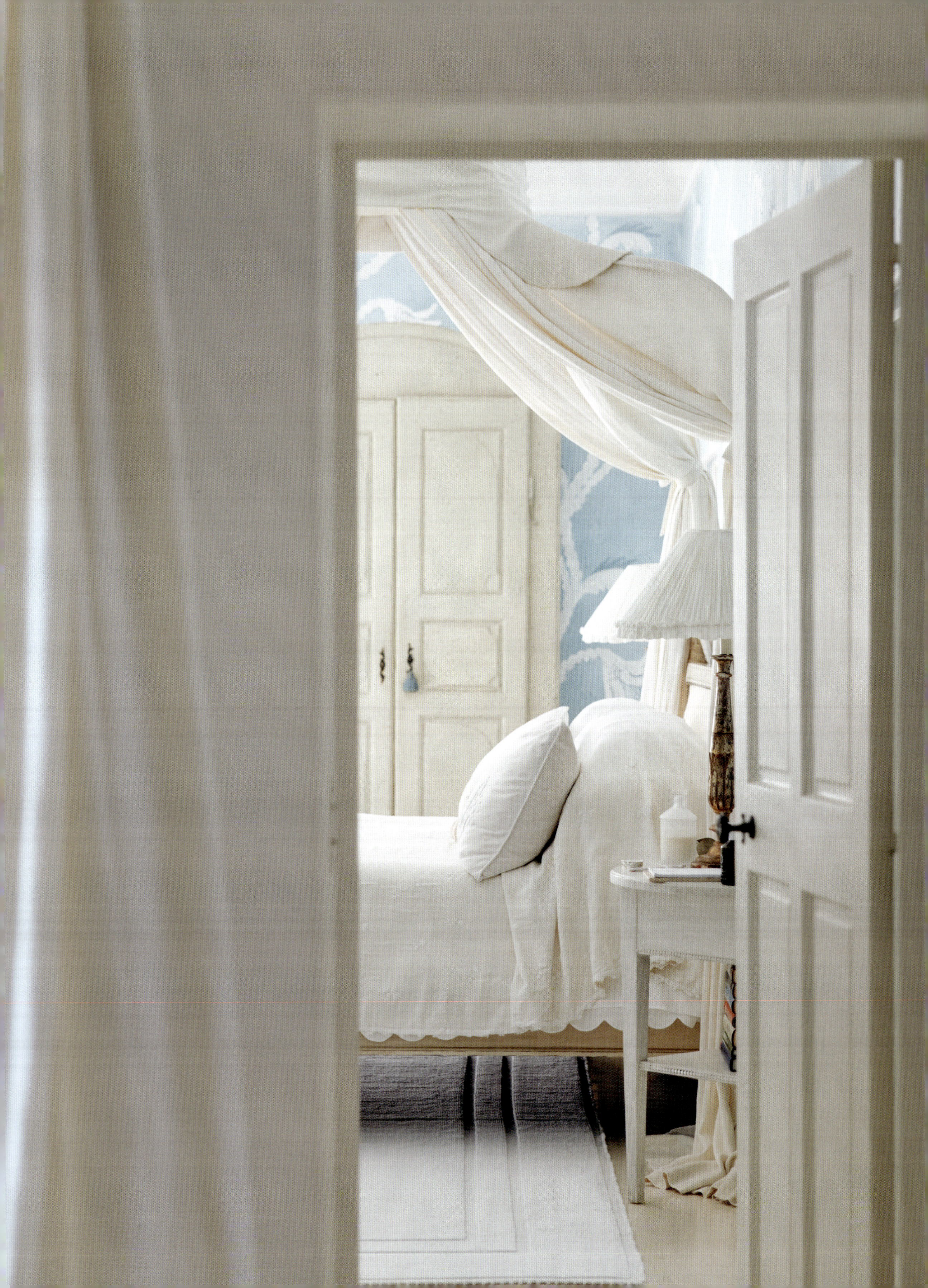

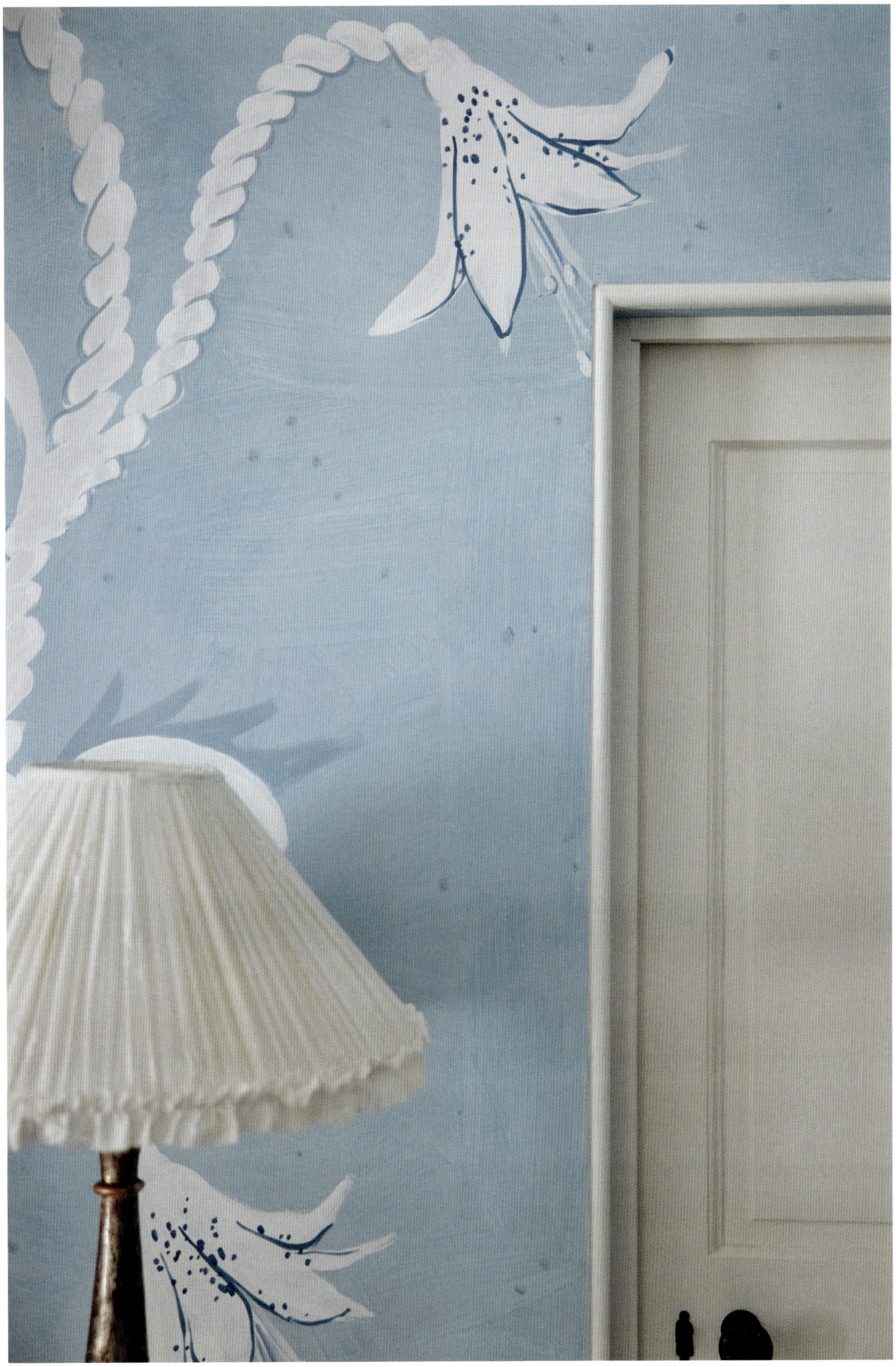

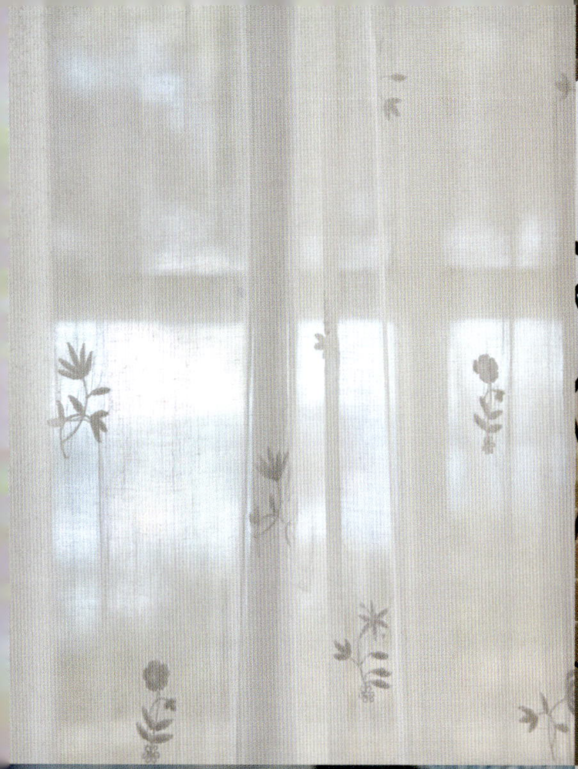
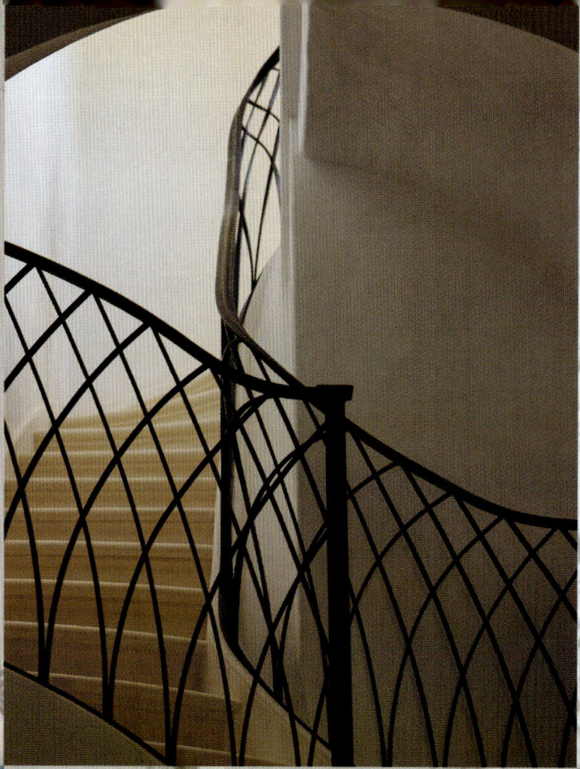

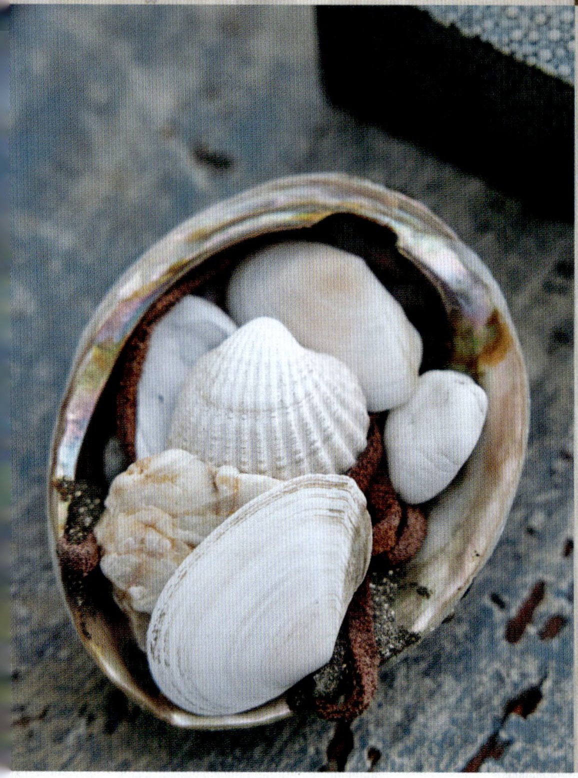
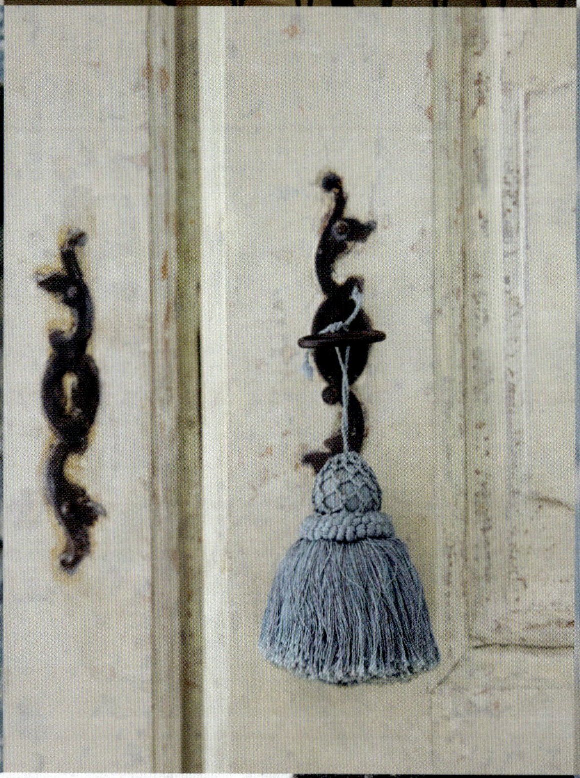
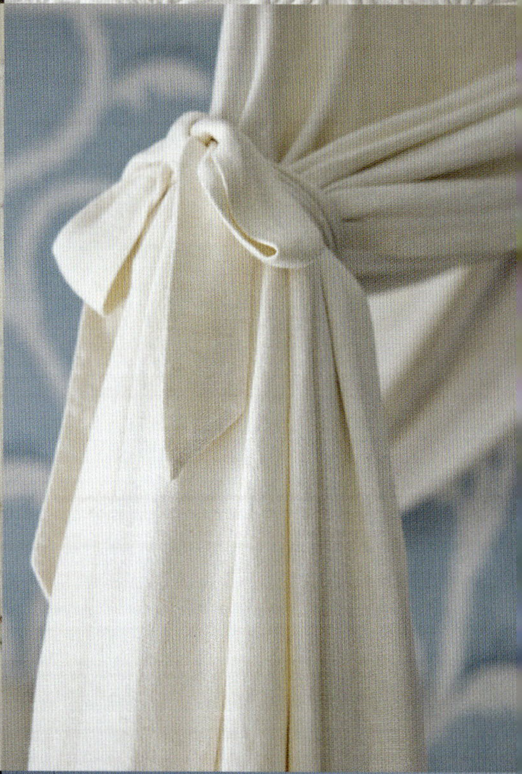
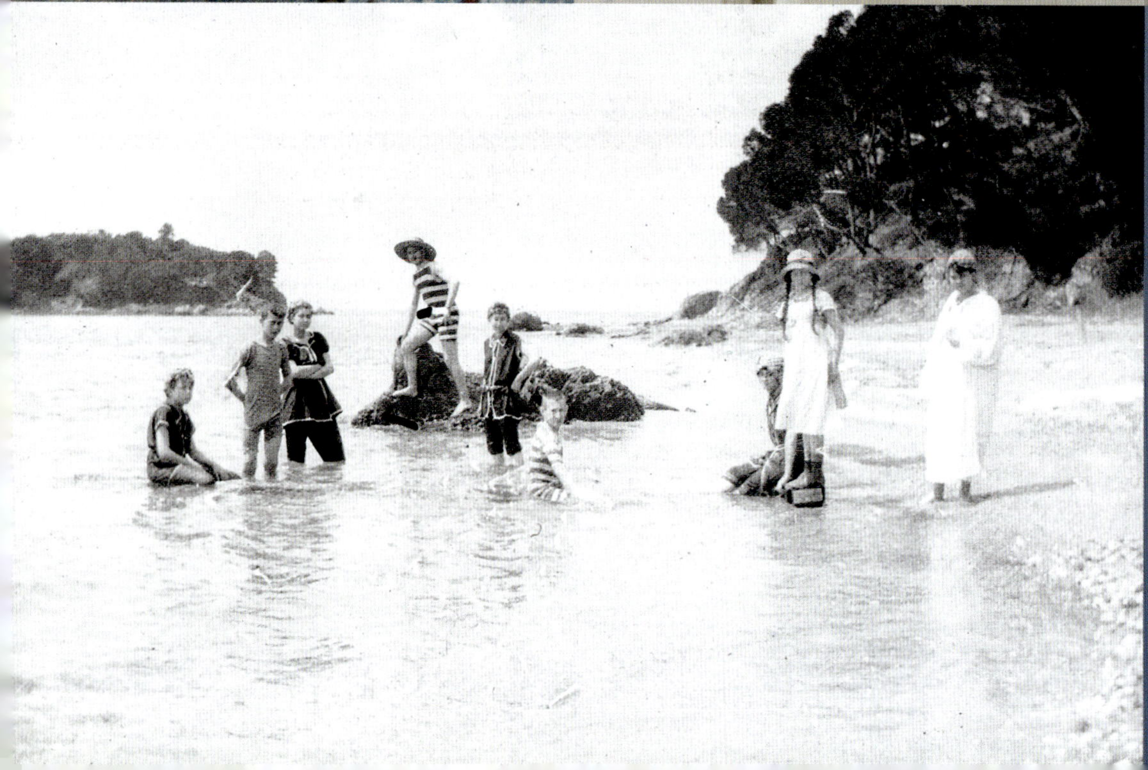
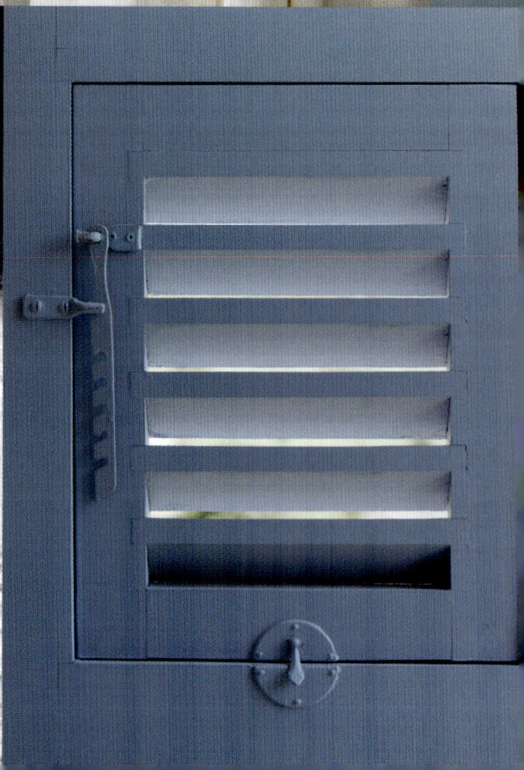

VILLA MARIA

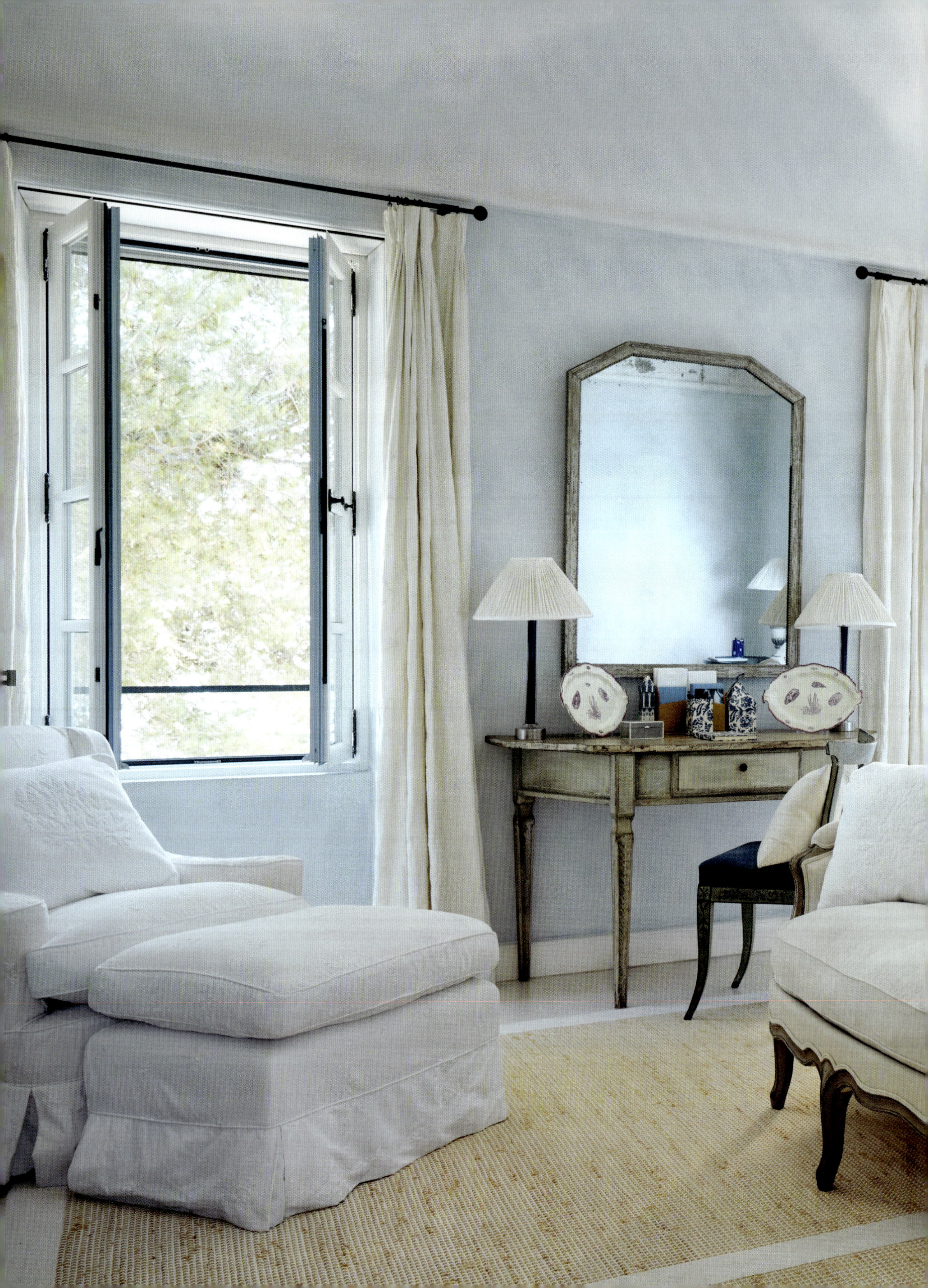

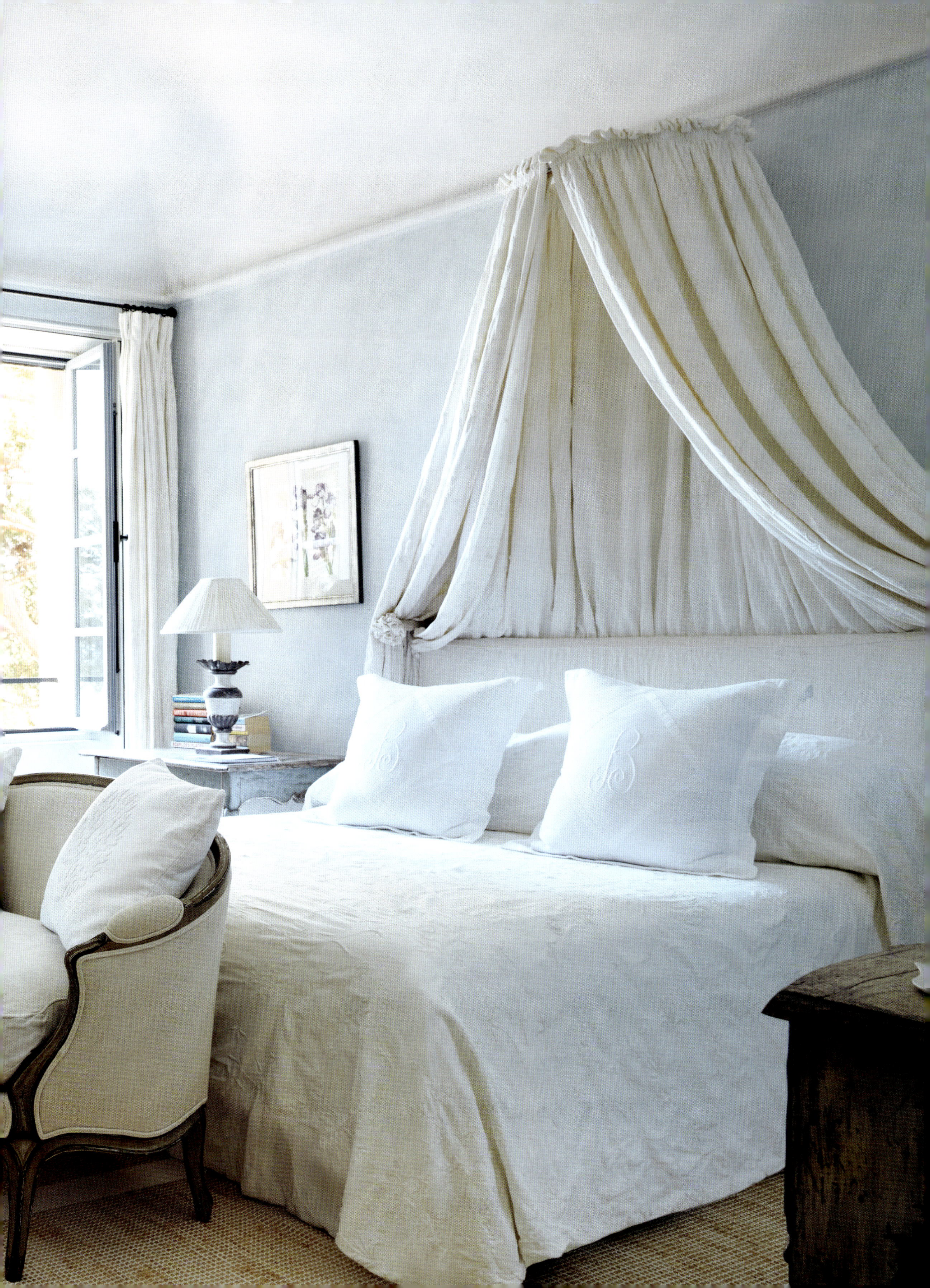

The room we still refer to as our bedroom is on the ground floor. The walls were hand-painted by a scene painter from Brighton who flew out to Léoube for about a week. The blue and white design – inspired by a Minoan painting of traditional Cretan sand lilies – is bold and striking. I've always loved the symbolism of flowers and these lilies are renowned as symbols of beauty and purity: the whole design feels very at home in Villa Maria.

We'll try to have lunch on the terrace in front of the villa overlooking the sea as often as we can, particularly when guests are with us, to soak up the magnificent Mediterranean views. In the summer months the heat of the early afternoon can be so stifling that if we sit at table too long we often have to pull across the white drapes or the heat just becomes unbearable and we have to retreat indoors.

OPPOSITE One of the upstairs bedrooms looks out to the the *Îlot de Léoube*, the Léoube islet, which is part of the Port-Cros National Park, a conservation area that protects its fauna, flora and marine life.

VILLA MARIA 201

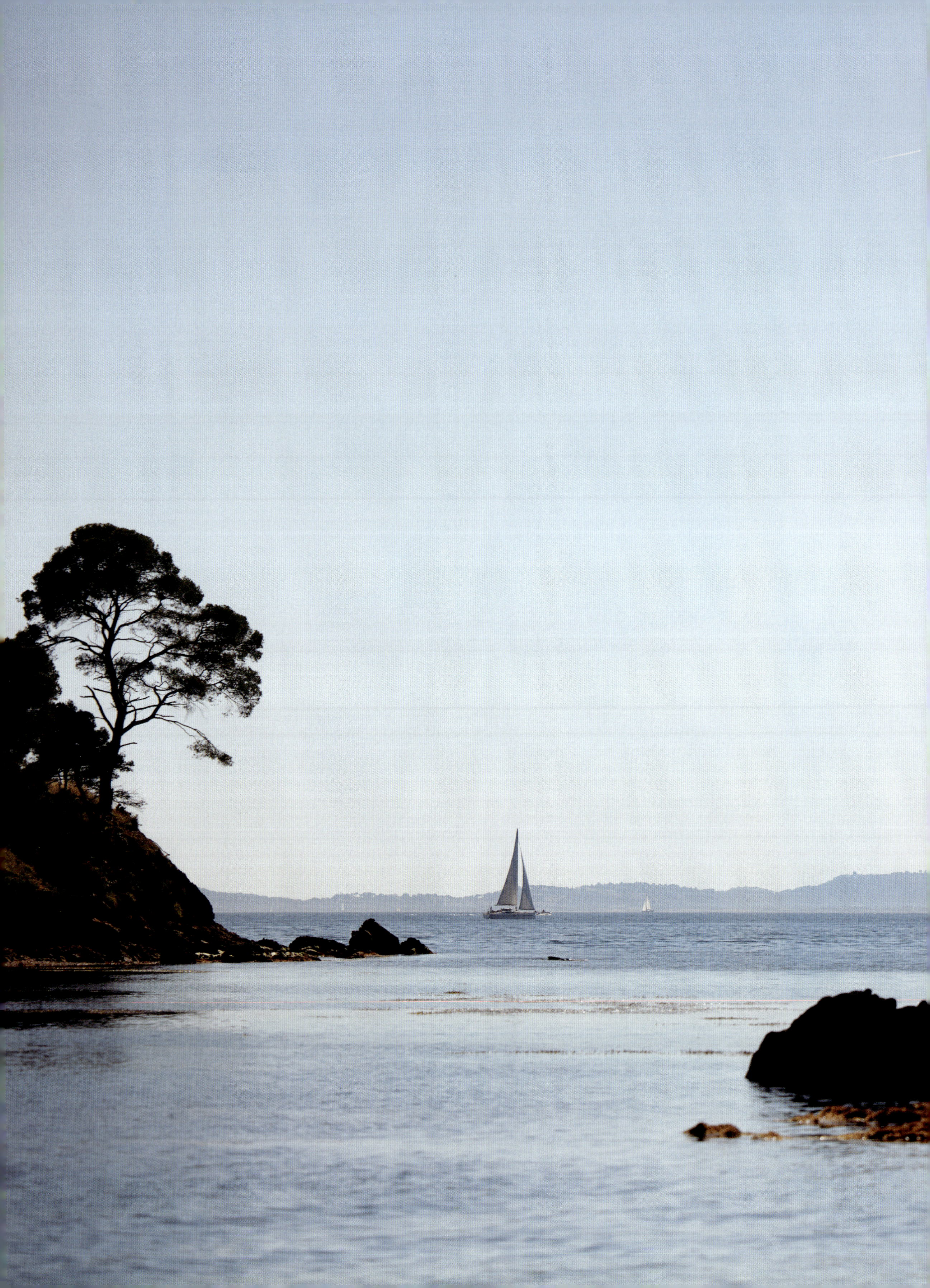

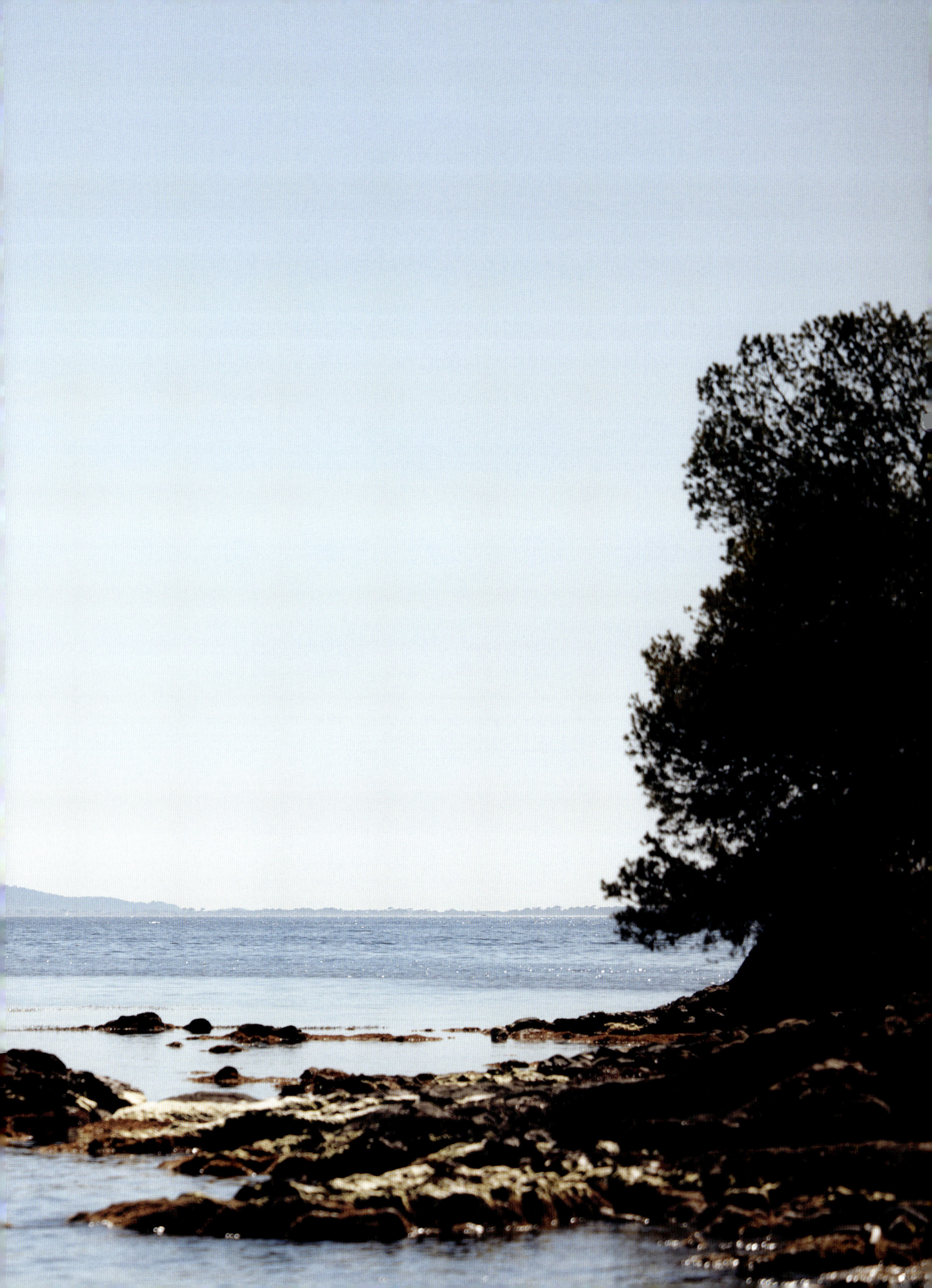

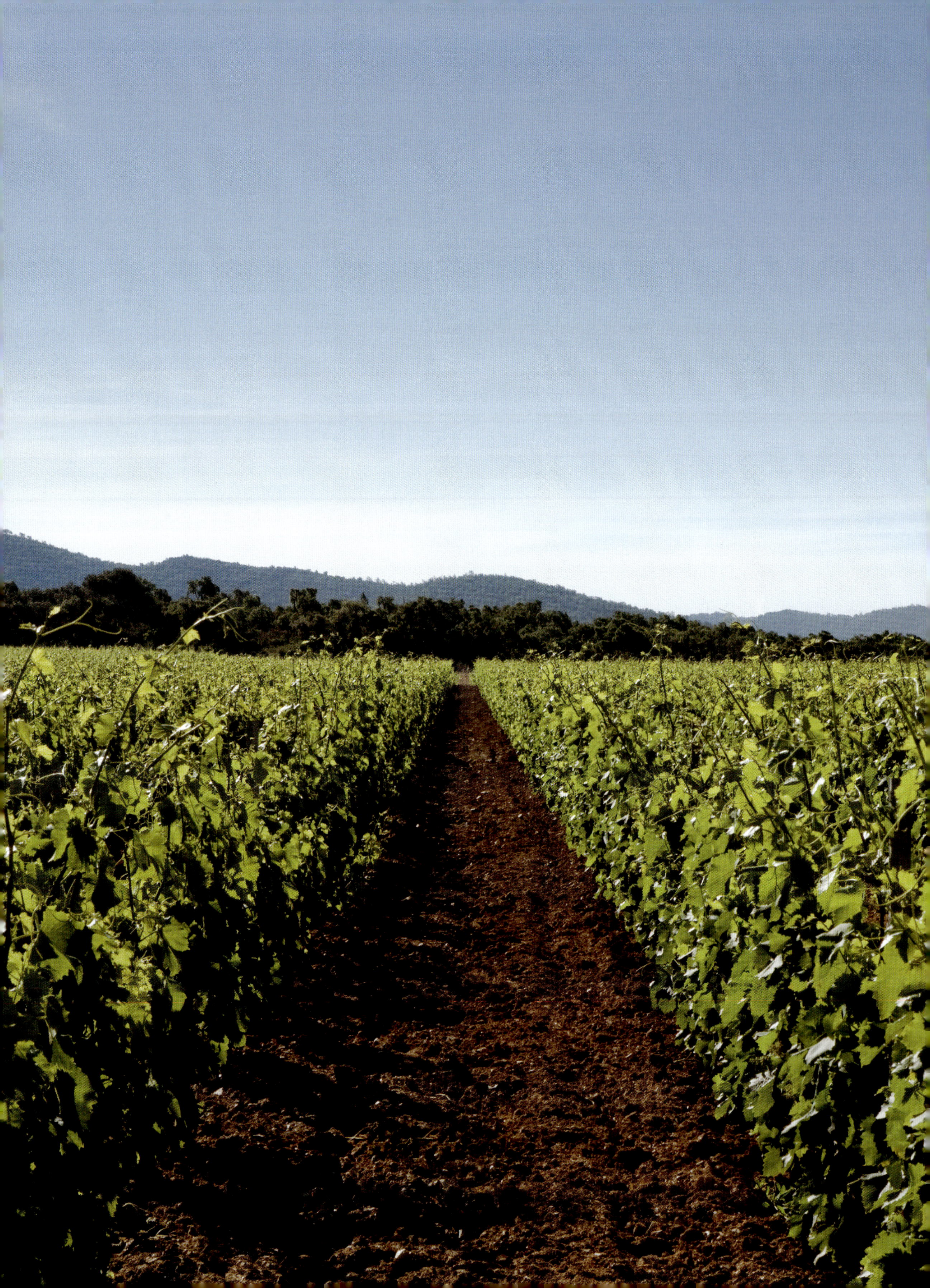

# THE VINEYARD

AND OLIVE GROVE

Provence's mild Mediterranean climate means that it has one of the most perfect settings for winemaking. The winters are mild and the summer's dry daytime heat is tempered by the gentle but cooling nighttime breezes. The occasional gust of the region's Mistral wind keeps the vines aerated and dry and prevents them attracting mildew or disease.

One of my favourite things to do at Léoube is to take a car up to the very top of the estate just as the dawn is breaking. It is difficult to walk up as the terrain is rough and bumpy but when you reach the highest point the ground flattens and as you step out of the car you are rewarded with the most spectacular panoramic vista of the estate. As the morning light spills over the horizon, you look down over vast patches of greenery bordered by dense maquis. Vines cling to the gentle curve of the slopes with clusters of silvery olive trees below them and the bright blue of the sea glistens beyond. It's breathtaking.

But what is most special about the land at Léoube, and what fascinates me more than anything else, is its soil. Provence is home to some of the oldest vineyards in France and the soil here dates back over 800 million years. The seabed once sat on the estate's land, saturating the soil with an array of minerals that not only feed the vines with nutrients but give the wines a unique character, a hint of salinity coming through in each vintage.

A respect for the soil and its ability to give life runs through everything I do but it's particularly important in the context of winemaking, because of the region's 'terroir'. Terroir is a concept that has been written about and argued over for centuries and yet is hard to define because opinions are divided over what it truly means. Simple definitions observe that it is the environment of a vineyard – its soil, climate and the human interaction with them – that shapes the quality and flavour of the wine. But at its broadest interpretation, terroir simply represents 'a sense of place', the idea that there are countless factors, each unique to that vineyard's situation, that will affect the expression of the wine. The term holds a wonderful sense of mysticism for me and perhaps that is the secret to a terroir's allure.

OPPOSITE Seasonal *vendangeurs* arrive to help us with our grape and olive harvest, collecting the fruit by hand.

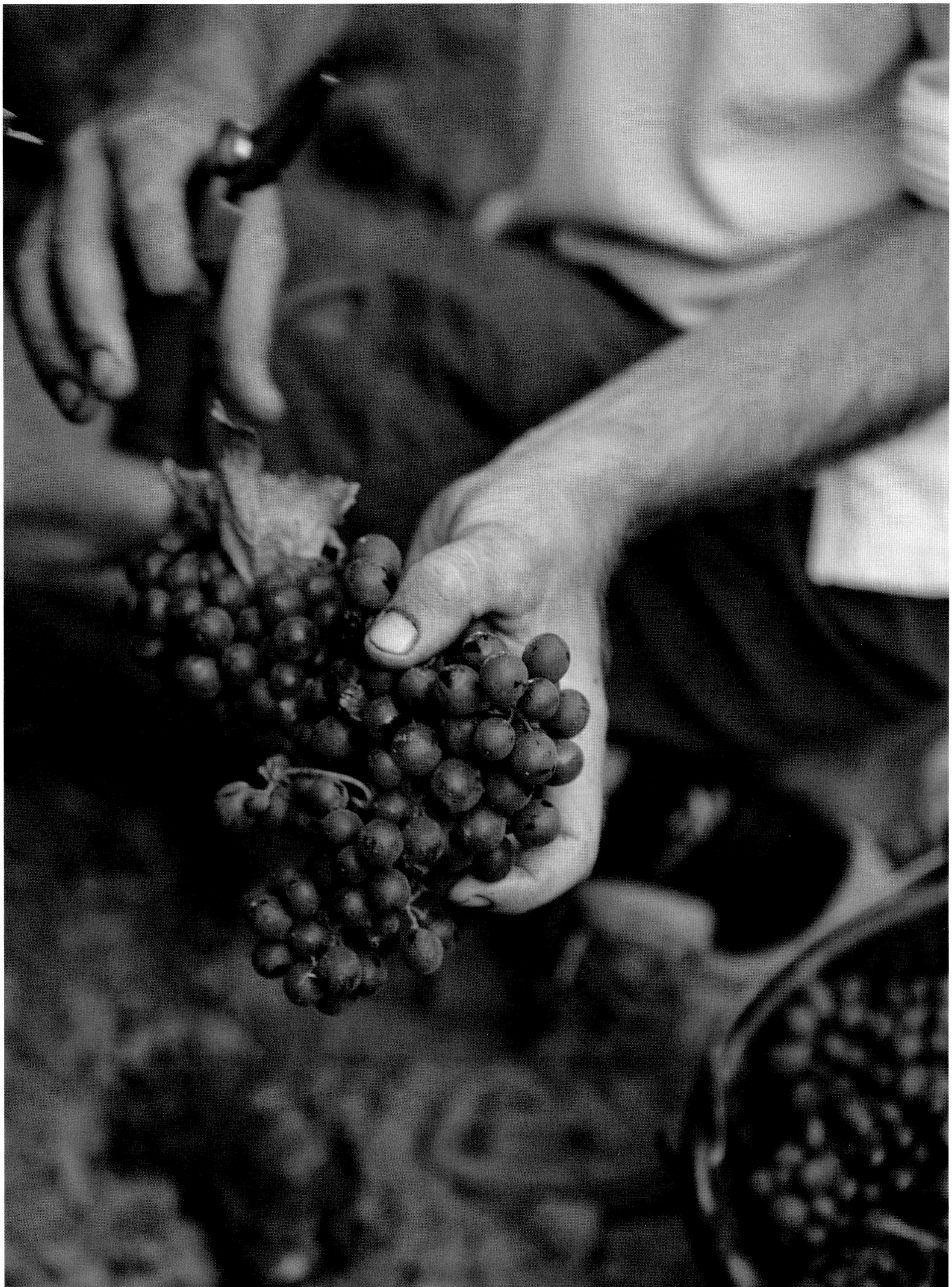

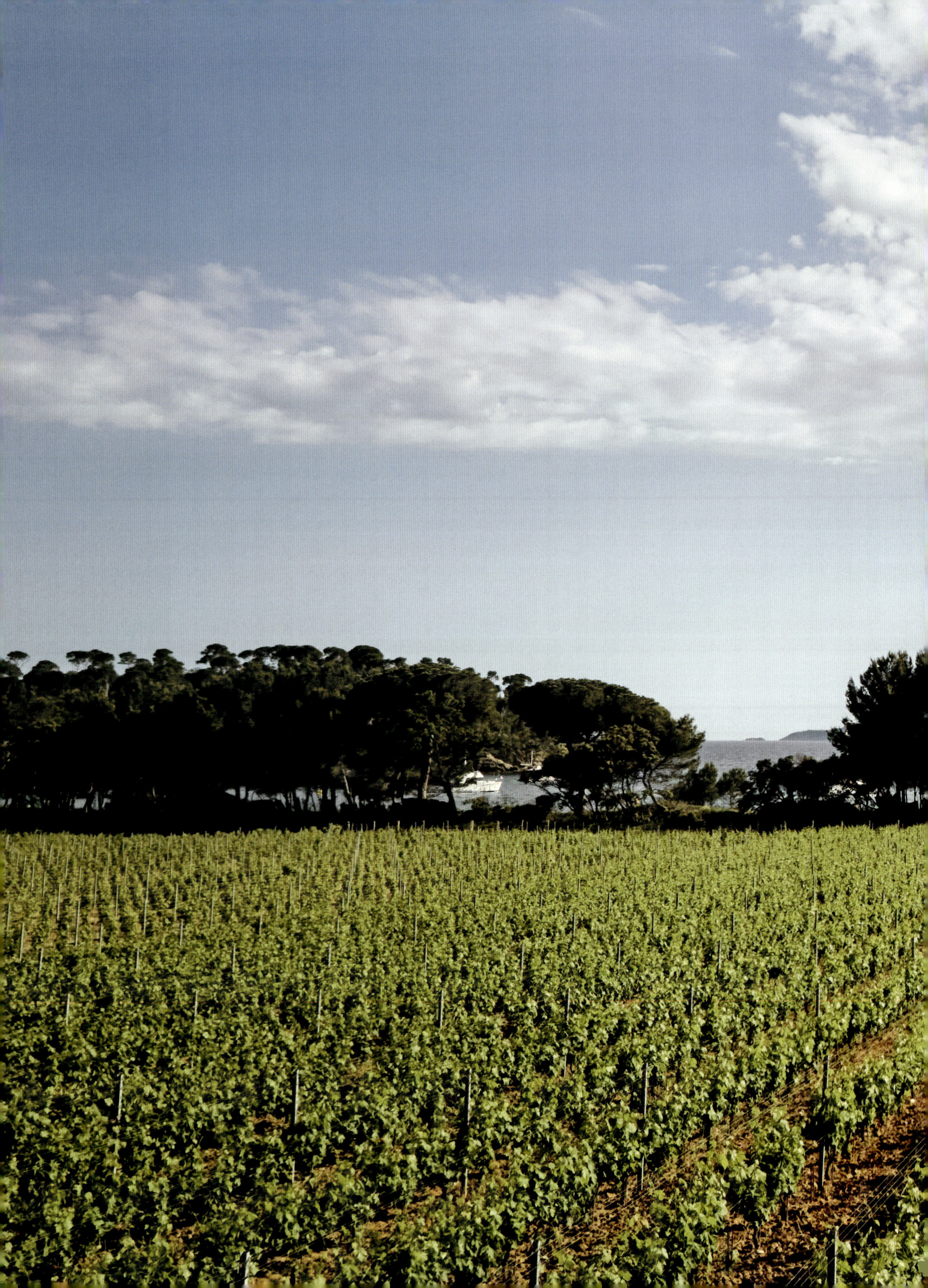

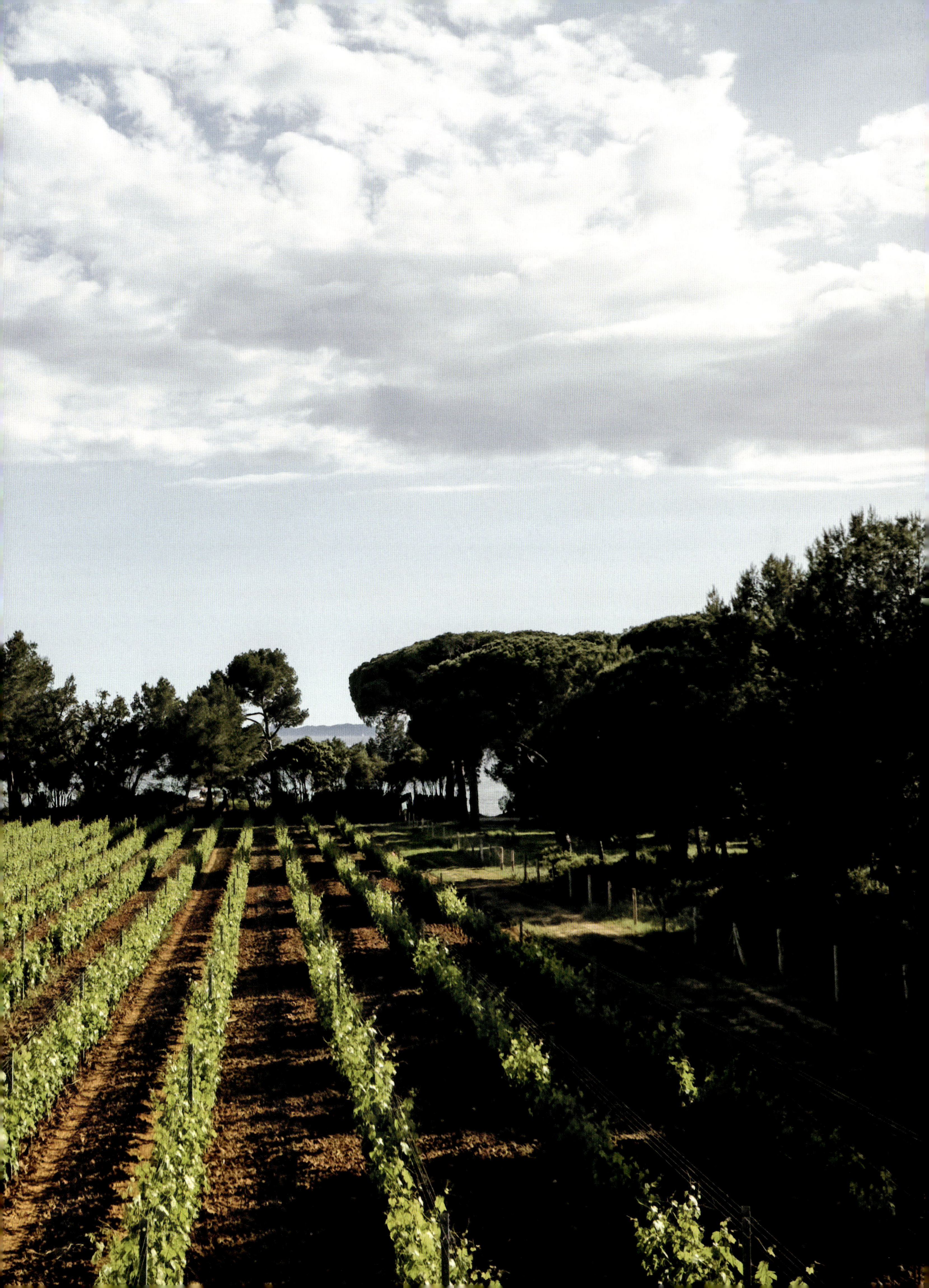

CHÂTEAU LÉOUBE

'The garden of the world has no limits. Except in your mind. Its presence is more beautiful than the stars. With more clarity than the polished mirror of your heart.'

– RUMI

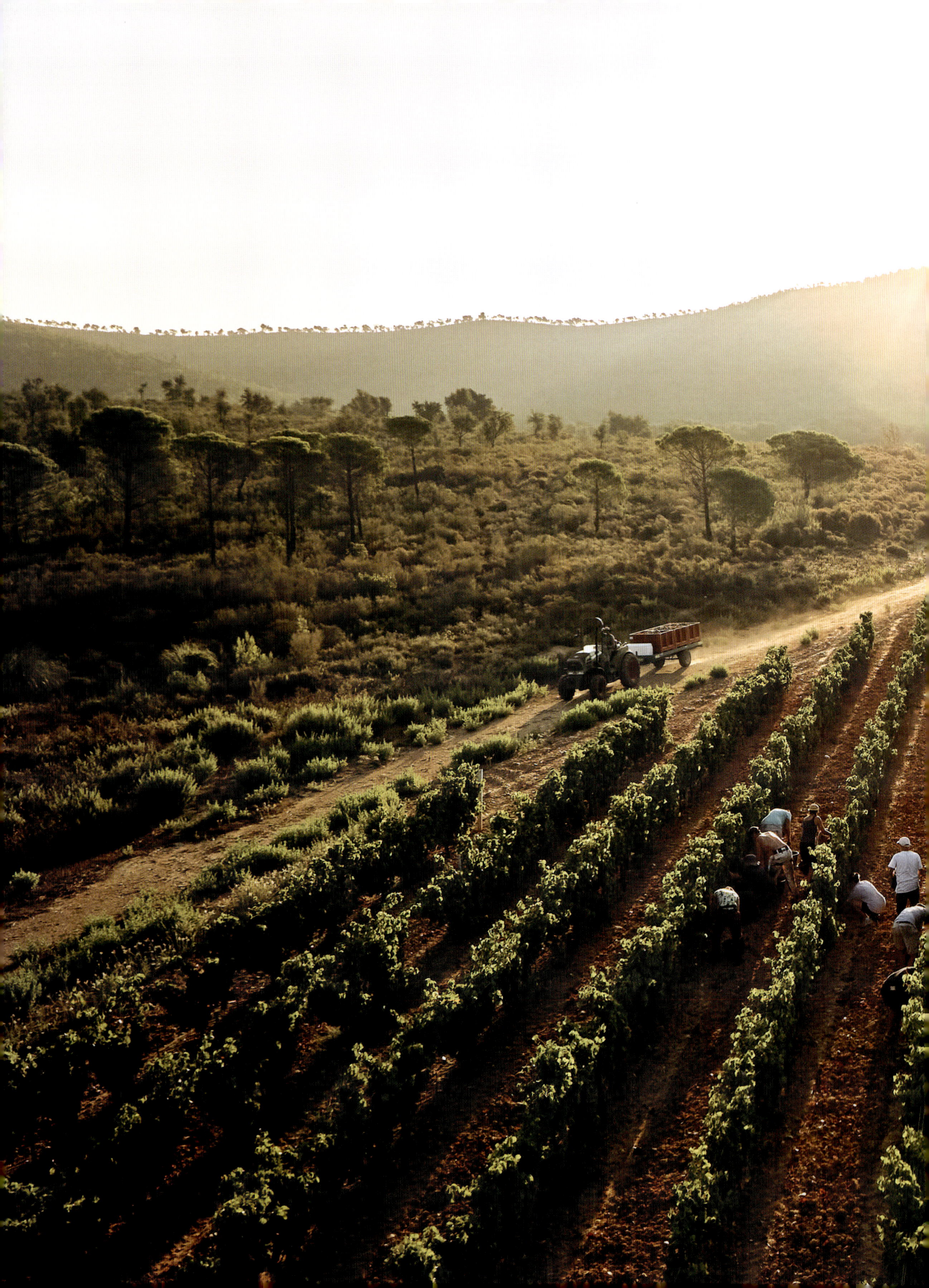

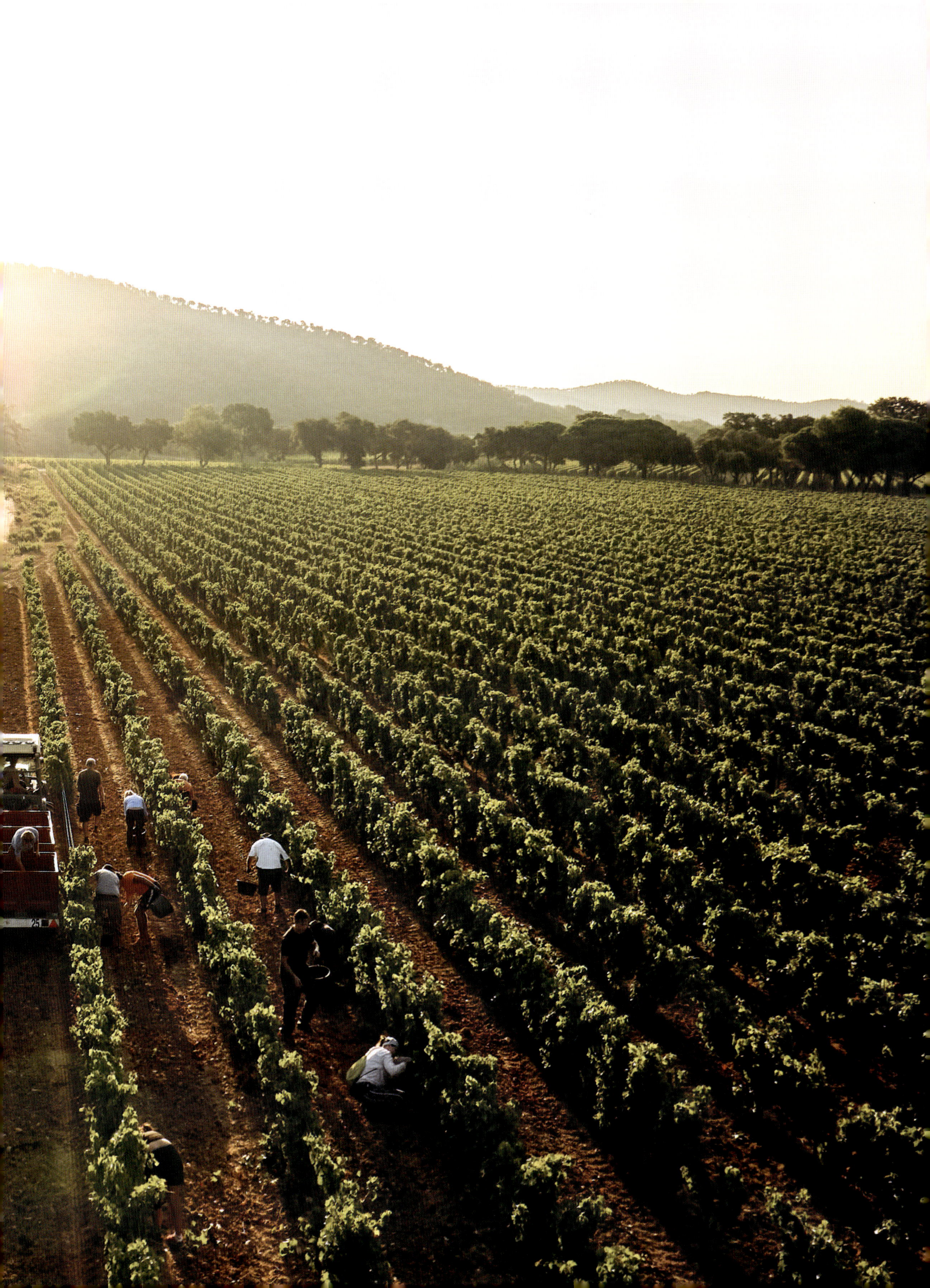

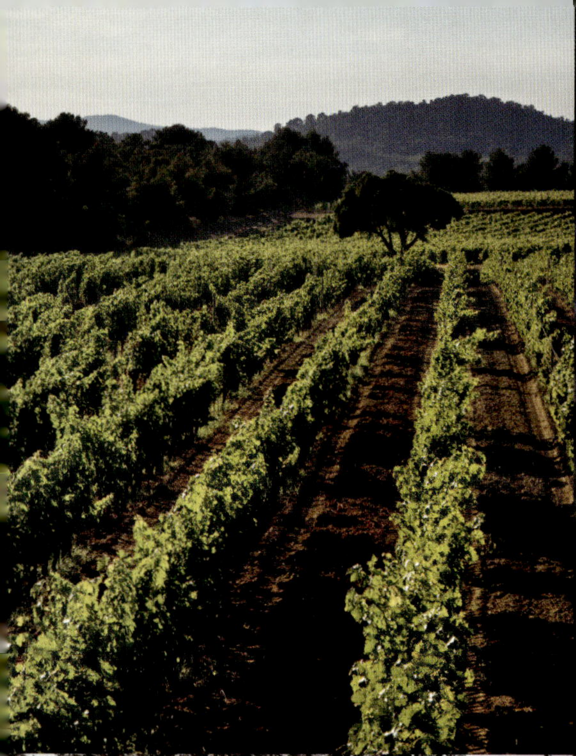
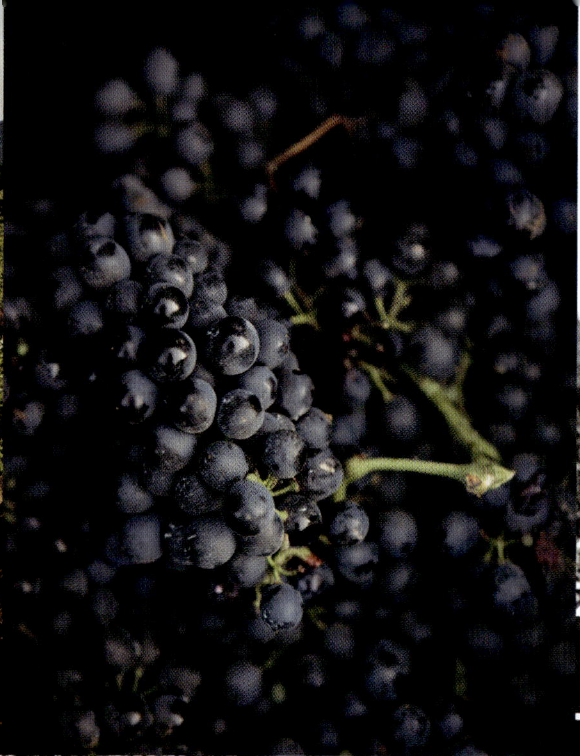
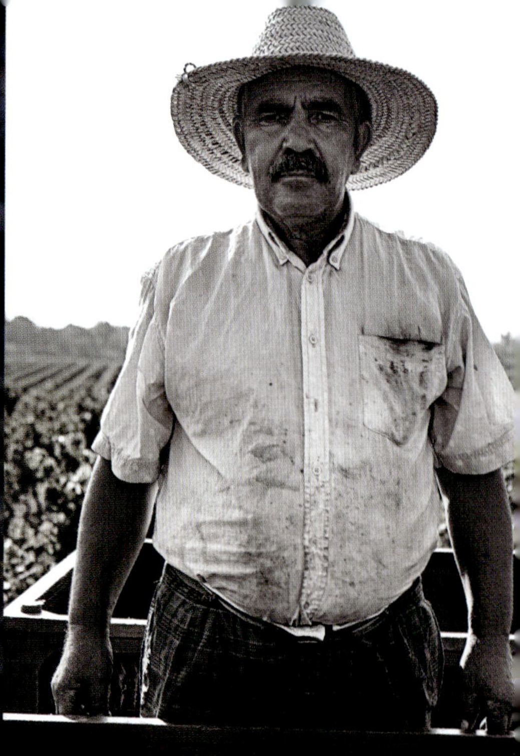
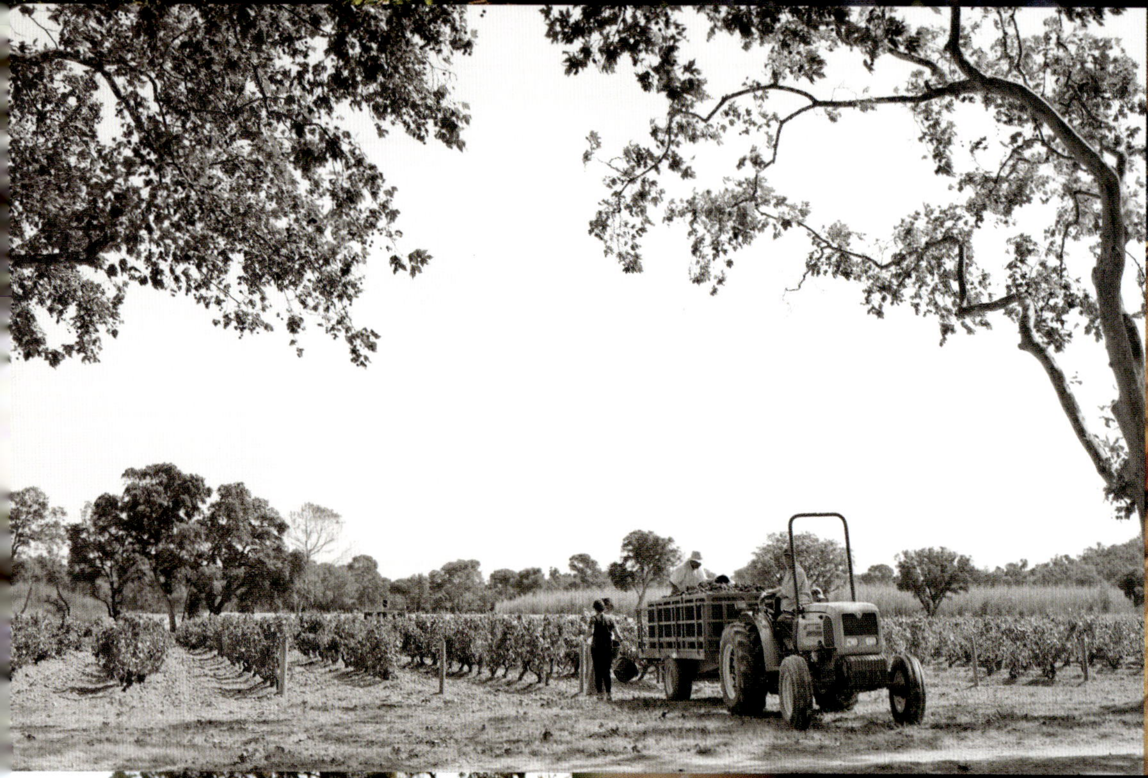
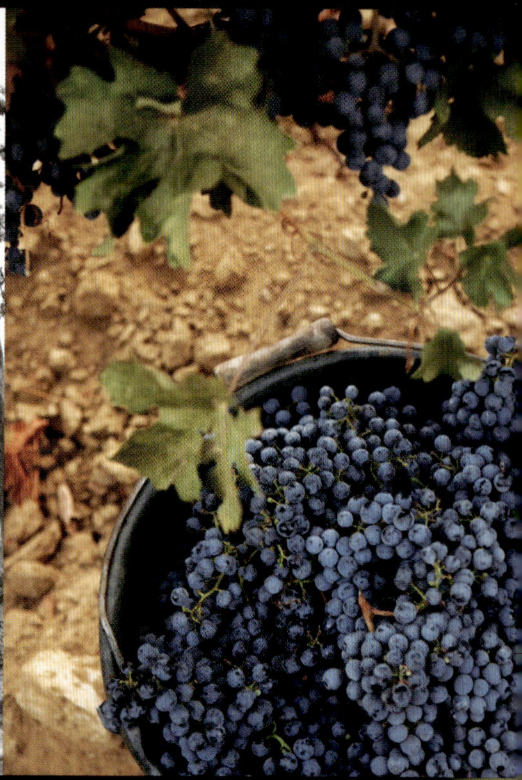
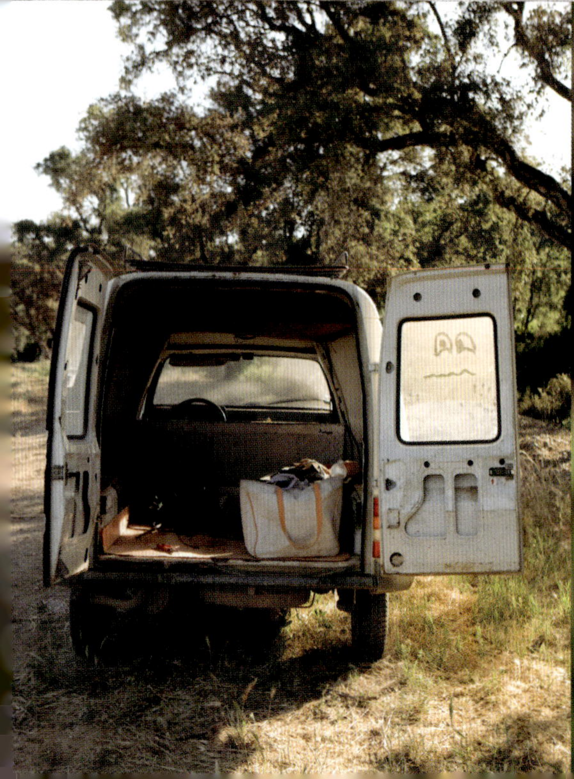
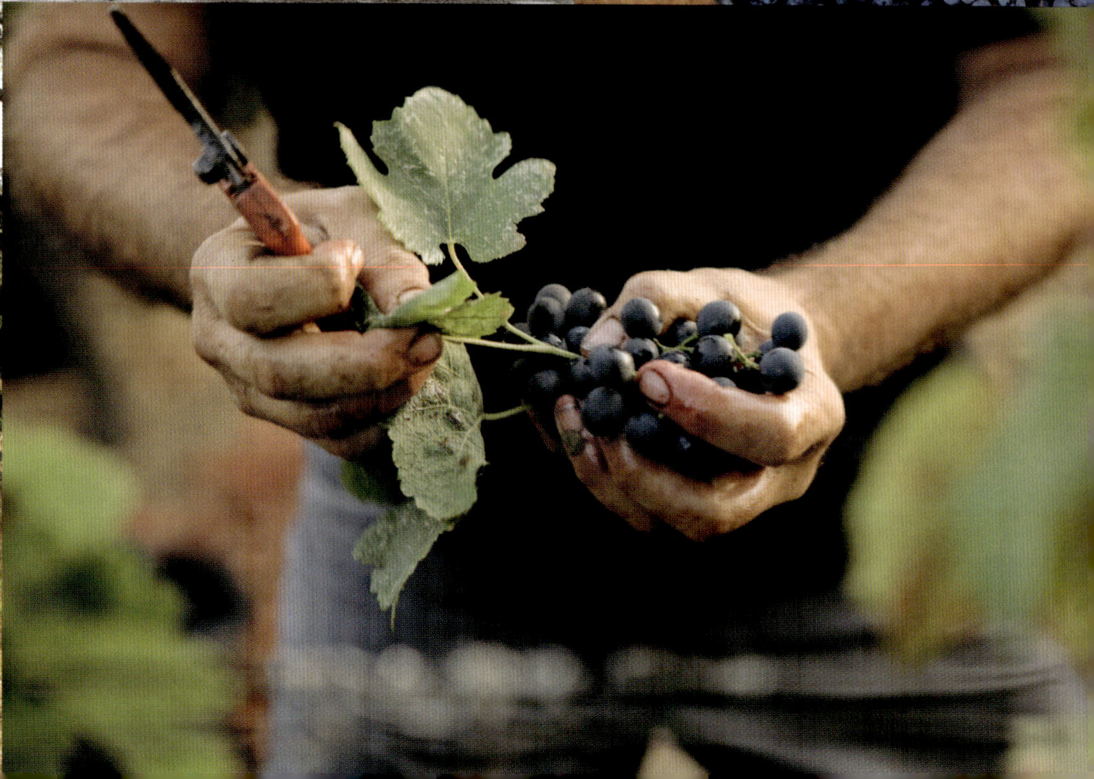

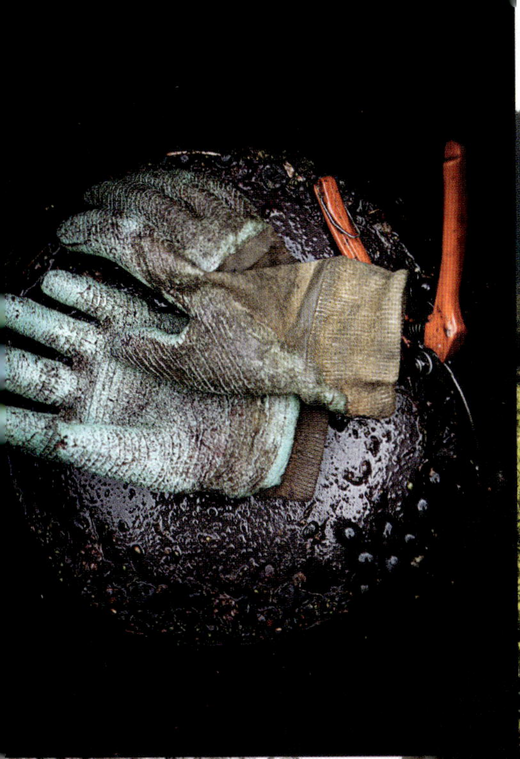

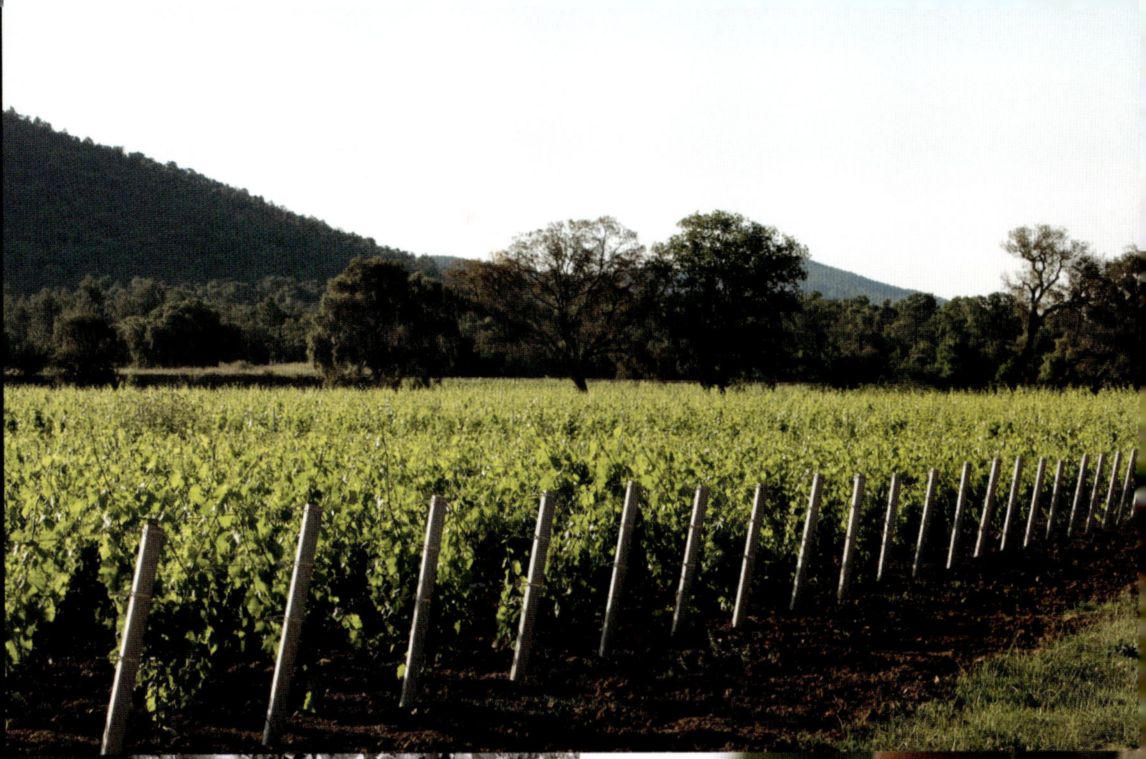

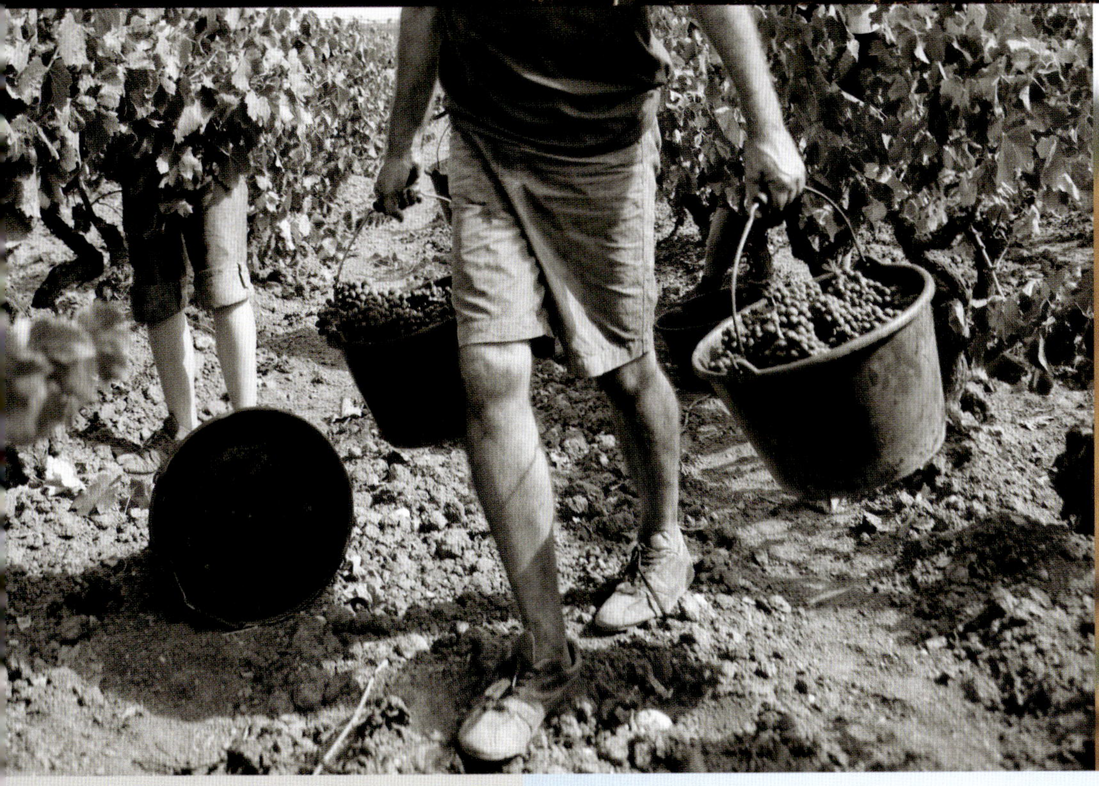

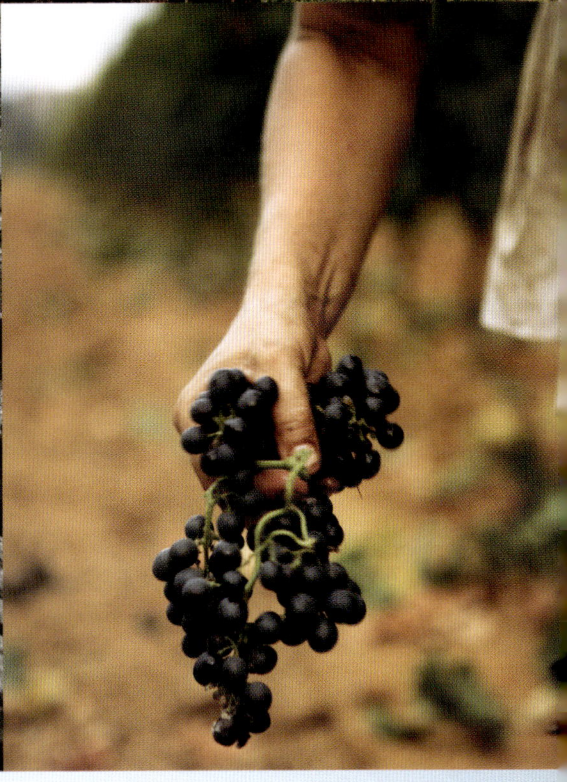

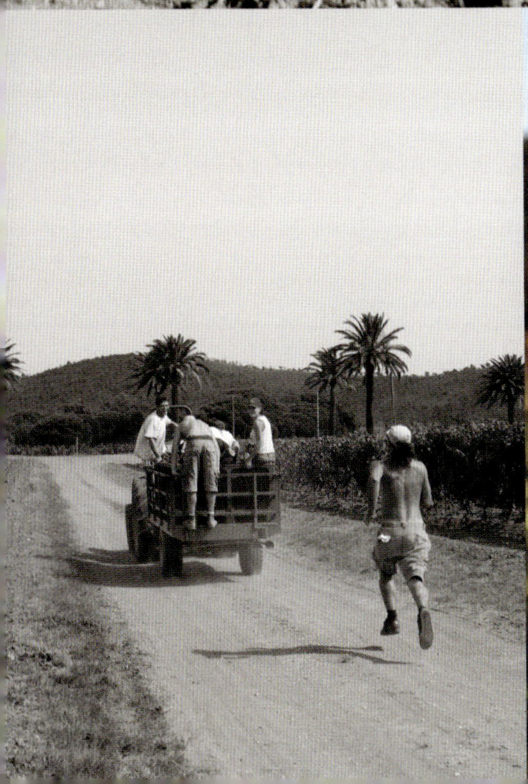

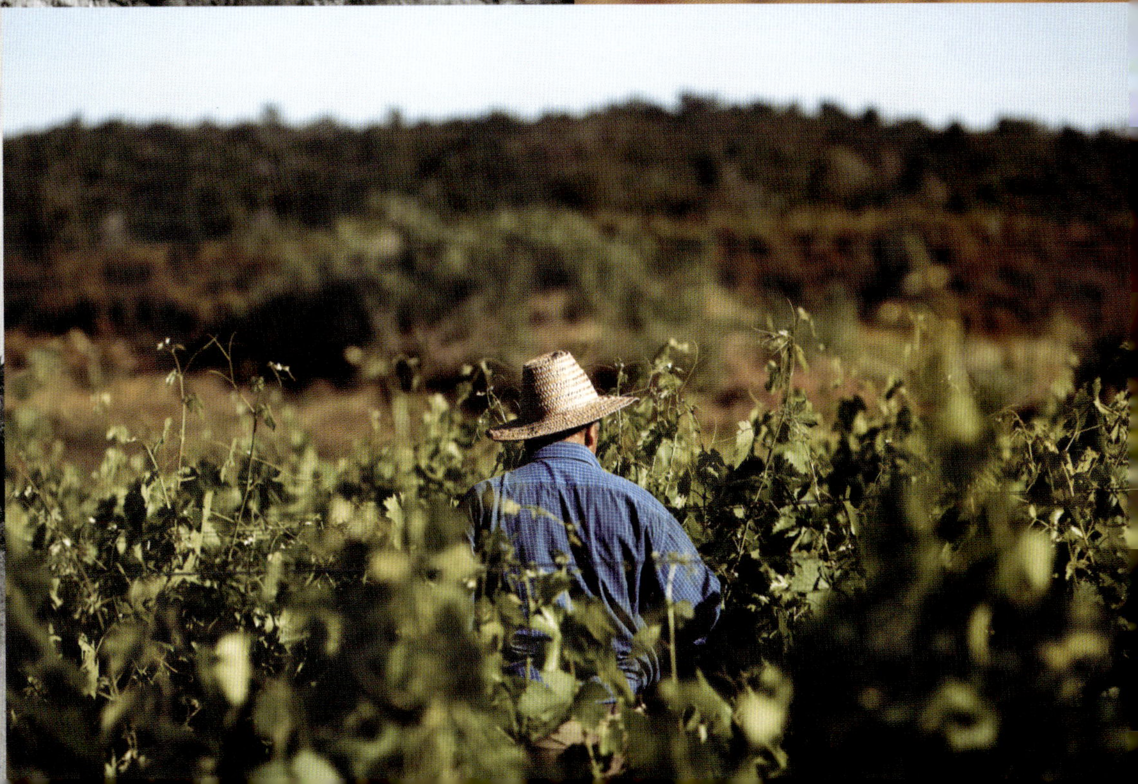

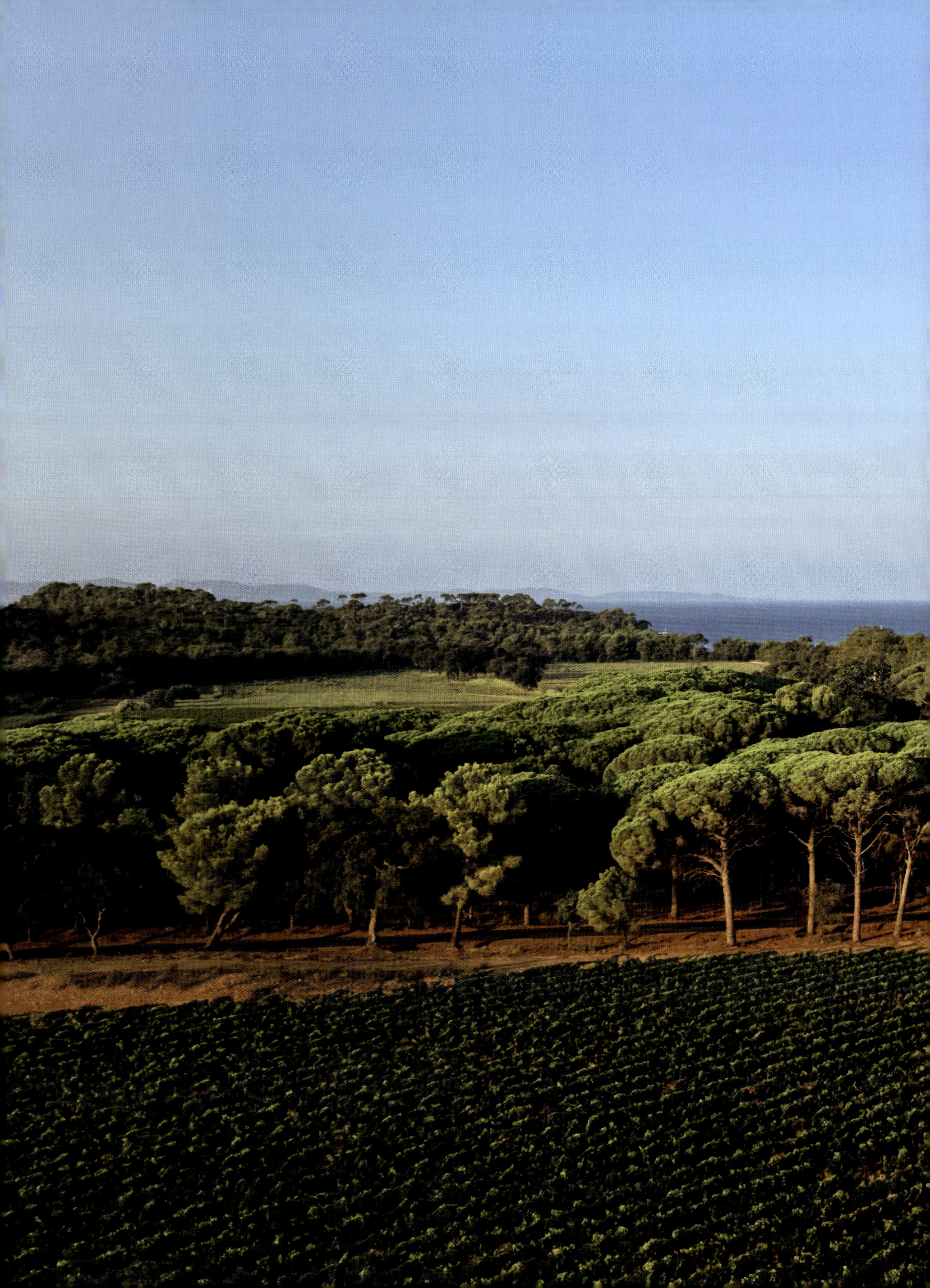

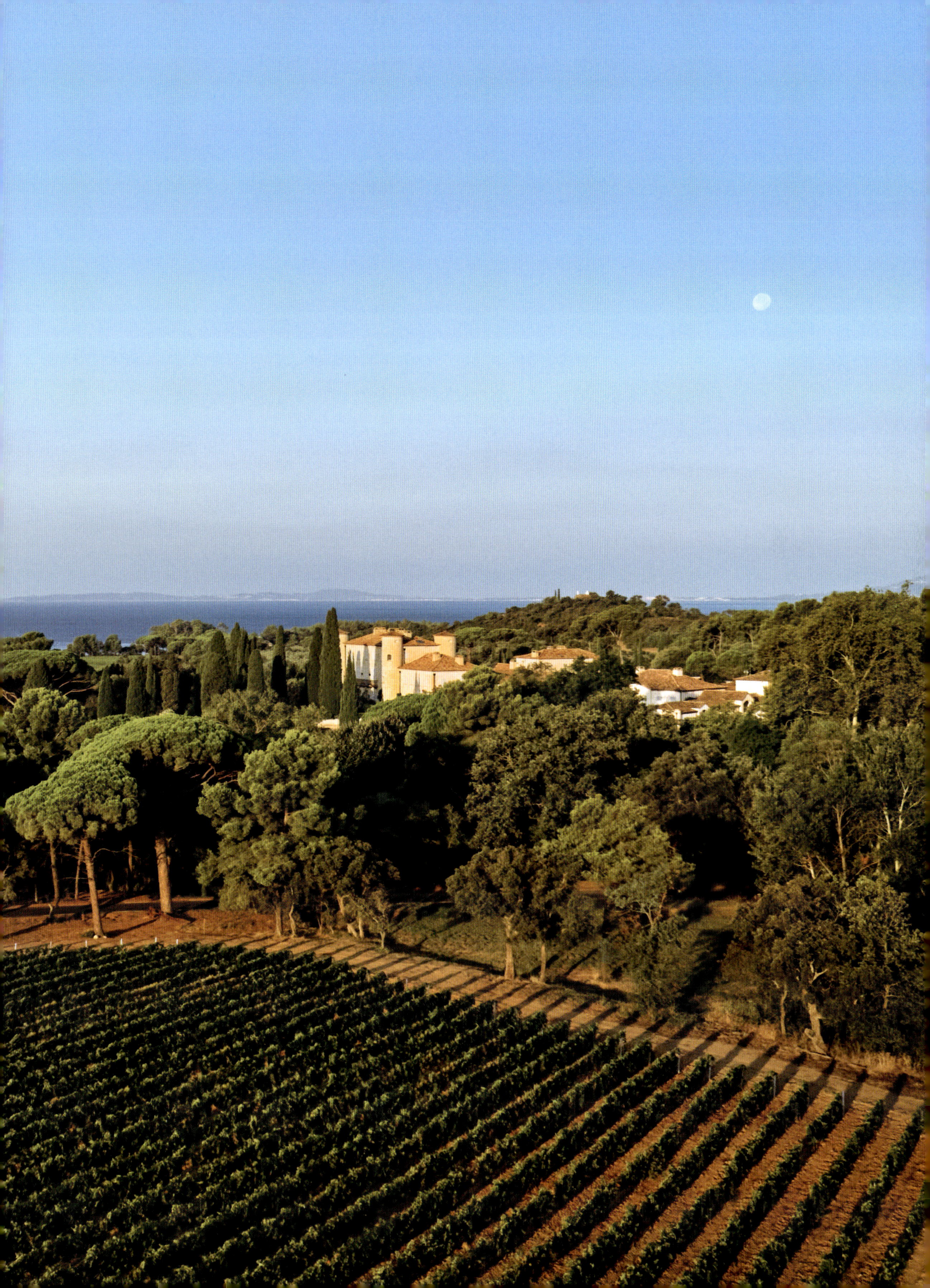

Honouring our terroir and protecting our mineral-rich marine soil has been fundamental to the way we produce our wines at Léoube, which is very much aligned with the philosophy of my farm and businesses in England. Everything is governed by a profound respect for nature and a desire to produce in accordance with its timelines, only harvesting what the land gives us. We grow our grapes organically – without the use of pesticides or chemicals – and follow the principles of biodynamic farming, by which produce is harvested in line with the moon's cycles and rhythms. To me, that makes so much sense on a vineyard as the gravitational pull of the moon affects the sap and juices in the vines so that helps determine how you should cultivate them and when you should harvest.

When we arrived on the estate, it was clear that the soil hadn't been looked after as well as it might have been. We worked hard to breathe life into it, replanting the parcels to ensure each grape varietal was suited to the different soil types around the estate, which allowed the vines time – over a decade – to regain their strength and vitality before we tried to harness their potential.

Like so much in nature, vineyards are a delicate ecosystem, at the mercy of their surroundings and the weather, and they need to be treated holistically in order to thrive. We work with every element of the land's flora and fauna to preserve its harmony and balance. In early spring, the estate is carpeted in a blanket of bright white when wild chamomile covers the corridors between the vines. The flowers are indigenous to the estate and not only are they a very beautiful sight but they help protect the soil from erosion and encourage pollinators to visit us. They also provide a food source for our sheep. We're very fond of the sheep and look forward to their arrival every year. They arrive as soon as the warmer days set in, roaming the estate, grazing amongst the vines, helping to control the weeds naturally and providing a source of fertilisation to nourish the soil. They're treasures to us in countless ways and an important part of the story that creates our wines.

We owe a great deal to Romain Ott, who joined us from the next door domaine to be our winemaker. His family has been producing exemplary Provençal wines for generations – we'd been drinking Ott wines long before we bought Léoube – and we met Romain's father when we arrived. He advised us and came to help us with the wines, before Romain joined us when he was just twenty-six. He's stayed with us for over twenty-five years and it is his expertise, his passion for his craft and his belief in our values that have allowed us to produce wines that are consistently recognised as excellent examples of their terroir.

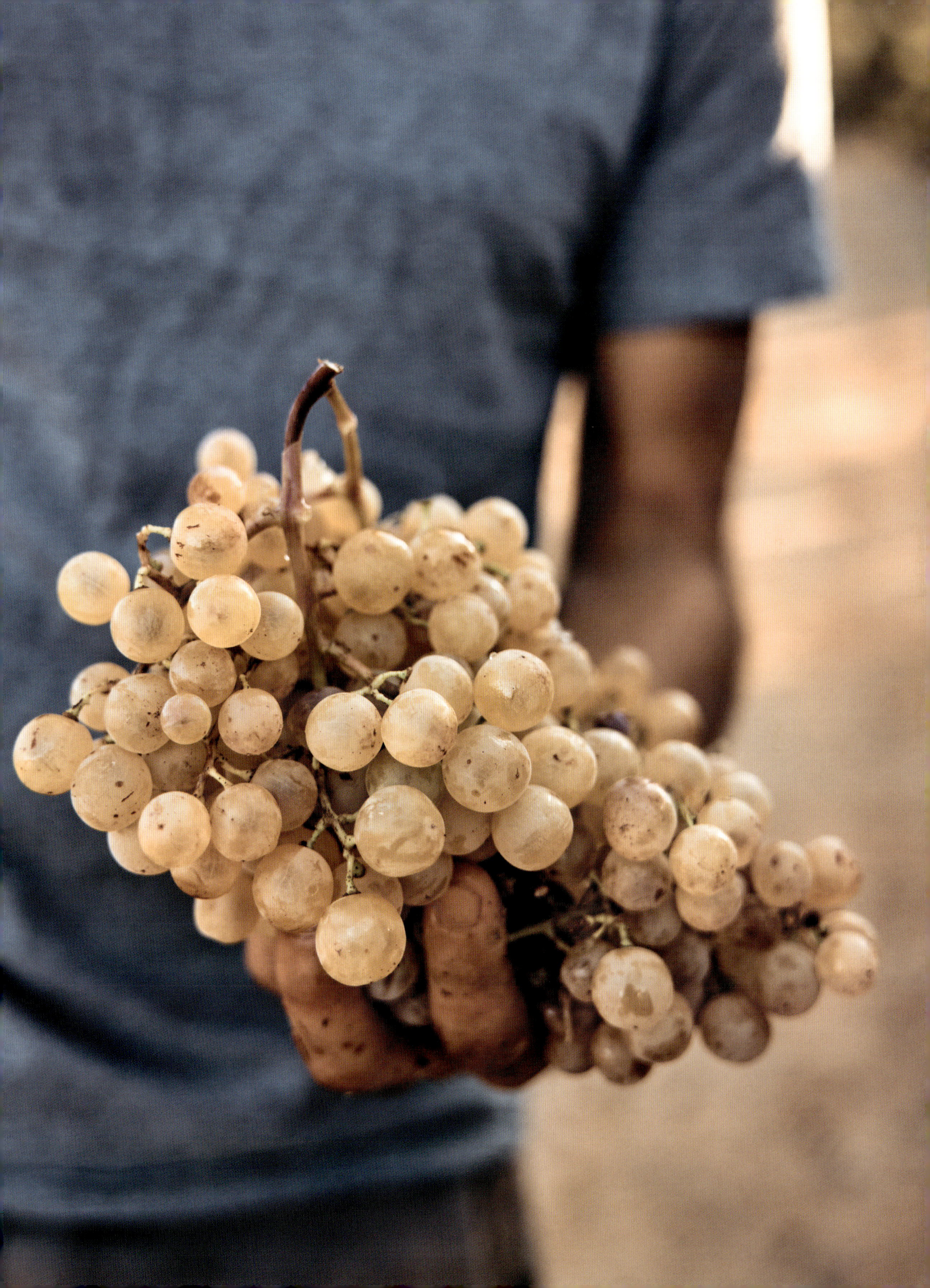

But we've also chosen to step outside the norms in this region, daring to take risks and do things differently by questioning the traditional methods and codes of winemaking in Provence. It was my husband Anthony who, inspired by the Super Tuscan wines, was the first person to plant Cabernet Franc grapes in the area. He realised that the latitude here was the same as that of the famous red wines from Tuscany and thought that we could try producing a full-bodied red with a similar profile to Chianti's revered wines by including a percentage of Cabernet Franc grapes in one of our red wines. Everybody around here was absolutely horrified by the idea of using grapes that weren't permitted by the *appellation*.

An *appellation* is a legally defined and protected geographical designation for wine that identifies where the grapes were grown and provides information about a wine's origin and characteristics. The appellation governs what vines you grow, where you grow them and how, and sometimes it even controls the flavour profile of the wine. You have to use whatever grape varietals the appellation recommends in order to be awarded its coveted AOC (*Appellation d'Origine Contrôlée*) classification of authenticity. Our appellation here is *Côtes de Provence* and Cabernet Franc grapes are not included in the list of varietals accepted by the appellation. There used to be a similar situation in Tuscany but in the 1960s and 1970s a group of Chianti winemakers decided to rebel and reject the rules of their appellation. Sassicaia from the Tenuta San Guido estate was the forerunner but there were others. They decided they would intentionally produce wines with non-indigenous and non-accepted grape varietals or blends to try and redress the falling status and quality of Chianti wines, but this meant that their wines were automatically given the lowest status classification – *vino da tavola* (table wine) – without the appellation's stamp of approval. What began as lowly table wines are now some of the most expensive and sought-after in the world.

While most of Léoube's wines have been granted the AOC certification, the red wine in our Collector range has followed a similar path to the Super Tuscans – we produce it using Cabernet Sauvignon and Cabernet Franc grapes. This means it hasn't been granted the Côtes de Provence appellation but it is nevertheless recognised as a *Grand Vin* and widely acknowledged to be a complex, elegant and beautiful wine.

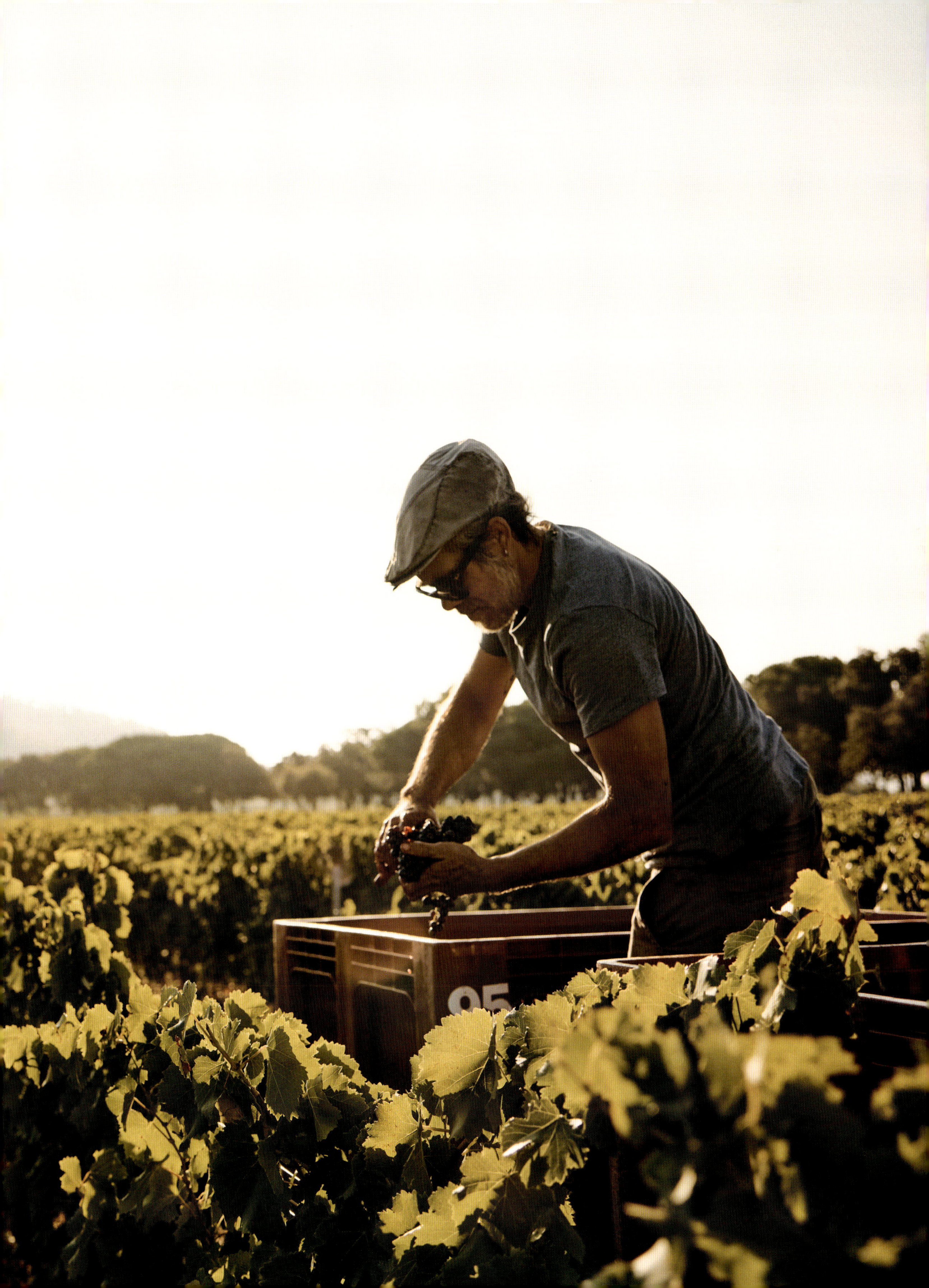

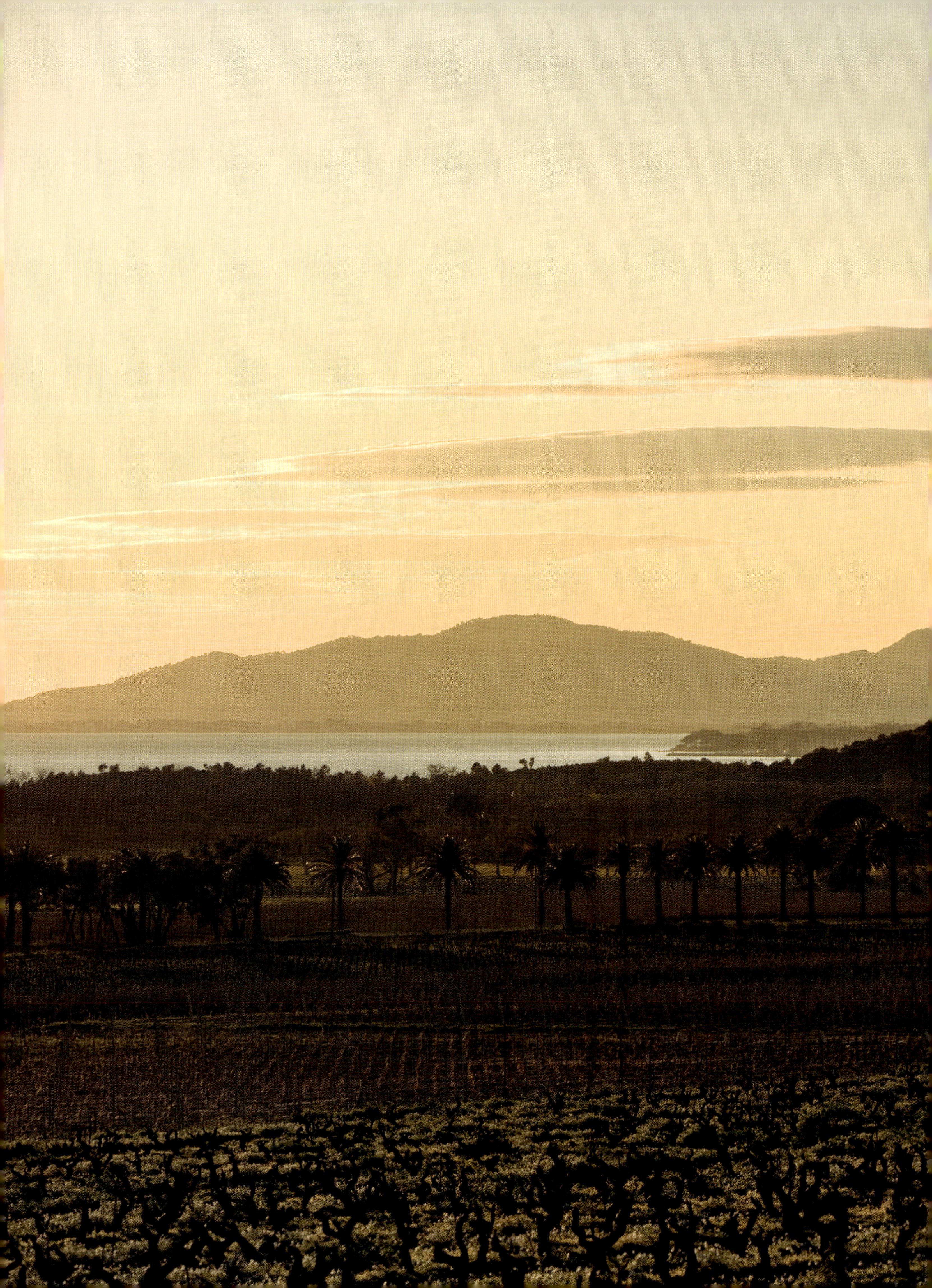

# THE VENDANGE

We believe in honouring the knowledge and skills of tradition in winemaking but not at the expense of innovation and progress. The trimming of the vines and the harvesting and sorting of the grapes are all carried out by hand, but we also draw on the capabilities of modern technology to ensure the utmost precision and consistency in the wines.

The annual grape and olive harvests – the *vendanges* – are very special times of the year. Around 50 pickers will arrive to help us harvest the grapes over three weeks, gathering around 30 tonnes of the ripe fruit each day. There's a group who return to visit us every year and we know them well now so there's a lovely sense of continuity and camaraderie to the process. The *vendange* will usually start around the third week in August, which means the heat can be suffocating. The pickers begin early, just as the sun is rising, so as to get as much harvested as possible before the most stifling temperatures of the day set in. Watching them as they move methodically along the rows of vines is mesmerising, their concentration infectious. They work fast. Baskets fill quickly as practised hands snip the bunches of ripe grapes with secateurs then toss them into the tractor's trailer. A sorter presides over the grapes that have been chosen, meticulously inspecting each bunch and discarding any damaged fruit. There's little noise – the occasional cheerful shout of somebody asking for a bottle of water or remarking on how much ground is left to cover – but really all you can hear is the throaty grumble of the tractor's engine as it paces along ahead of the pickers.

The grapes are then driven back up to the *chai* – the cellar – where they are carefully pressed immediately to extract their juice at its freshest. This is then left to ferment and mature slowly, allowing the flavours to develop fully before the wines are blended.

As with any artisan product, the wine changes year to year but our aim with Léoube's wines was to create balanced, elegant wines that were consistently true expressions of our terroir and we're very proud to have maintained that style year after year. The range ensures that there is a wine to cater for each taste. Sometimes you want a bottle that is easy to drink, refreshing and moreish; at other times you want something elegant to match your food. Above all, the wines are full of character and a perfect accompaniment to the Provençal sunshine.

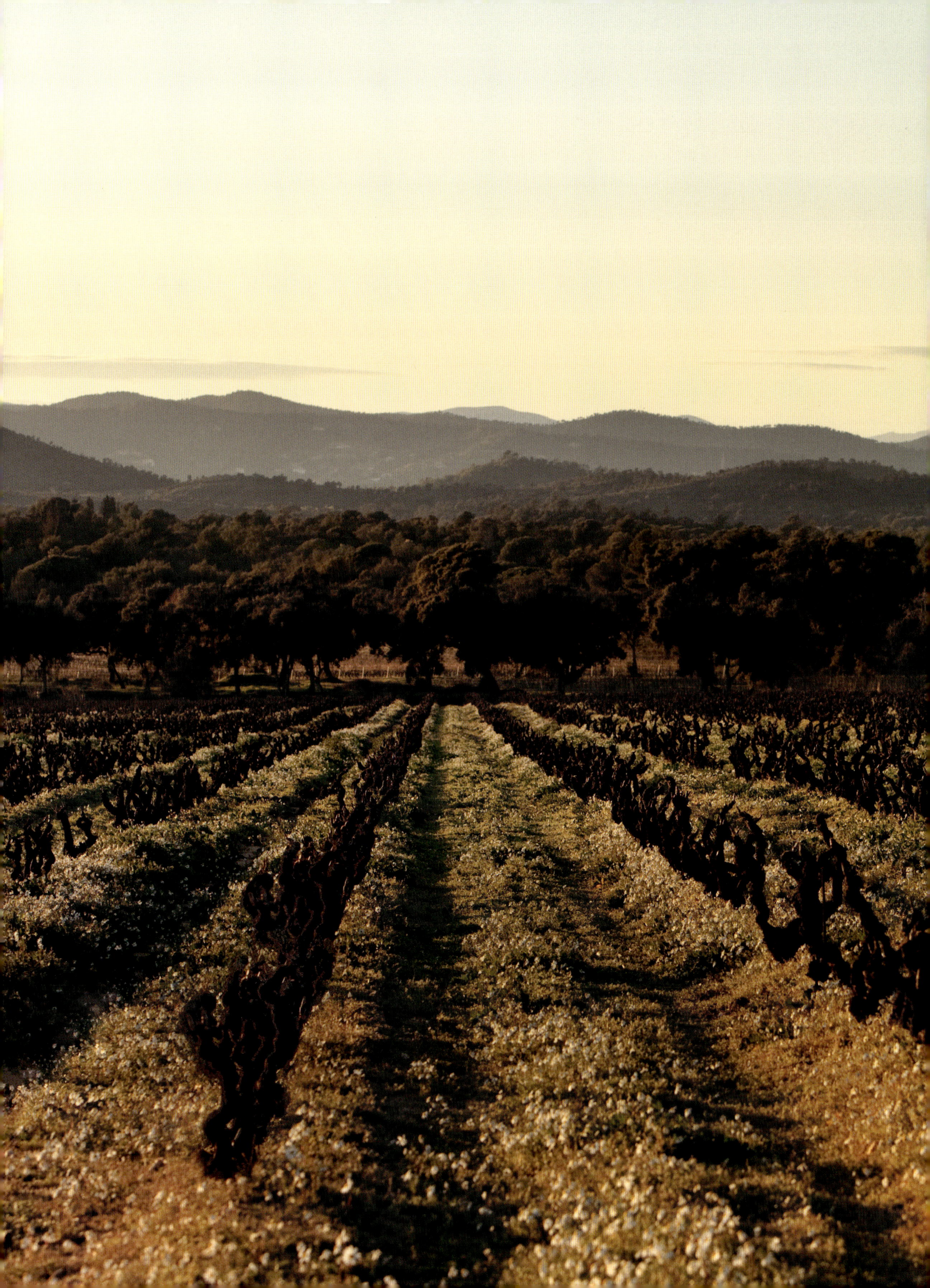

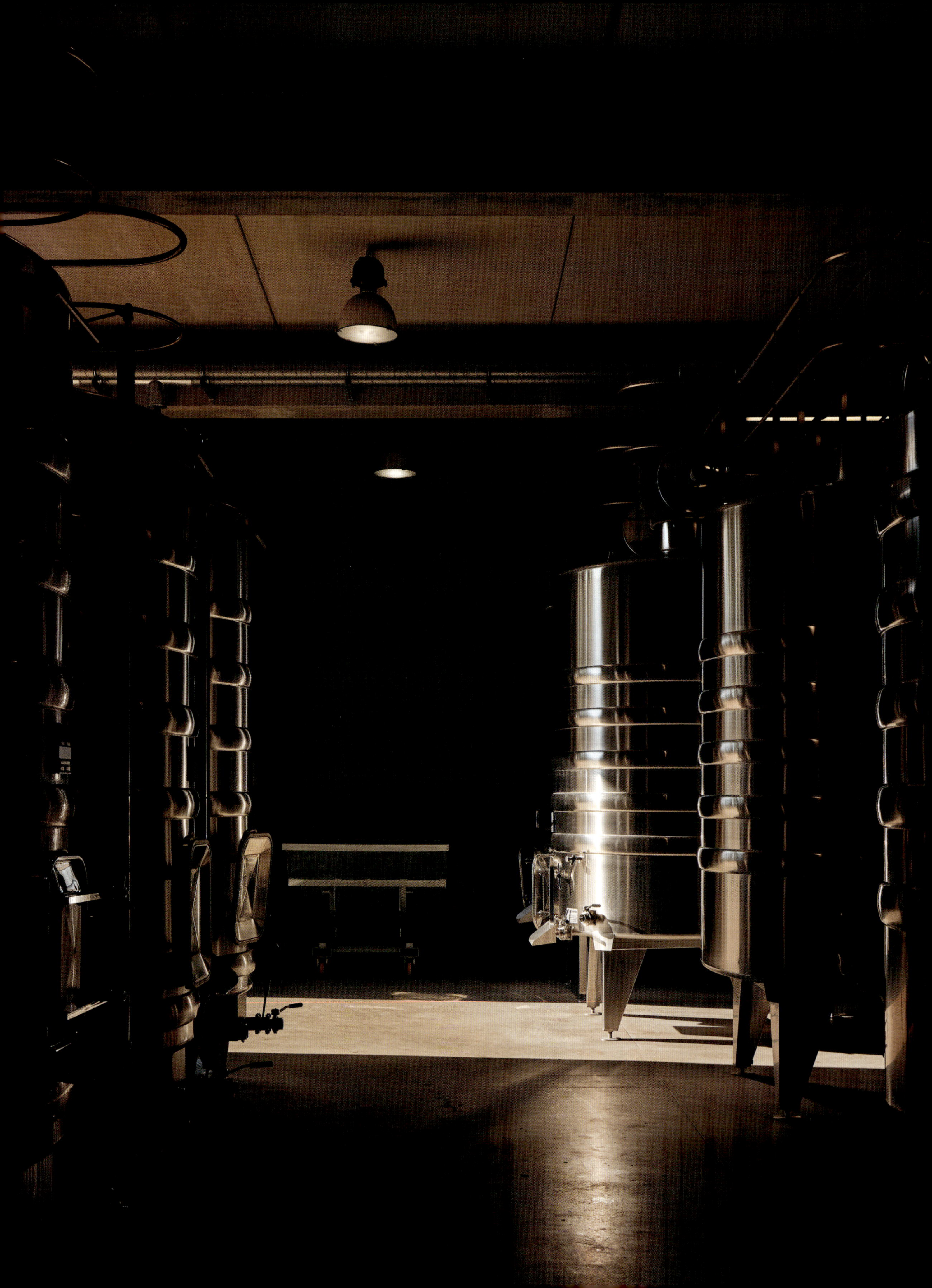

OPPOSITE We ferment the wine in in temperature-controlled stainless-steel tanks for alcoholic fermentation. After fermentation, the clarification cycle begins, to produce wines ready to be bottled in the spring following harvest.
ABOVE Being sustainable – following nature's cycles and reaping what the land gives us – is instinctive to Romain Ott, our winemaker, who has been with us for over 25 years.

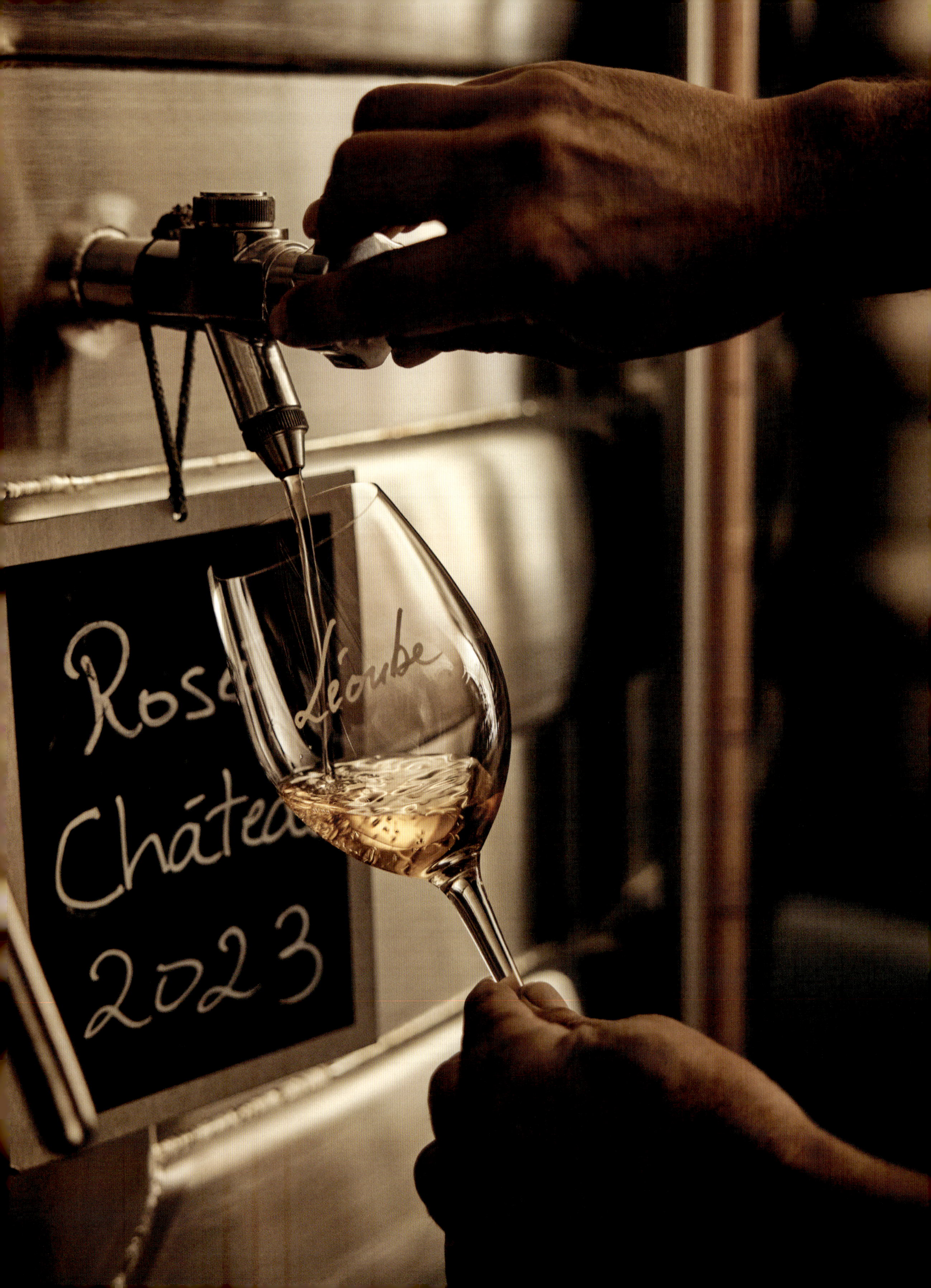
Léoube
2023

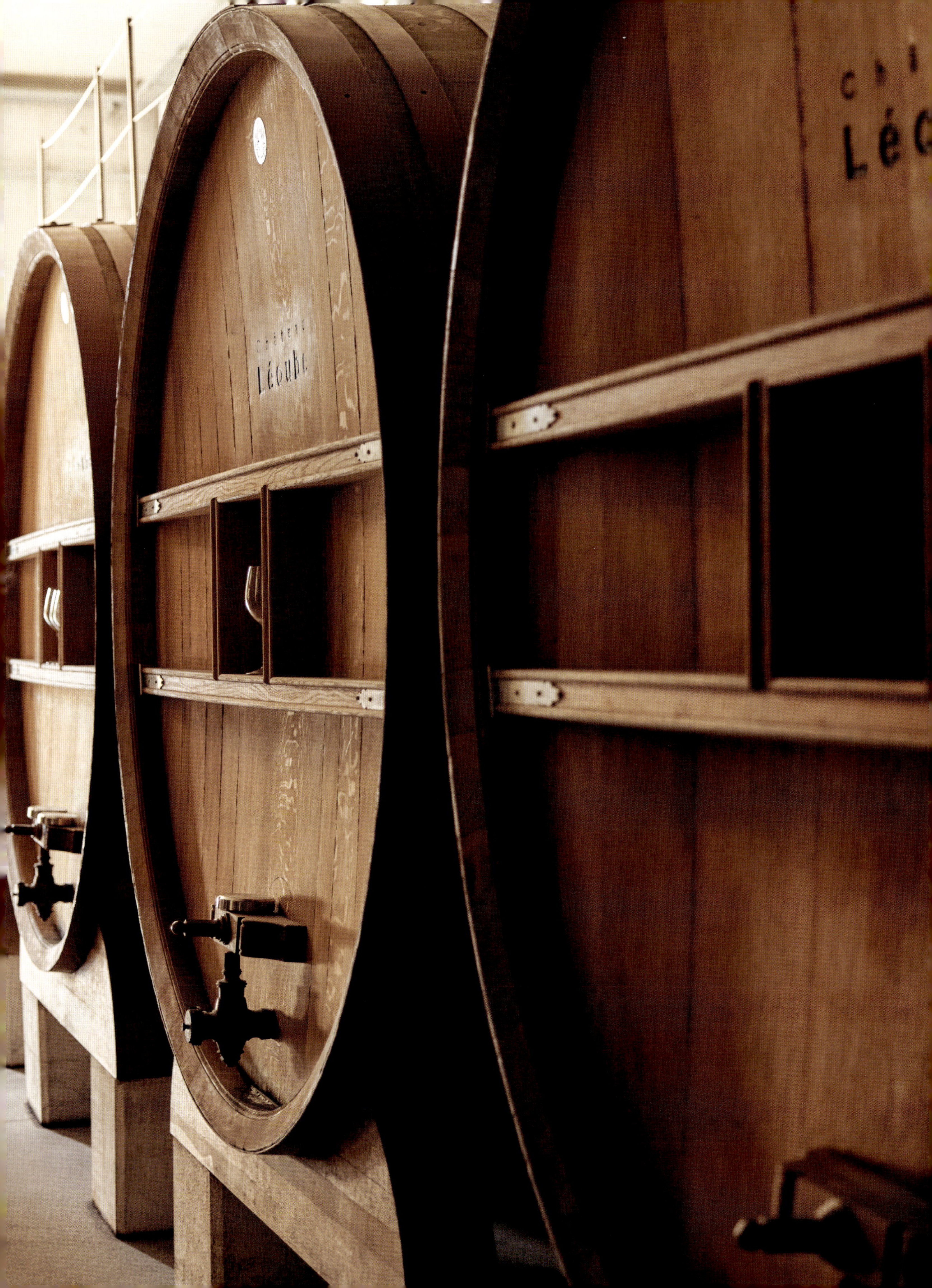

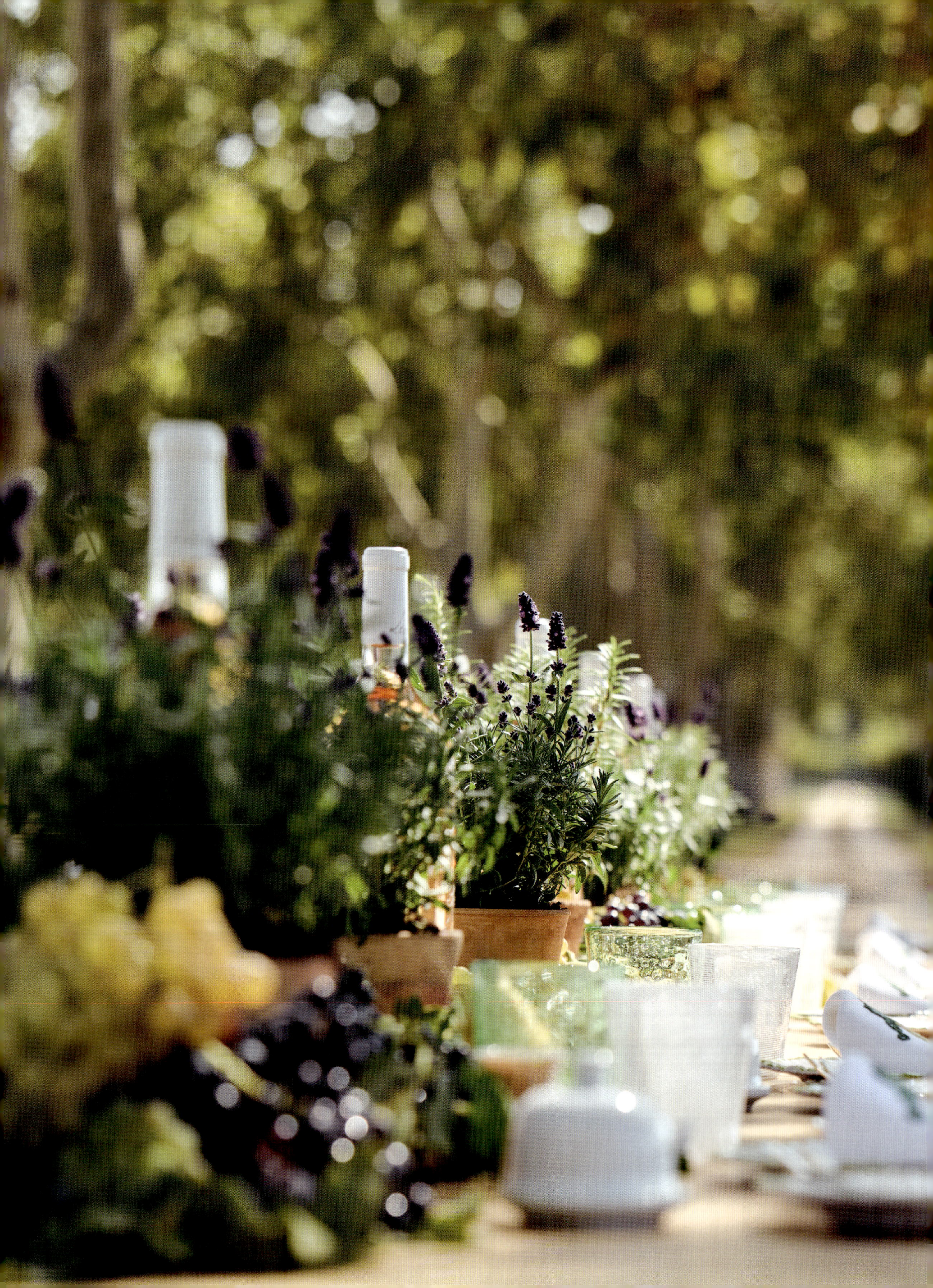

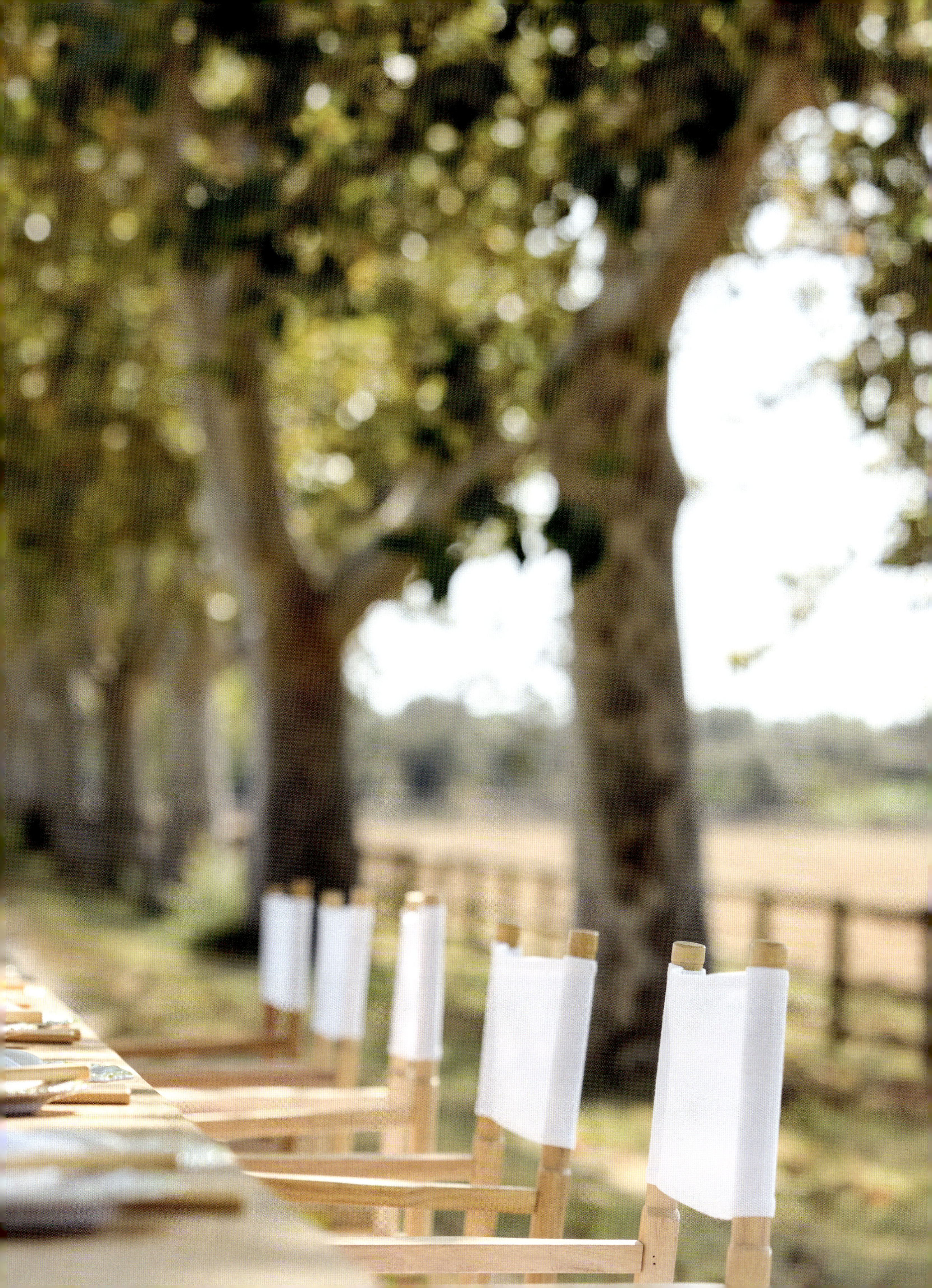

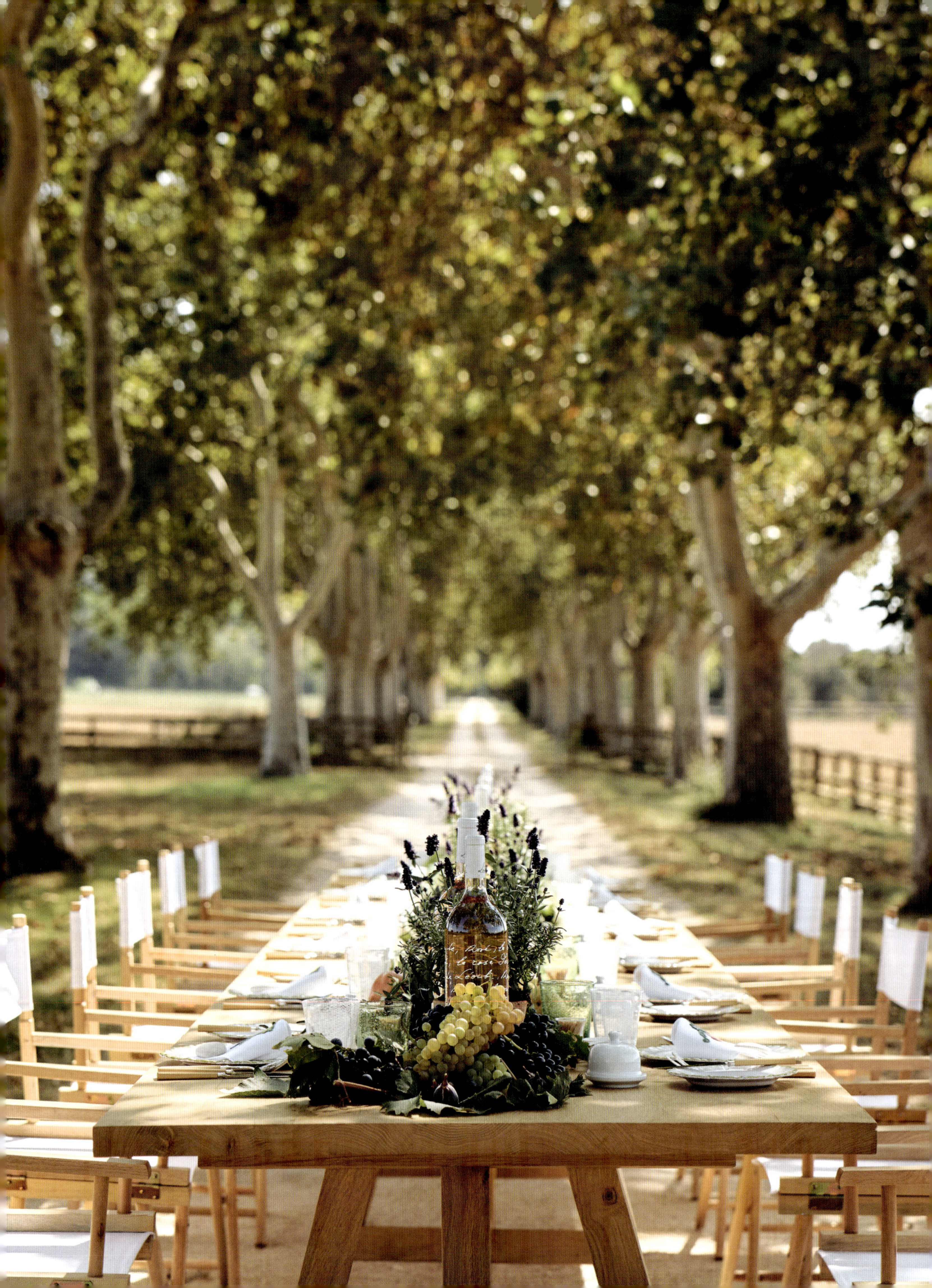

THE VINEYARD AND OLIVE GROVE

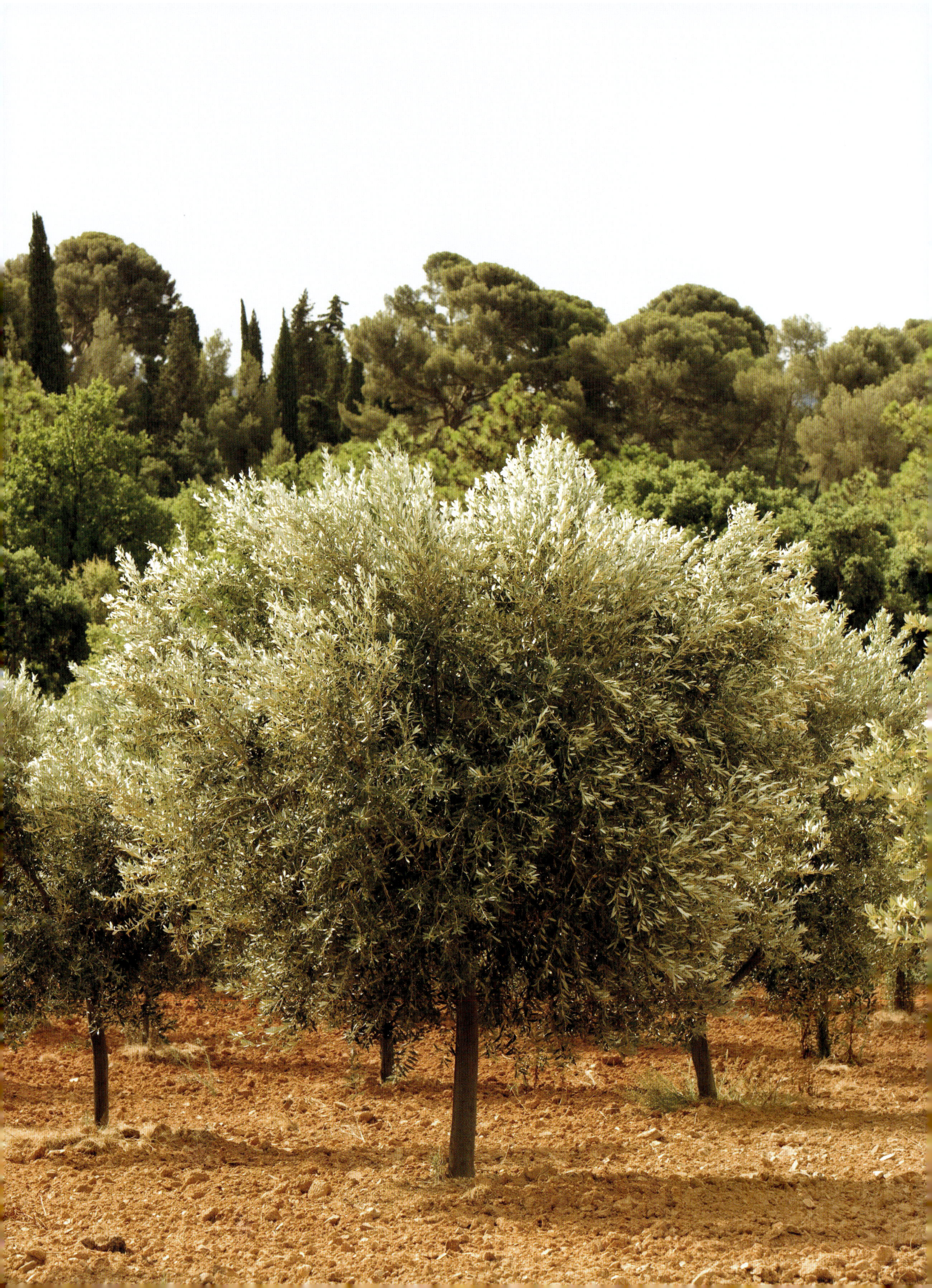

# THE OLIVE GROVE

A few years after arriving at Léoube, we decided to start producing olive oil too. We laid down 5,000 olive trees, a blend of 25 different Provençal and Italian varieties. Our aim is to produce oils that are rich and densely flavoured, designed to be cooked with or used raw to accompany and enrich the local cuisine. Romain does this by keeping the extracted oil from each variety separate before tasting and assessing the flavours of each one, then blending them to create the final olive oil. It's a meticulous process that ensures we can sustain the quality and bring out the best of the harvest each year. We now have two different kinds of olive oil, both beautiful, fragrant, pale liquids that are carefully balanced – one fruity, nutty and rich, the other more delicate and leaning on herbaceous notes.

Like the grapes, the olives are handled very delicately and carefully to harness their flavours. We harvest using nets and gently vibrating tongs before washing them in natural spring water. The production is quite small as we only press oil from what we grow and one year we couldn't produce any at all. The trees were infected by a bug and there was nothing we could do – the year's bounty was lost. That's just part of being artisan – you're at the mercy of what nature chooses to throw at you. But it makes the oil even more special when you do get that first taste of the freshly pressed nectar.

OPPOSITE Léoube has more than 20 hectares of olive groves that benefit from the same unique terroir as its wines. We grow 25 varietals of olive, chosen to produce extra virgin olive oils that are smooth and rich in flavour.

Bour Laoube

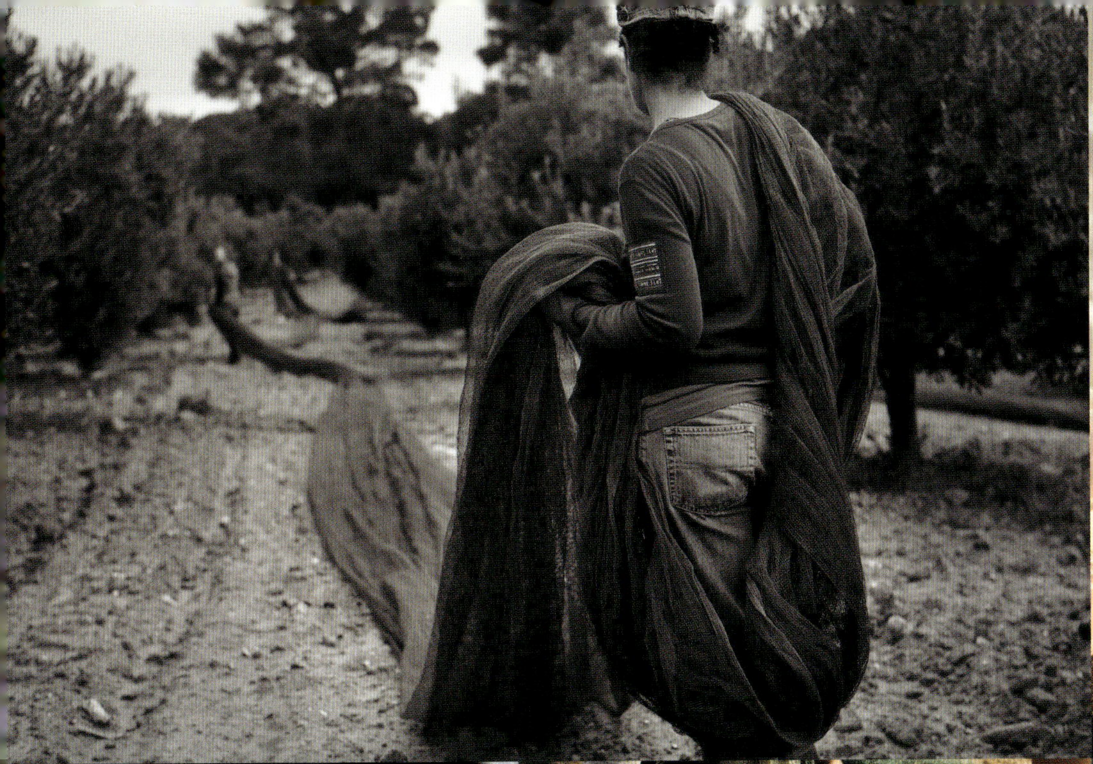
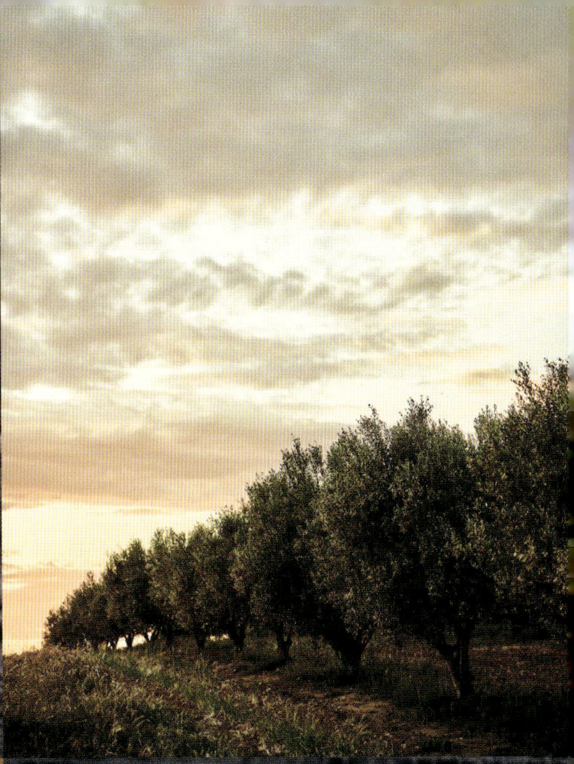
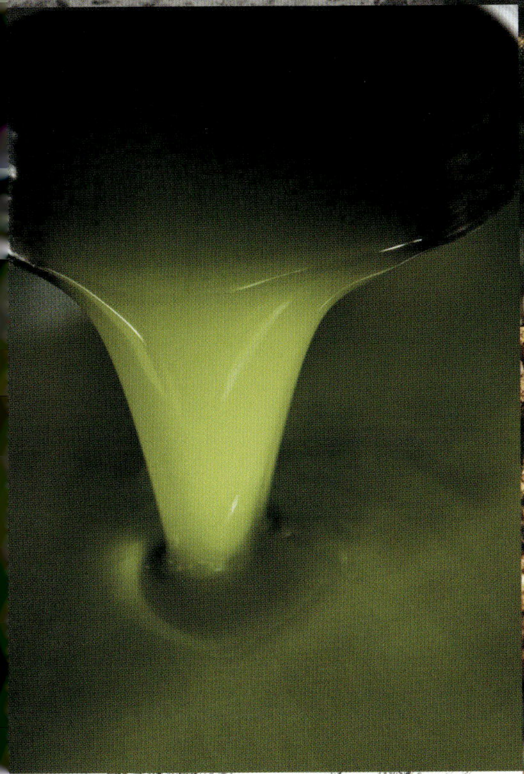
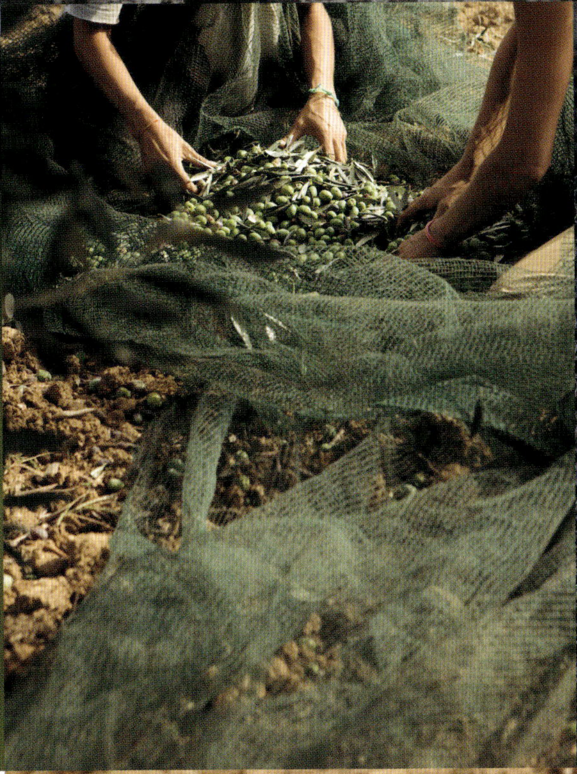
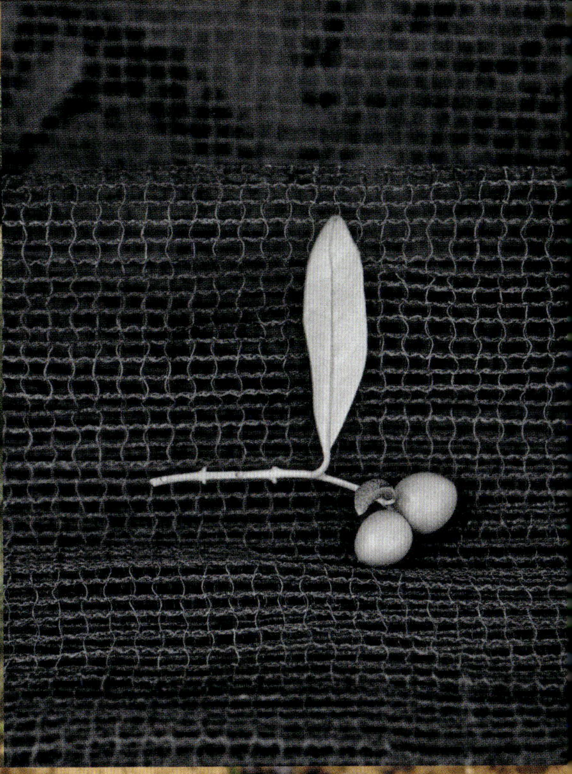
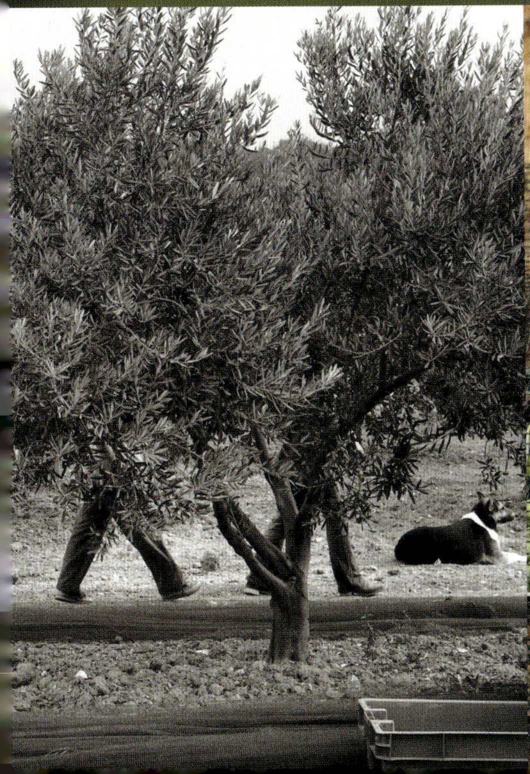
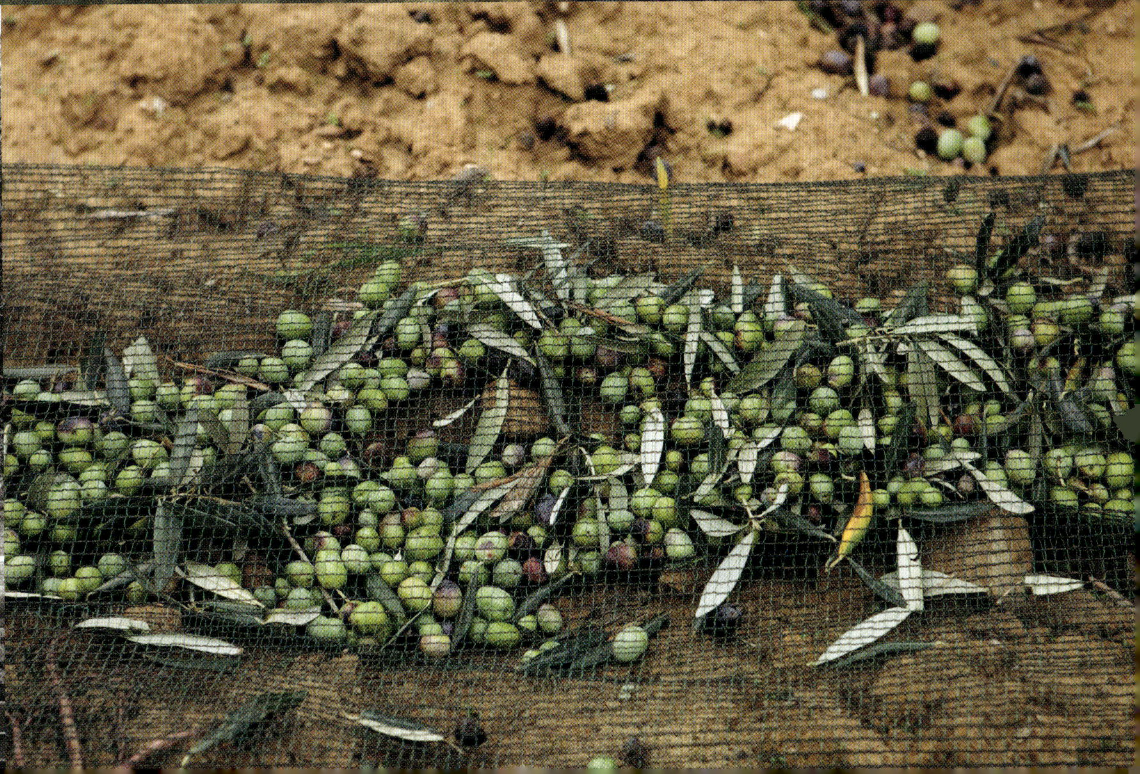

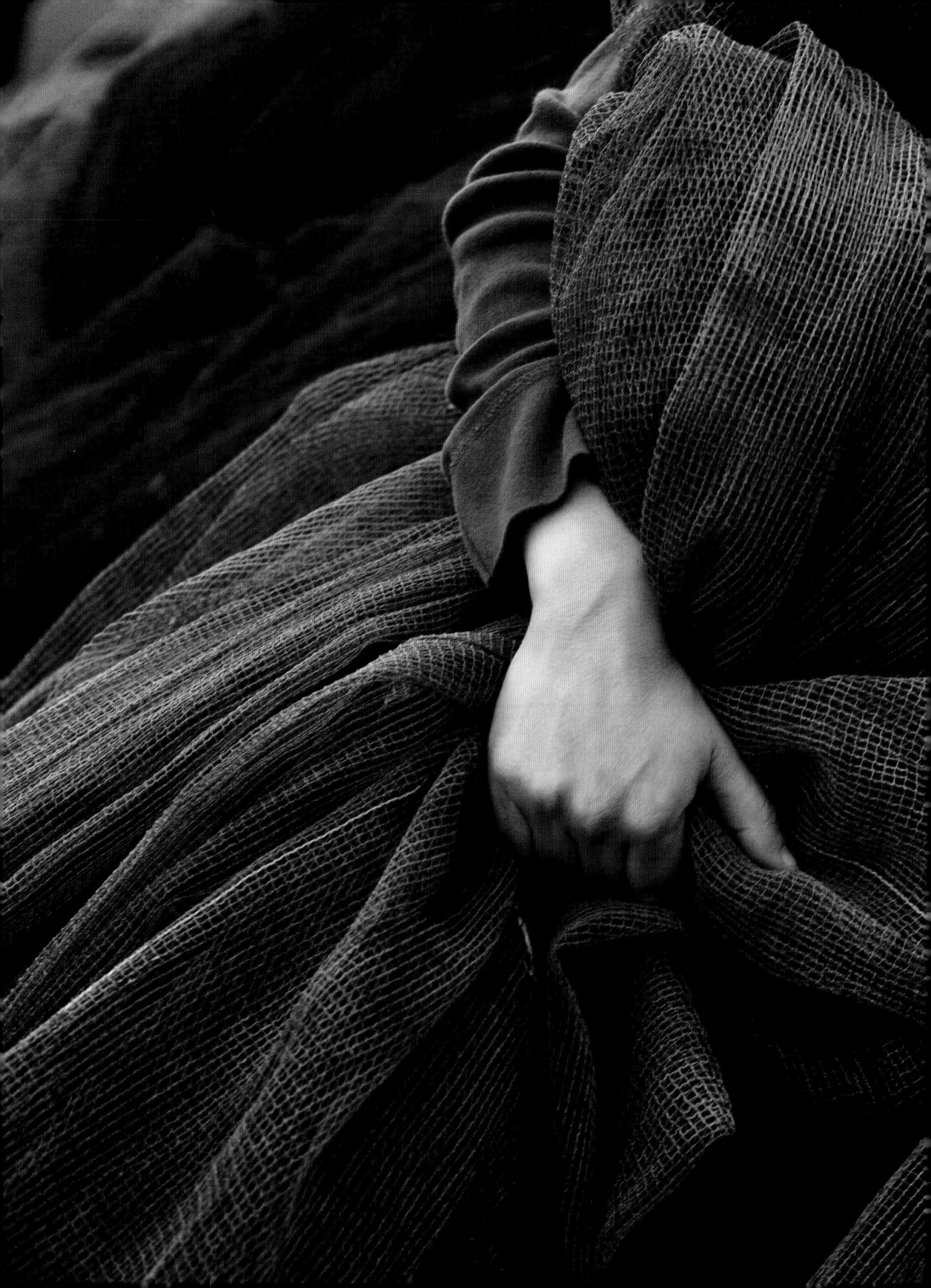

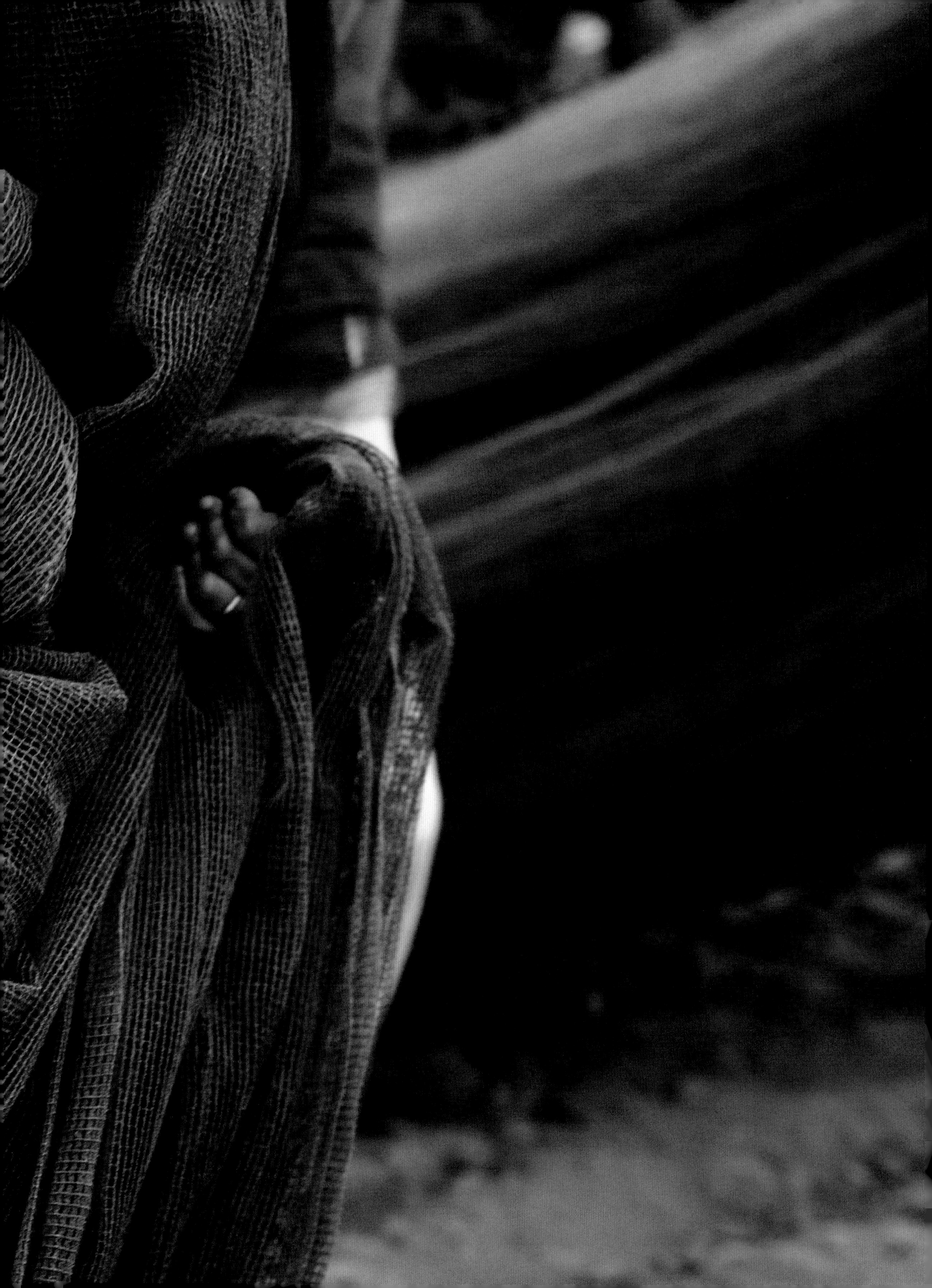

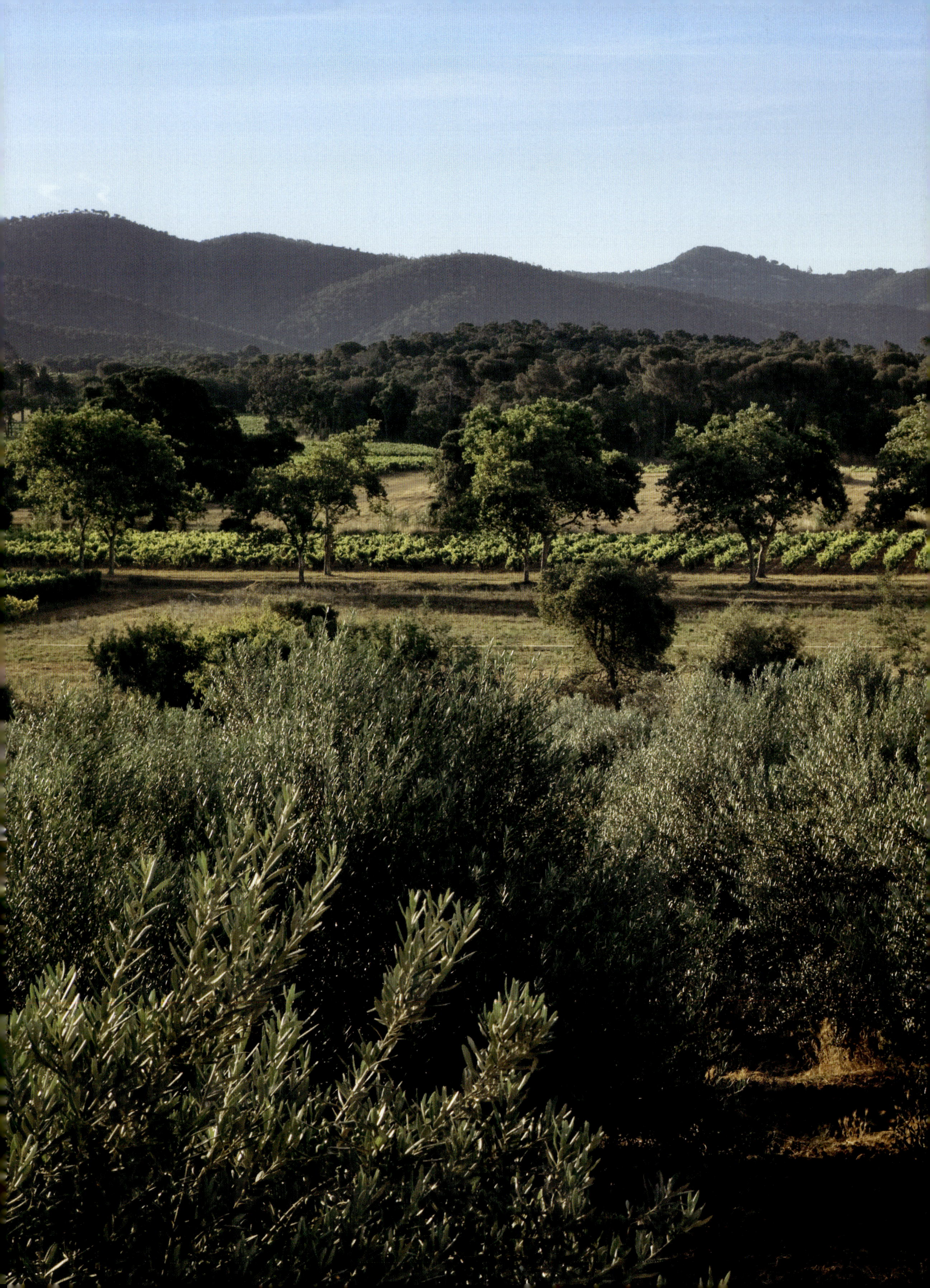

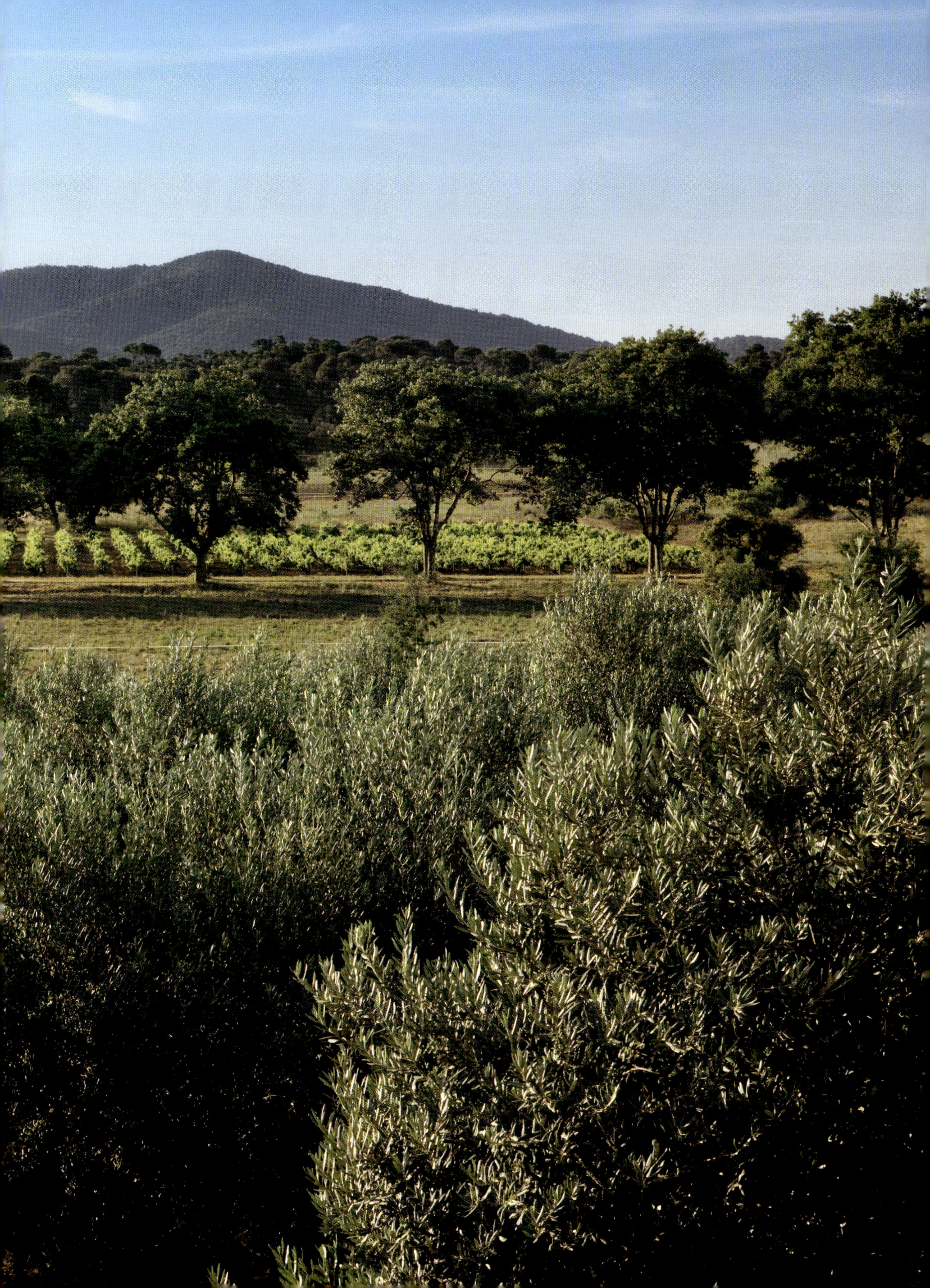

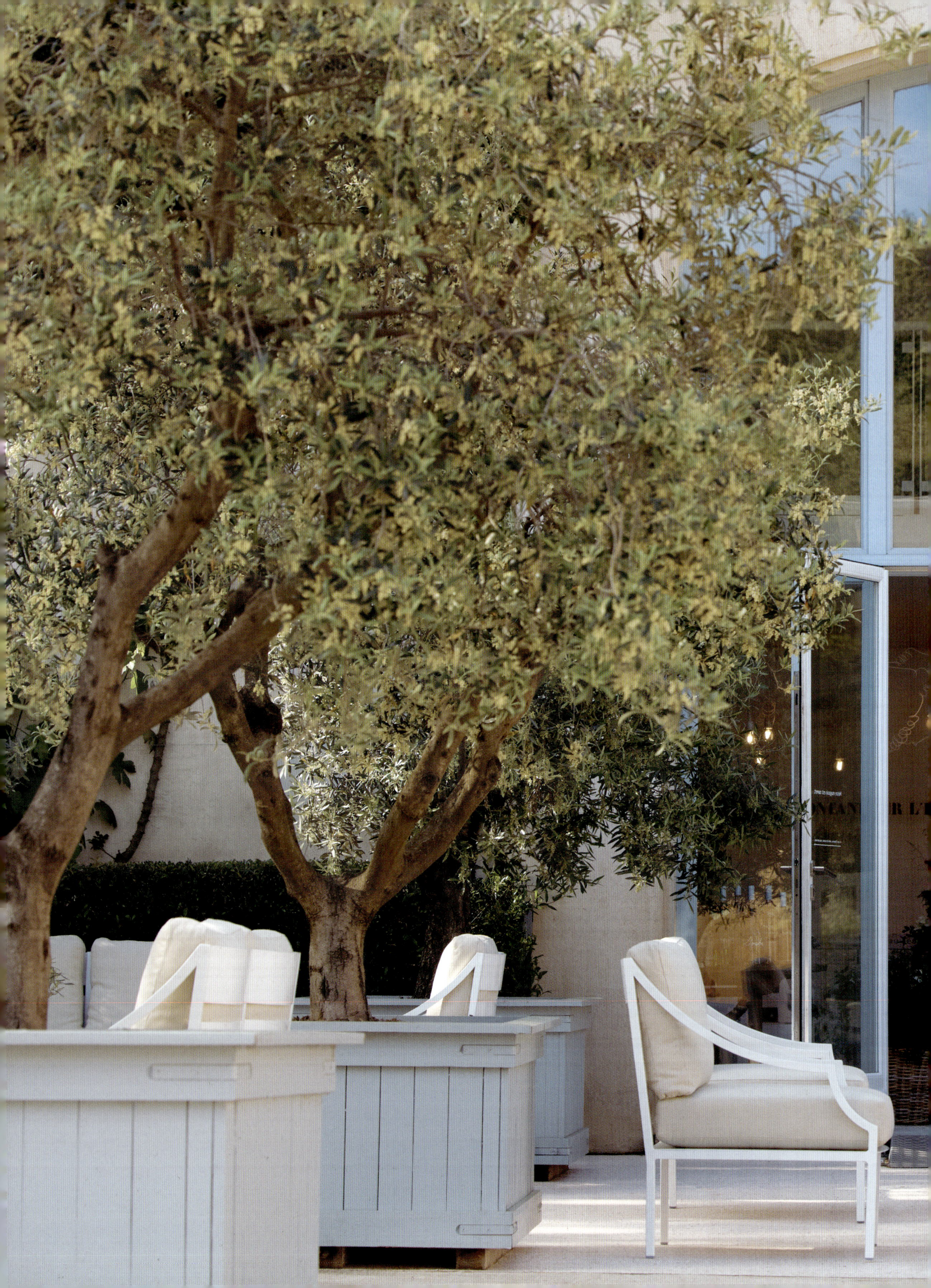

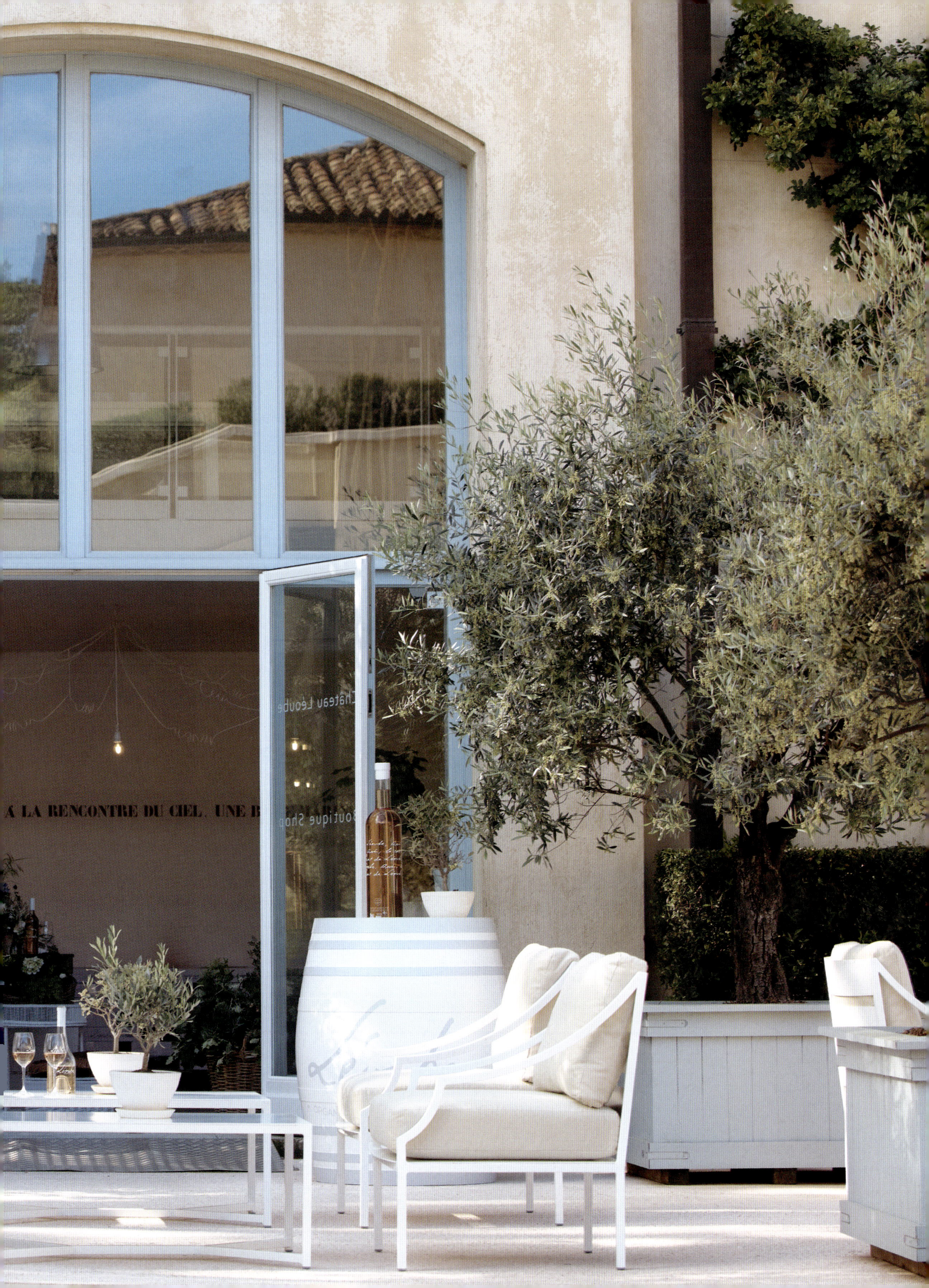
A LA RENCONTRE DU CIEL. UNE

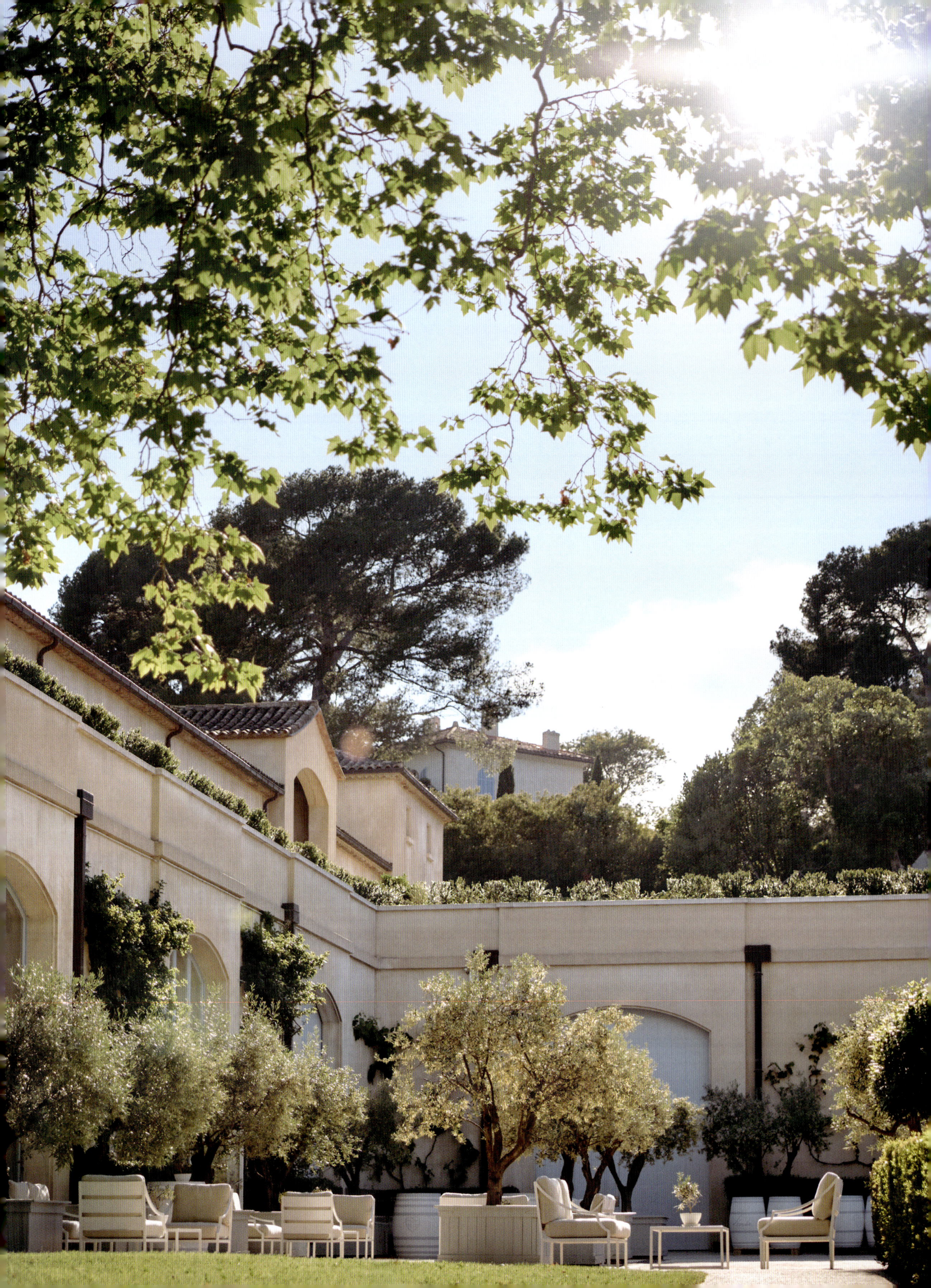

OPPOSITE AND PREVIOUS PAGE The boutique allows us to engage with our visitors and share the essence and spirit of the vineyard. ABOVE The Collector Rosé is part of a limited-edition collection of wines. It is a sophisticated wine that showcases the ageing potential of rosé and will offer further complexity and depth over time.

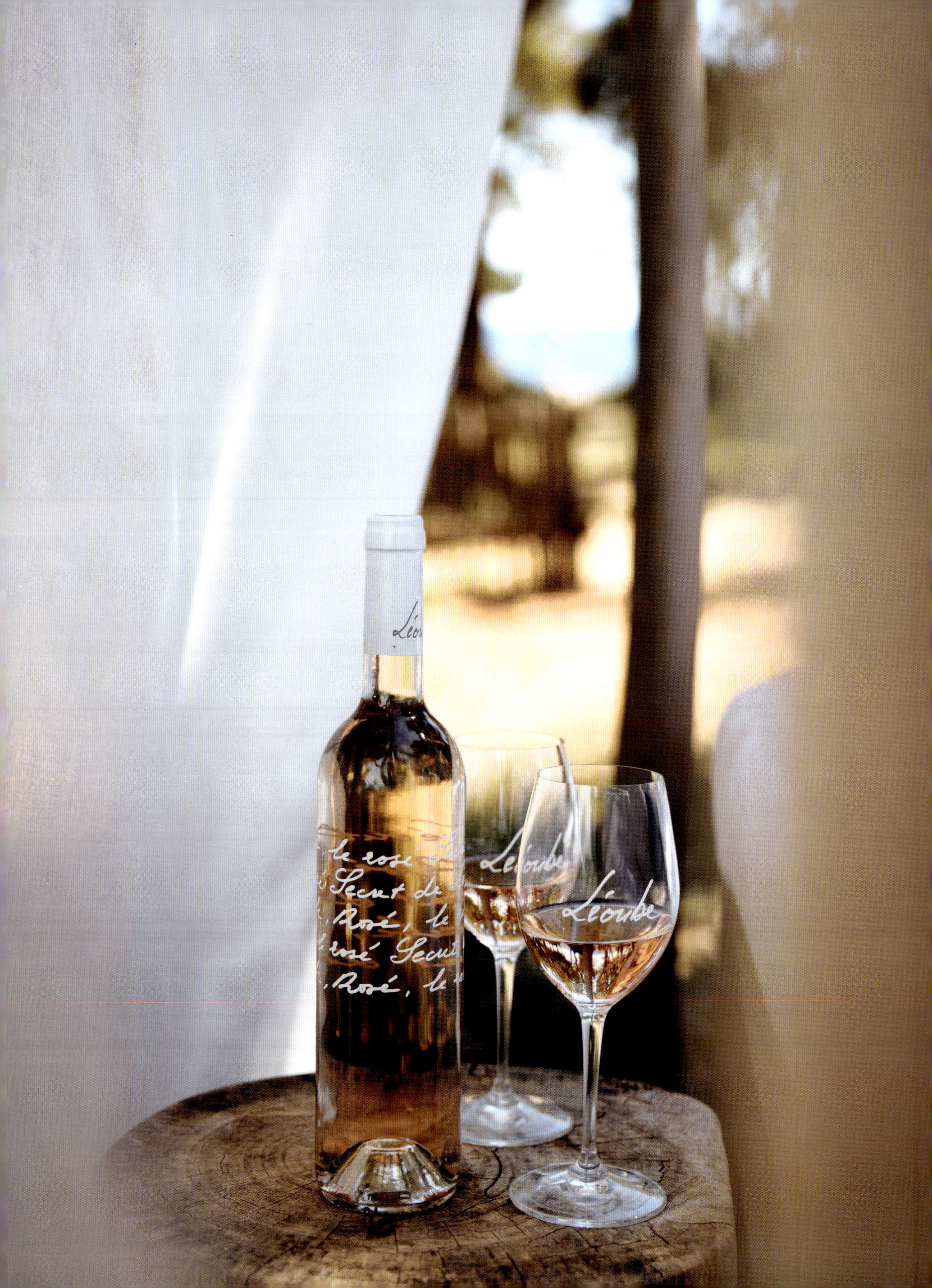
Léoube
Léoube

# THE BOUTIQUE DU CHAI

I wanted the boutique at the domaine to be more than just a shop. A vineyard is not only about cultivation and production: it is about celebrating craftsmanship and – most importantly – the joy of getting people together to share a bottle of beautifully crafted wine. The shop is our portal, allowing us to connect with those who visit us and share the essence of the vineyard. Having a place where guests can taste our wines, learn about our philosophy and engage in conversation lets us share the story behind what we do. I think it helps enhance the experience and deepens the appreciation of drinking our wines, transforming bottles from simply a product that's plucked from a shelf to one that has a meaning which reflects our commitment to the land and the dedication that goes into making every bottle.

The boutique provides an opportunity for us to explain about the design of the labels on our wine bottles because many visitors are quite surprised by them. They certainly caused quite a stir when I first unveiled them because in France, it's traditional to use a very classical style of labelling with an image of the estate's château, communicating a sense of the heritage, history and continuity of the domaine. But I wanted our labels to feel fresh and modern – to stand out.

OPPOSITE The Secret Rosé is one of Léoube's most popular wines: elegant and rounded. The unexpected design of the bottle always sparks conversation and curiosity.

The labels were designed by Jacqueline Morabito, who would also later help me with the vision for the boutique and the café, and I instantly loved her concept of the cursive handwriting but above all the idea of doing something different: elegant, eye-catching, minimalist and – hopefully – intriguing. I like the fact that the labels get people talking. It's in my nature to appreciate the unexpected – I love to have my own expectations challenged and be continuously surprised by life's eccentricities and so I think there's a part of me that enjoys doing the same for others. Life would be very boring if we all conformed always. And, despite many people's reservations, Léoube's label designs have proved that straying from the norm can invite success.

It's nearly 30 years since we bought Château Léoube and yet every time I return I am struck by an overwhelming feeling that it is a very special place. I'm not sure I've arrived at a definitive answer as to why or how but what I've come to realise is that it is not simply the beauty of the landscape or its tangible connection to nature but the way it brings people together – to share, to savour and, above all, to slow down. Whether it's an afternoon spent with your toes in the sand and a glass of rosé, a film watched under the stars, or the pleasure of lingering over a meal with the scent of pine, lavender and sea salt in the air, time spent here is an invitation to embrace a slower, more intentional way of life. It is a life attuned to nature, to craftsmanship, to simple yet profound joys. It's a place that, once visited, never leaves you.

OPPOSITE Alongside the boutique, all the wines can be tried at the café and a lounge area by the beach where these white linens are hung from branches to resemble sails billowing in the breeze.

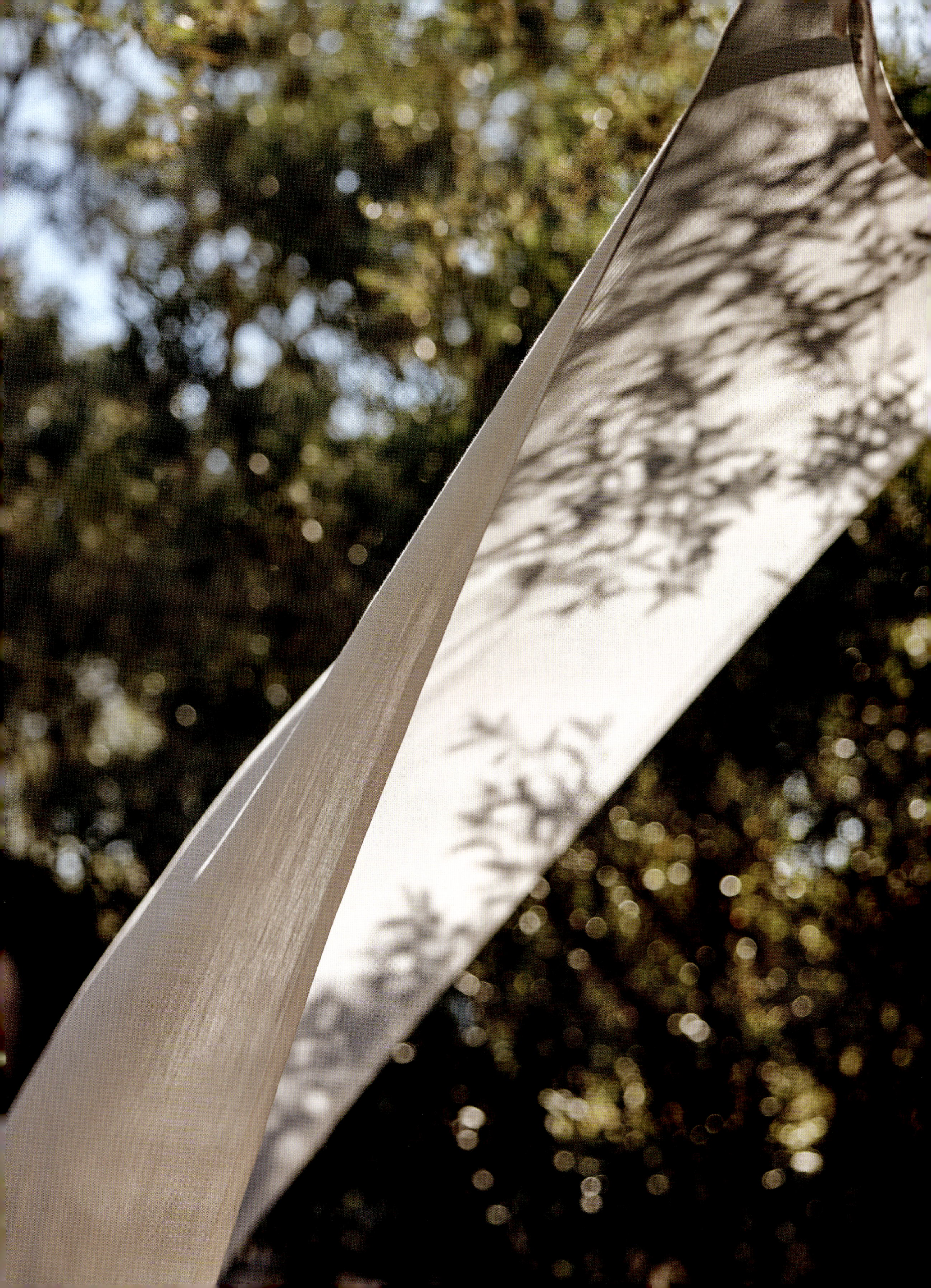

OPPOSITE Our tasting room, fondly known as the '*poulailler*', meaning 'henhouse' is a charming space next to the boutique where we invite guests to discover the flavours of our wines.

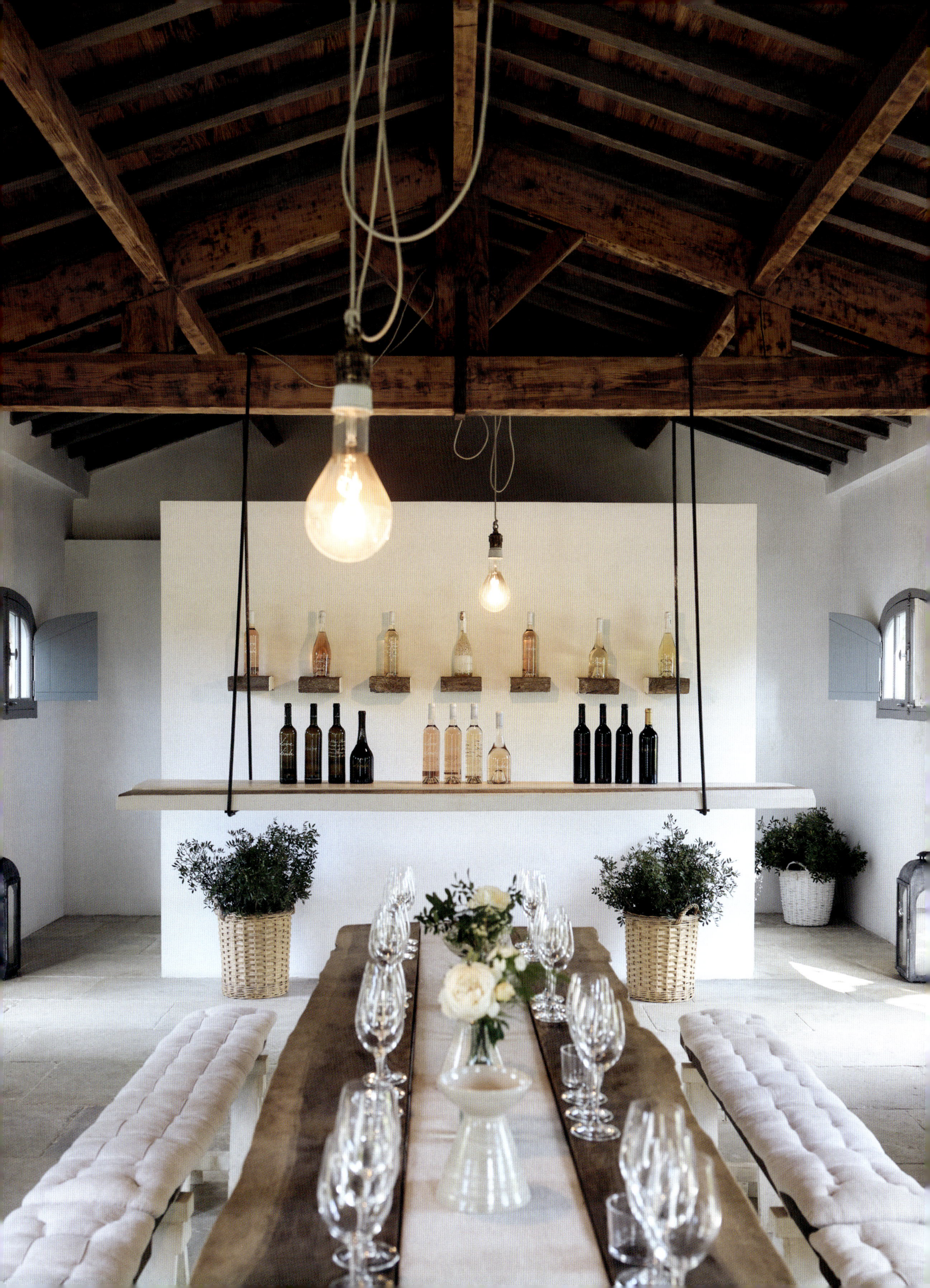

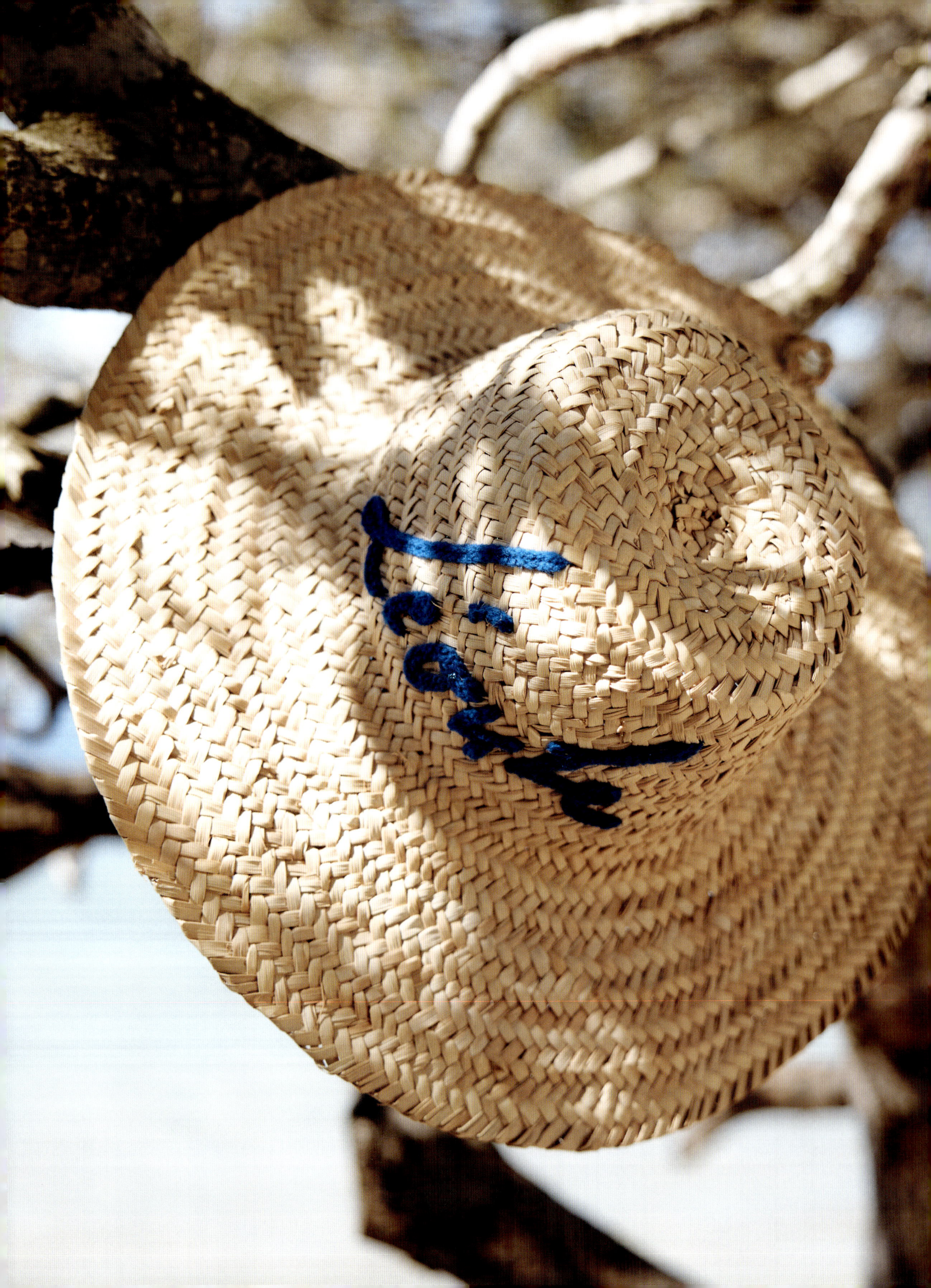

# THE BEACH

AND CAFÉ

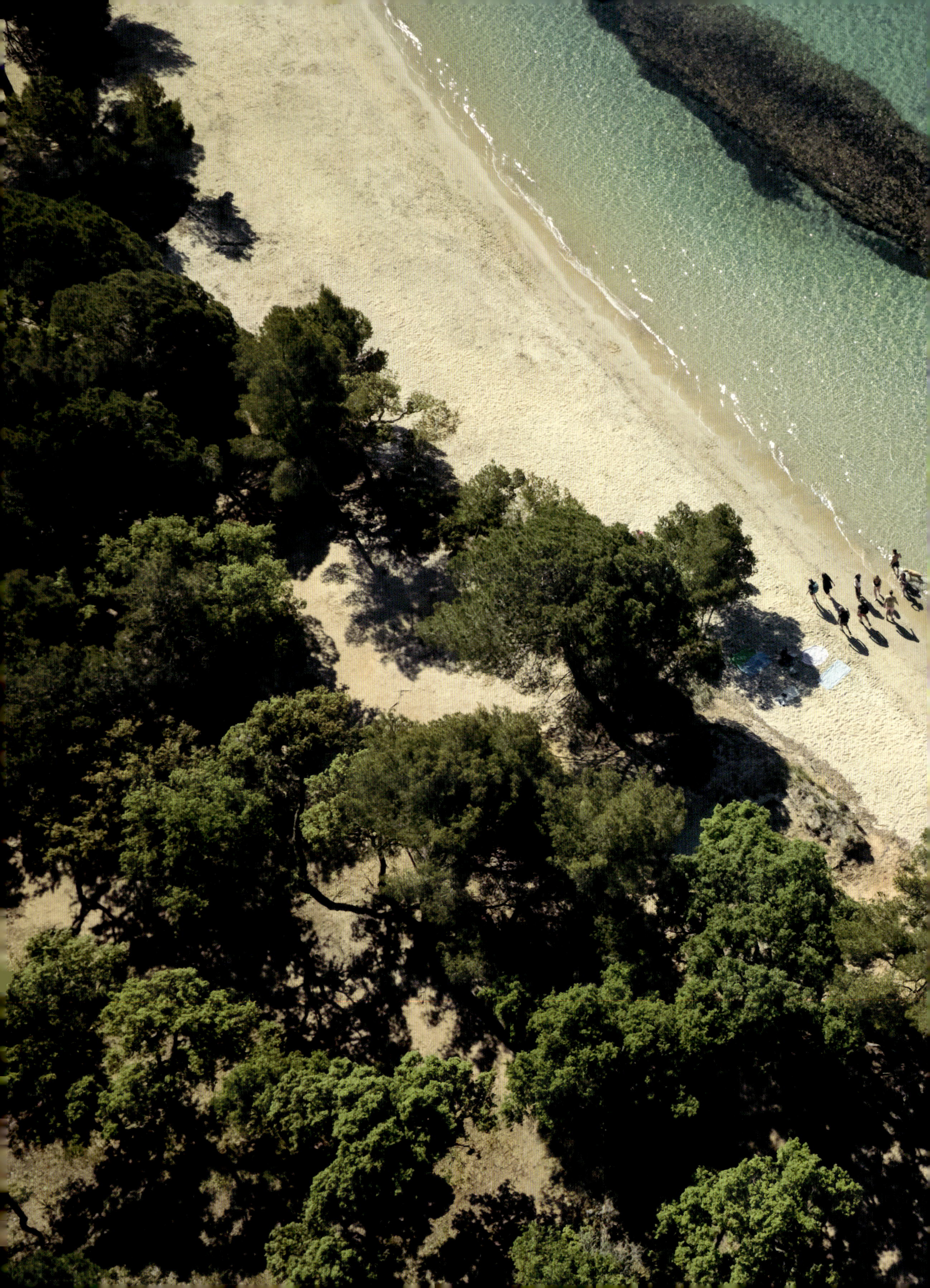

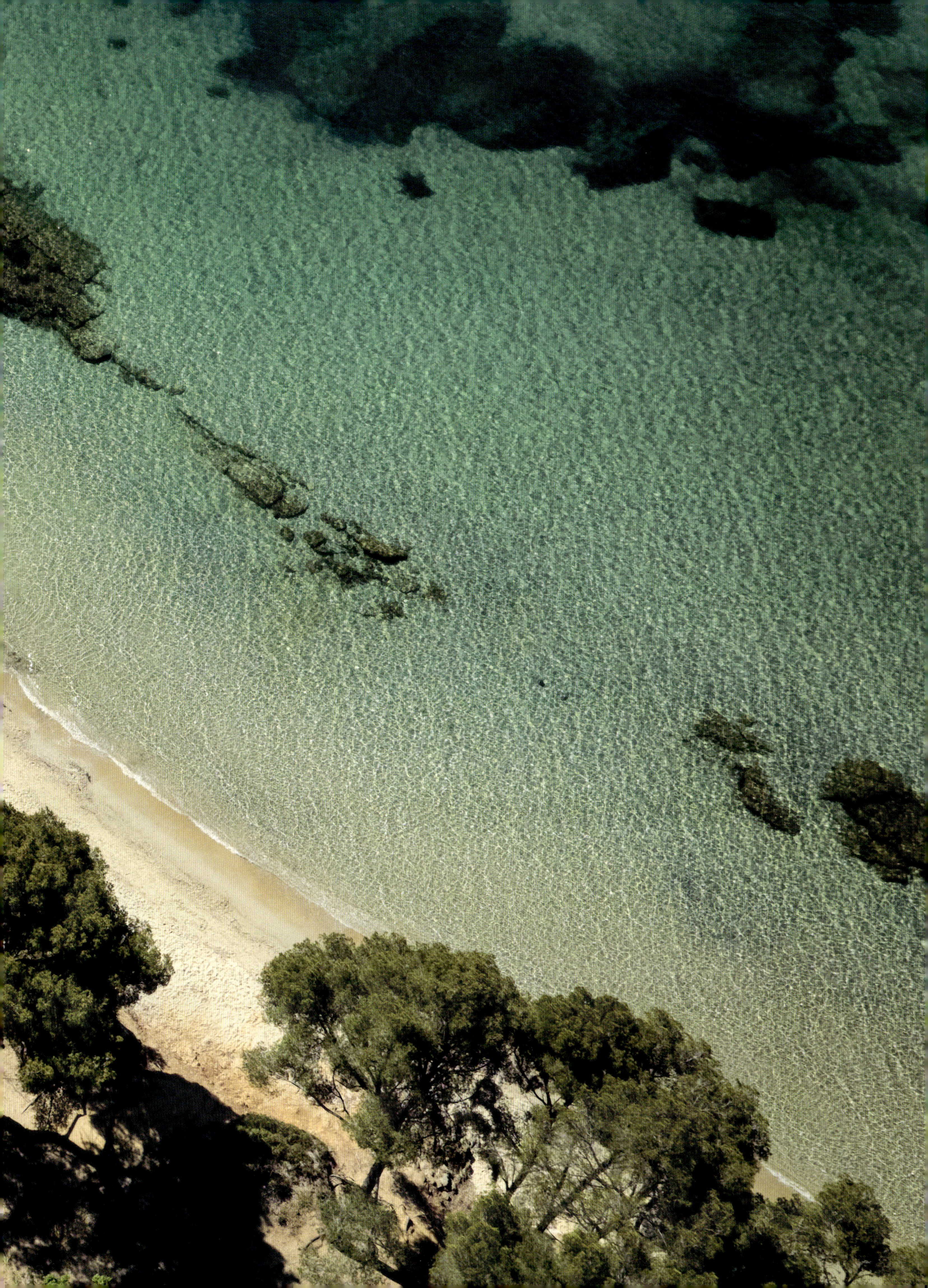

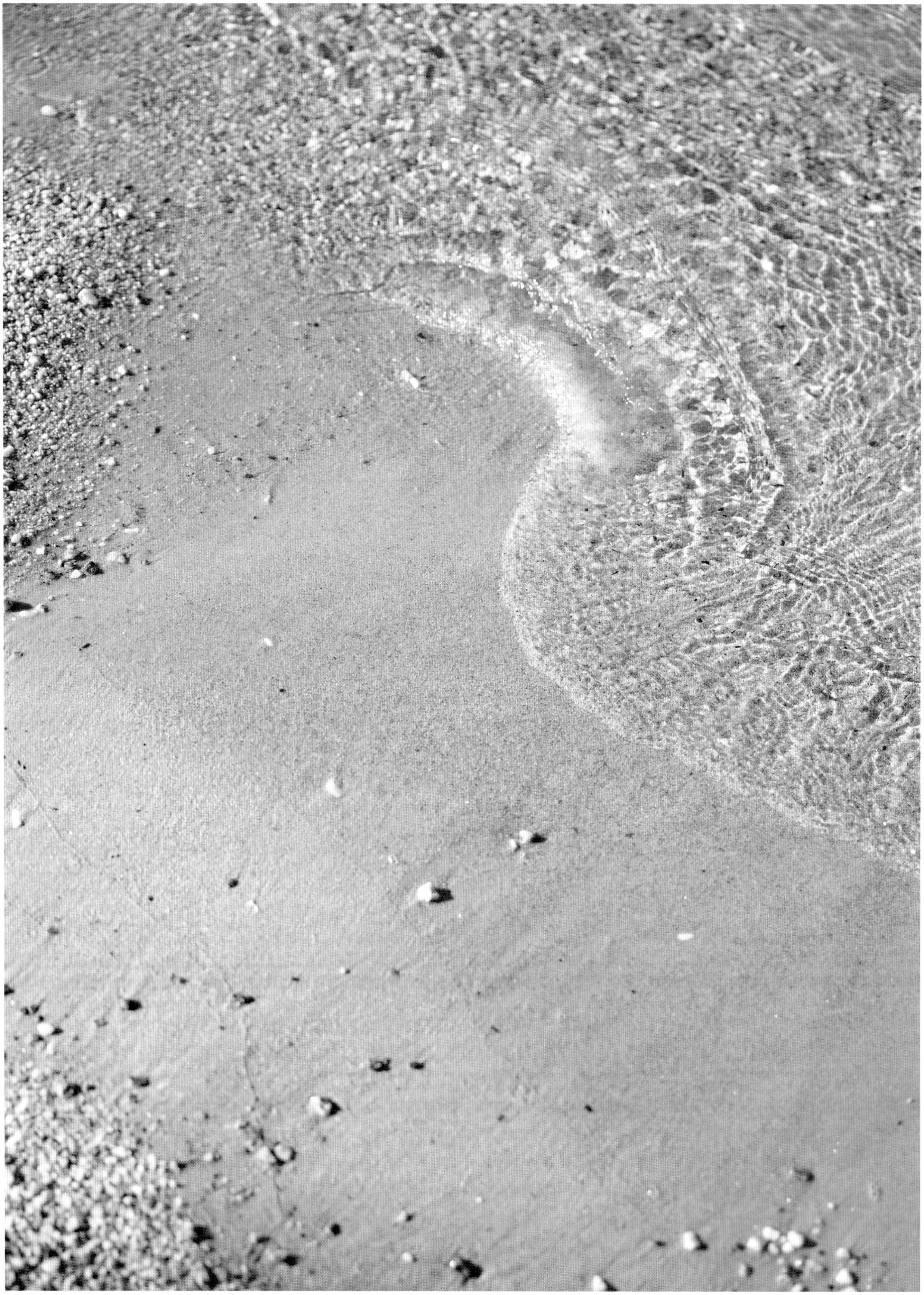

As you drive along the main road to Léoube from Brégançon, you pass a sign to the château and its boutique and a little further on is a turning off to the left. The road winds its way through an olive grove, its gnarled trunks lined up in orderly rows, the silvery-green leaves catching the sunlight. Eventually the road becomes a sandy track before you pull into a car park. Glimpses of bright turquoise break through the canopy of pine trees that borders the sand, welcoming you to what I truly believe is one of the most beautiful places on the Côte d'Azur.

In fact, while I might be considered biased, I've yet to experience a beach in Europe to rival the untainted wild beauty of the *Plage du Pellegrin*. The beach is part of a protected area, which means that its precious natural resources – nearly a kilometre of honeyed golden sand, crystal-clear warm waters and ancient pines – have been preserved. It's tucked inside a small cove and because it's away from the hustle and bustle of Saint Tropez, Nice and Cannes, it doesn't draw their large crowds and remains quiet, calm and secluded.

When we bought the house, there was a little café by the beach and we thought we could carry on the previous owner's tradition and keep it. Ours started out very small too – we were simply serving filled baguettes alongside our wines, but as time went on we felt we could do a little more with the space. There's so much shelter under the trees, which provide much needed respite from the heat of high summer, and we thought we could share a little more of Léoube with our visitors.

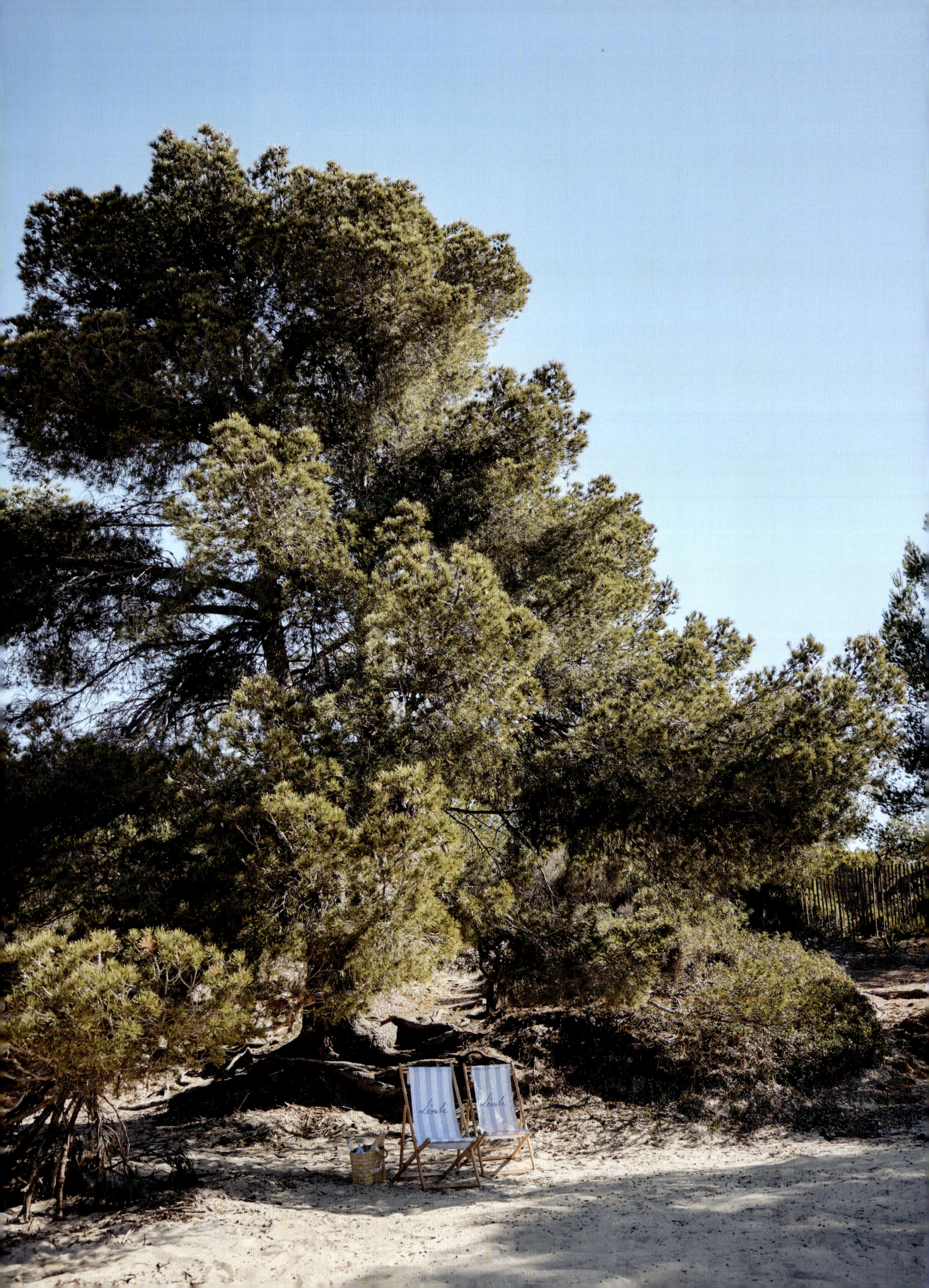

THE BEACH AND CAFÉ

The café is a place where time seems to stand still. Its setting under the olive trees, with a view out to the sea and the sound of the lapping waves, the white linens hung from branches and made to look like sails billowing in the breeze, and the fact that the sand is a mere metre from your feet, all make it feel very special. The beach is of course somewhere families come for the day, so we have a very laidback crowd in flip flops and T-shirts who wander up for a late lunch after a morning's swimming but it's also somewhere people dress up for and you can tell they've travelled quite far or are here for a special occasion. I think it's because the café has such a warmth to it – there's a strong sense of generous hospitality that our wonderful teams create, seemingly effortlessly, and such a contrast to some of the other more bustling trendy beach cafés in the area.

The menu is very simple and restrained. We want to celebrate produce and good ingredients so we like to showcase them and not play around by dressing them up too much. As much as is possible, the fruit and vegetables are sourced from the market garden on the estate and we serve a selection of traditional Provençal specialities – crudités served with anchoïade and goats' cheese from a nearby farm with our olive oil – alongside other Mediterranean-inspired favourites like a really good burrata, beef carpaccio and the catch of the day. There are always plenty of other light seafood options too, as well as pizzas – fired in our pizza oven – and homemade ice creams.

We also have a lounge area overlooking the beach where visitors can sink into reclining daybeds, order a bottle of rosé or a hand-crafted cocktail and settle in for the afternoon or evening. I think what draws people back is that our beach and café teams are so very committed to fostering a sense of connection between visitors and locals, sharing a slice of that slow, simple Provençal way of life. Throughout the summer, the beach comes alive with plenty of different activities designed to celebrate this sense of community, enabling all to enjoy the setting in so many different ways. When dusk falls, we often host open-air film nights, the beach taking on a magical ambiance as the lights on the big screen go up. Alternatively there are live music evenings and DJ sets and every year we host a mid-summer party before closing the season at the estate's annual harvest festival.

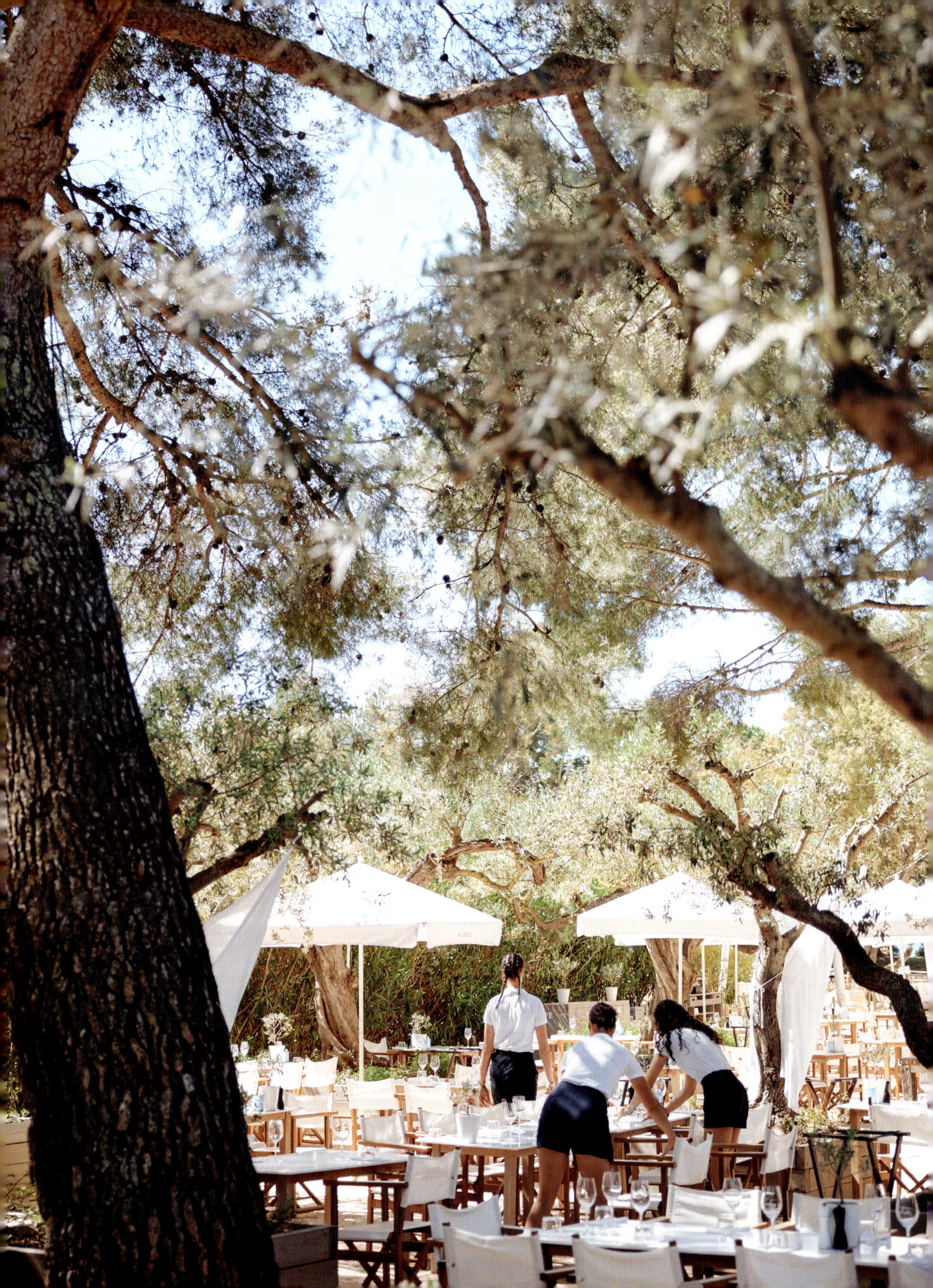

ABOVE AND OPPOSITE The shaded lounge area is set just back from the beach.
Visitors can settle into reclining daybeds to enjoy a glass of wine or a cocktail.

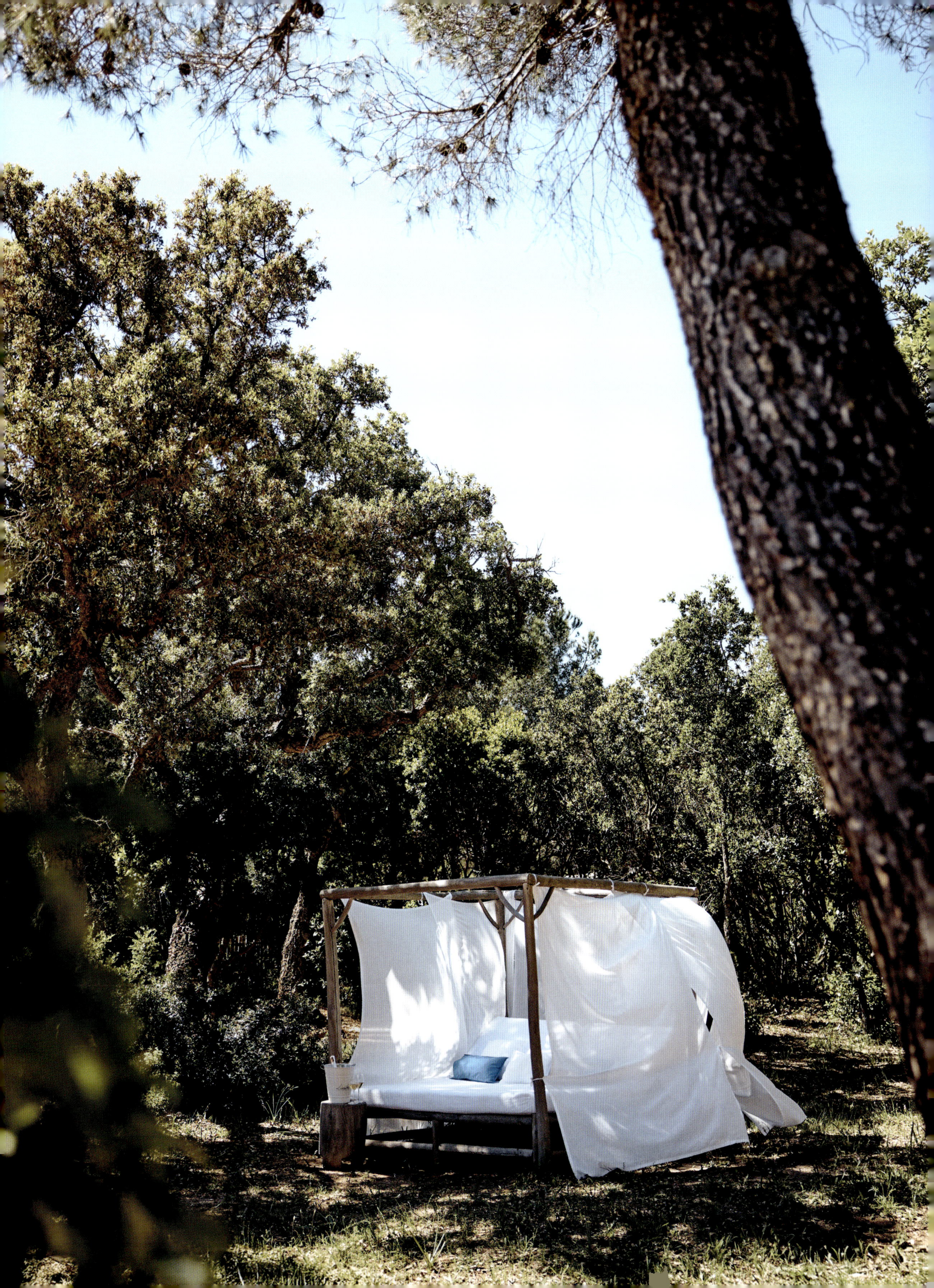

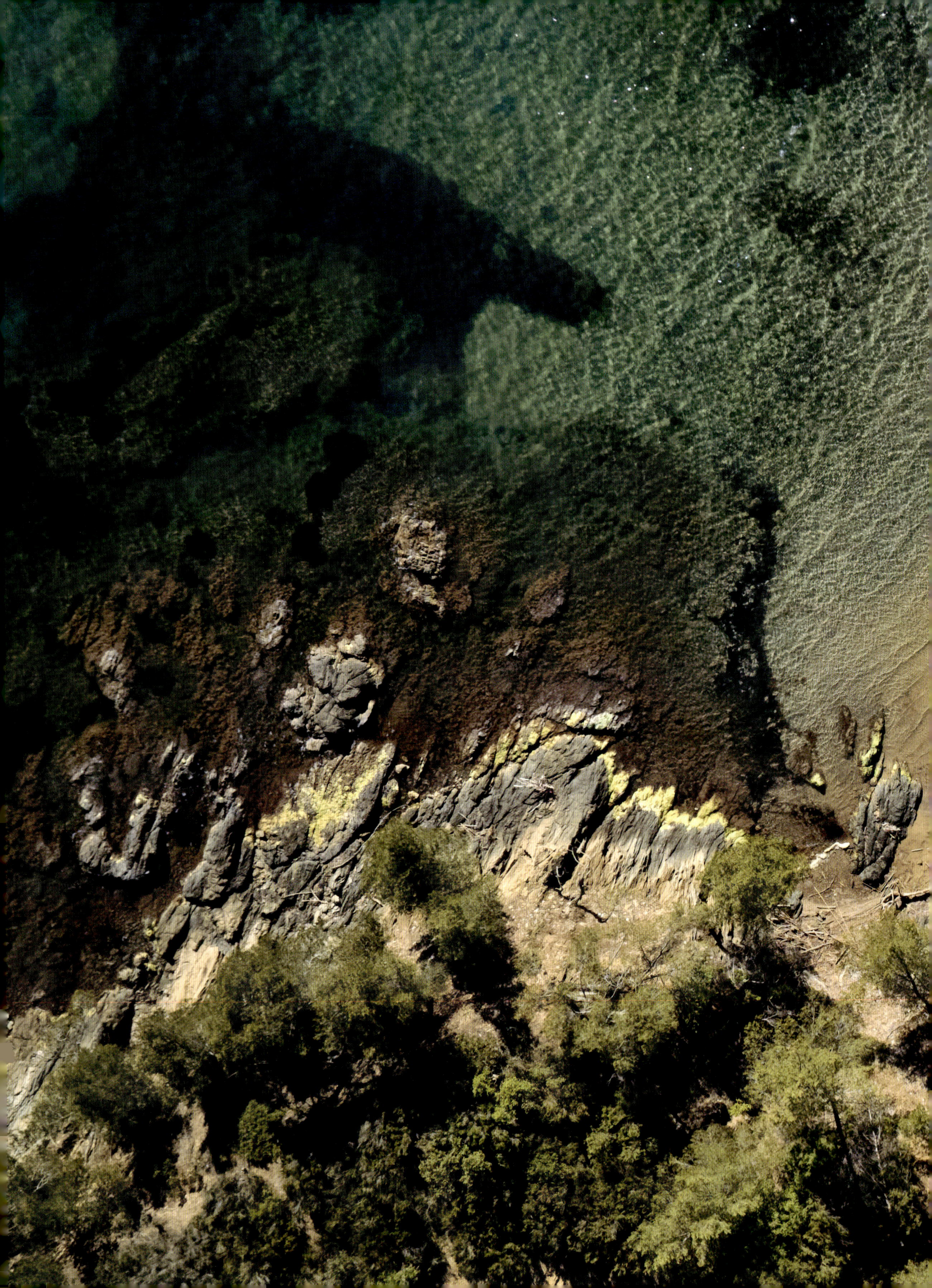

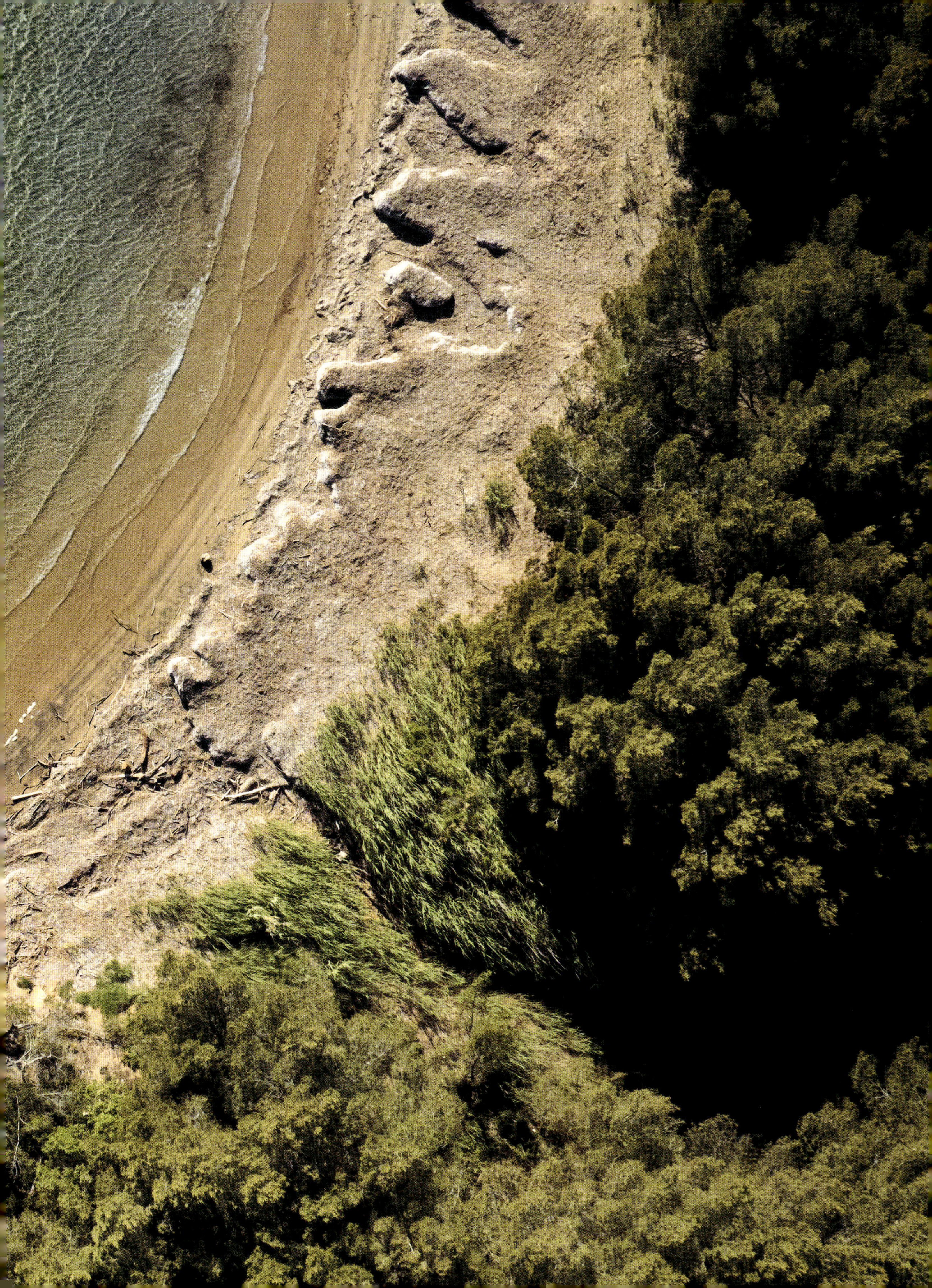

CHÂTEAU LÉOUBE

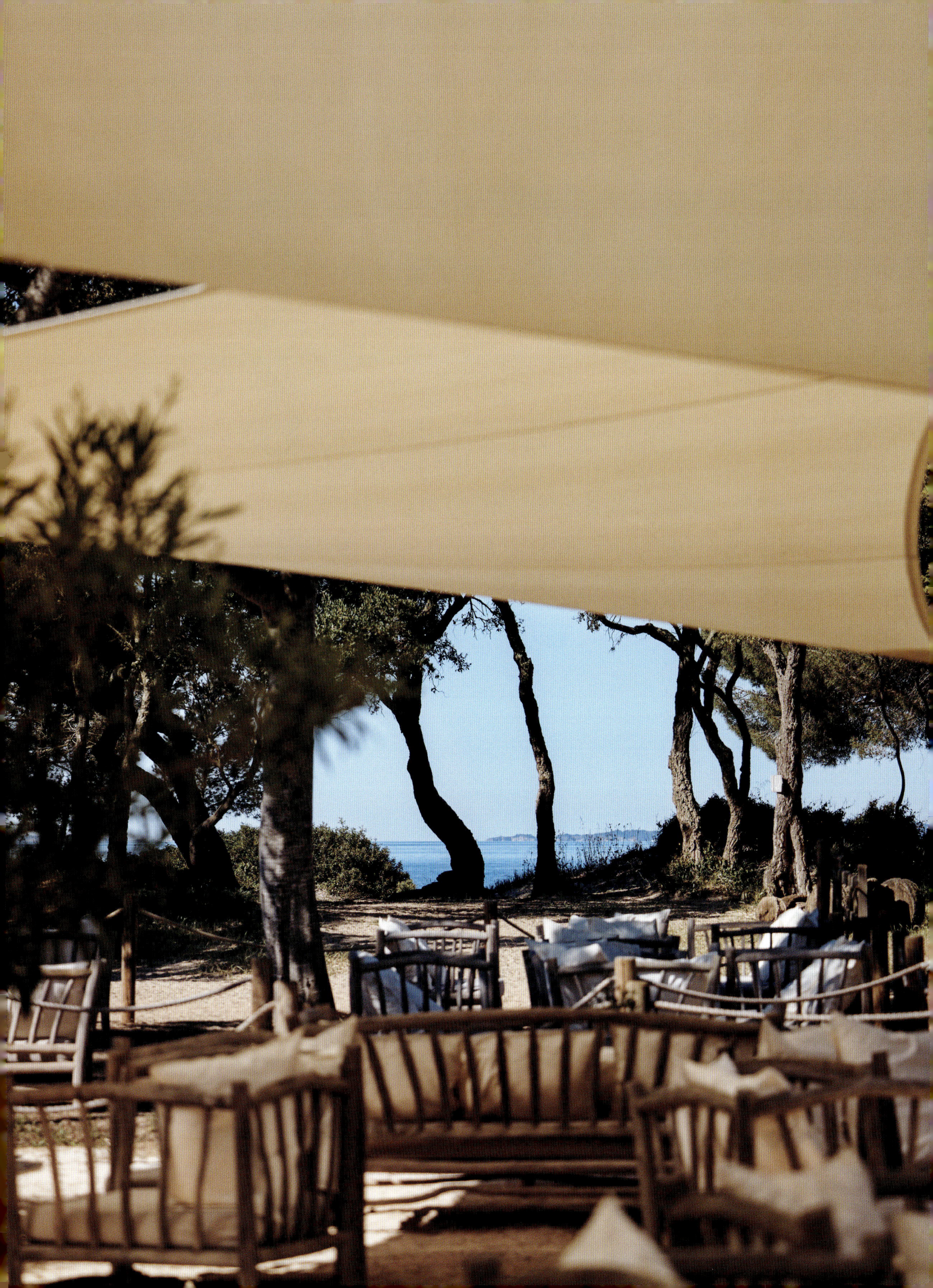

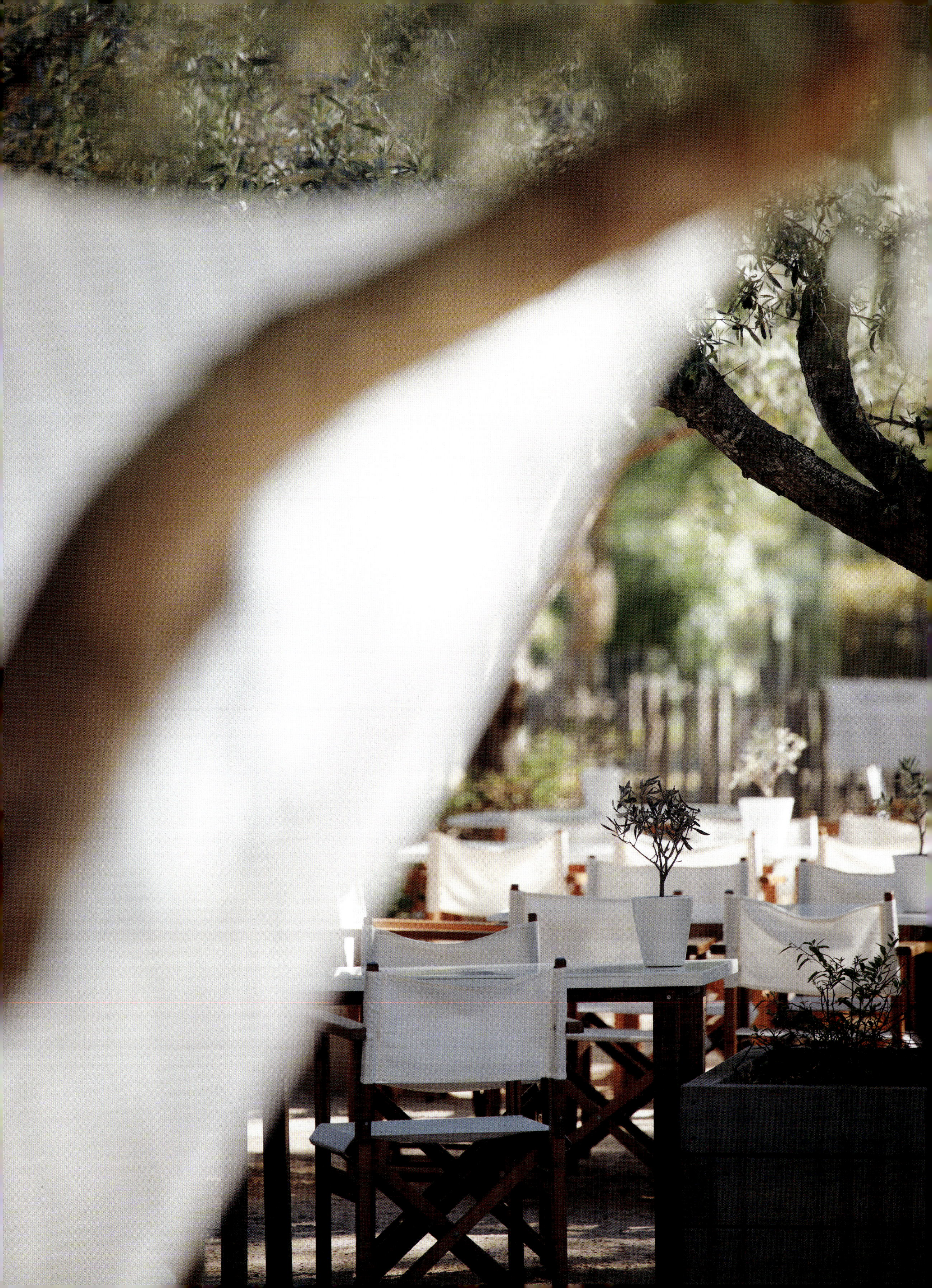

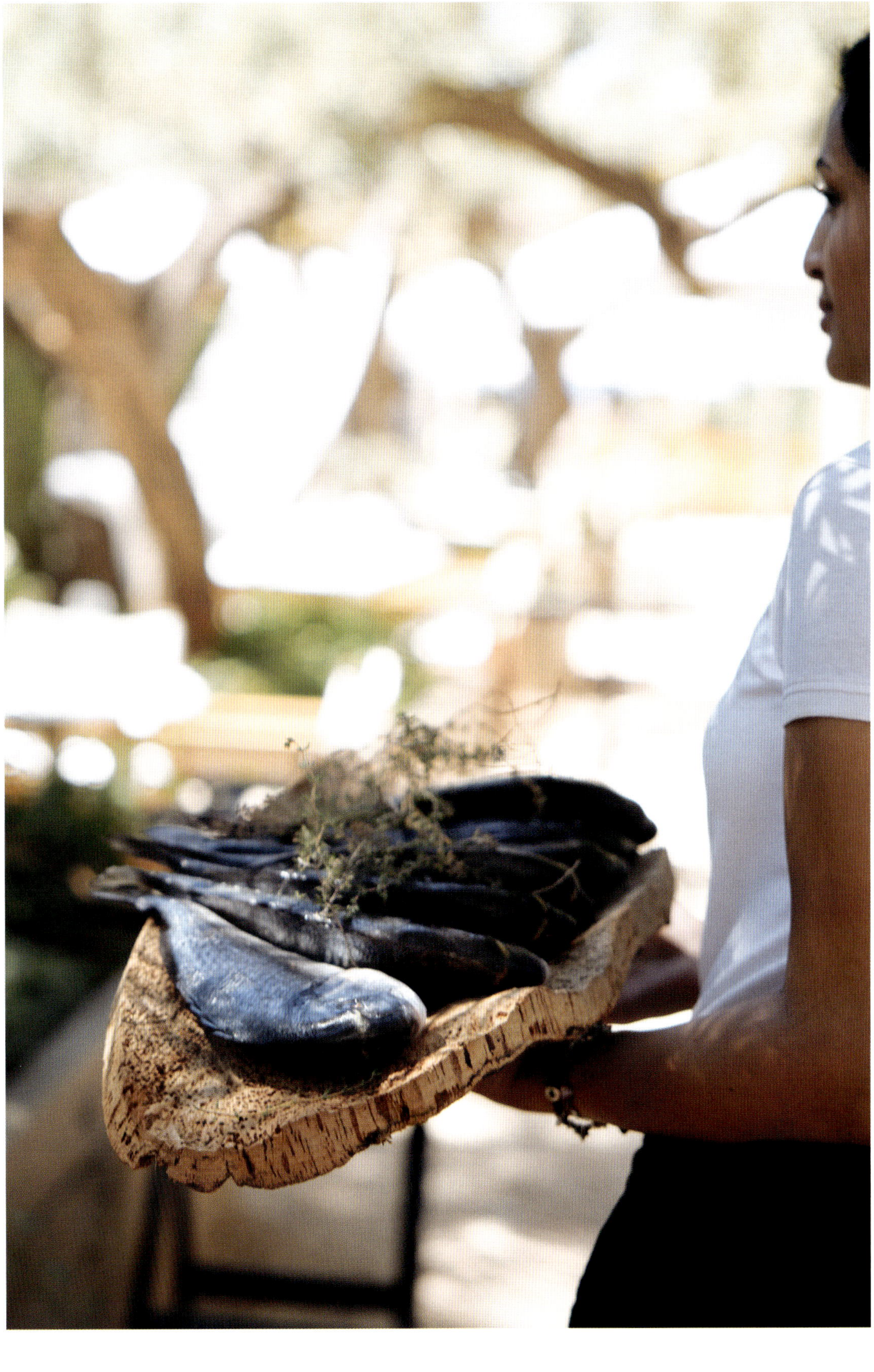

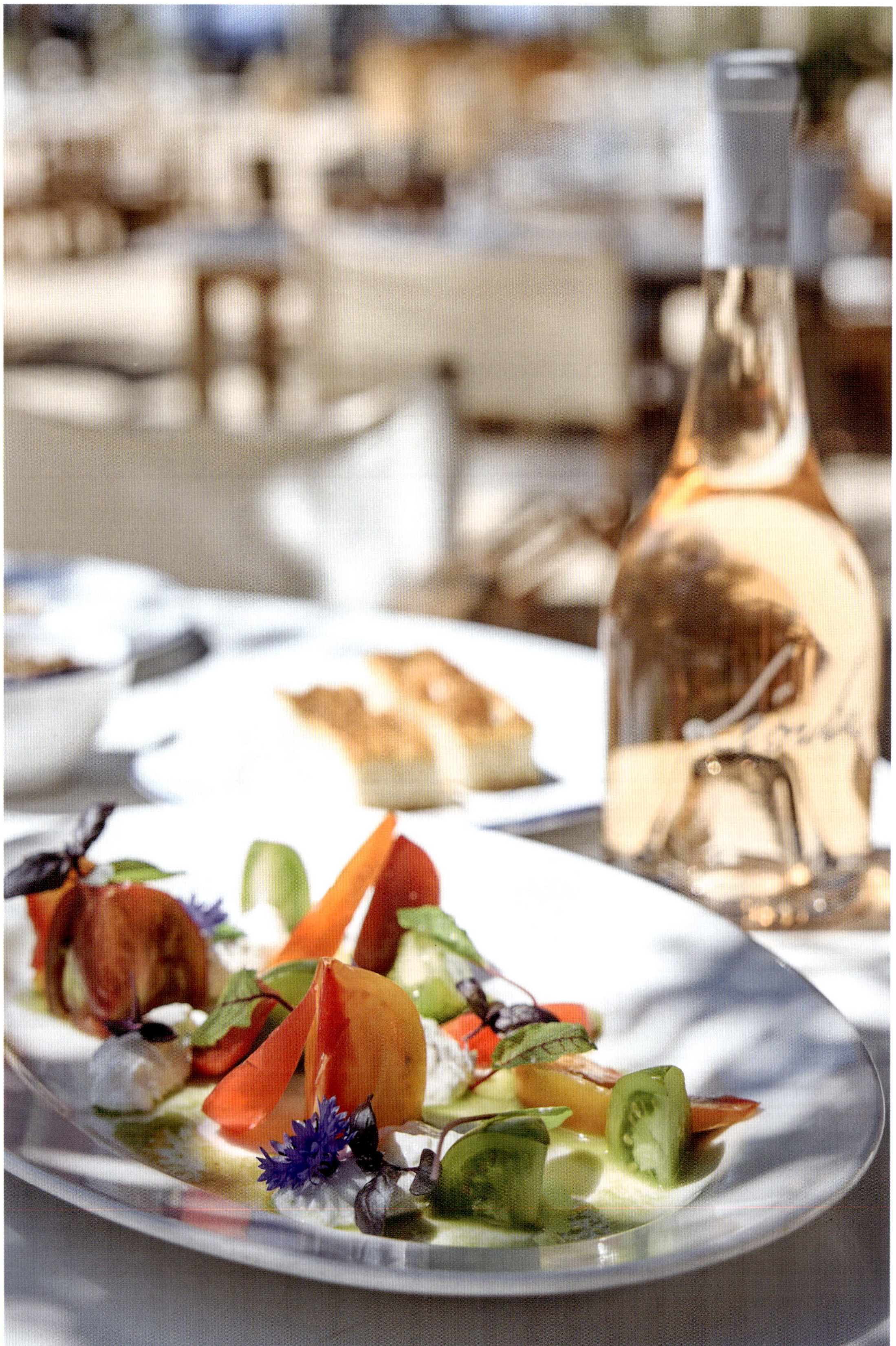

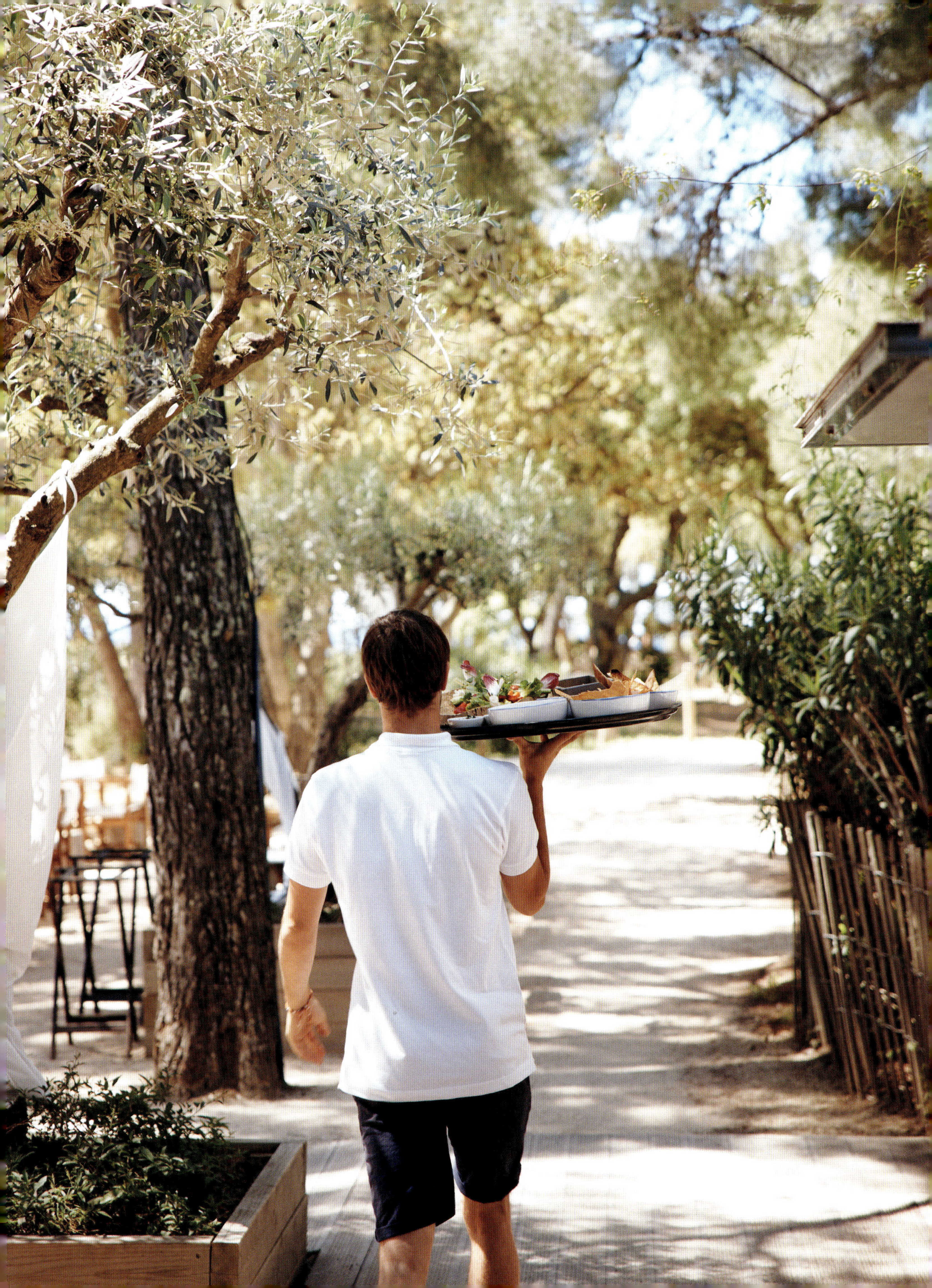

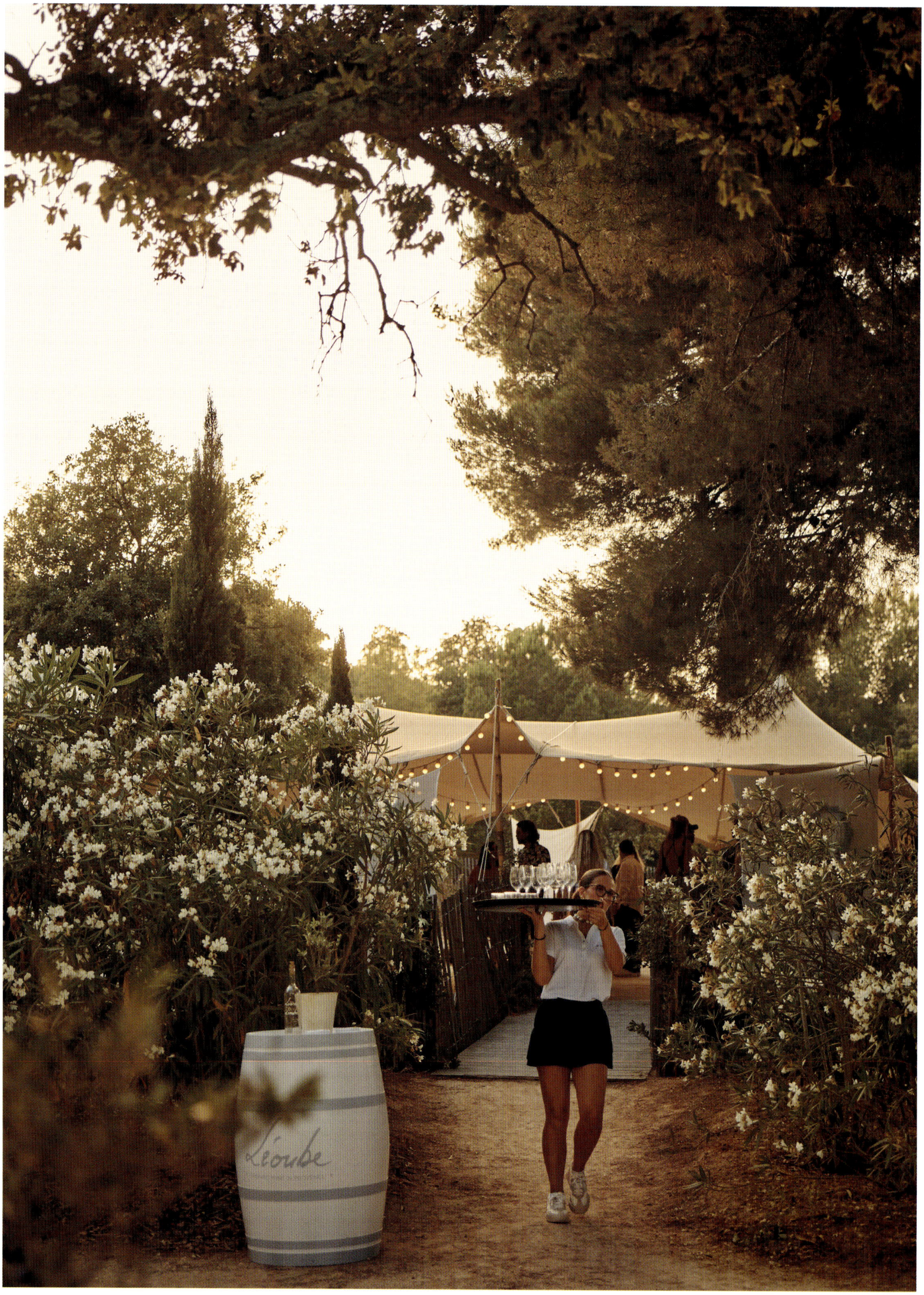
Léoube

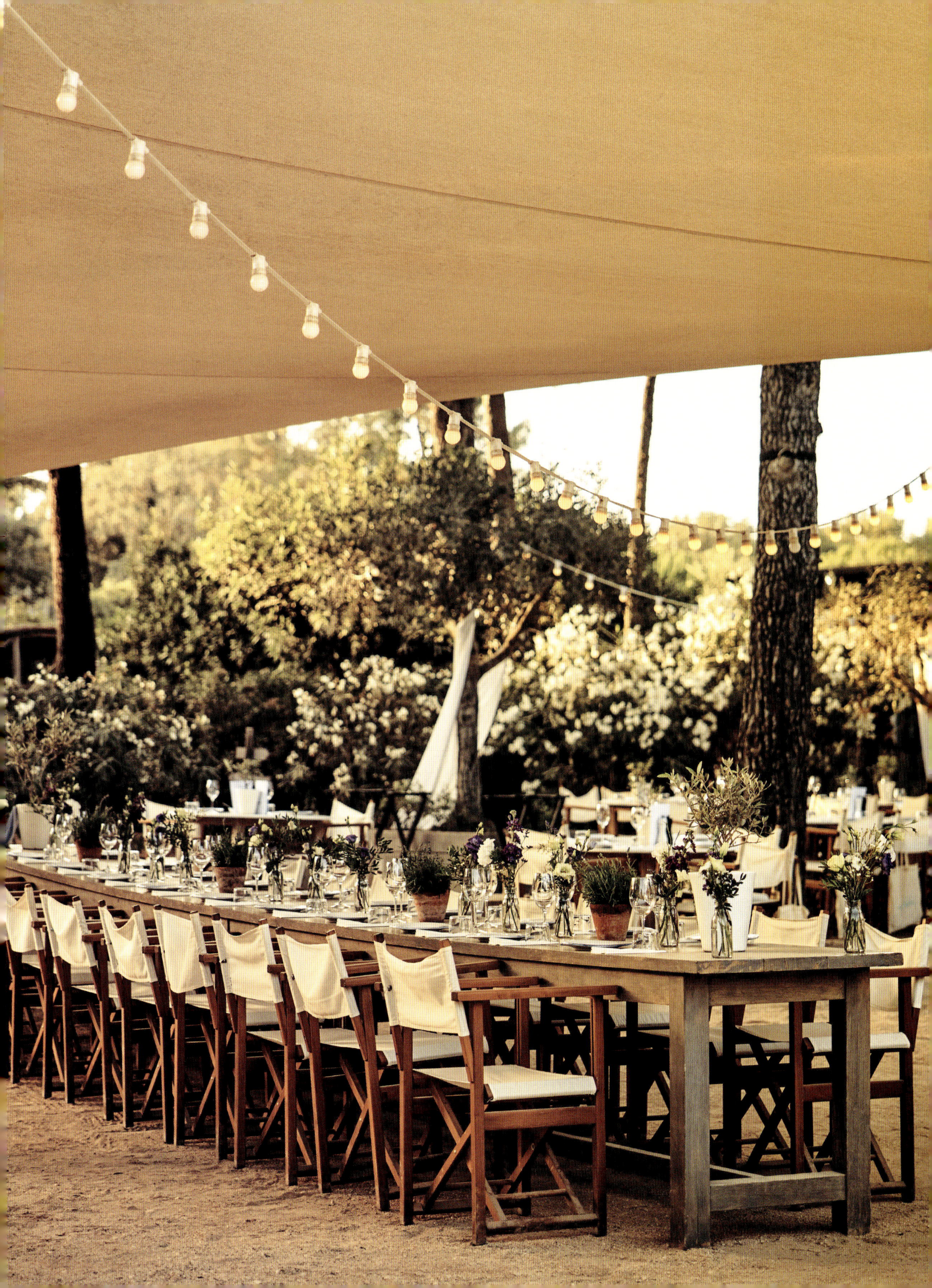

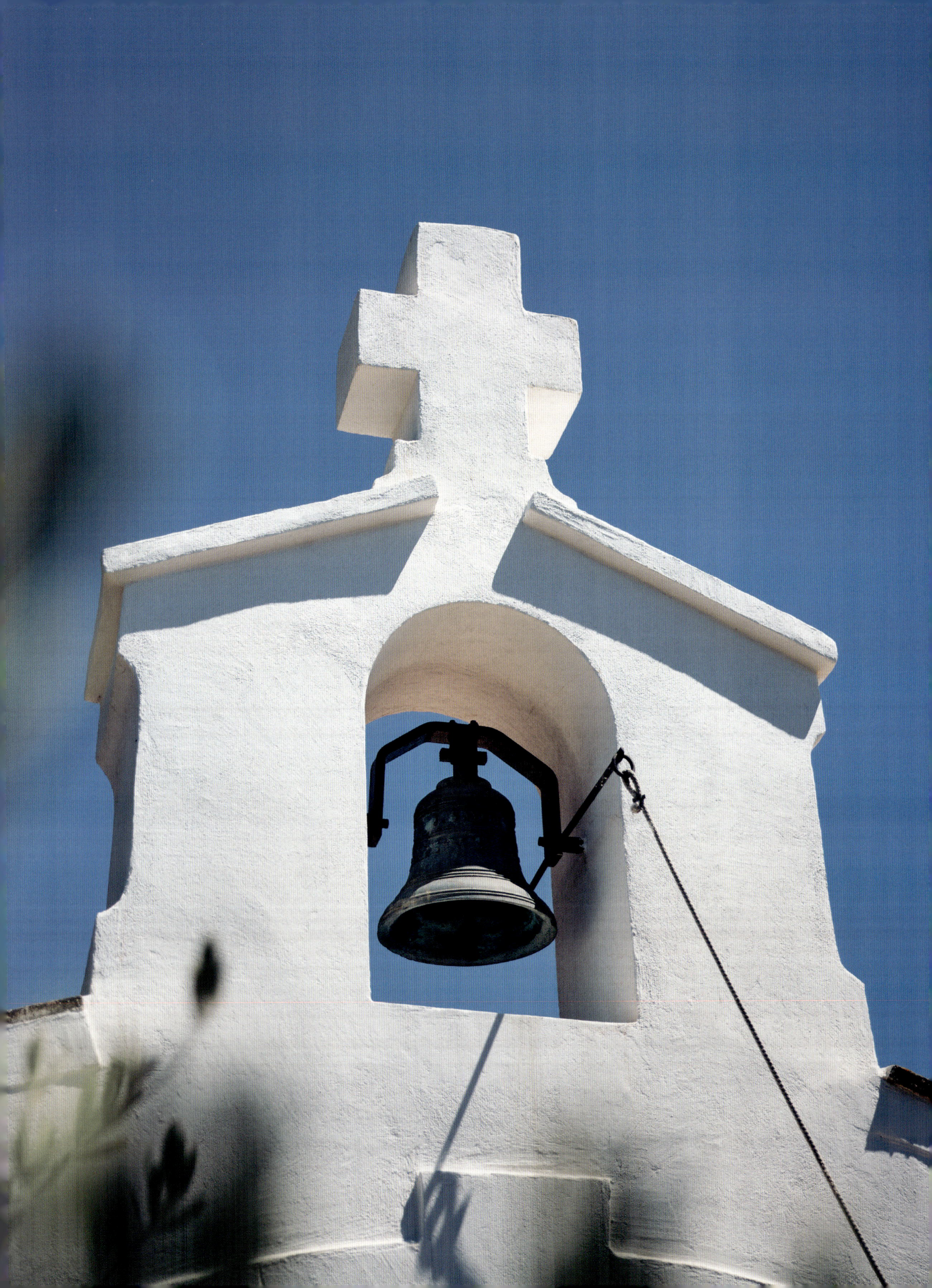

# THE CHAPELLE SAINT-GEORGES

Perched on one of the highest points on the estate is a tiny painted white chapel, the Chapelle Saint-Georges. It's one of the stops along the region's pilgrim way.

The chapel building was restored in 1891 and it sits at around 37 metres above sea level so the views it affords over the bay are spectacular. The land around it is very wild – it's mostly scrubland and maquis, and the ground is craggy and rough, with a steep climb to get up there, but inside the walls of the chapel are painted white with simple accents of blue and there's a purity and simplicity to the building that I find so moving and peaceful. I'm a very spiritual person, with strong faith, so to me the chapel is a calming refuge and I will always try and get up there to light a candle when I'm at Léoube.

The statue of the Virgin on its roof faces another representation of the mother of Christ erected on the northern part of the estate which is believed to protect the land, and we've always felt like the estate was being watched over and kept safe. The chapel feels like a very sacred place, and it holds many special memories for my family because it was here that we held my grandson Otis's christening in 2016 over my birthday weekend. Family and friends joined us to celebrate and at the end of the ceremony a choir from the local school sang John Lennon's 'Imagine', one of my favourite songs – and sentiments – and for all of us it represents a very, very happy day, a treasured memory and a place that holds so much meaning.

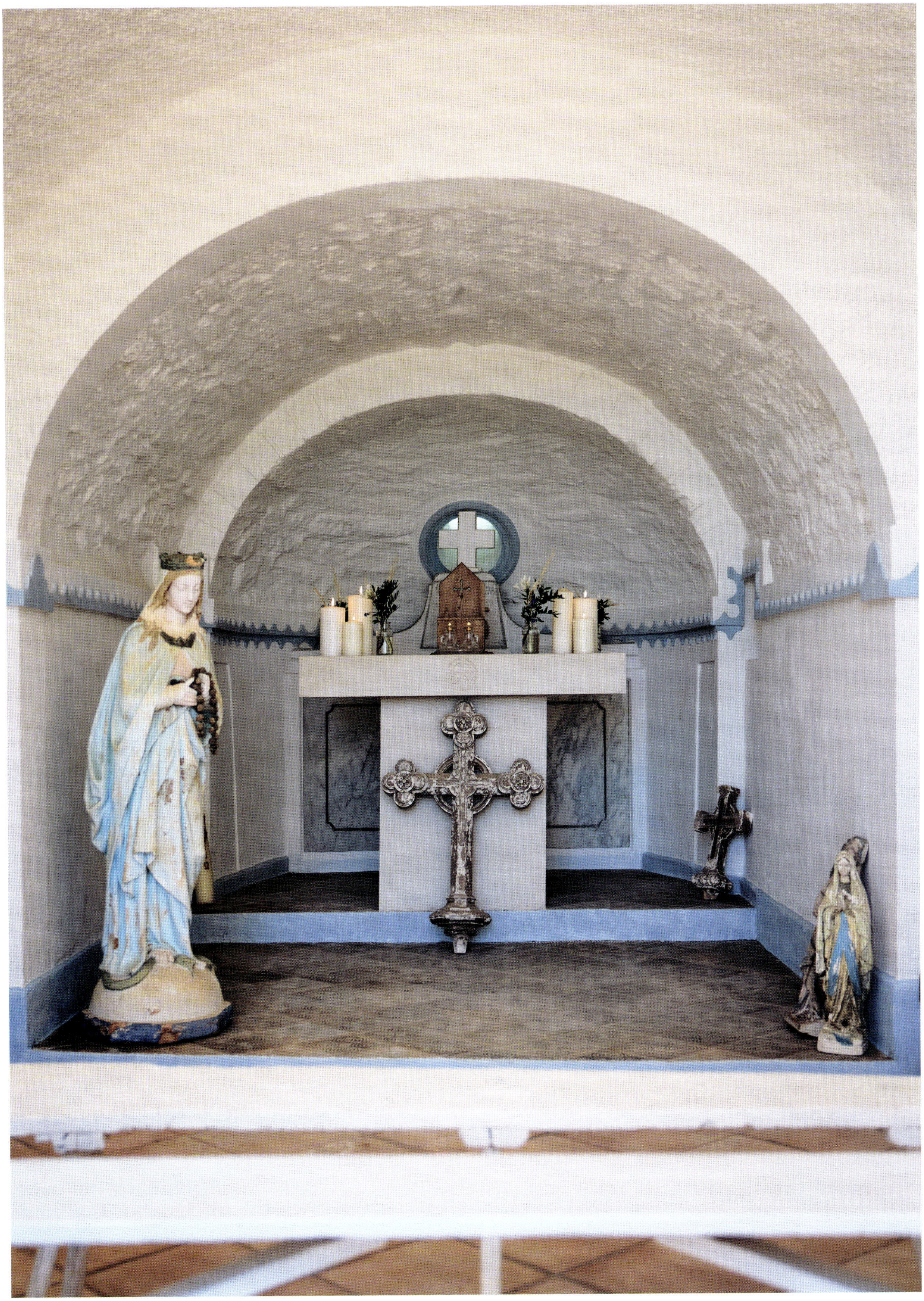

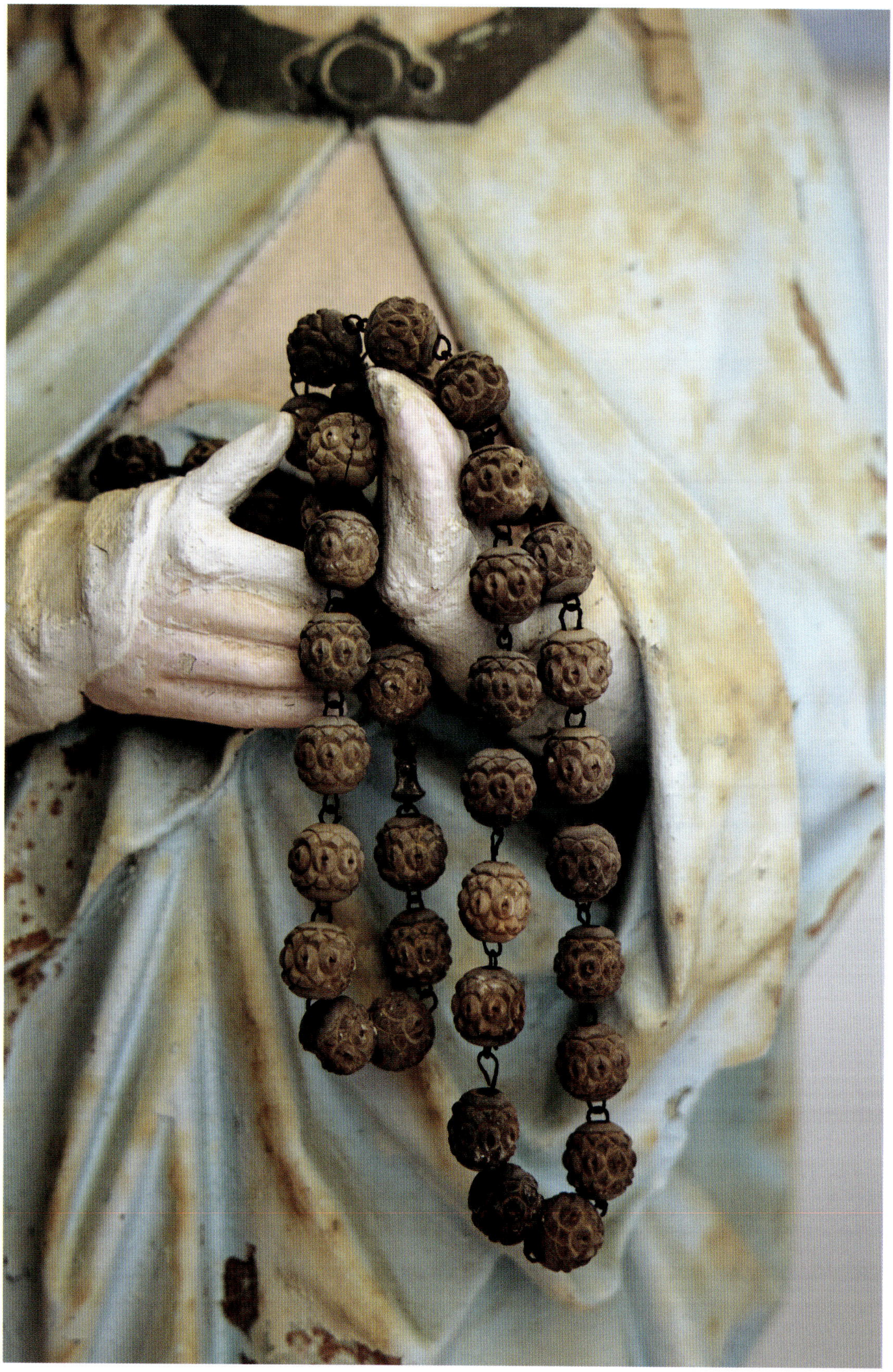

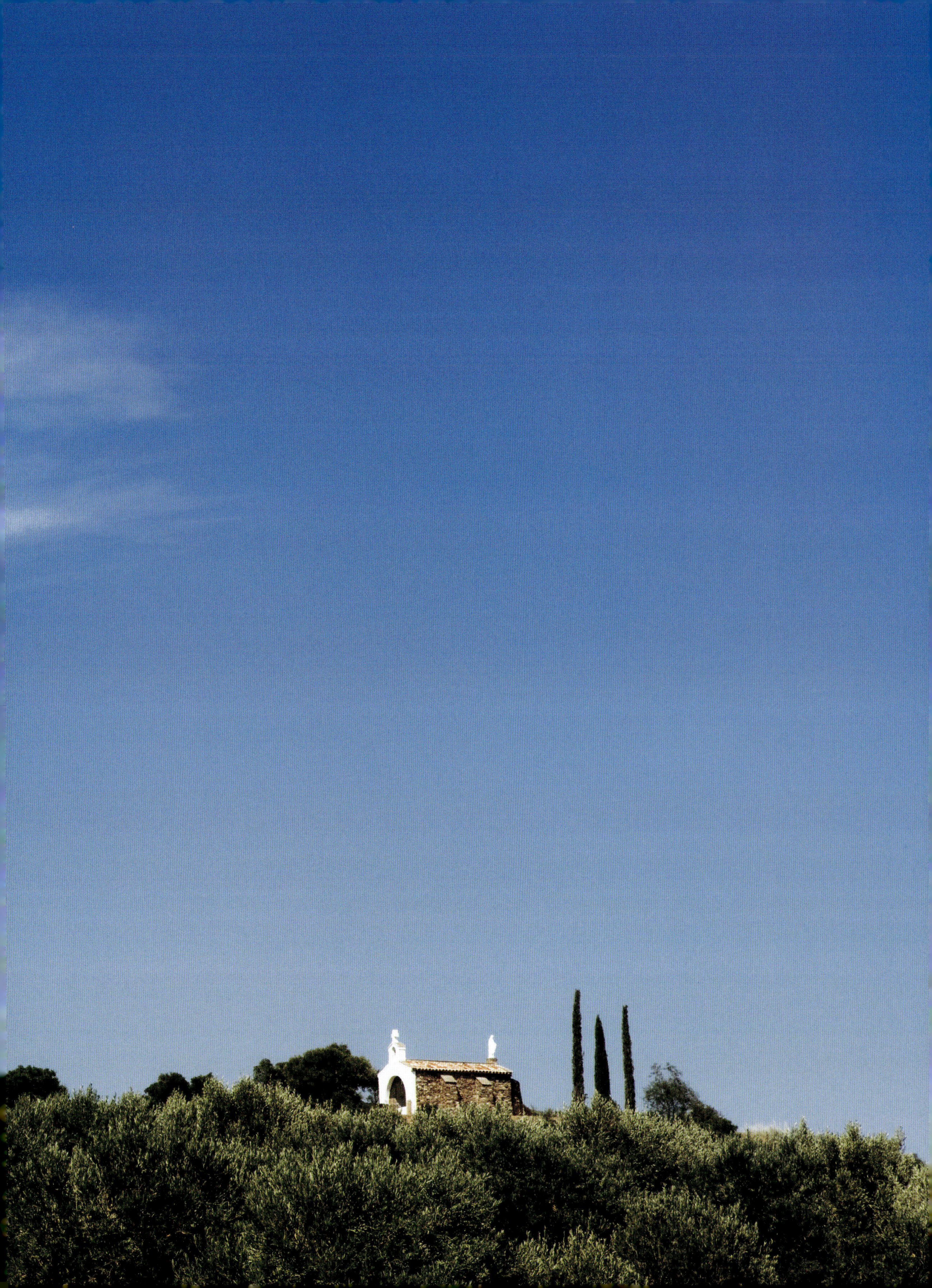

Perched on one of the highest points on the estate is a tiny painted white chapel, the Chapelle Saint-Georges. It's one of the stops along the region's pilgrim way.

The chapel building was restored in 1891 and it sits at around 37 metres above sea level so the views it affords over the bay are spectacular. The land around it is very wild – it's mostly scrubland and maquis, and the ground is craggy and rough, with a steep climb to get up there, but inside the walls of the chapel are painted white with simple accents of blue and there's a purity and simplicity to the building that I find so moving and peaceful. I'm a very spiritual person, with strong faith, so to me the chapel is a calming refuge and I will always try and get up there to light a candle when I'm at Léoube.

The statue of the Virgin on its roof faces another representation of the mother of Christ erected on the northern part of the estate which is believed to protect the land, and we've always felt like the estate was being watched over and kept safe. The chapel feels like a very sacred place, and it holds many special memories for my family because it was here that we held my grandson Otis's christening in 2016 over my birthday weekend. Family and friends joined us to celebrate and at the end of the ceremony a choir from the local school sang John Lennon's 'Imagine', one of my favourite songs – and sentiments – and for all of us it represents a very, very happy day, a treasured memory and a place that holds so much meaning.

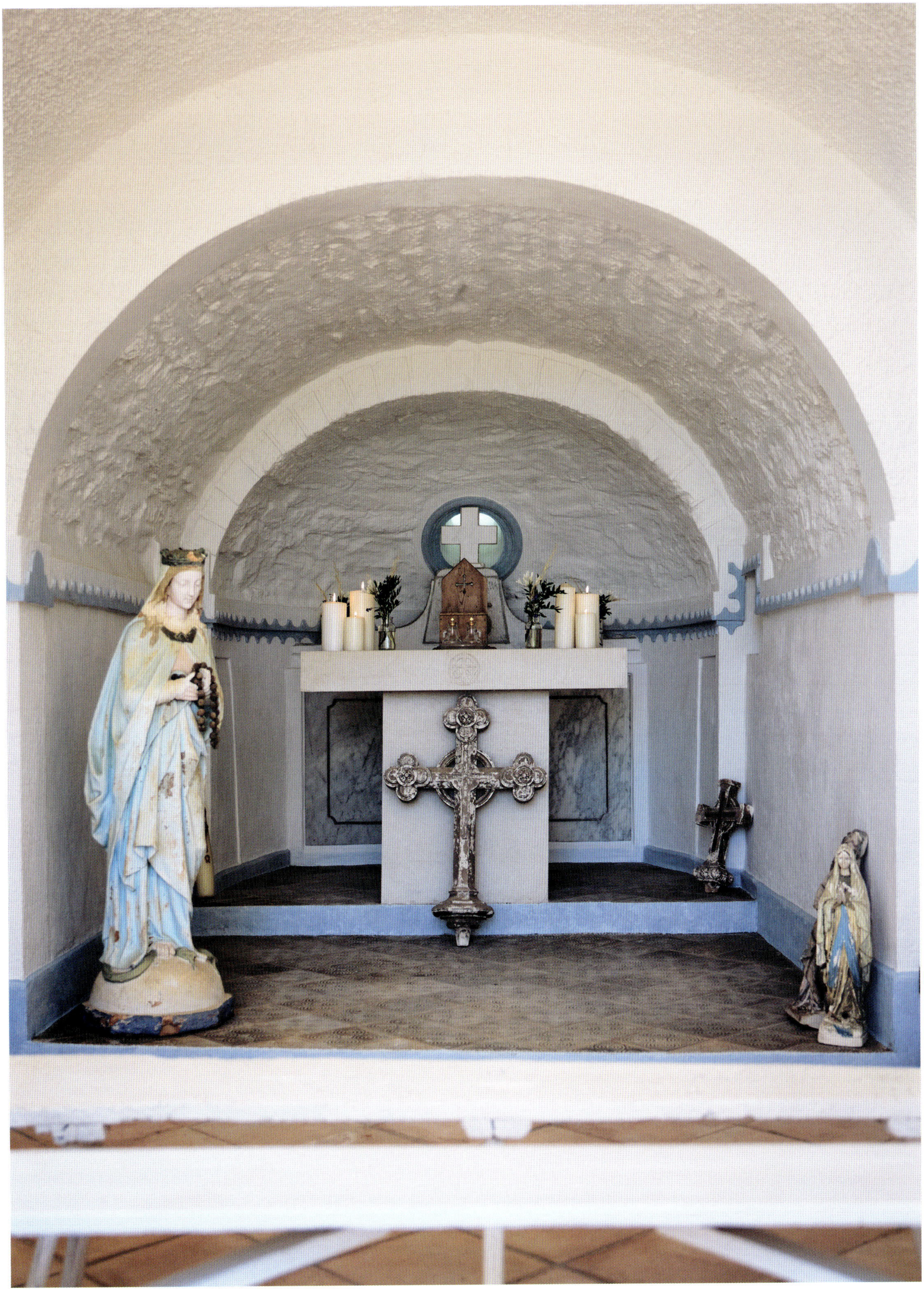

CHÂTEAU LÉOUBE

'Only from the heart can you
touch the sky.'

– RUMI

RECONNAISSANCE
A LA SAINTE VIERGE
ET A ST GEORGES
POUR NOTRE LIBERATION
LEOUBE-BREGANÇON
15 AOUT 1944

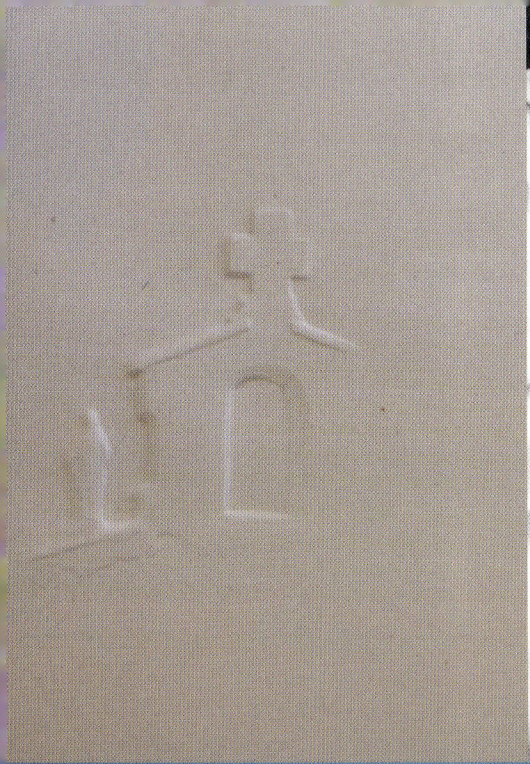

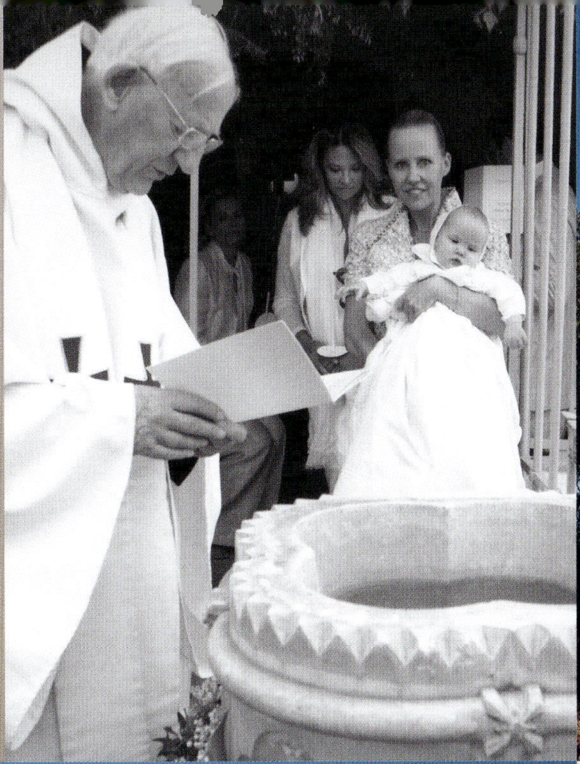

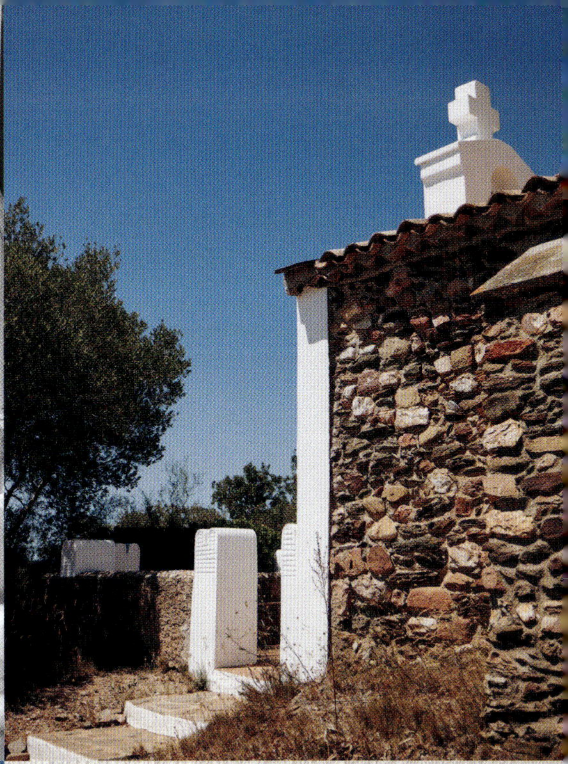

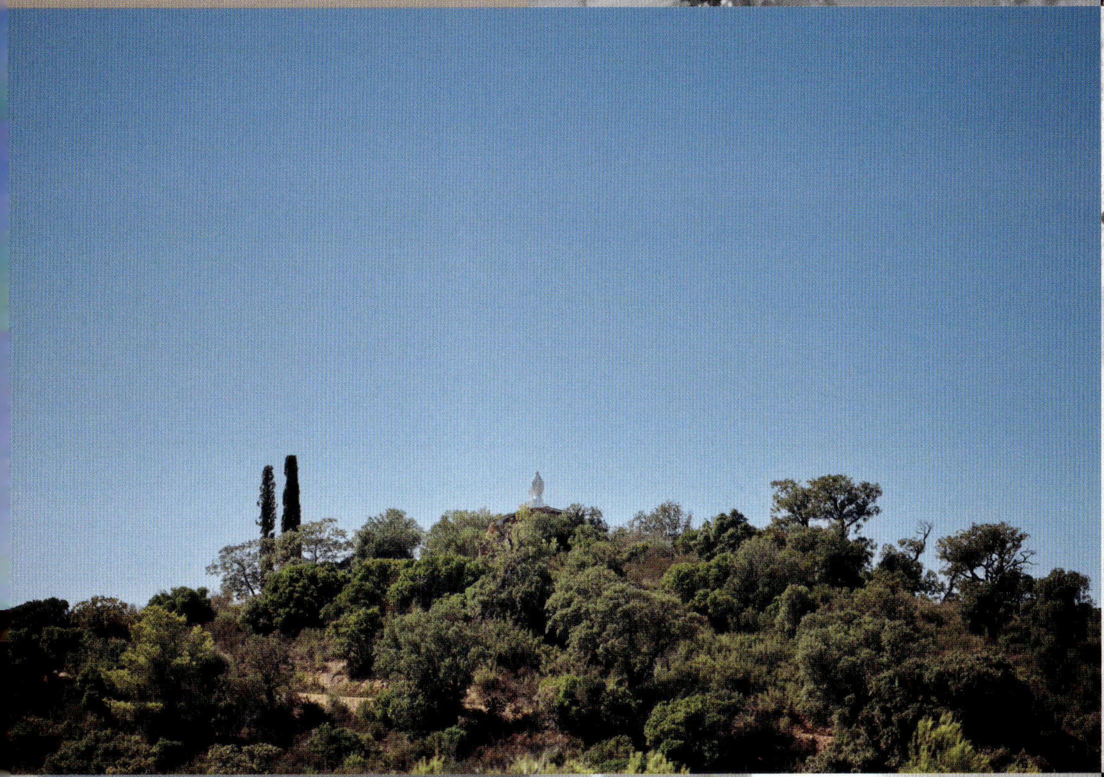

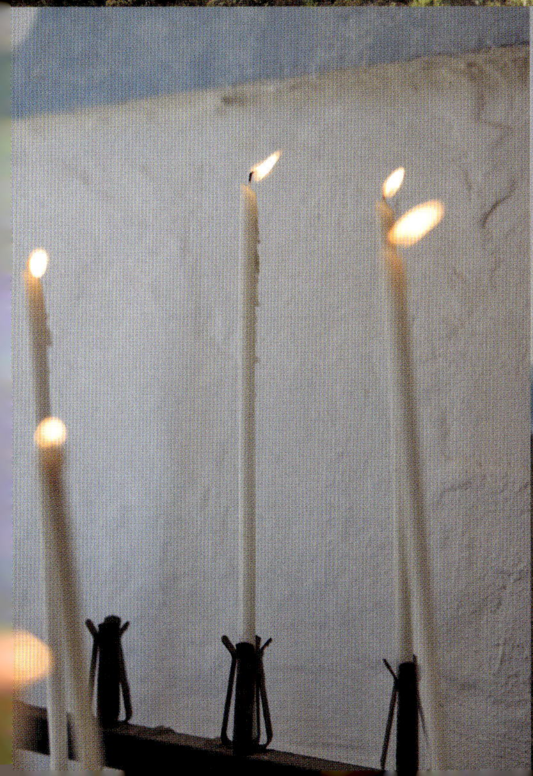

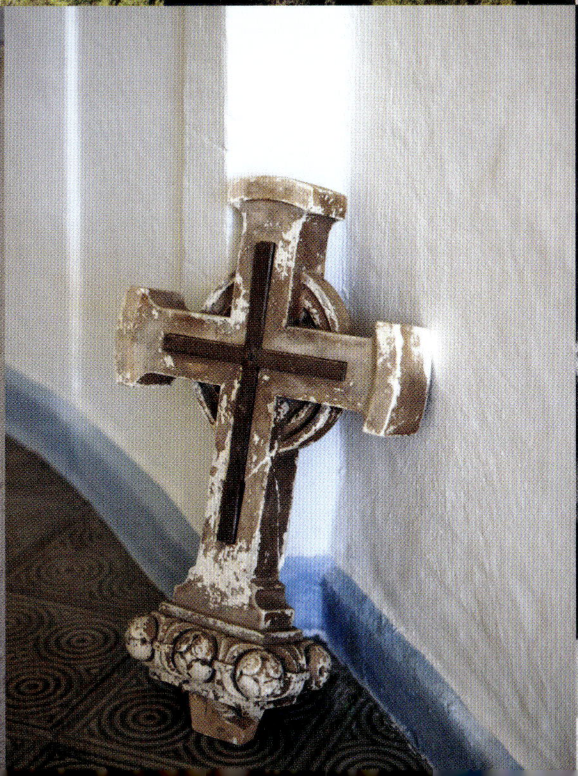

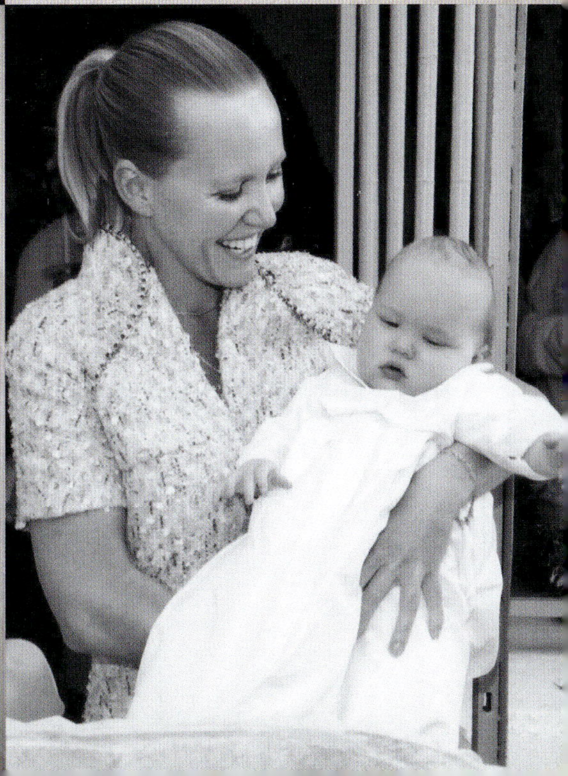

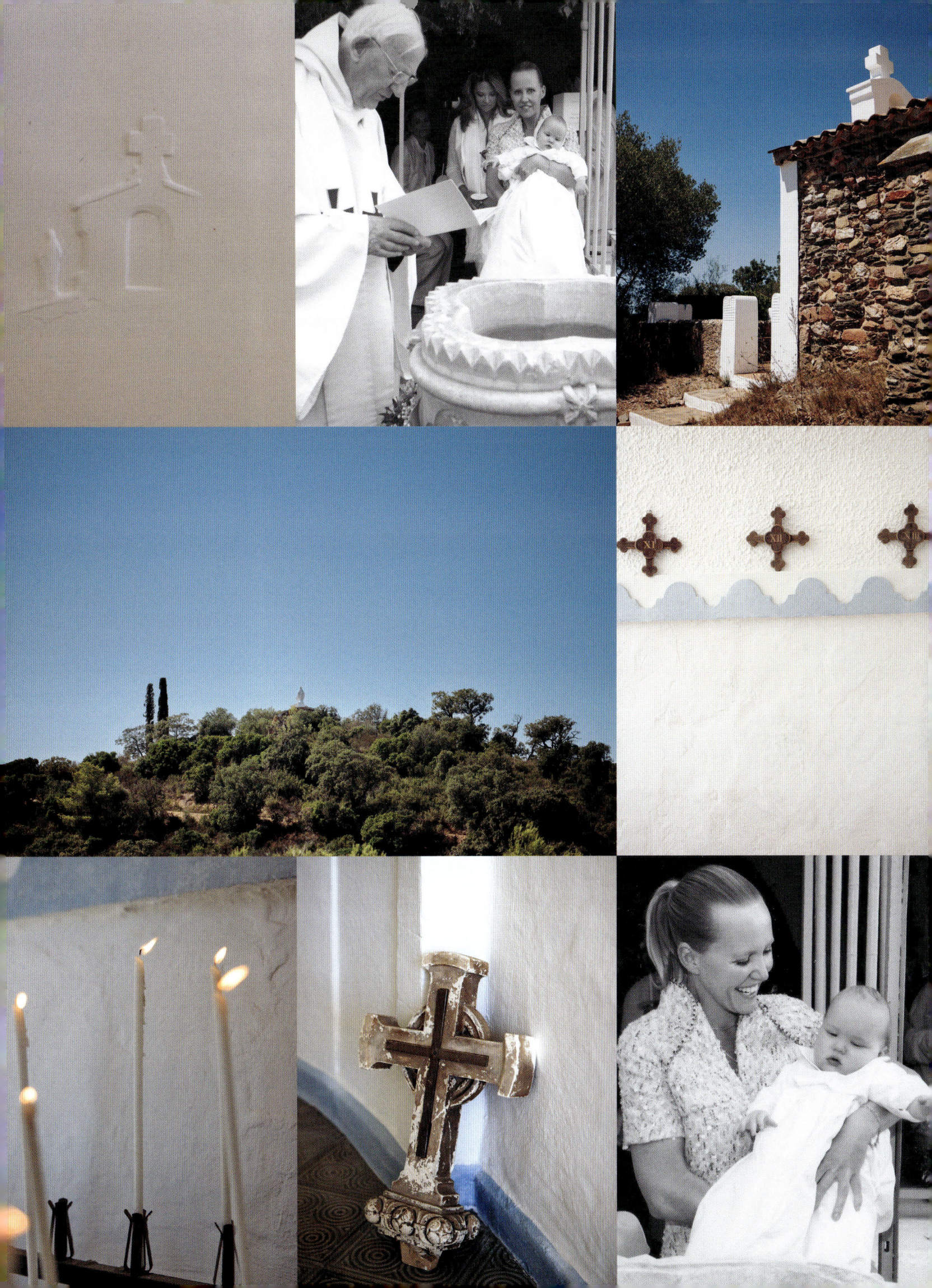

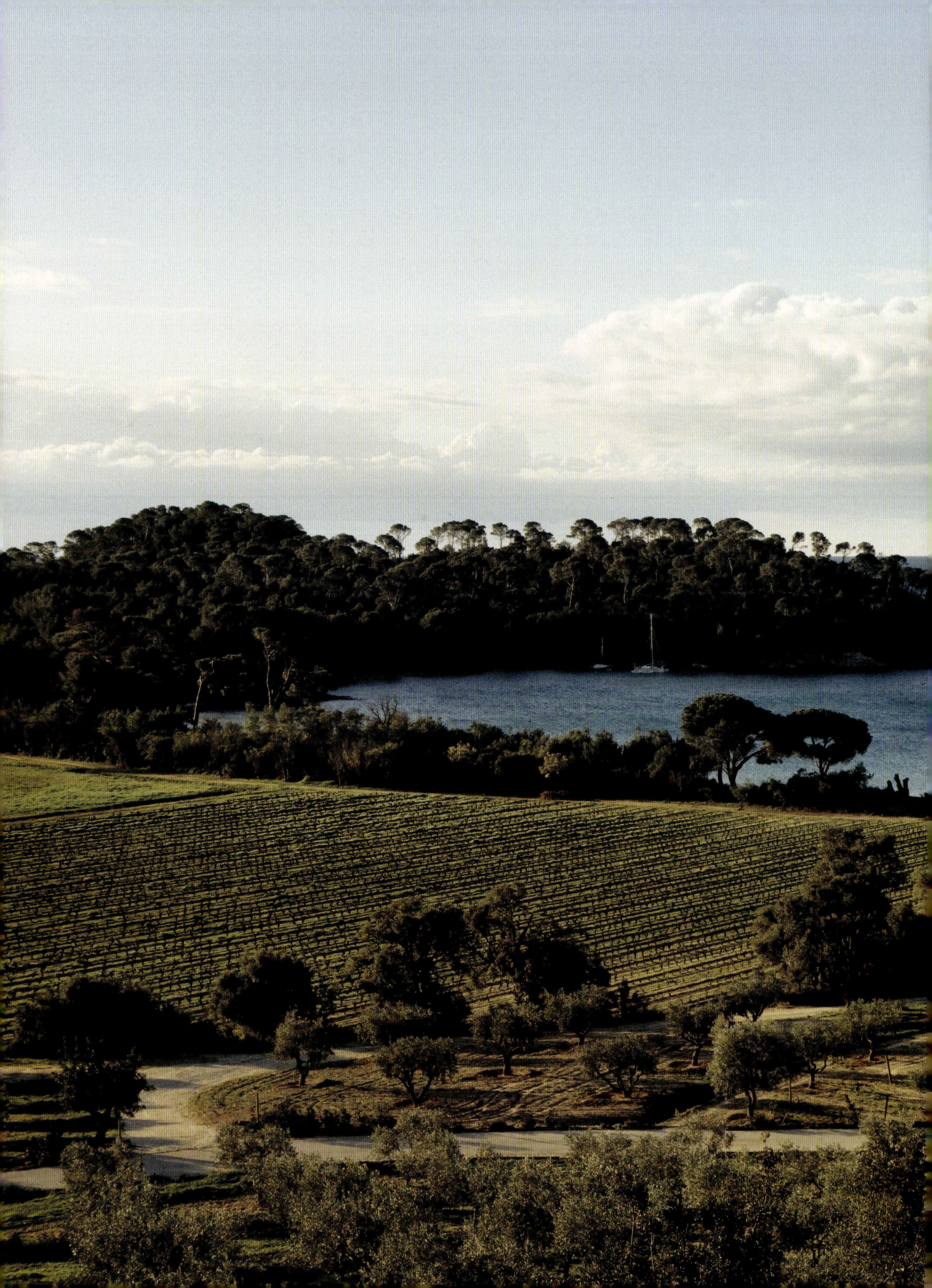

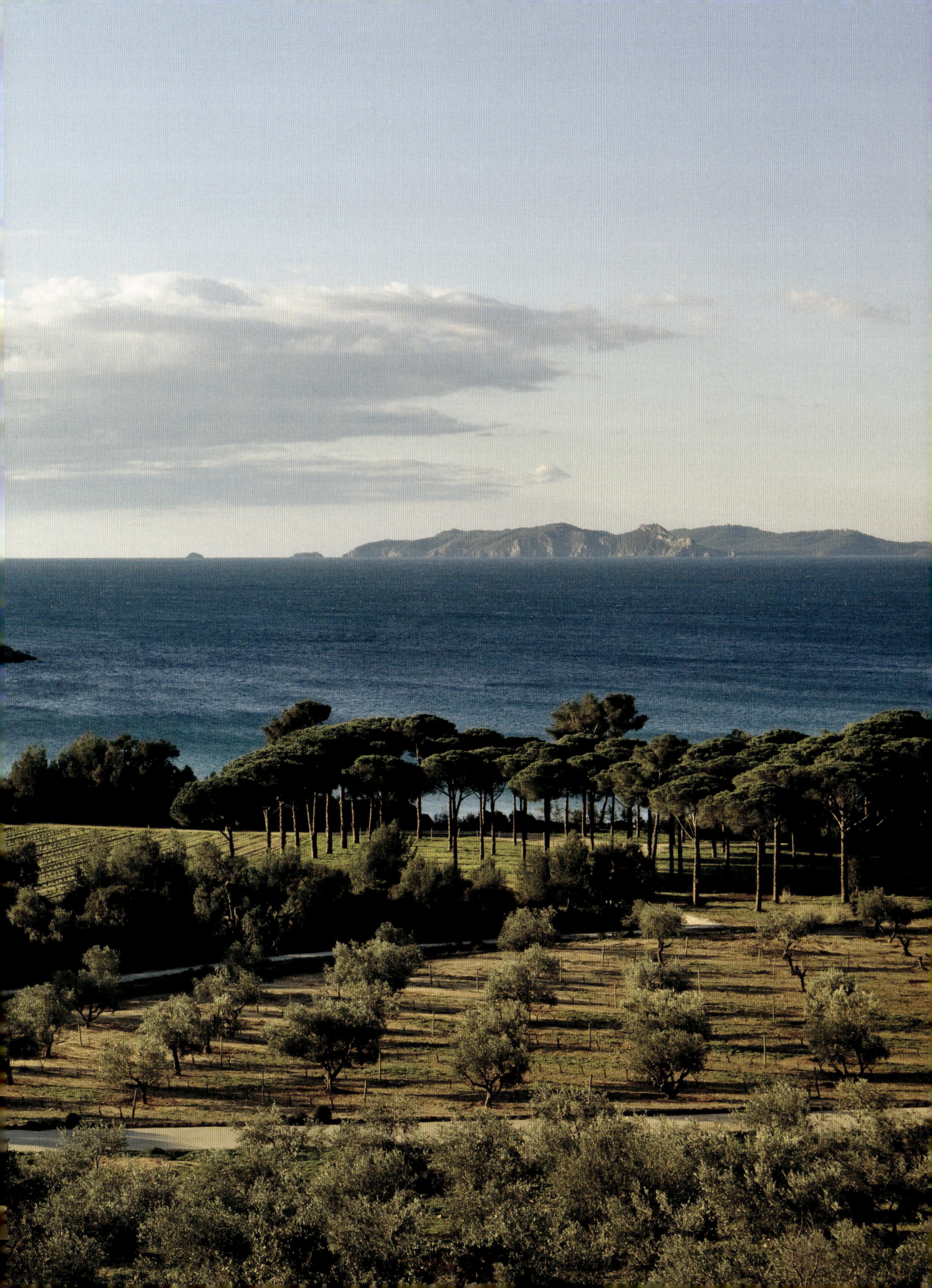

# ACKNOWLEDGEMENTS

Many people have left their mark on Château Léoube over the years and I am indebted to them all.

Alain Raynaud, Wendy Nicholls, Tommaso del Buono and Jacqueline Morabito. There aren't words to express my gratitude. Your work and your skills are part of the fabric of this home and its surroundings, and I will forever be grateful for all that you have helped me to create.

I owe enormous thanks to the wonderful team at Léoube, in particular Jérome Pernot, Romain Ott, Charles and Rose-Marie Goupilleau, Sandy Roux, Guillaume Duverger and Françoise Rausch who ensure that the house, the vineyard and the estate are nurtured and tended to with the utmost care, and that our wines reach hands far beyond our corner of Provence. Léoube would not be what it is without your hard work.

Martin Morrell, even after all the years we've worked together, I remain in awe of your ability to create such timeless and magnificent images. Thank you for capturing the magic and beauty of Léoube with your lens.

Claudie Dubost, *un énorme merci* for designing a book that reflects what this house means to me so elegantly. You understood and honoured our home and these beautiful pages fill me with joy.

Heartfelt thanks to Beatrice Vincenzini, my publisher and friend, for your support of this project and for allowing it to look and feel like the book I wanted it to be. And my thanks to the whole team at Vendôme Press and to Catharine Snow, for your attention to detail and editorial guidance.

And to Imogen Fortes, for helping me to express my love for Léoube just as I'd hoped to.

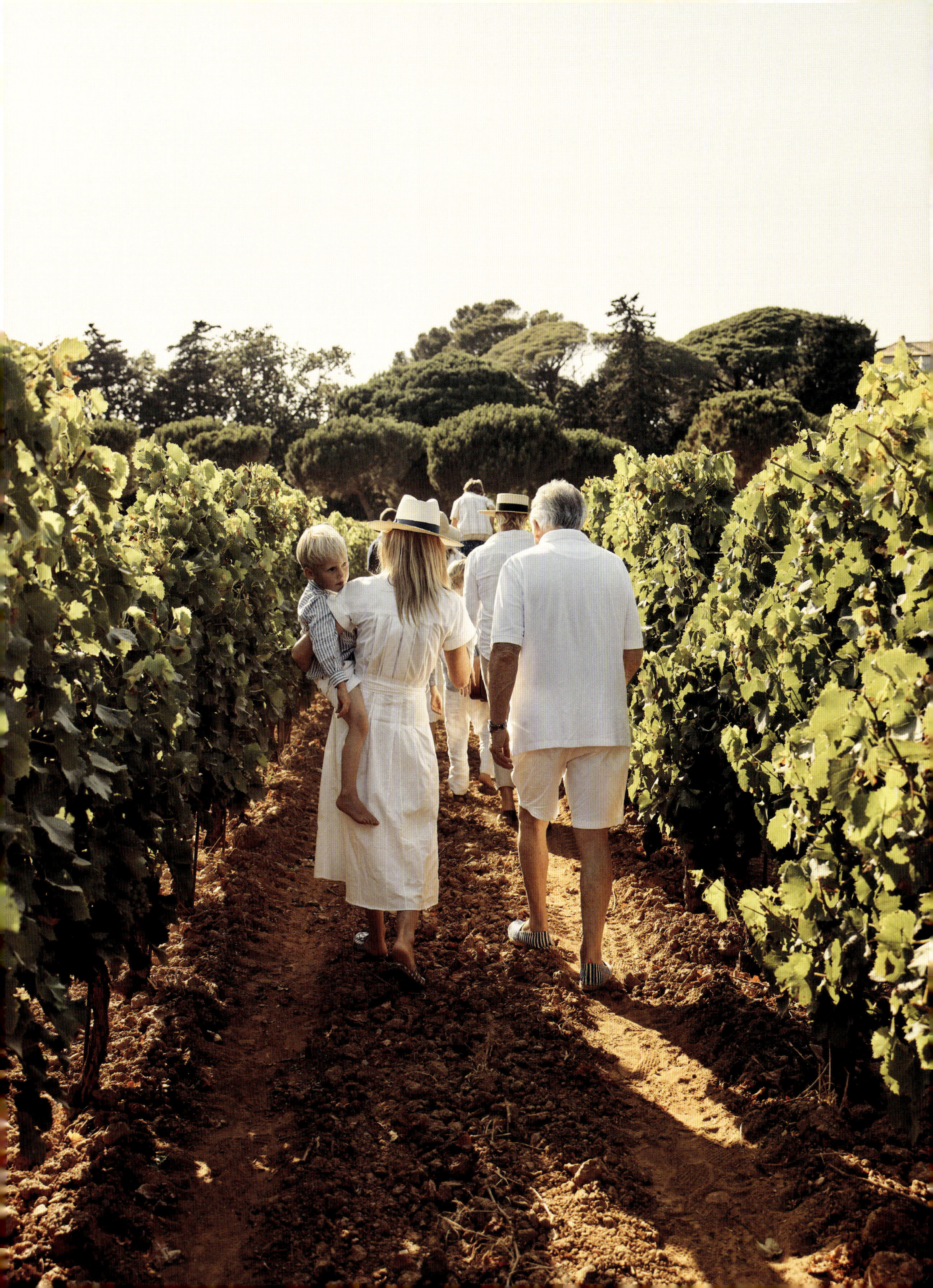

*Château Léoube: Provence Living*
First published in 2025 by The Vendome Press
Vendome is a registered trademark of The Vendome Press LLC

VENDOME PRESS US
PO Box 566
Palm Beach, FL 33480

VENDOME PRESS UK
Worlds End Studio
132-134 Lots Road
London SW10 0RJ

www.vendomepress.com

COPYRIGHT © 2025 The Vendome Press LLC
TEXT Copyright © Carole Bamford
PHOTOGRAPHY Copyright © Martin Morrell
Copyright © Eliya Ca pages 16, 82, 83, 84, 85

All rights reserved. No part of the contents of this book may be reproduced in whole or in part without prior written permission from the publishers.

Any use of this book to train generative artificial intelligence ("AI") technologies is expressly prohibited. Vendome Press, their authors, and their photographers reserve all rights to license uses of this work for generative AI training and development of machine learning language models.

ISBN (English edition): 978-0-86565-463-1

PUBLISHERS Beatrice Vincenzini, Mark Magowan, and Francesco Venturi
EDITOR Catharine Snow
PRODUCTION MANAGER Amanda Mackie
CREATIVE CONSULTANT Peter Dawson
CONTRIBUTING EDITOR Imogen Fortes
MAP ILLUSTRATION Léa Souchon
DESIGN CONCEPT AND LAYOUT Claudie Dubost

Library of Congress Cataloging-in-Publication Data available upon request

Distributed in North America by
Abrams Books
www.abramsbooks.com

Distributed in the rest of the world by
Thames & Hudson Ltd.
6-24 Britannia Street
London WC1X 9JD
United Kingdom
www.thamesandhudson.com

EU Authorized Representative
Interart S.A.R.L.
19 Rue Charles Auray
93500 Pantin, Paris
France
productsafety@vendomepress.com
www.interart.fr

Printed and bound in China

FIRST PRINTING